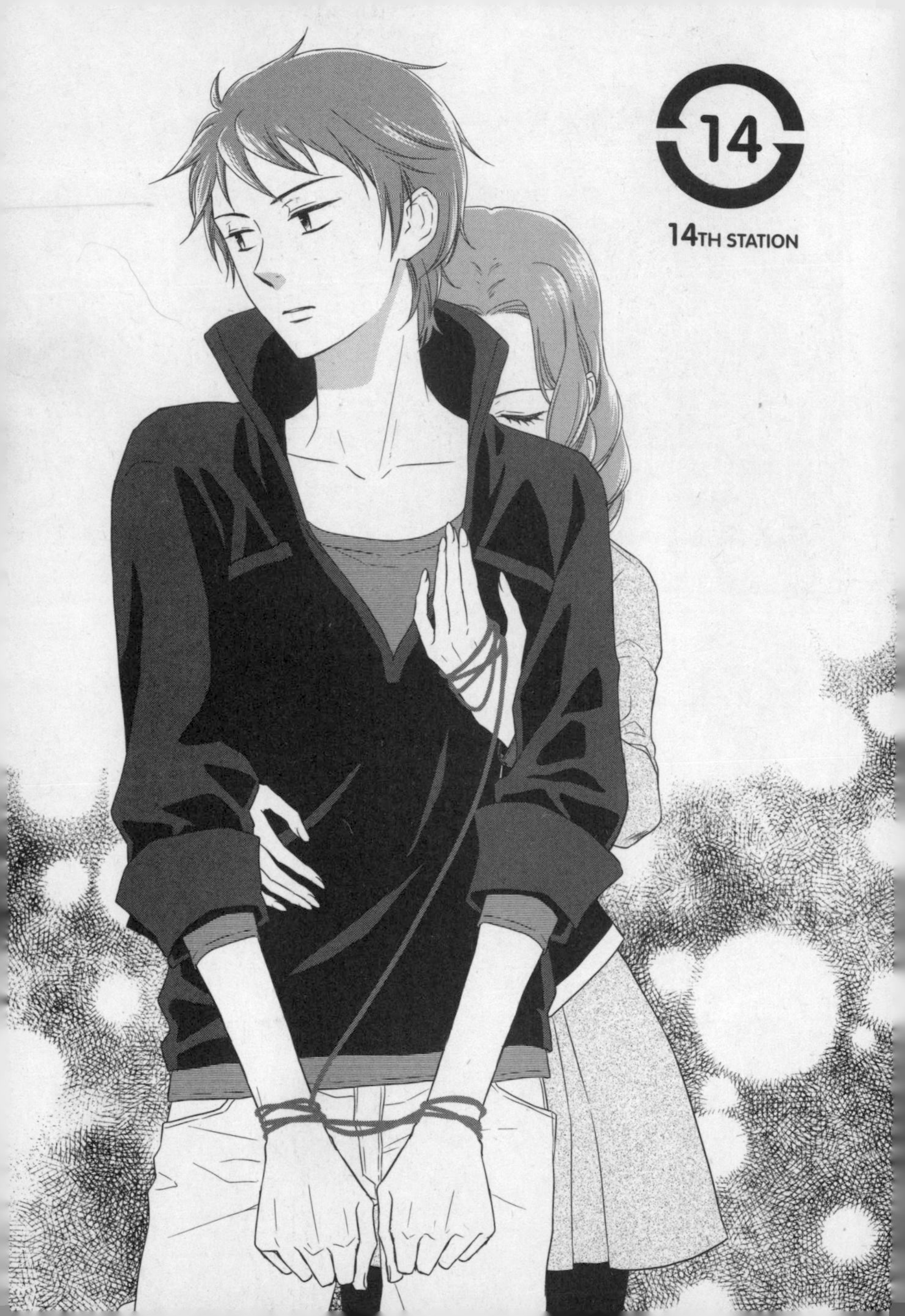
14
14TH STATION

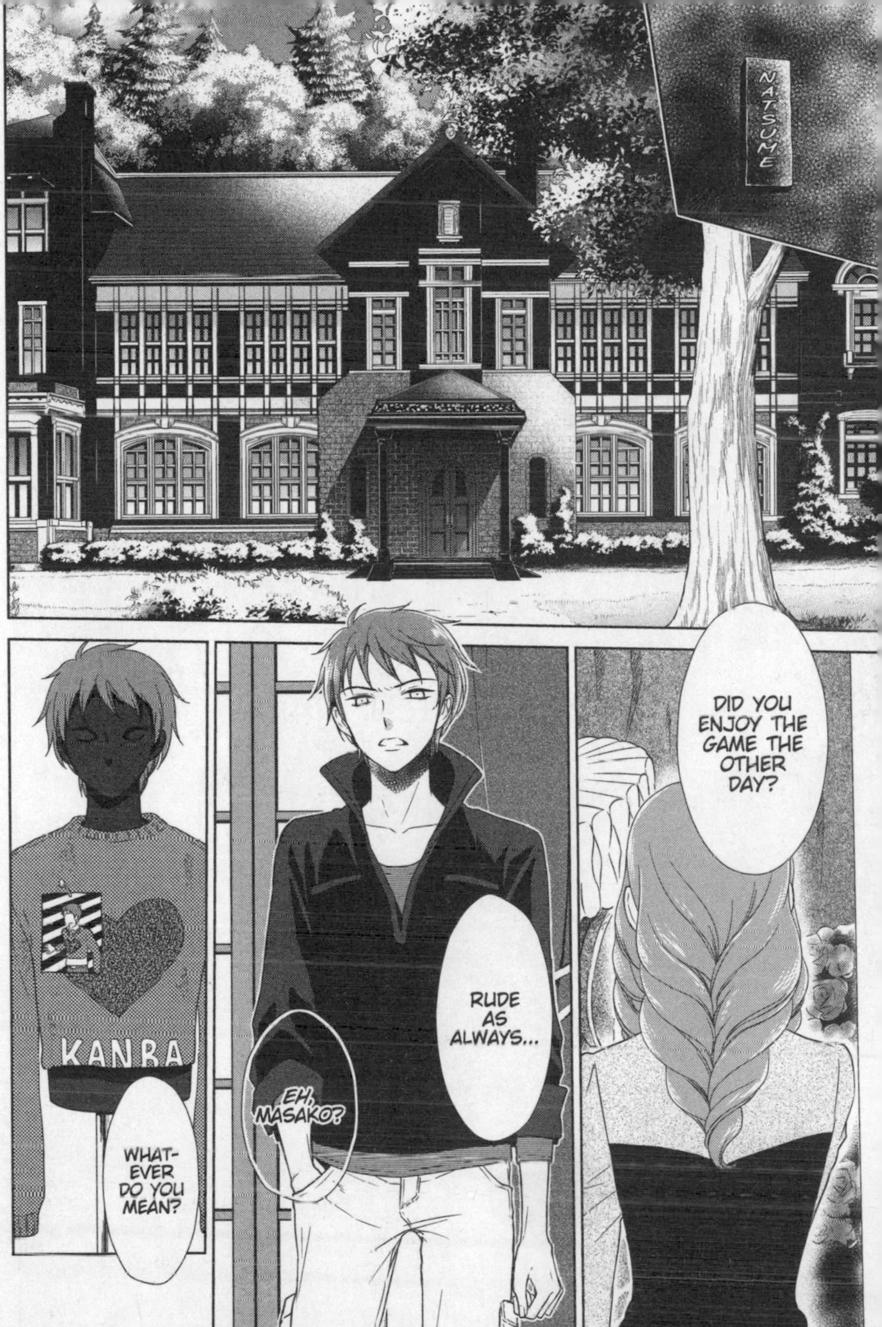
NATSUME
DID YOU ENJOY THE GAME THE OTHER DAY?
RUDE AS ALWAYS...
EH, MASAKO?
KANBA
WHAT-EVER DO YOU MEAN?

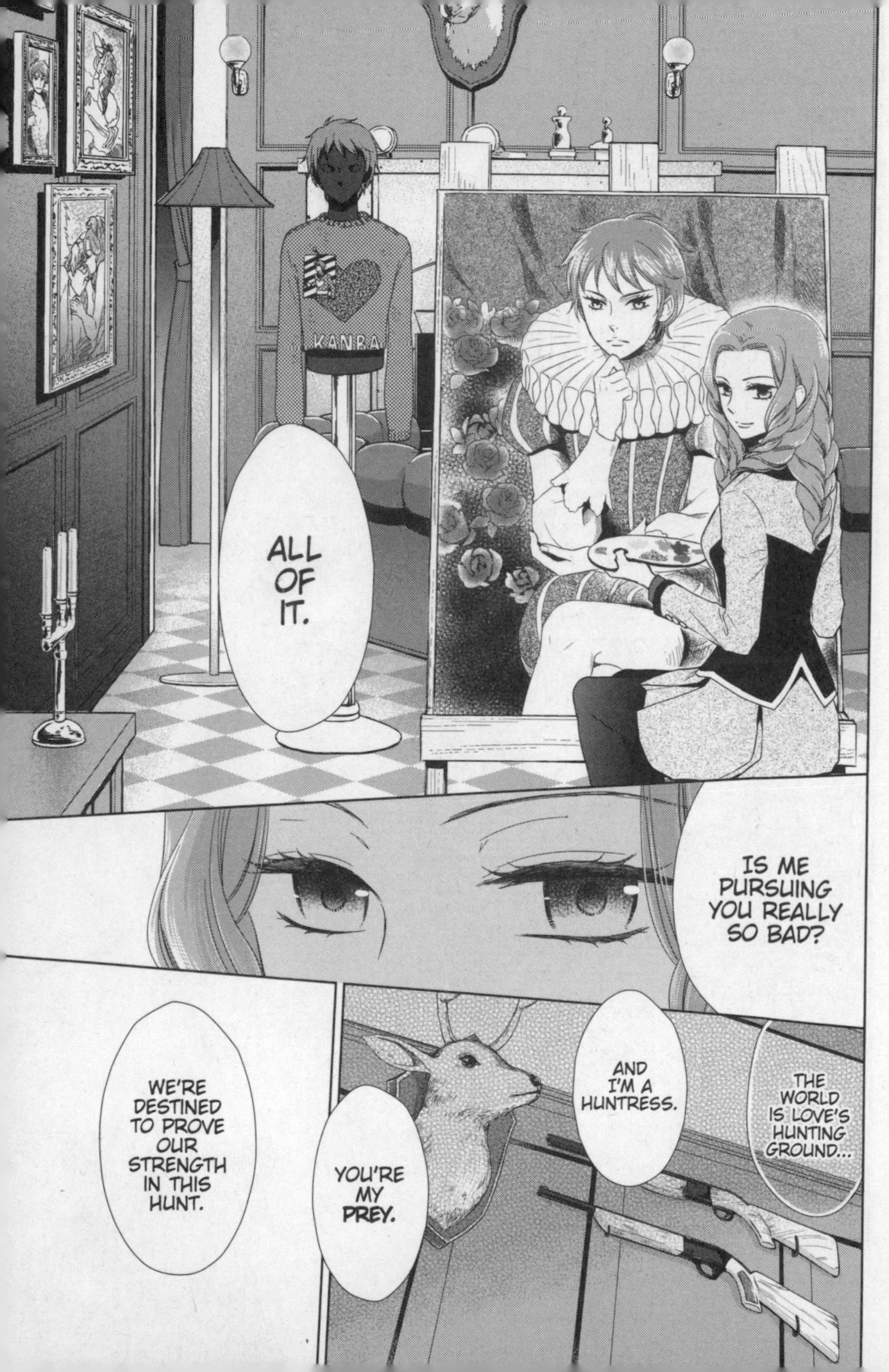
KANBA
ALL OF IT.
IS ME PURSUING YOU REALLY SO BAD?
THE WORLD IS LOVE'S HUNTING GROUND...
AND I'M A HUNTRESS.
YOU'RE MY PREY.
WE'RE DESTINED TO PROVE OUR STRENGTH IN THIS HUNT.

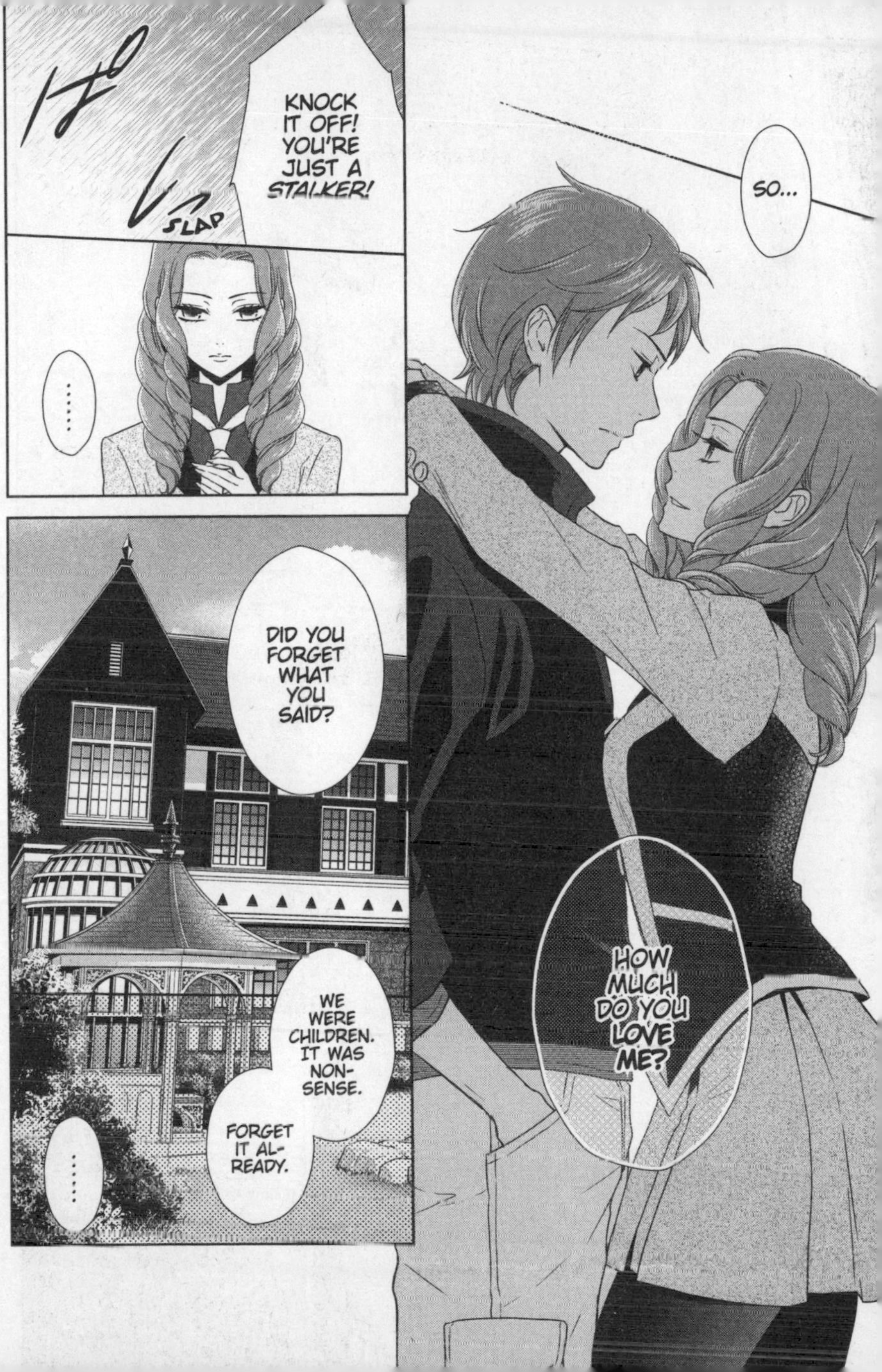
SO...
HOW MUCH DO YOU LOVE ME?
KNOCK IT OFF! YOU'RE JUST A STALKER!
SLAP
......
DID YOU FORGET WHAT YOU SAID?
WE WERE CHILDREN. IT WAS NON-SENSE.
FORGET IT AL-READY.
......

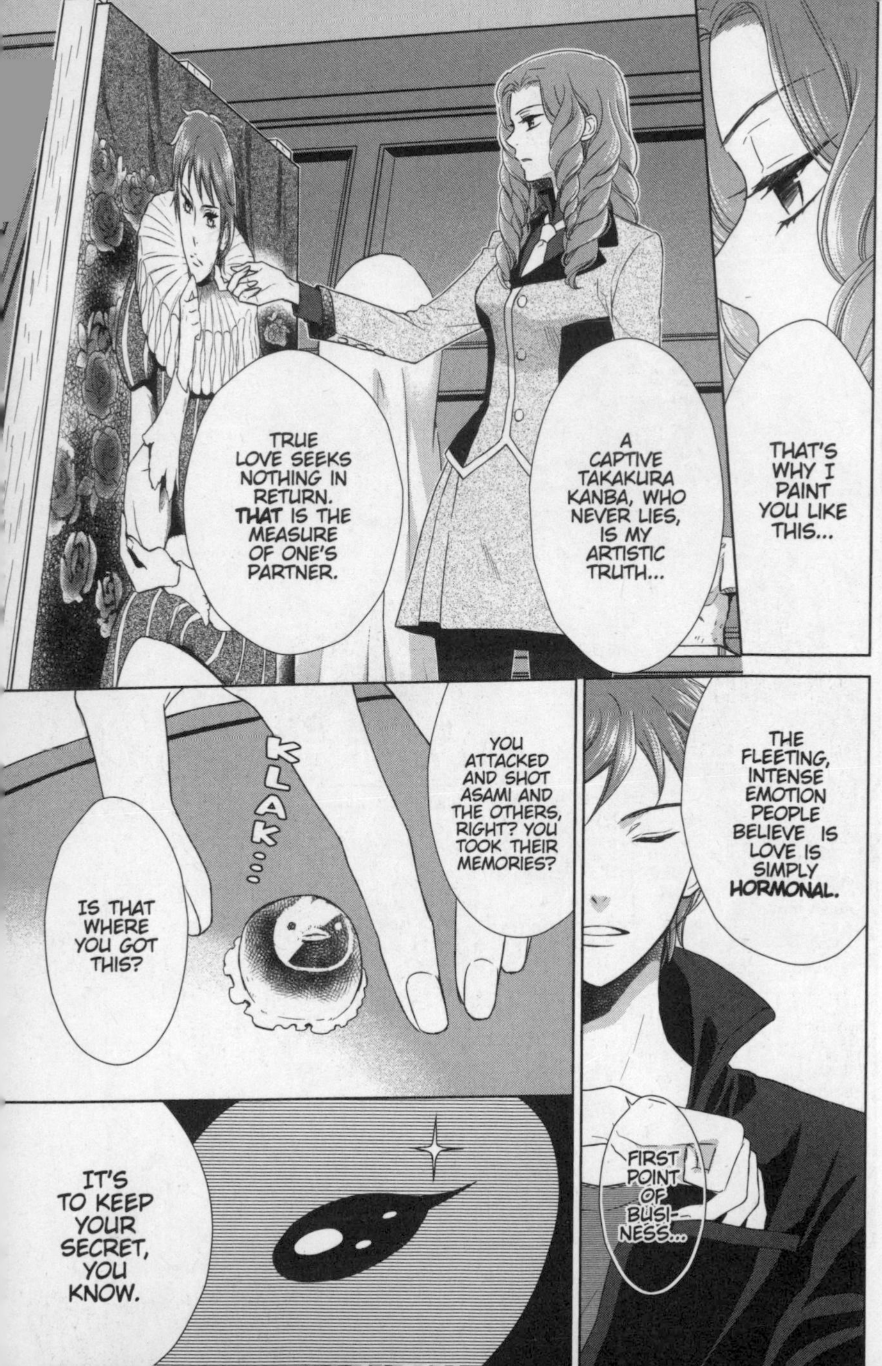
THAT'S WHY I PAINT YOU LIKE THIS...
A CAPTIVE TAKAKURA KANBA, WHO NEVER LIES, IS MY ARTISTIC TRUTH...
TRUE LOVE SEEKS NOTHING IN RETURN. THAT IS THE MEASURE OF ONE'S PARTNER.
THE FLEETING, INTENSE EMOTION PEOPLE BELIEVE IS LOVE IS SIMPLY HORMONAL.
FIRST POINT OF BUSI-NESS...
YOU ATTACKED AND SHOT ASAMI AND THE OTHERS, RIGHT? YOU TOOK THEIR MEMORIES?
KLAK...
IS THAT WHERE YOU GOT THIS?
IT'S TO KEEP YOUR SECRET, YOU KNOW.

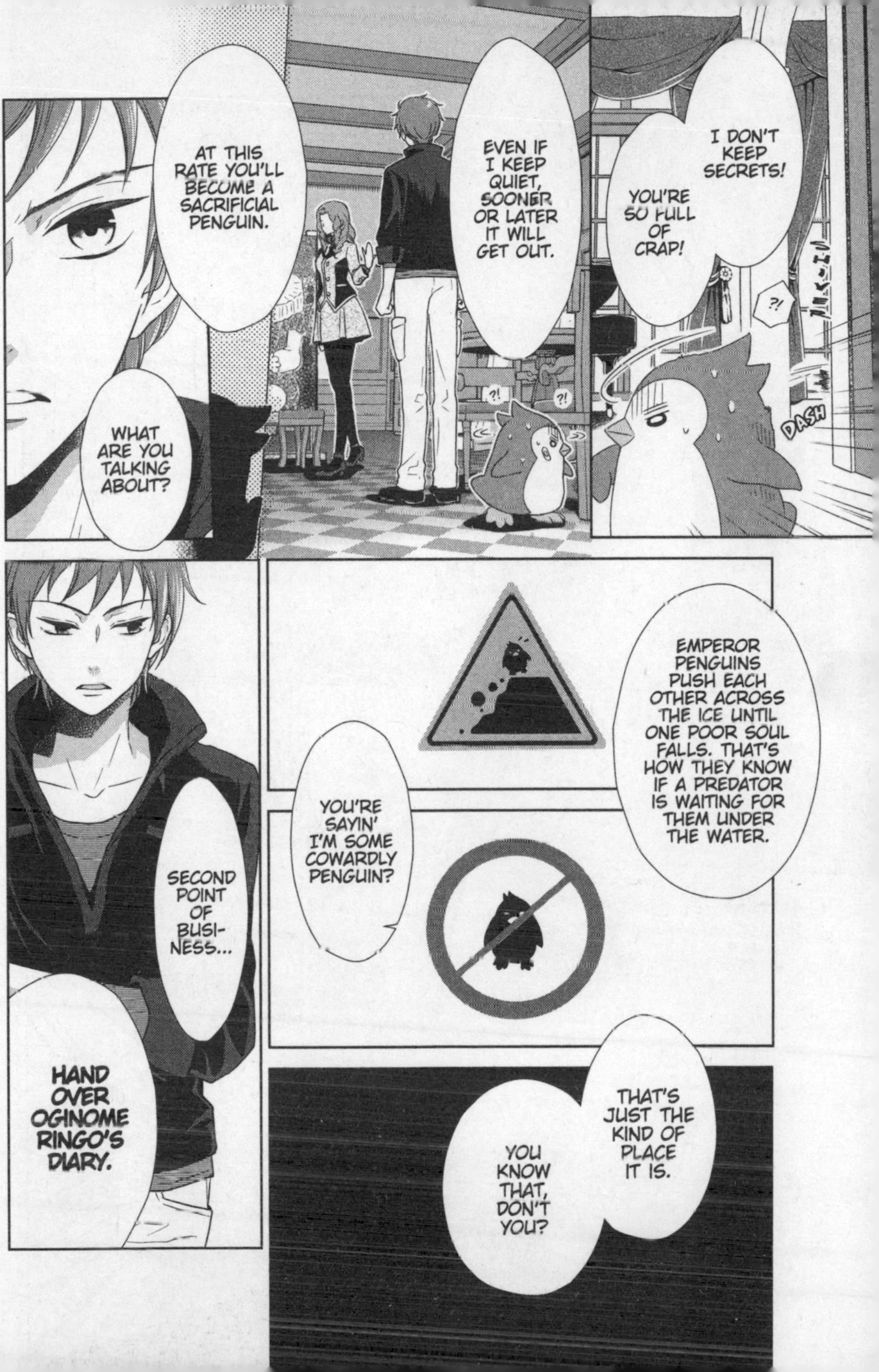
I DON'T KEEP SECRETS!
YOU'RE SO FULL OF CRAP!
?!
DASH
EVEN IF I KEEP QUIET, SOONER OR LATER IT WILL GET OUT.
?!
?!
AT THIS RATE YOU'LL BECOME A SACRIFICIAL PENGUIN.
WHAT ARE YOU TALKING ABOUT?
EMPEROR PENGUINS PUSH EACH OTHER ACROSS THE ICE UNTIL ONE POOR SOUL FALLS. THAT'S HOW THEY KNOW IF A PREDATOR IS WAITING FOR THEM UNDER THE WATER.
YOU'RE SAYIN' I'M SOME COWARDLY PENGUIN?
THAT'S JUST THE KIND OF PLACE IT IS.
YOU KNOW THAT, DON'T YOU?
SECOND POINT OF BUSINESS...
HAND OVER OGINOME RINGO'S DIARY.

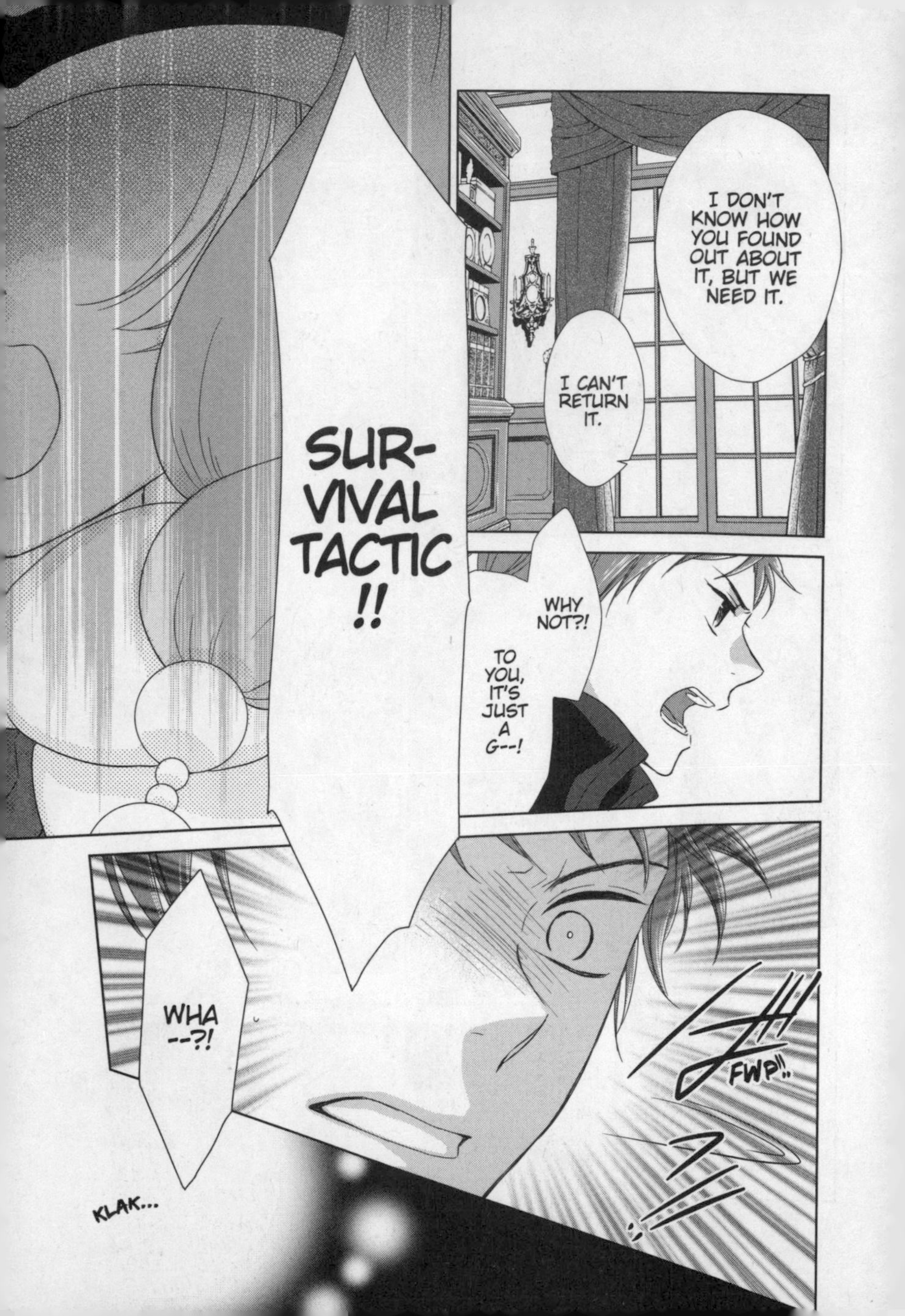

I DON'T KNOW HOW YOU FOUND OUT ABOUT IT, BUT WE NEED IT.
I CAN'T RETURN IT.
WHY NOT?!
TO YOU, IT'S JUST A G--!
SUR-VIVAL TACTIC!!
FWP!!
WHA--?!
KLAK...

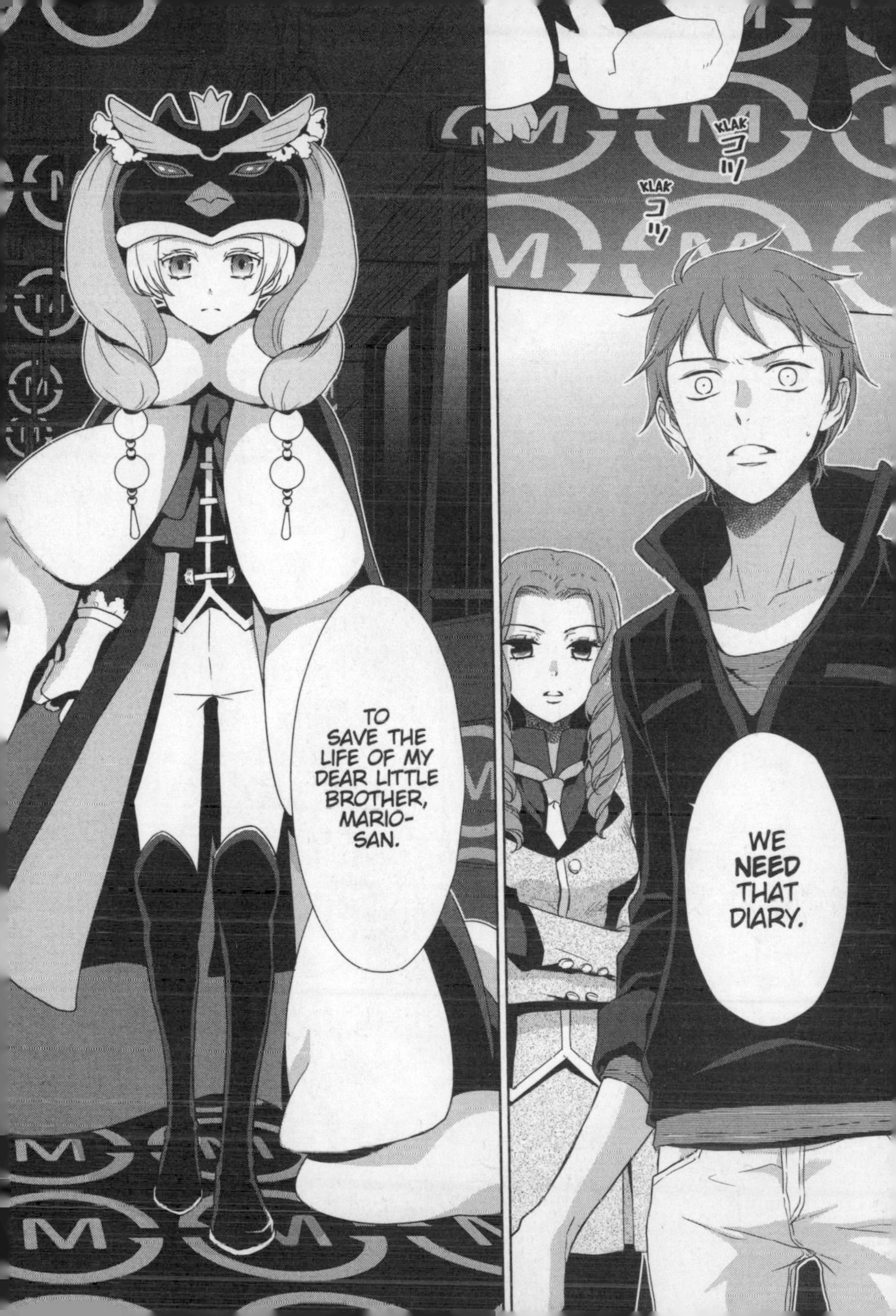
KLAK コッ
KLAK コッ
WE NEED THAT DIARY.
TO SAVE THE LIFE OF MY DEAR LITTLE BROTHER, MARIO-SAN.

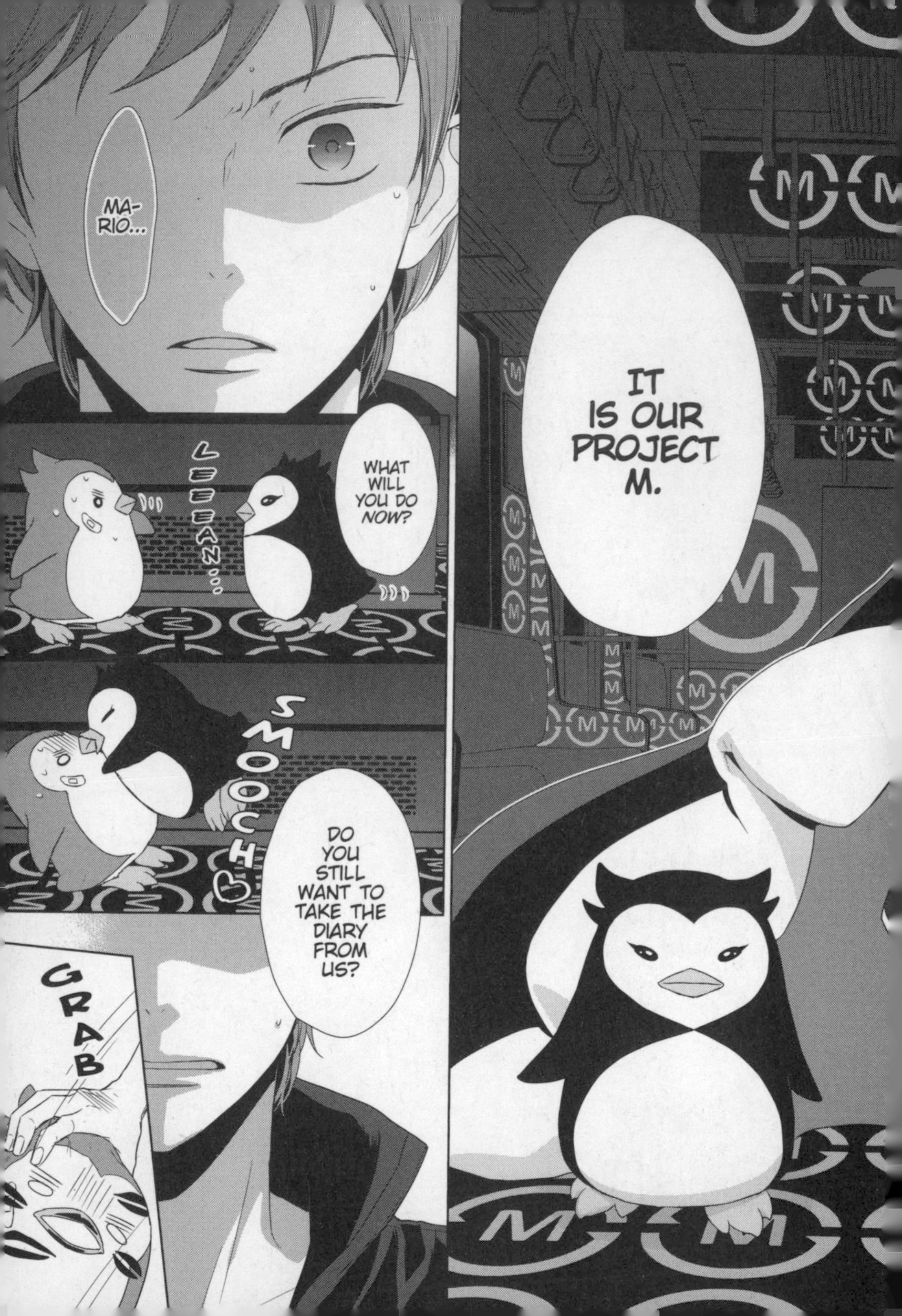
IT IS OUR PROJECT M.
MA-RIO...
WHAT WILL YOU DO NOW?
LEEEEAN...
SMOOCH
DO YOU STILL WANT TO TAKE THE DIARY FROM US?
GRAB

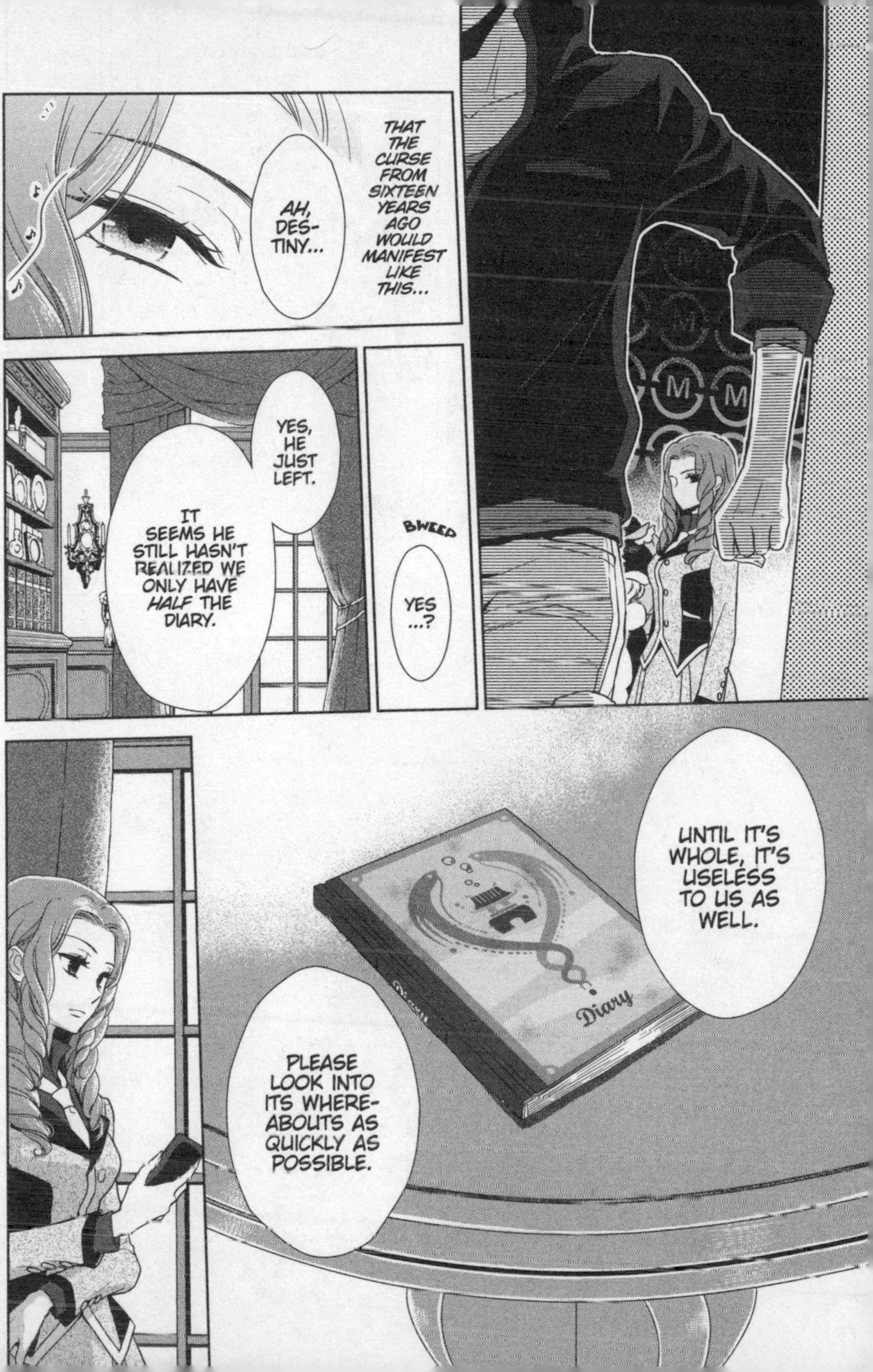
THAT THE CURSE FROM SIXTEEN YEARS AGO WOULD MANIFEST LIKE THIS...
AH, DES-TINY...
BWEED
YES ...?
YES, HE JUST LEFT.
IT SEEMS HE STILL HASN'T REALIZED WE ONLY HAVE *HALF* THE DIARY.
UNTIL IT'S WHOLE, IT'S USELESS TO US AS WELL.
Diary
PLEASE LOOK INTO ITS WHERE-ABOUTS AS QUICKLY AS POSSIBLE.

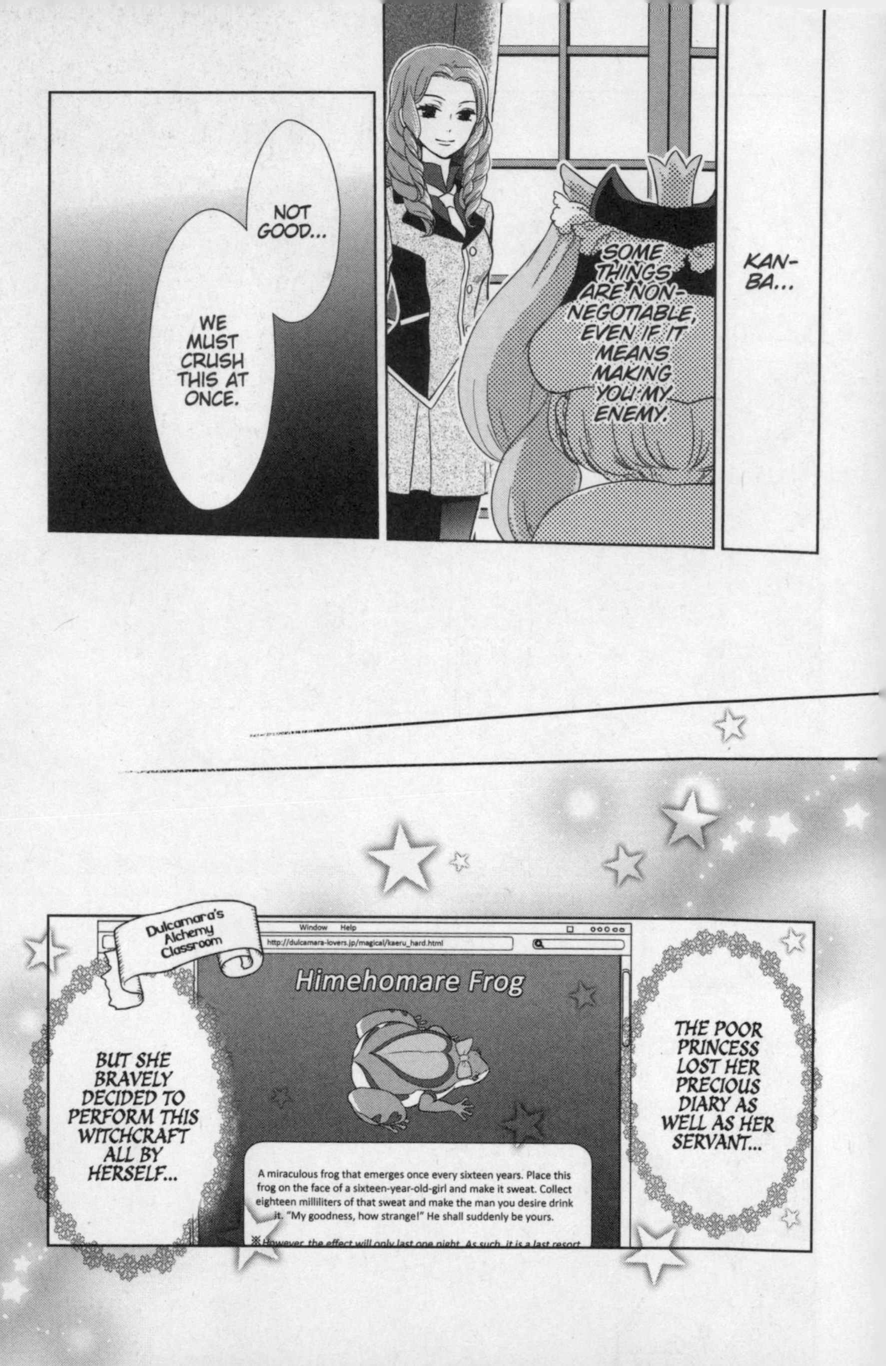
KAN-BA...
SOME THINGS ARE NON-NEGOTIABLE, EVEN IF IT MEANS MAKING YOU MY ENEMY.
NOT GOOD...
WE MUST CRUSH THIS AT ONCE.
THE POOR PRINCESS LOST HER PRECIOUS DIARY AS WELL AS HER SERVANT...
Dulcamara's Alchemy Classroom
Window Help
http://dulcamara-lovers.jp/magical/kaeru_hard.html
Himehomare Frog
A miraculous frog that emerges once every sixteen years. Place this frog on the face of a sixteen-year-old-girl and make it sweat. Collect eighteen milliliters of that sweat and make the man you desire drink it. "My goodness, how strange!" He shall suddenly be yours.
※However, the effect will only last one night. As such, it is a last resort
BUT SHE BRAVELY DECIDED TO PERFORM THIS WITCHCRAFT ALL BY HERSELF...

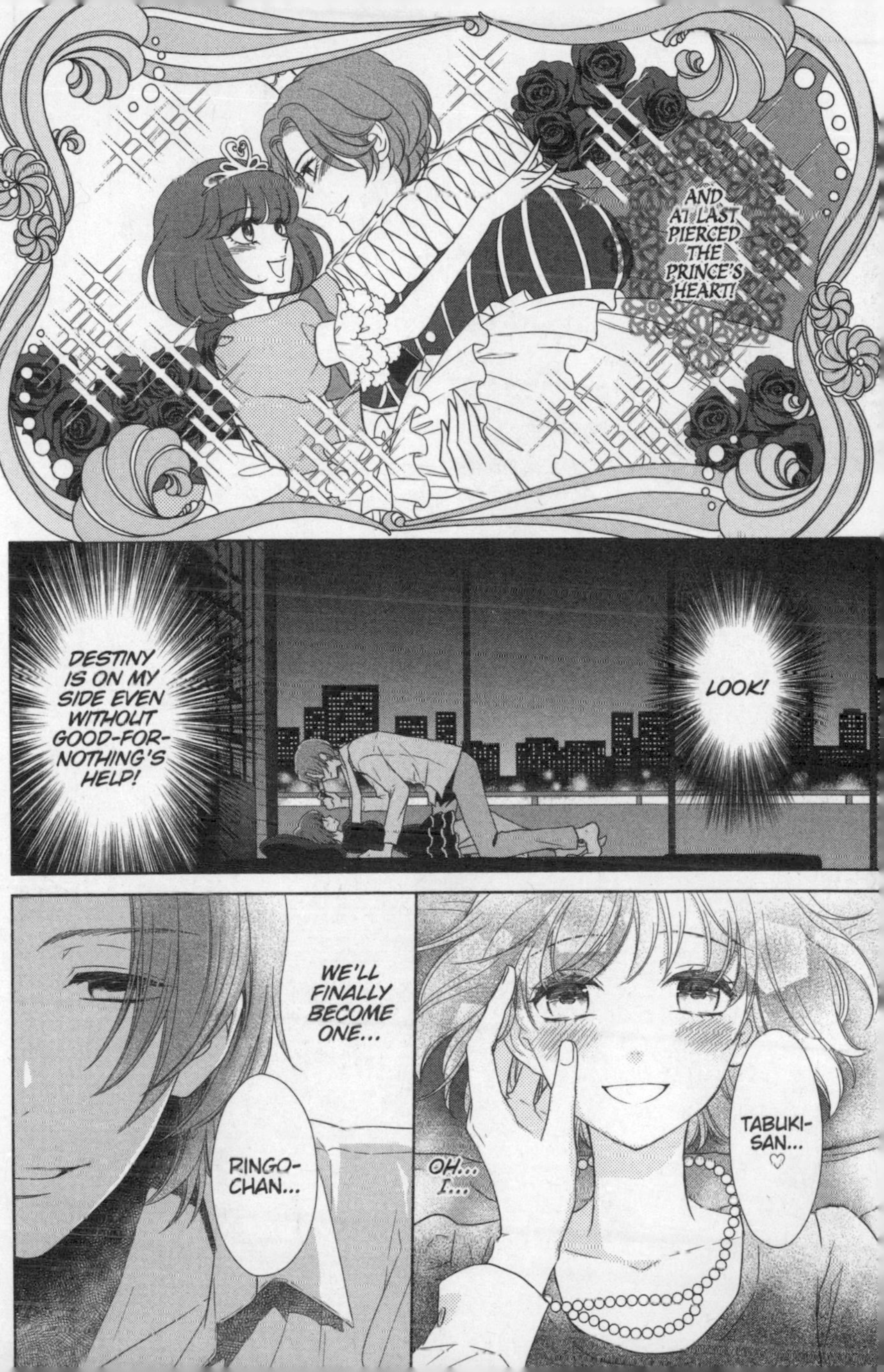
AND AT LAST PIERCED THE PRINCE'S HEART!
LOOK!
DESTINY IS ON MY SIDE EVEN WITHOUT GOOD-FOR-NOTHING'S HELP!
TABUKI-SAN... ♡
OH... I...
WE'LL FINALLY BECOME ONE...
RINGO-CHAN...

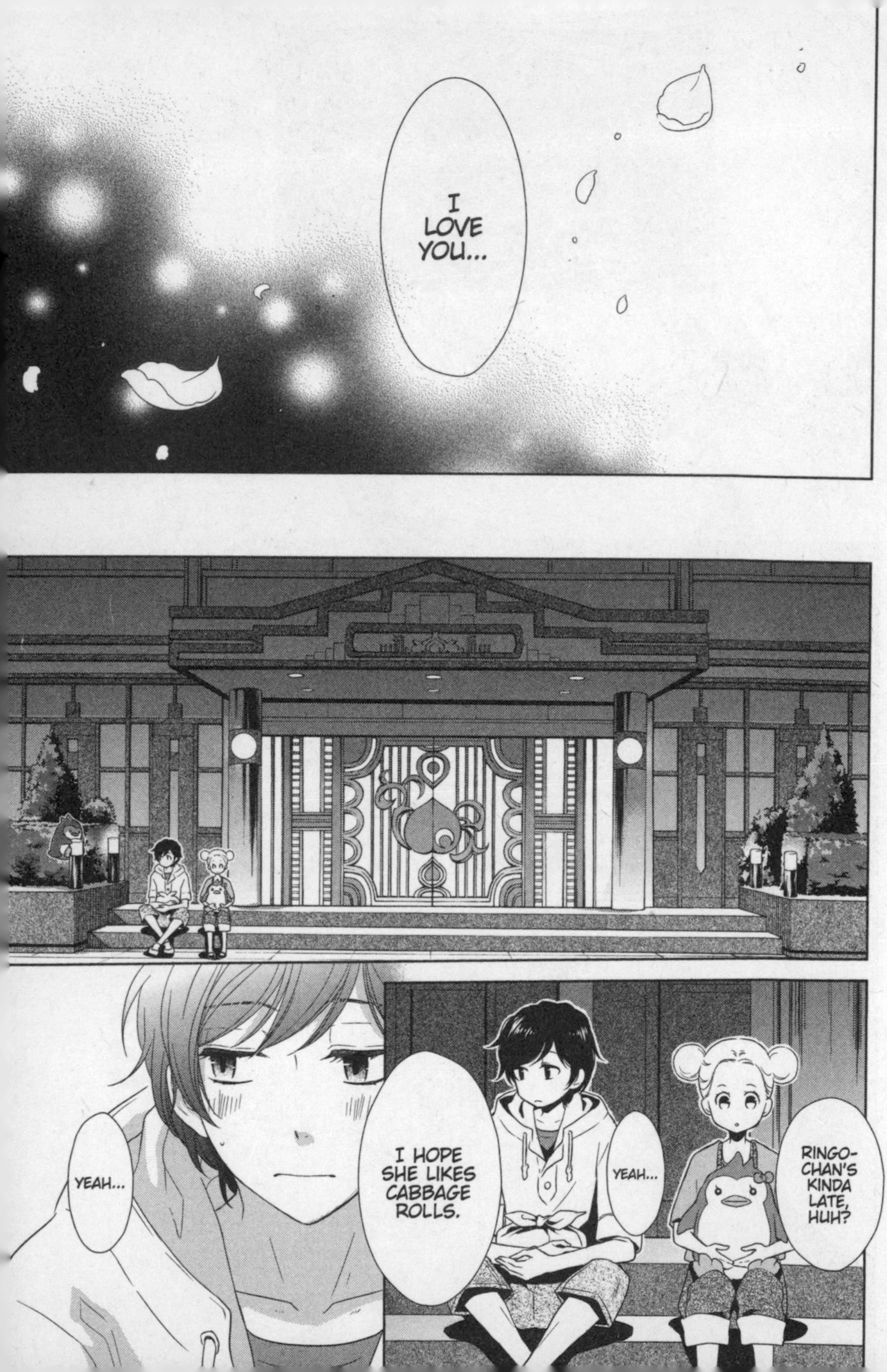
I LOVE YOU...
RINGO-CHAN'S KINDA LATE, HUH?
YEAH...
I HOPE SHE LIKES CABBAGE ROLLS.
YEAH...

Flashback

Shoma

Takakura Kitchen

Cabbage Rolls Himari and Shoma Made

Takakura Cabbage Rolls are an apologetic symbol. That's why...

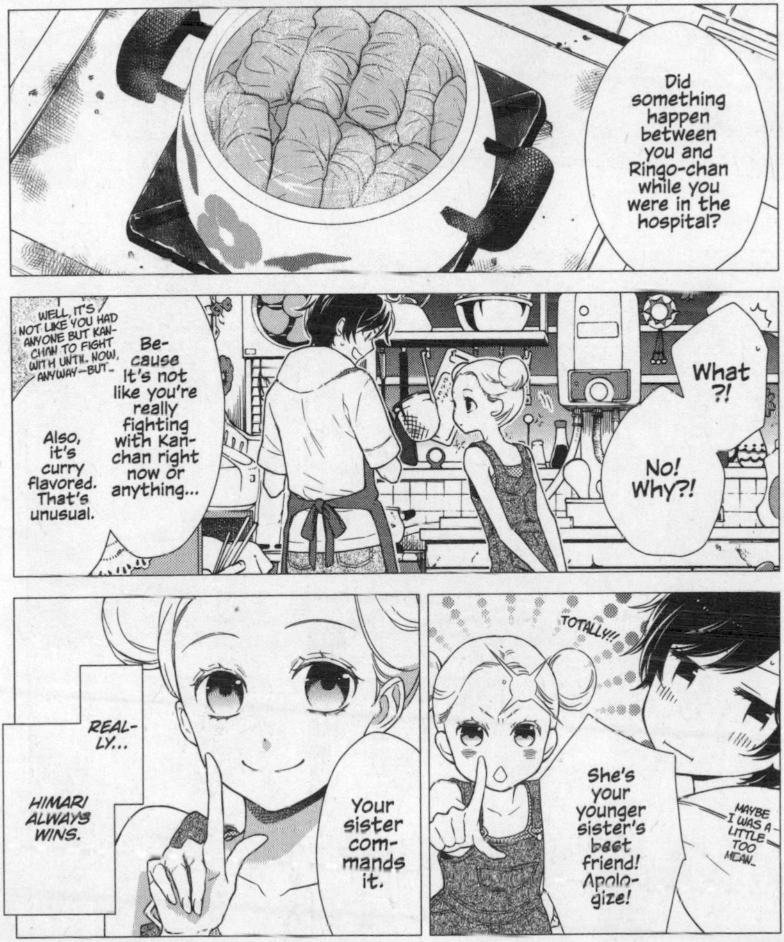

Did something happen between you and Ringo-chan while you were in the hospital?
What?!
No! Why?!
Because it's not like you're really fighting with Kan-chan right now or anything...
WELL, IT'S NOT LIKE YOU HAD ANYONE BUT KAN-CHAN TO FIGHT WITH UNTIL NOW, ANYWAY—BUT—
Also, it's curry flavored. That's unusual.
TOTALLY!!!
She's your younger sister's best friend! Apologize!
MAYBE I WAS A LITTLE TOO MEAN...
Your sister commands it.
REALLY... HIMARI ALWAYS WINS.

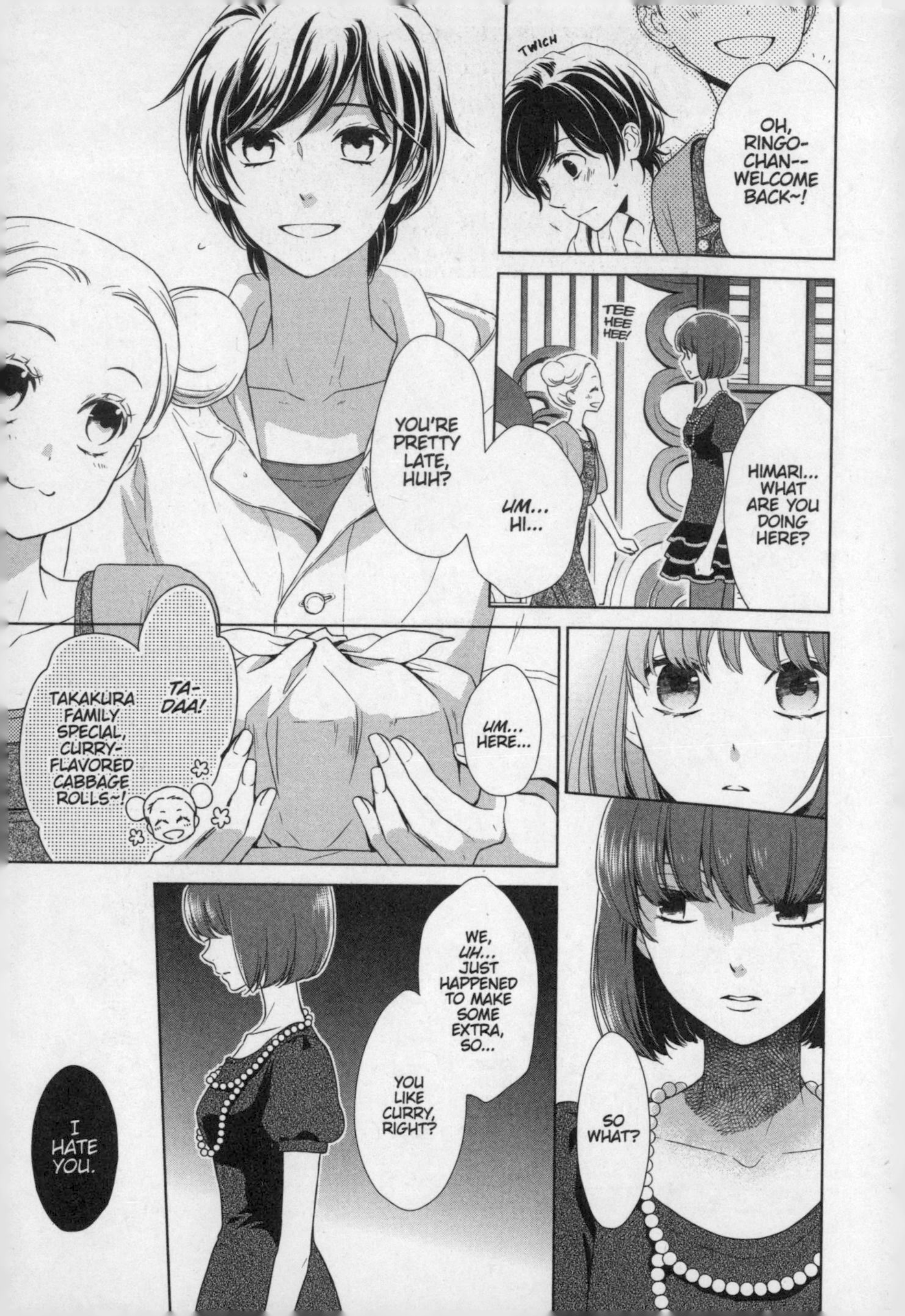
TWICH
OH, RINGO-CHAN-- WELCOME BACK~!
TEE HEE HEE!
HIMARI... WHAT ARE YOU DOING HERE?
UM... HI...
YOU'RE PRETTY LATE, HUH?
UM... HERE...
TA-DAA!
TAKAKURA FAMILY SPECIAL, CURRY-FLAVORED CABBAGE ROLLS~!
SO WHAT?
WE, UH... JUST HAPPENED TO MAKE SOME EXTRA, SO...
YOU LIKE CURRY, RIGHT?
I HATE YOU.

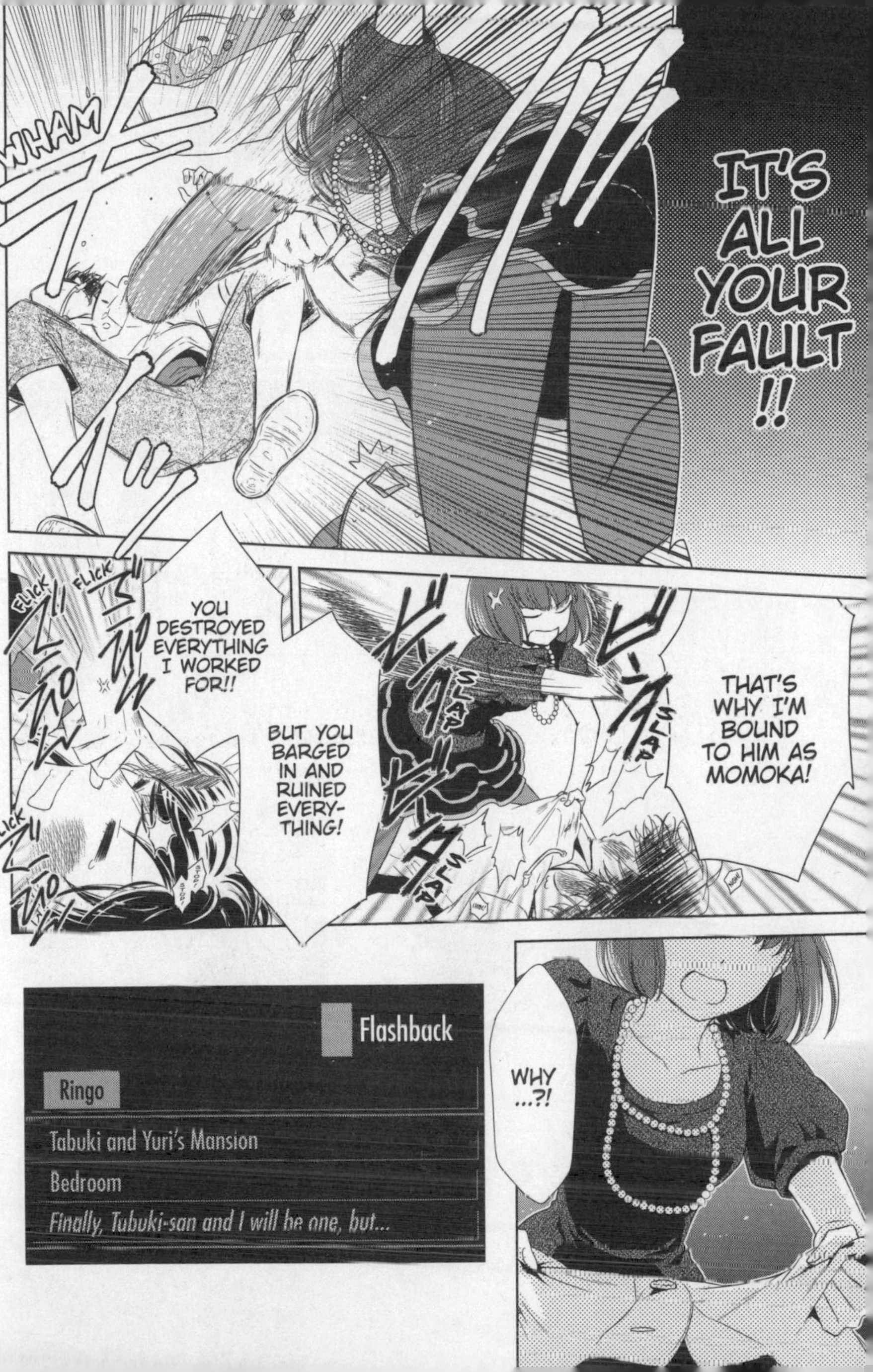
IT'S ALL YOUR FAULT!!
WHAM
THAT'S WHY I'M BOUND TO HIM AS MOMOKA!
SLAP
SLAP
SLAP
BUT YOU BARGED IN AND RUINED EVERYTHING!
YOU DESTROYED EVERYTHING I WORKED FOR!!
FLICK
FLICK
FLICK
WHY ...?!
Flashback
Ringo
Tabuki and Yuri's Mansion
Bedroom
Finally, Tubuki-san and I will be one, but...

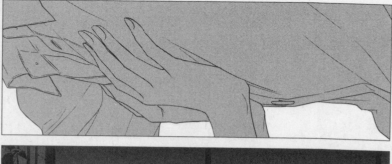

No...

Ahh...

This is wrong...

Why not?

I mean, we love each other, don't we? We're destined to be lovers.

19

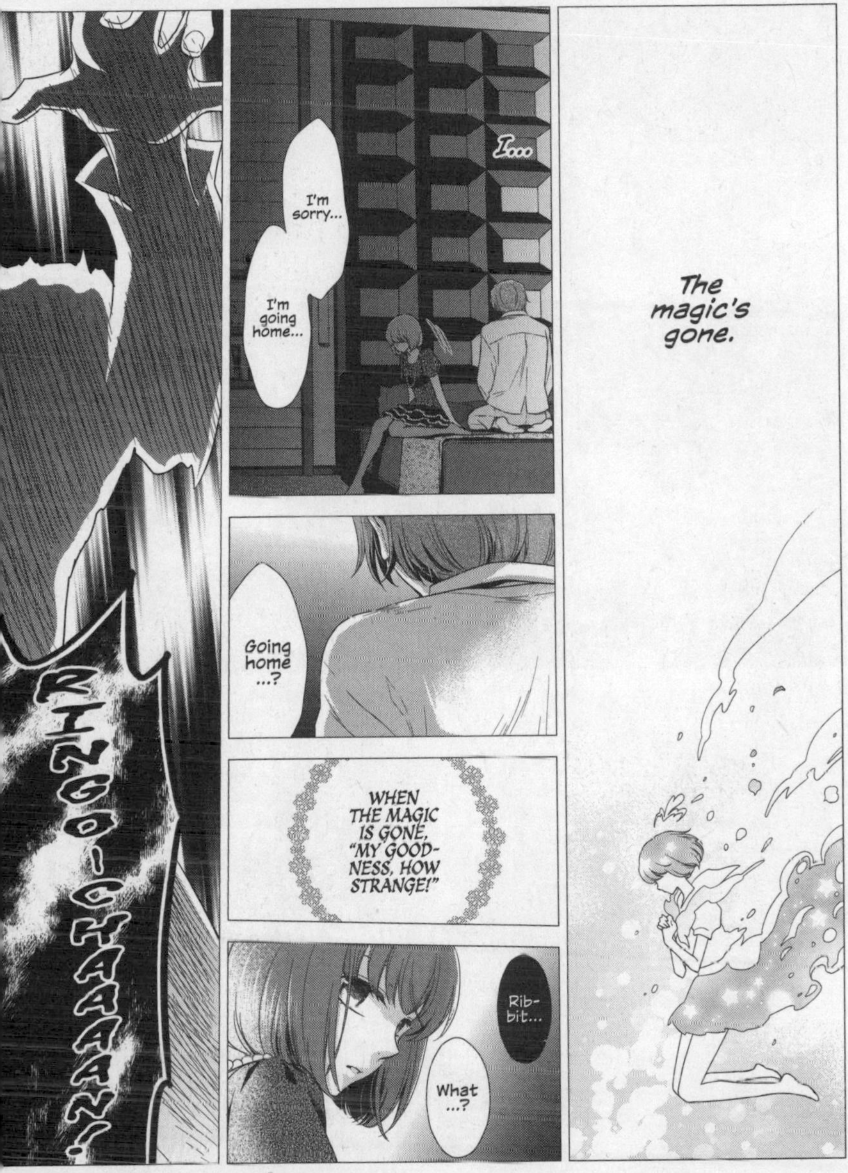
The magic's gone.
I...
I'm sorry...
I'm going home...
Going home ...?
WHEN THE MAGIC IS GONE, "MY GOODNESS, HOW STRANGE!"
Rib-bit...
What ...?
RINGO-CHAAAAAN!

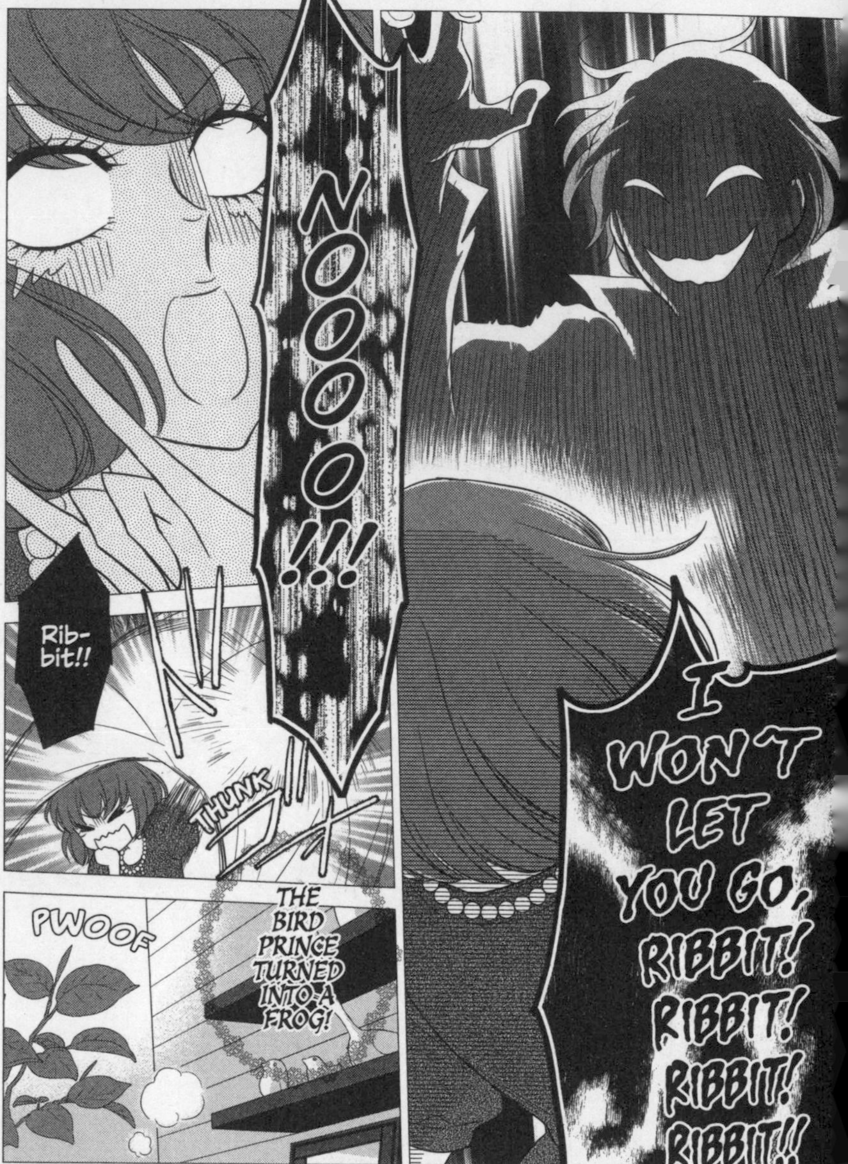
I WON'T LET YOU GO, RIBBIT! RIBBIT! RIBBIT! RIBBIT!!
NOOOOO!!!
Rib-bit!!
THUNK
PWOOF
THE BIRD PRINCE TURNED INTO A FROG!

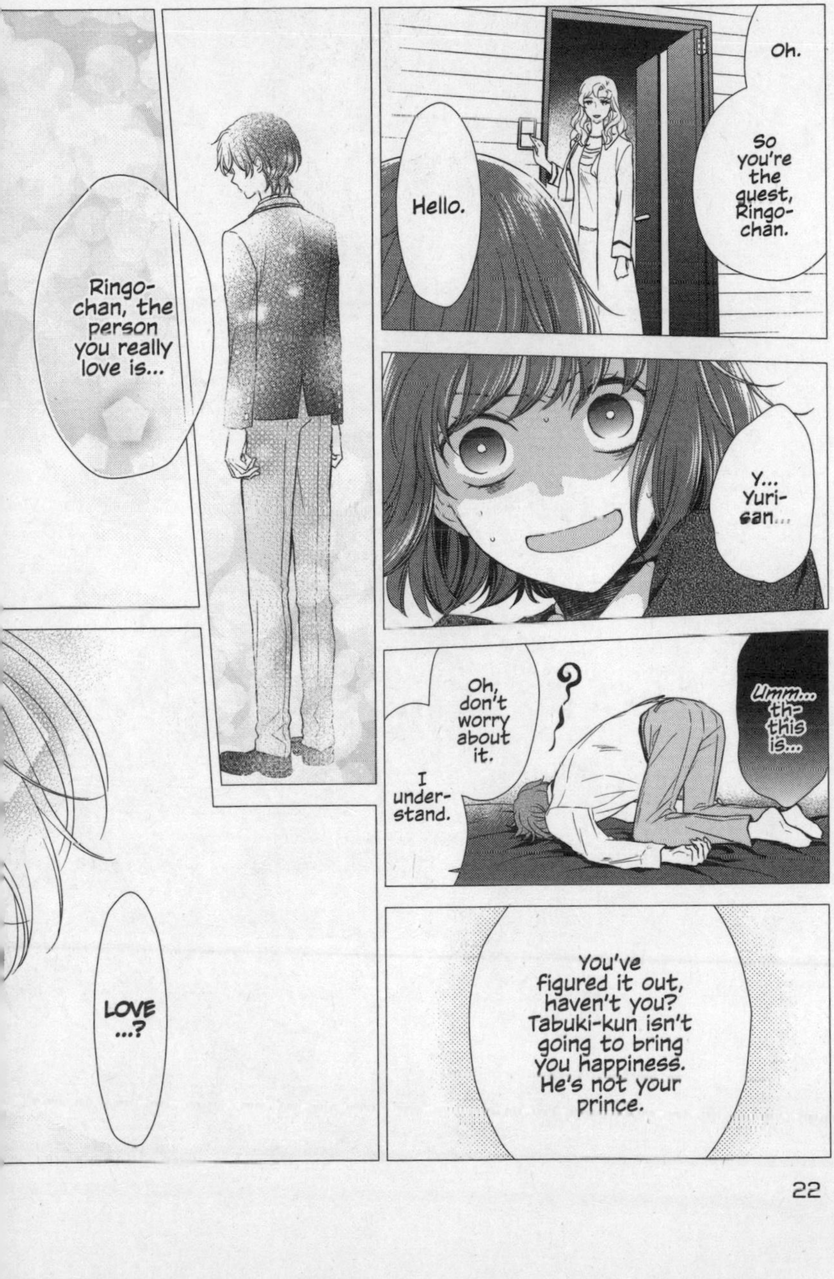

Oh.
So you're the guest, Ringo-chan.
Hello.
Y... Yuri-san...
Umm... th-this is...
Oh, don't worry about it.
I understand.
You've figured it out, haven't you? Tabuki-kun isn't going to bring you happiness. He's not your prince.
Ringo-chan, the person you really love is...
LOVE ...?

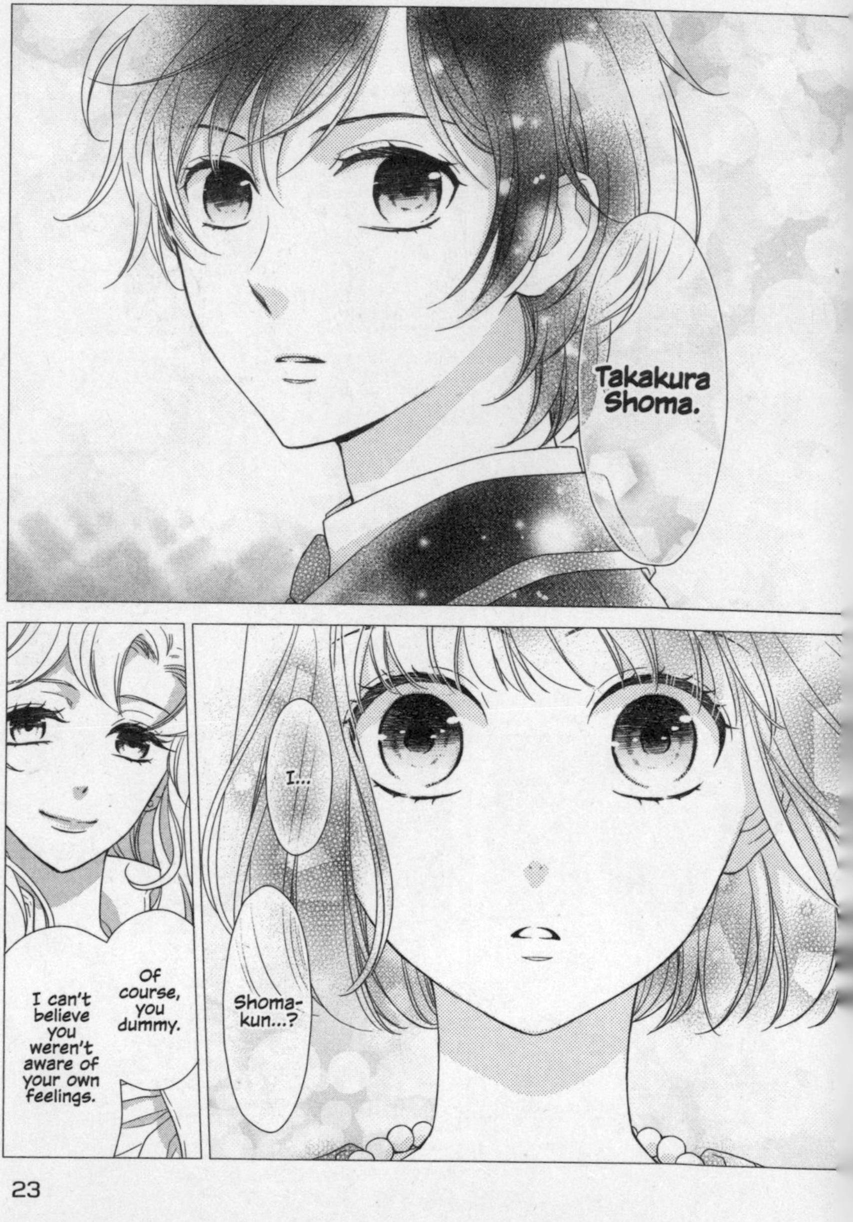
Takakura Shoma.
I...
Shoma-kun...?
Of course, you dummy.
I can't believe you weren't aware of your own feelings.

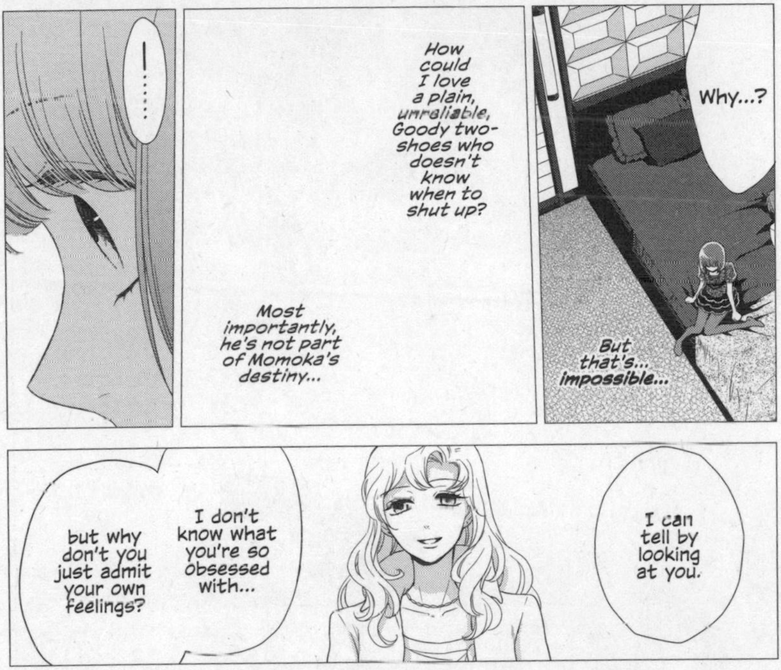
Why...?
But that's... impossible...
How could I love a plain, unreliable, Goody two-shoes who doesn't know when to shut up?
Most importantly, he's not part of Momoka's destiny...
......
I can tell by looking at you.
I don't know what you're so obsessed with...
but why don't you just admit your own feelings?

WHY DID YOU MAKE ME REALIZE?

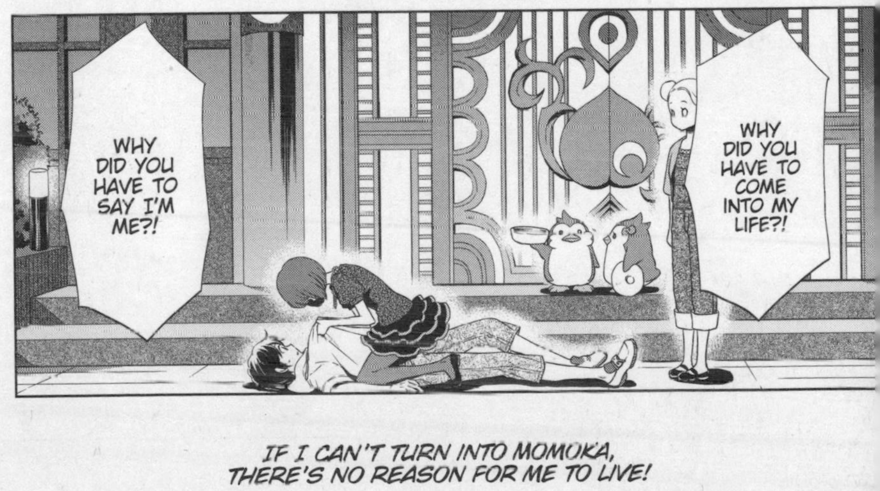
WHY DID YOU HAVE TO COME INTO MY LIFE?!
WHY DID YOU HAVE TO SAY I'M ME?!

*IF I CAN'T TURN INTO MOMOKA,
THERE'S NO REASON FOR ME TO LIVE!*

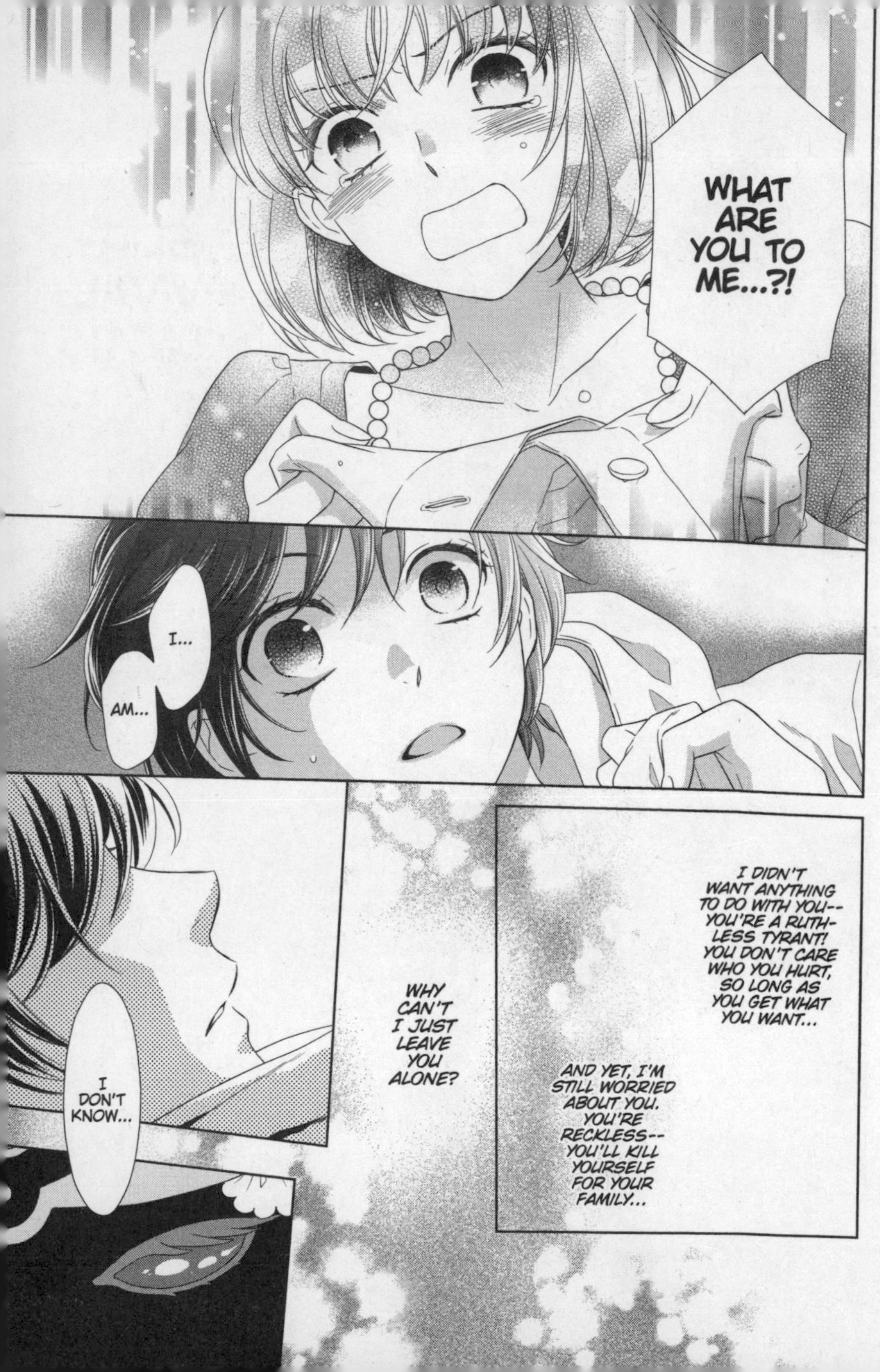
WHAT ARE YOU TO ME...?!
I...
AM...
I DIDN'T WANT ANYTHING TO DO WITH YOU-- YOU'RE A RUTH-LESS TYRANT! YOU DON'T CARE WHO YOU HURT, SO LONG AS YOU GET WHAT YOU WANT...
AND YET, I'M STILL WORRIED ABOUT YOU. YOU'RE RECKLESS-- YOU'LL KILL YOURSELF FOR YOUR FAMILY...
WHY CAN'T I JUST LEAVE YOU ALONE?
I DON'T KNOW...

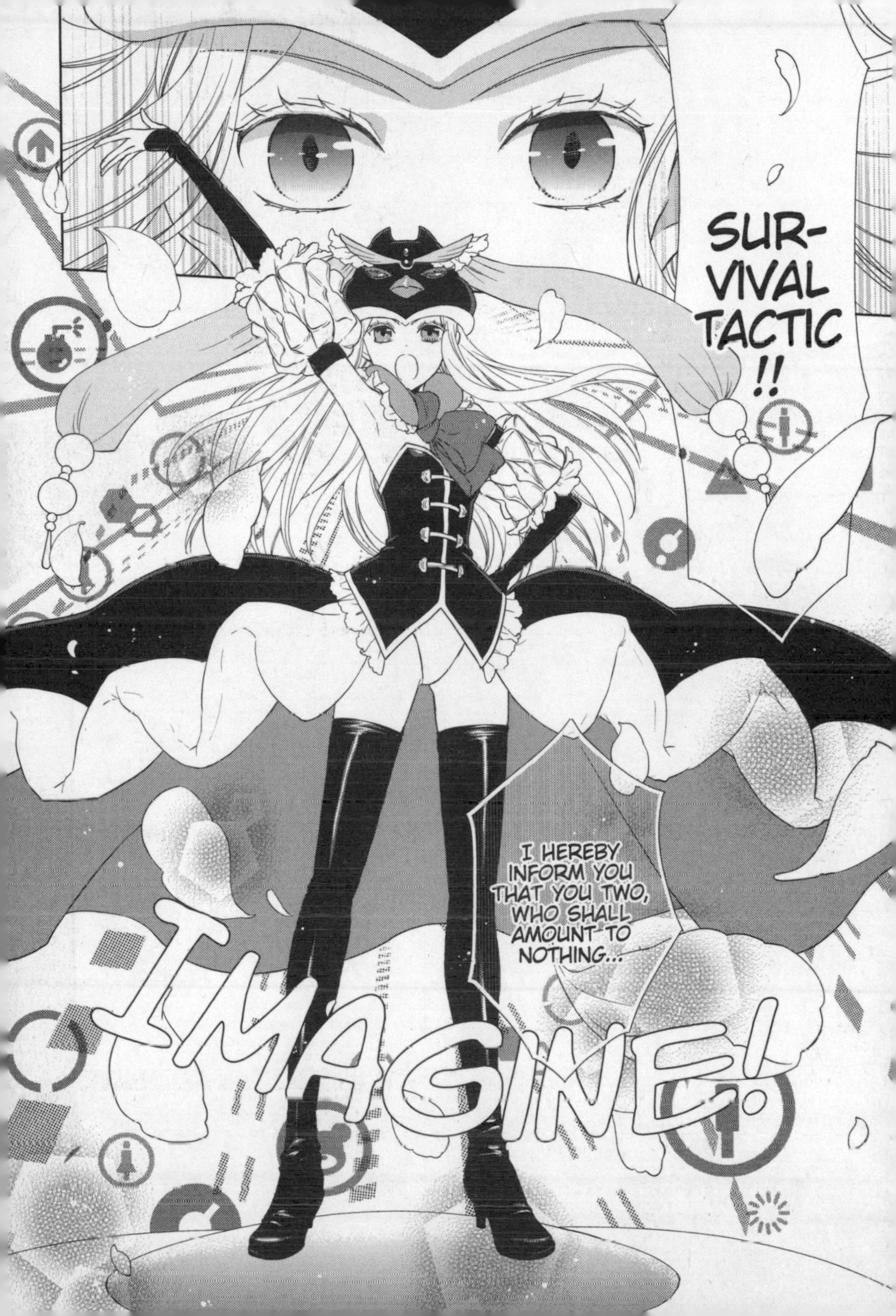
SUR-
VIVAL
TACTIC
!!
I HEREBY INFORM YOU THAT YOU TWO, WHO SHALL AMOUNT TO NOTHING...
IMAGINE!

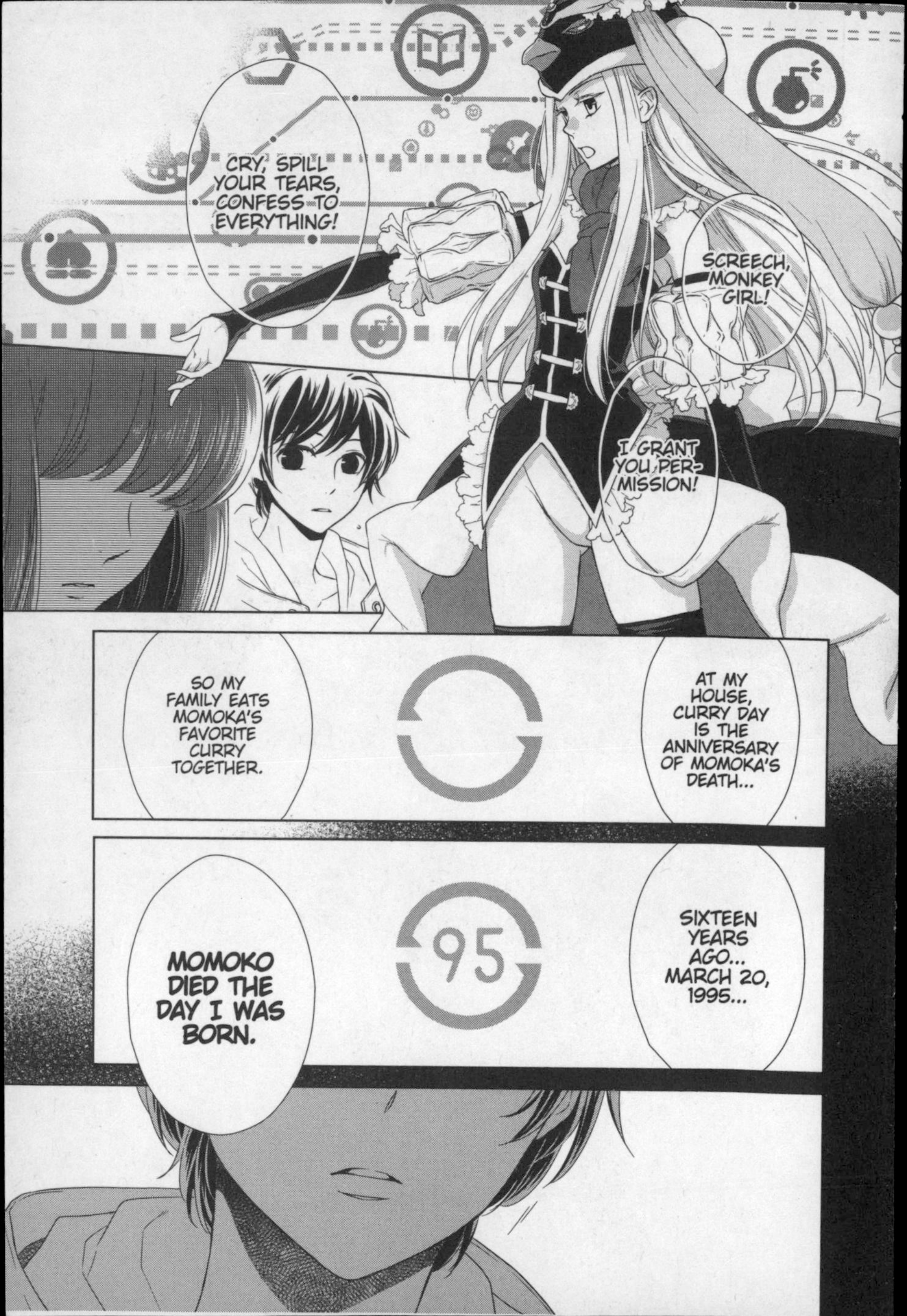
SCREECH, MONKEY GIRL!
I GRANT YOU PER-MISSION!
CRY, SPILL YOUR TEARS, CONFESS TO EVERYTHING!
AT MY HOUSE, CURRY DAY IS THE ANNIVERSARY OF MOMOKA'S DEATH...
SO MY FAMILY EATS MOMOKA'S FAVORITE CURRY TOGETHER.
SIXTEEN YEARS AGO... MARCH 20, 1995...
95
MOMOKO DIED THE DAY I WAS BORN.

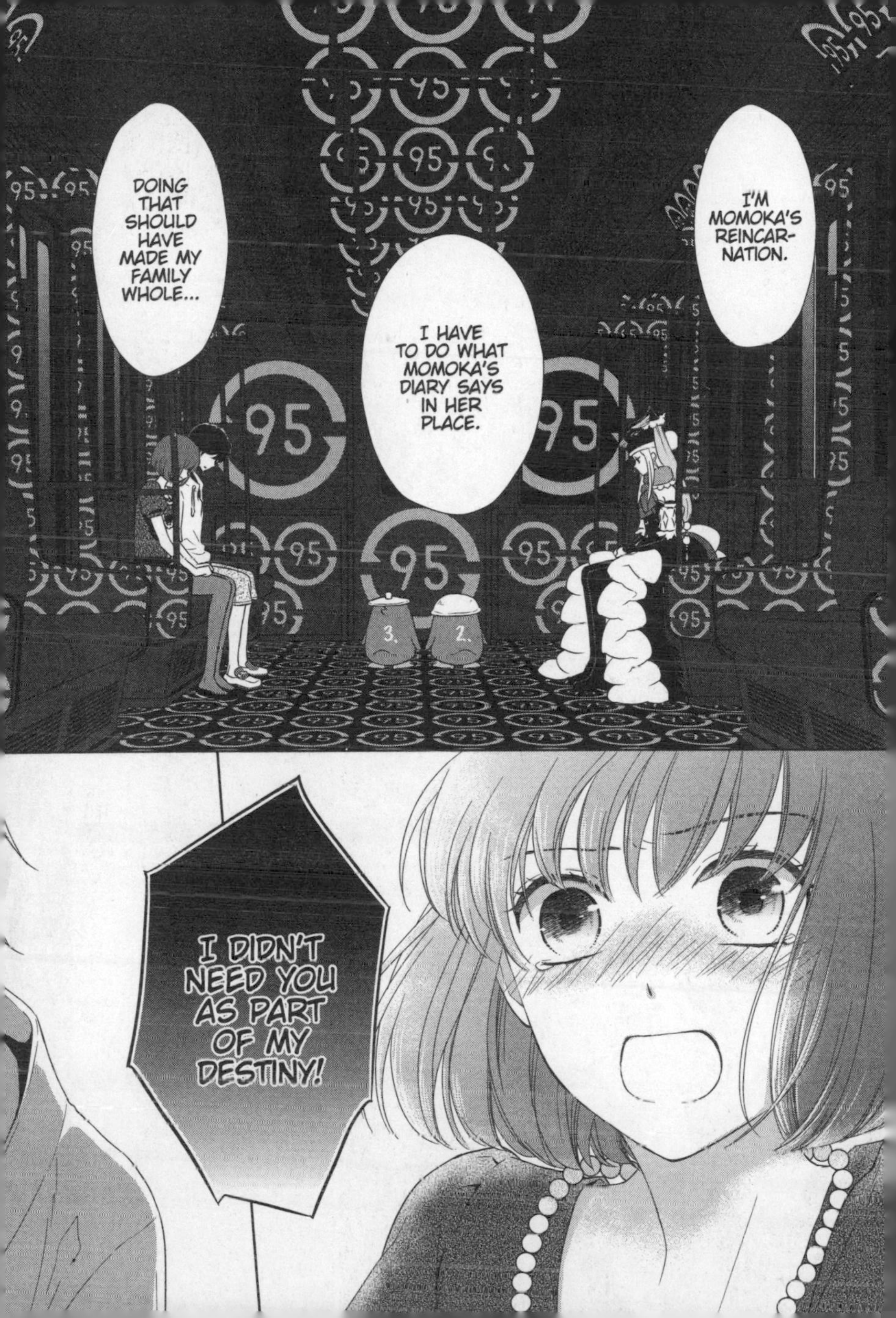
I'M MOMOKA'S REINCARNATION.
I HAVE TO DO WHAT MOMOKA'S DIARY SAYS IN HER PLACE.
DOING THAT SHOULD HAVE MADE MY FAMILY WHOLE...
I DIDN'T NEED YOU AS PART OF MY DESTINY!

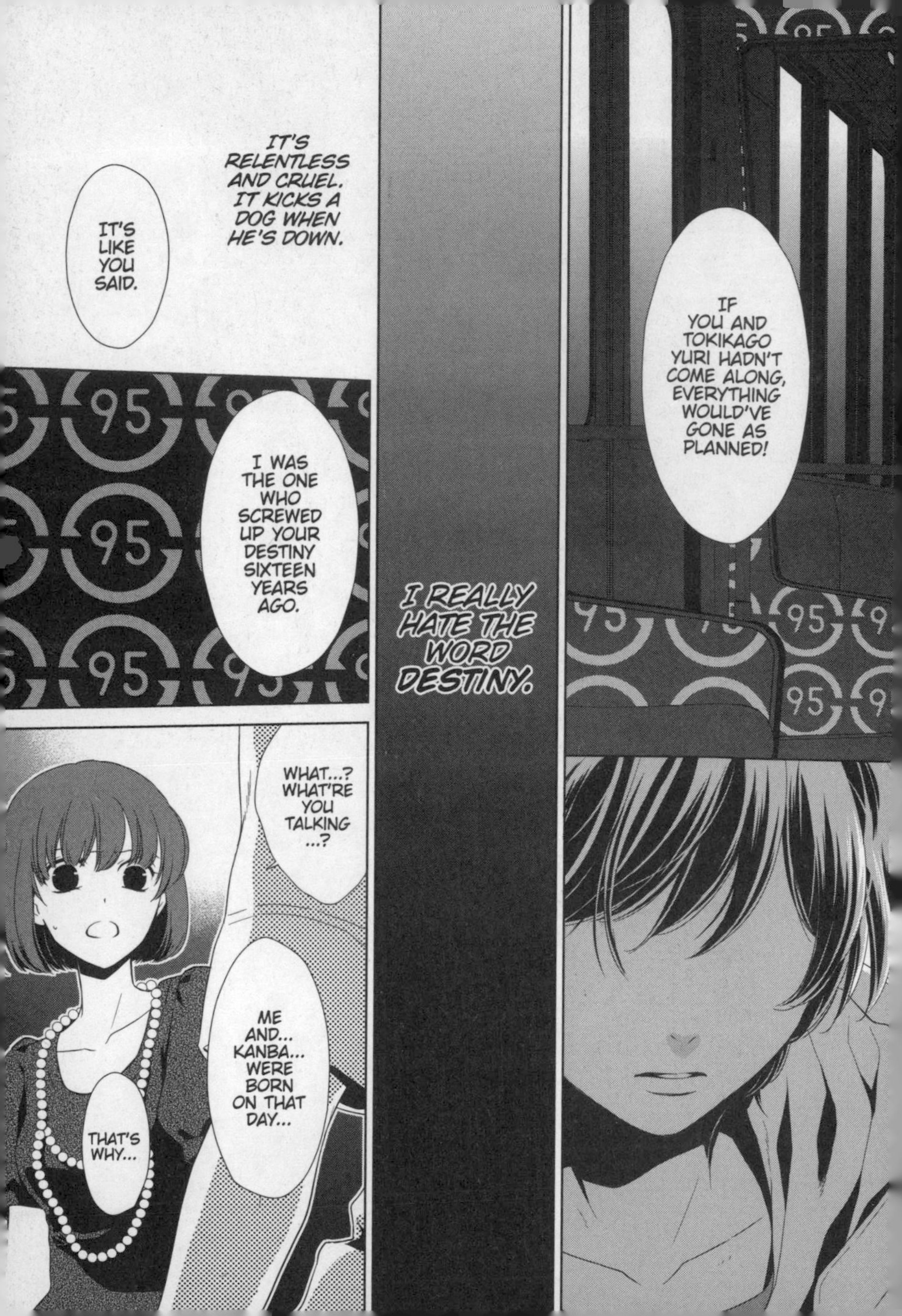
IF YOU AND TOKIKAGO YURI HADN'T COME ALONG, EVERYTHING WOULD'VE GONE AS PLANNED!
I REALLY HATE THE WORD DESTINY.
IT'S RELENTLESS AND CRUEL. IT KICKS A DOG WHEN HE'S DOWN.
IT'S LIKE YOU SAID.
I WAS THE ONE WHO SCREWED UP YOUR DESTINY SIXTEEN YEARS AGO.
WHAT...? WHAT'RE YOU TALKING ...?
ME AND... KANBA... WERE BORN ON THAT DAY...
THAT'S WHY...

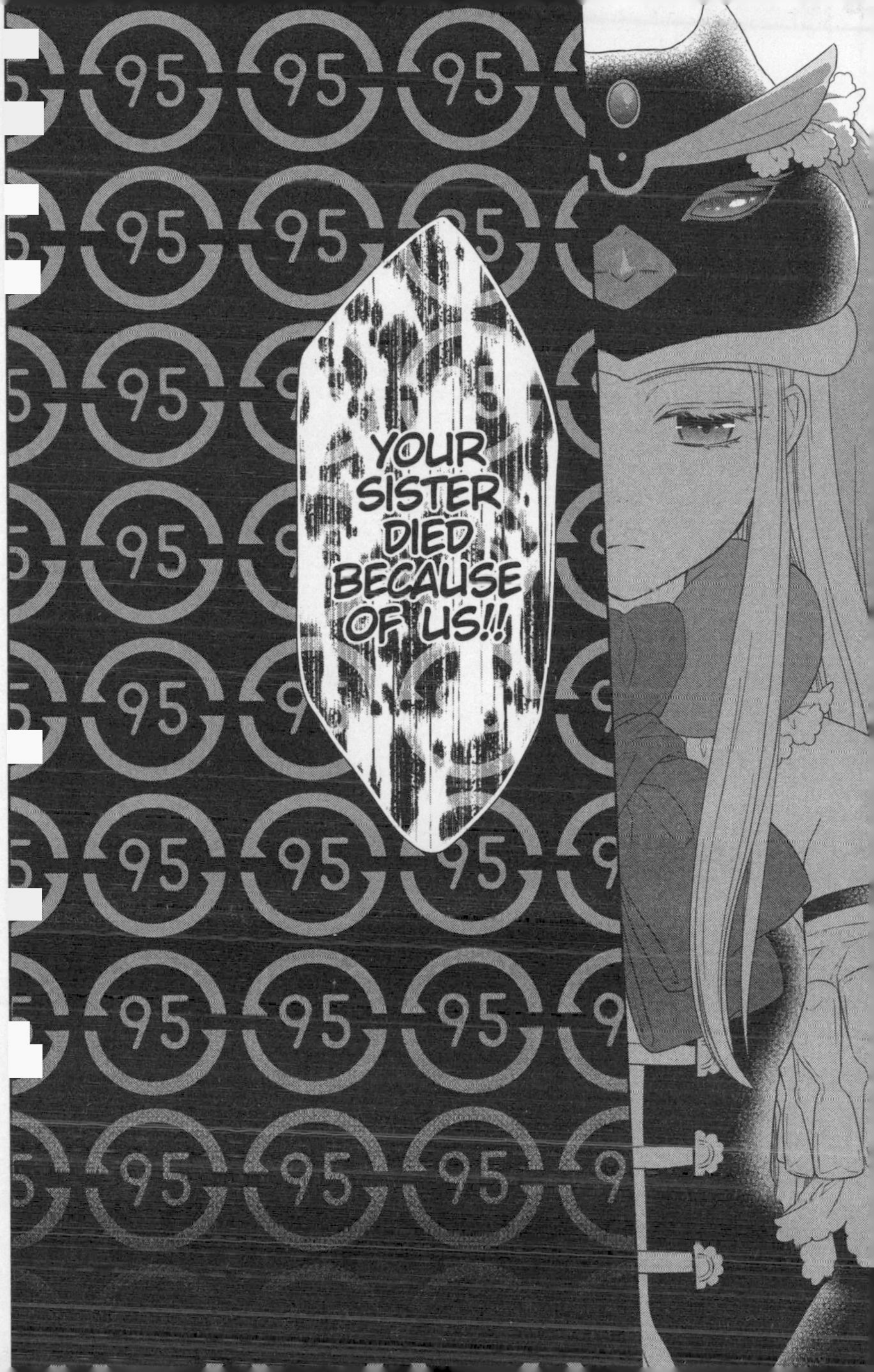
YOUR SISTER DIED BECAUSE OF US!!

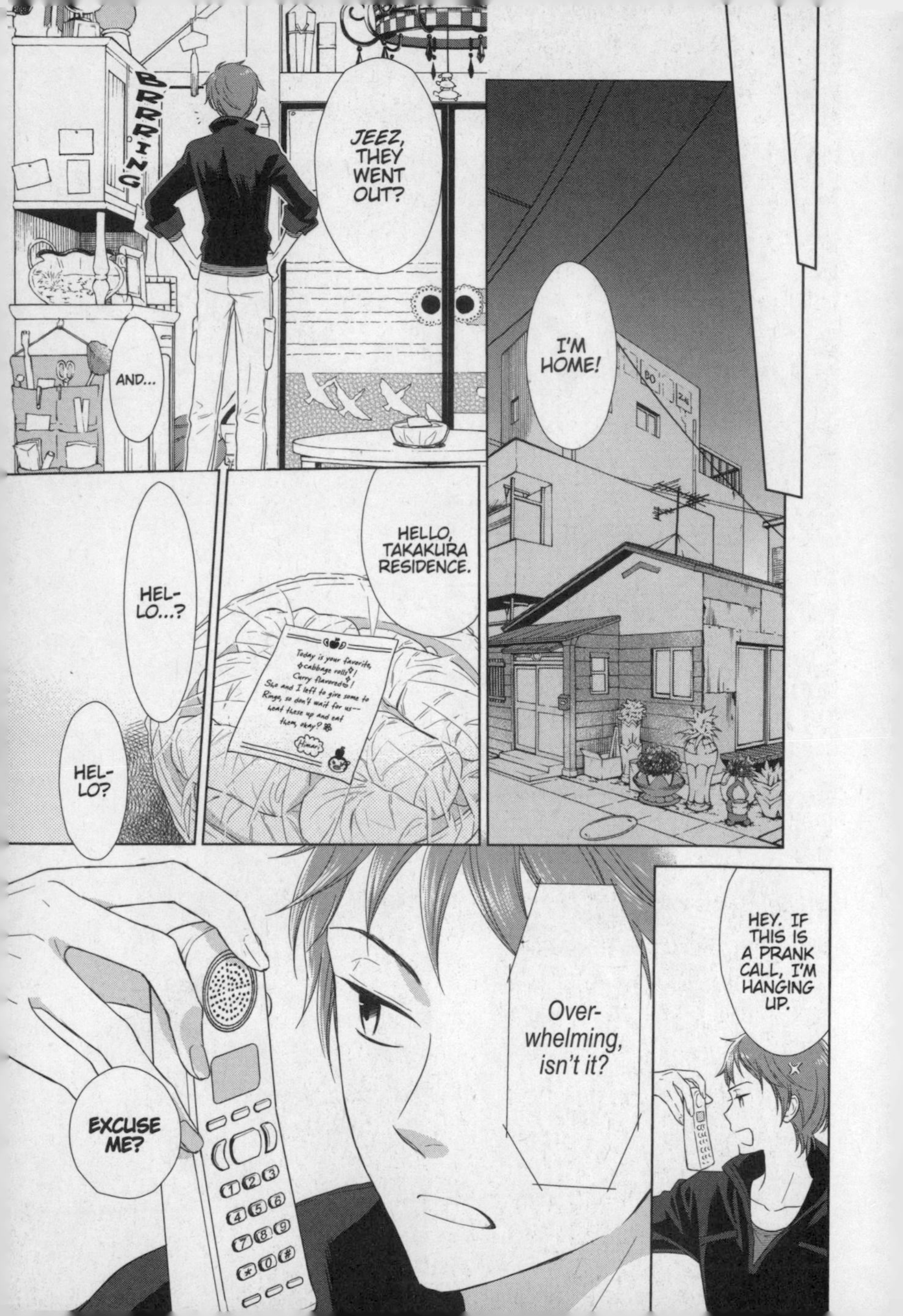
I'M HOME!
JEEZ, THEY WENT OUT?
BRRRING
AND...
HELLO, TAKAKURA RESIDENCE.
Today is your favorite, cabbage rolls! Curry flavored! She and I left to give some to Ringo, so don't wait for us-- heat these up and eat them, okay?
Himari
HEL-LO...?
HEL-LO?
HEY. IF THIS IS A PRANK CALL, I'M HANGING UP.
Over-whelming, isn't it?
EXCUSE ME?

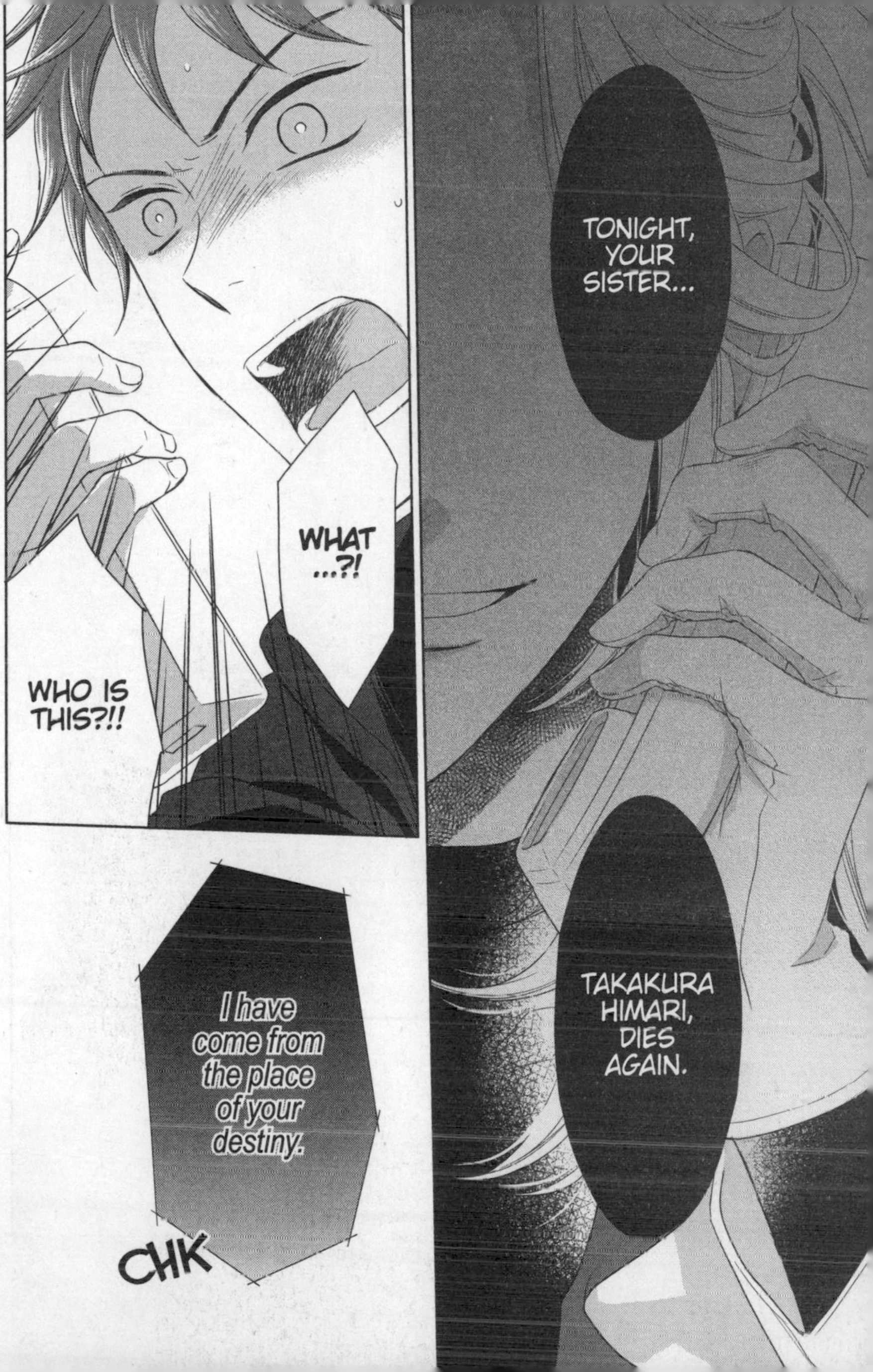
TONIGHT, YOUR SISTER...
TAKAKURA HIMARI, DIES AGAIN.
WHAT ...?!
WHO IS THIS?!!
I have come from the place of your destiny.
CHK

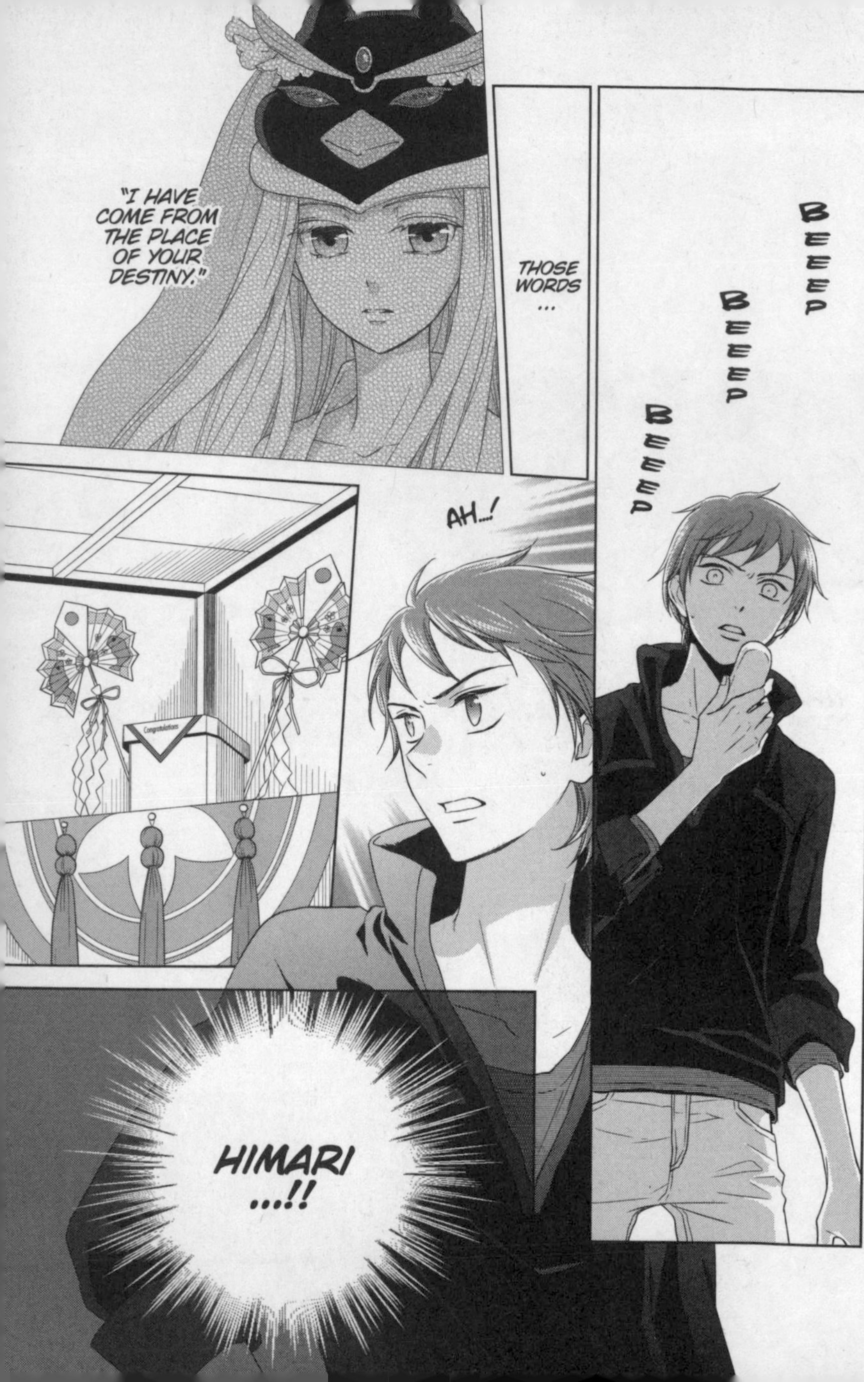

BEEEP
BEEEP
BEEEP
THOSE WORDS ...
"I HAVE COME FROM THE PLACE OF YOUR DESTINY."
AH...!
HIMARI ...!!

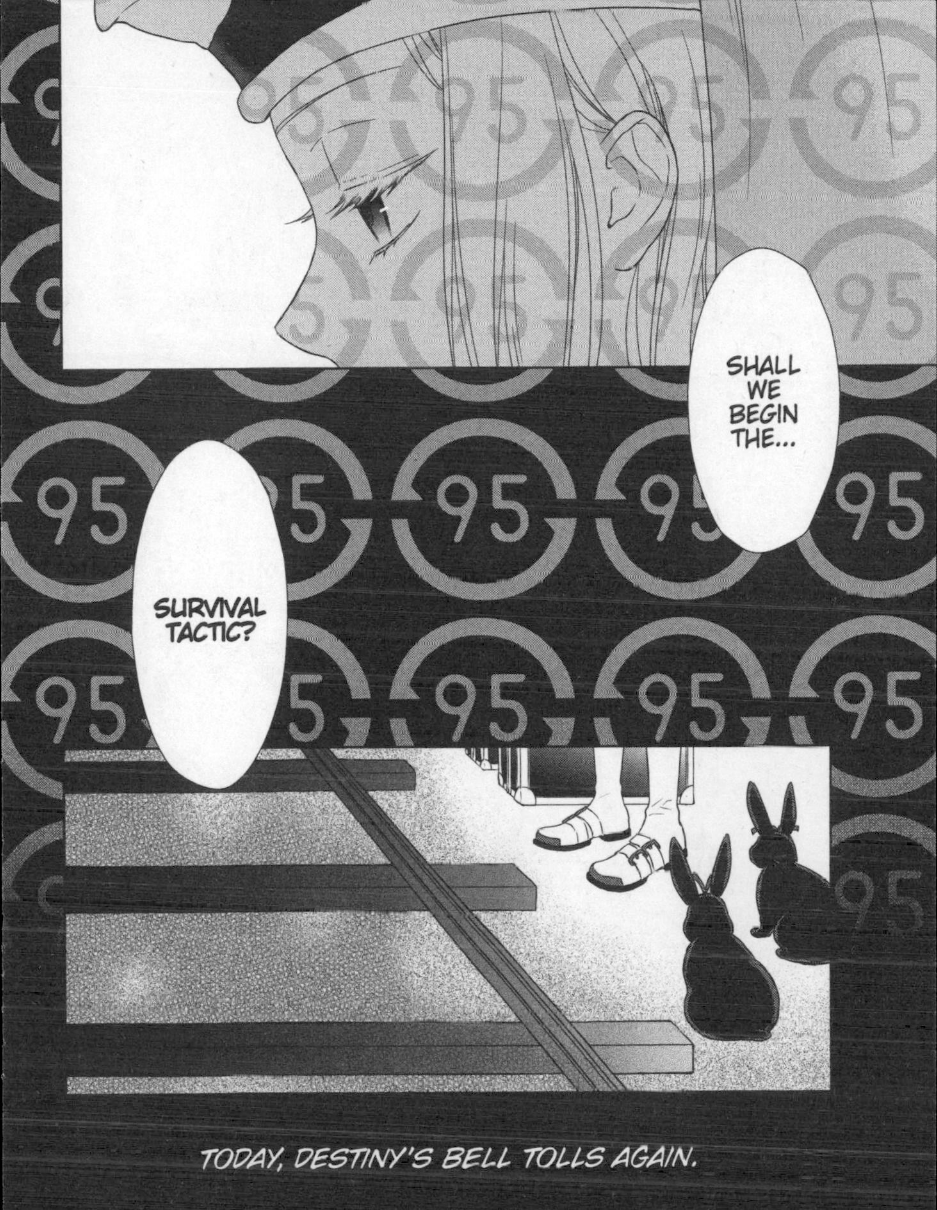
SHALL WE BEGIN THE...
SURVIVAL TACTIC?
TODAY, DESTINY'S BELL TOLLS AGAIN.

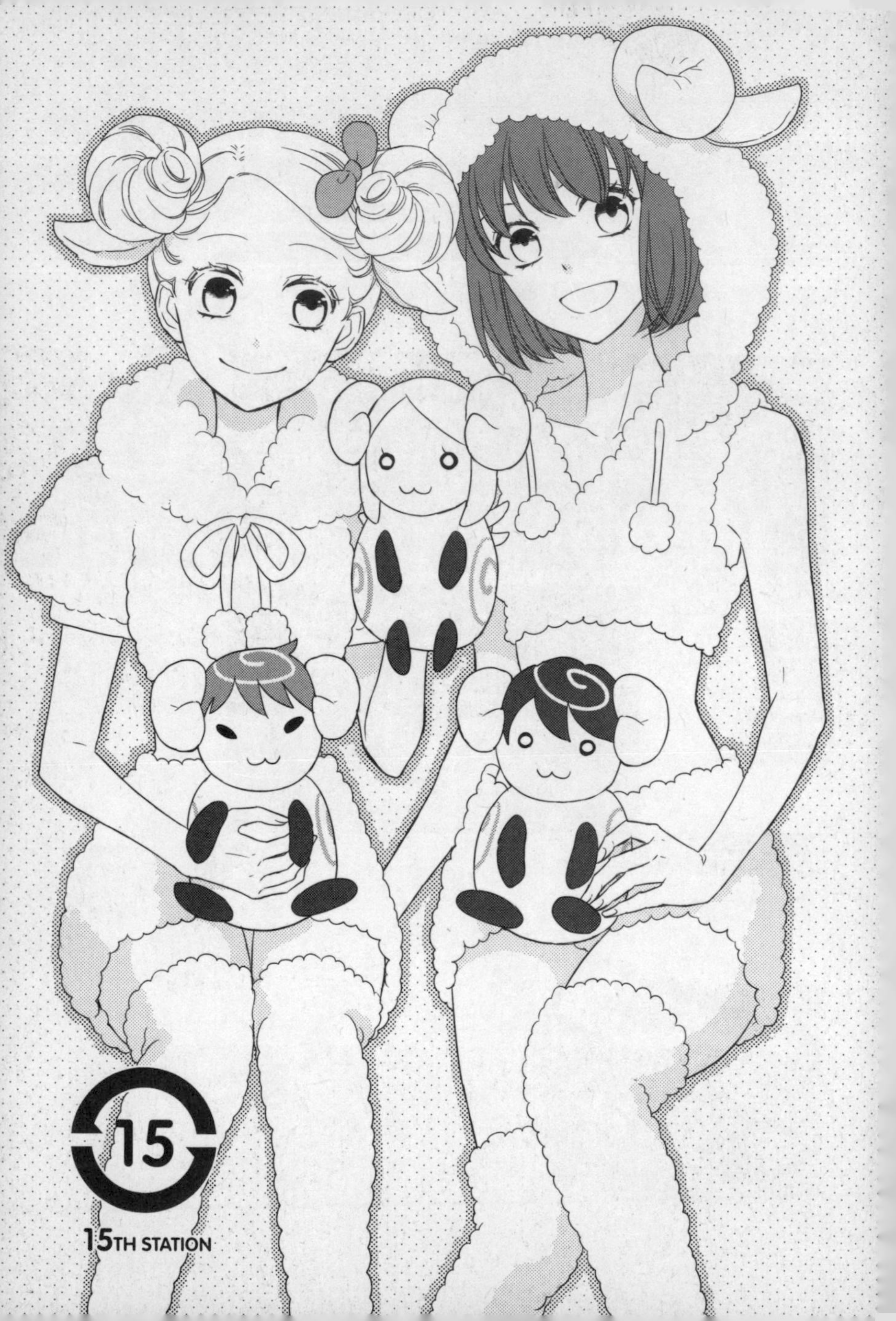
15
15TH STATION

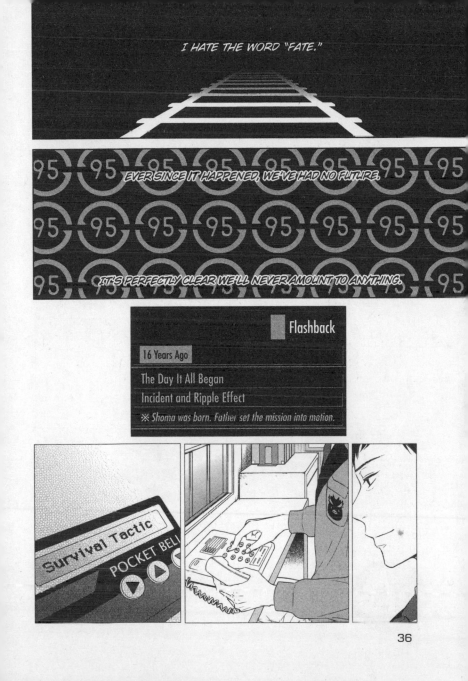

I HATE THE WORD "FATE."

EVER SINCE IT HAPPENED, WE'VE HAD NO FUTURE.

IT'S PERFECTLY CLEAR WE'LL NEVER AMOUNT TO ANYTHING.

Flashback

16 Years Ago

The Day It All Began

Incident and Ripple Effect

※ Shoma was born. Father set the mission into motion.

Survival Tactic

POCKET BELL

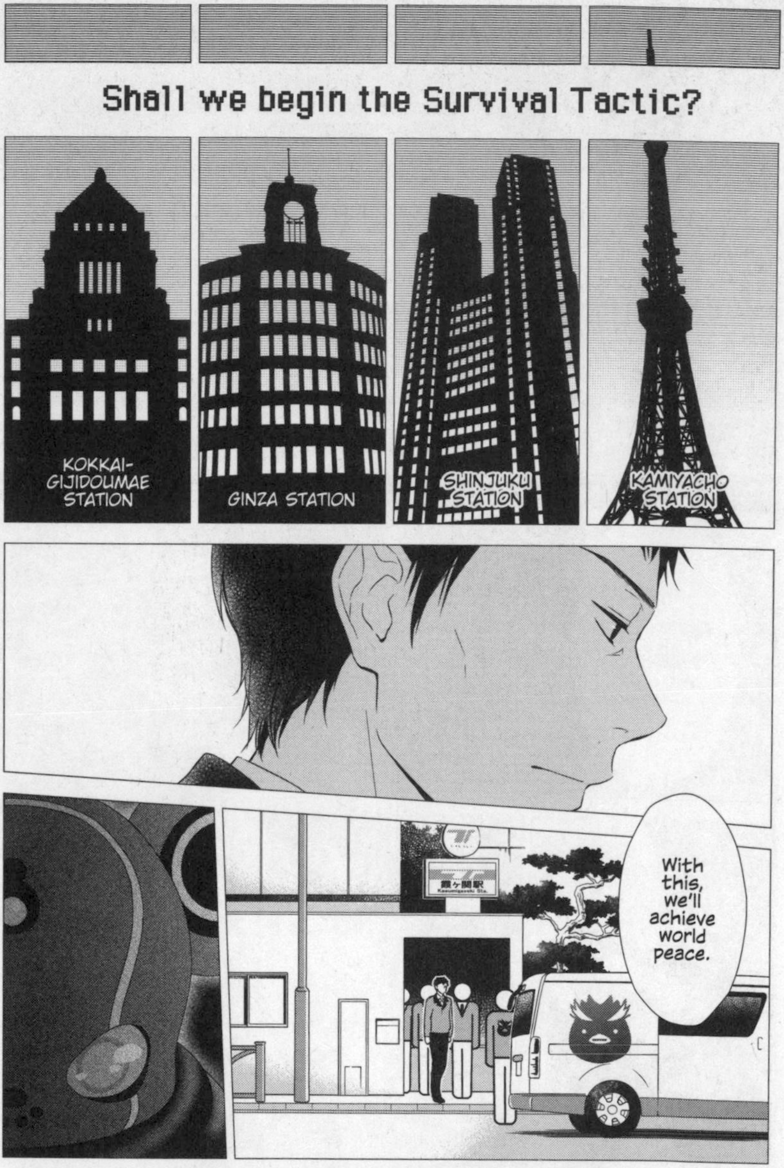
Shall we begin the Survival Tactic?
KAMIYACHO STATION
SHINJUKU STATION
GINZA STATION
KOKKAI-GIJIDOUMAE STATION
With this, we'll achieve world peace.

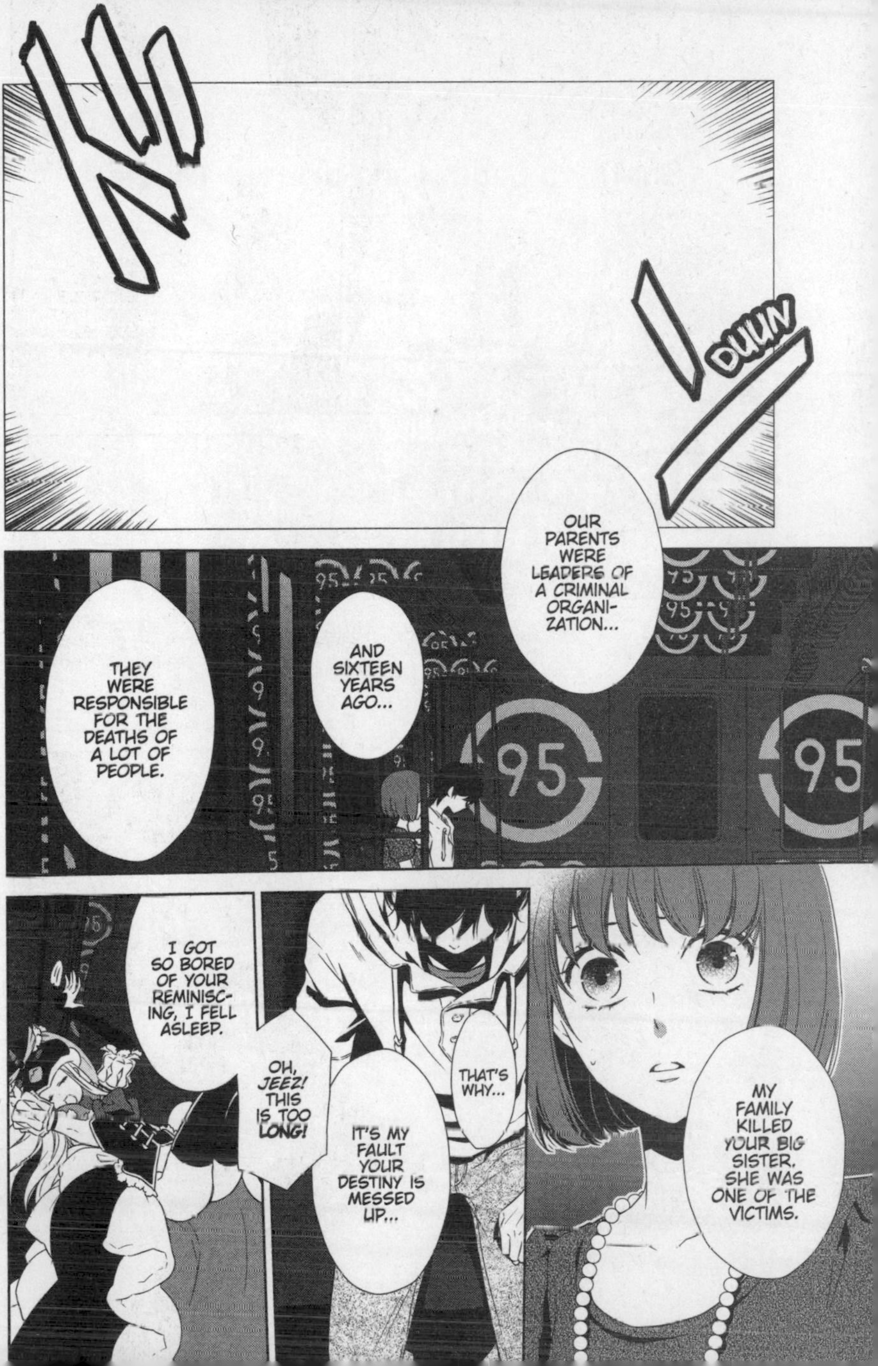
DUUN
OUR PARENTS WERE LEADERS OF A CRIMINAL ORGANIZATION...
AND SIXTEEN YEARS AGO...
THEY WERE RESPONSIBLE FOR THE DEATHS OF A LOT OF PEOPLE.
MY FAMILY KILLED YOUR BIG SISTER. SHE WAS ONE OF THE VICTIMS.
THAT'S WHY...
IT'S MY FAULT YOUR DESTINY IS MESSED UP...
OH, JEEZ! THIS IS TOO LONG!
I GOT SO BORED OF YOUR REMINISCING, I FELL ASLEEP.

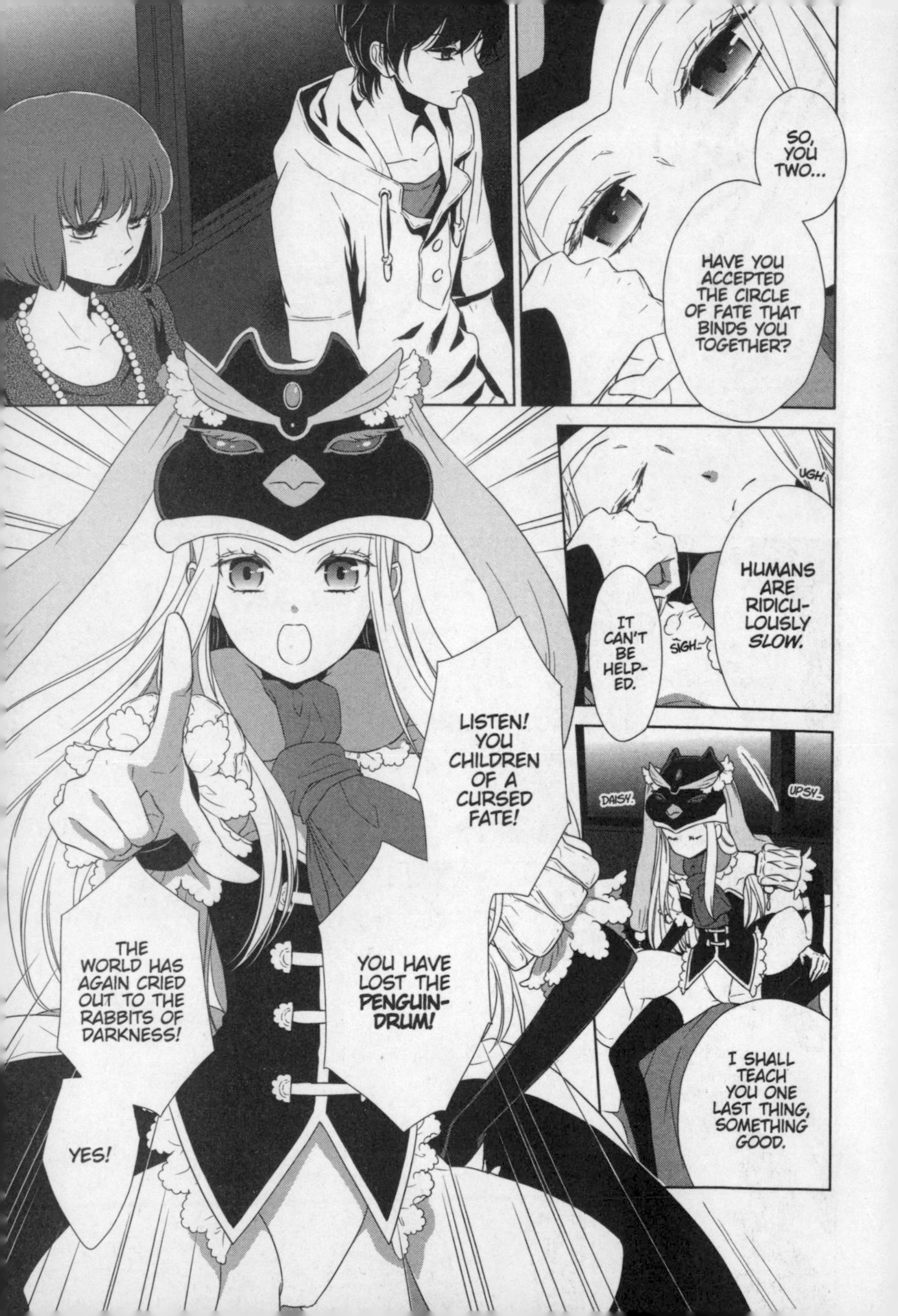
SO, YOU TWO...
HAVE YOU ACCEPTED THE CIRCLE OF FATE THAT BINDS YOU TOGETHER?
UGH.
HUMANS ARE RIDICULOUSLY SLOW.
SIGH...
IT CAN'T BE HELPED.
UPSY...
DAISY.
I SHALL TEACH YOU ONE LAST THING, SOMETHING GOOD.
LISTEN! YOU CHILDREN OF A CURSED FATE!
YOU HAVE LOST THE PENGUINDRUM!
THE WORLD HAS AGAIN CRIED OUT TO THE RABBITS OF DARKNESS!
YES!

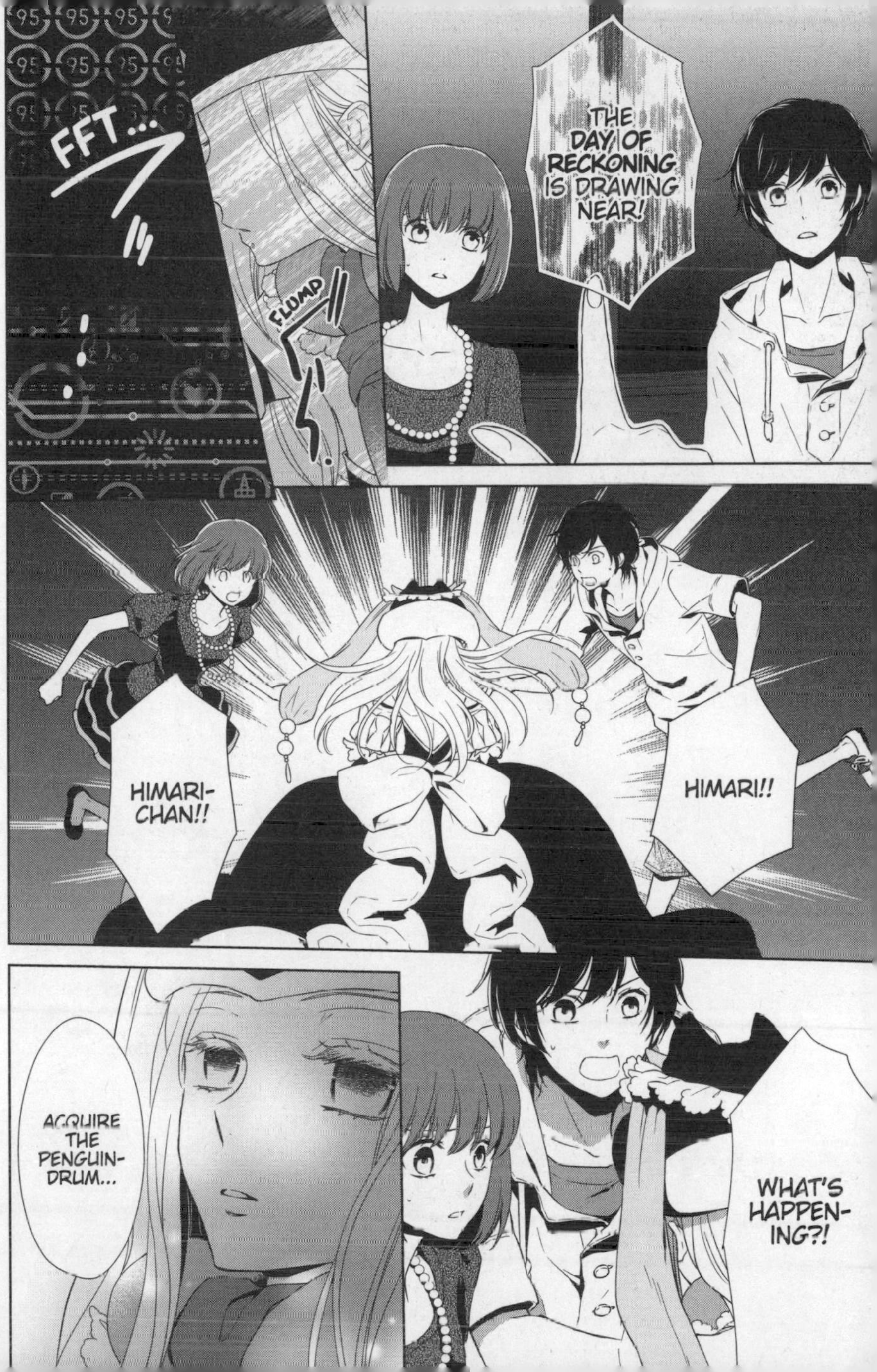
THE DAY OF RECKONING IS DRAWING NEAR!
FFT...
FLUMP
HIMARI!!
HIMARI-CHAN!!
WHAT'S HAPPEN-ING?!
ACQUIRE THE PENGUIN-DRUM...

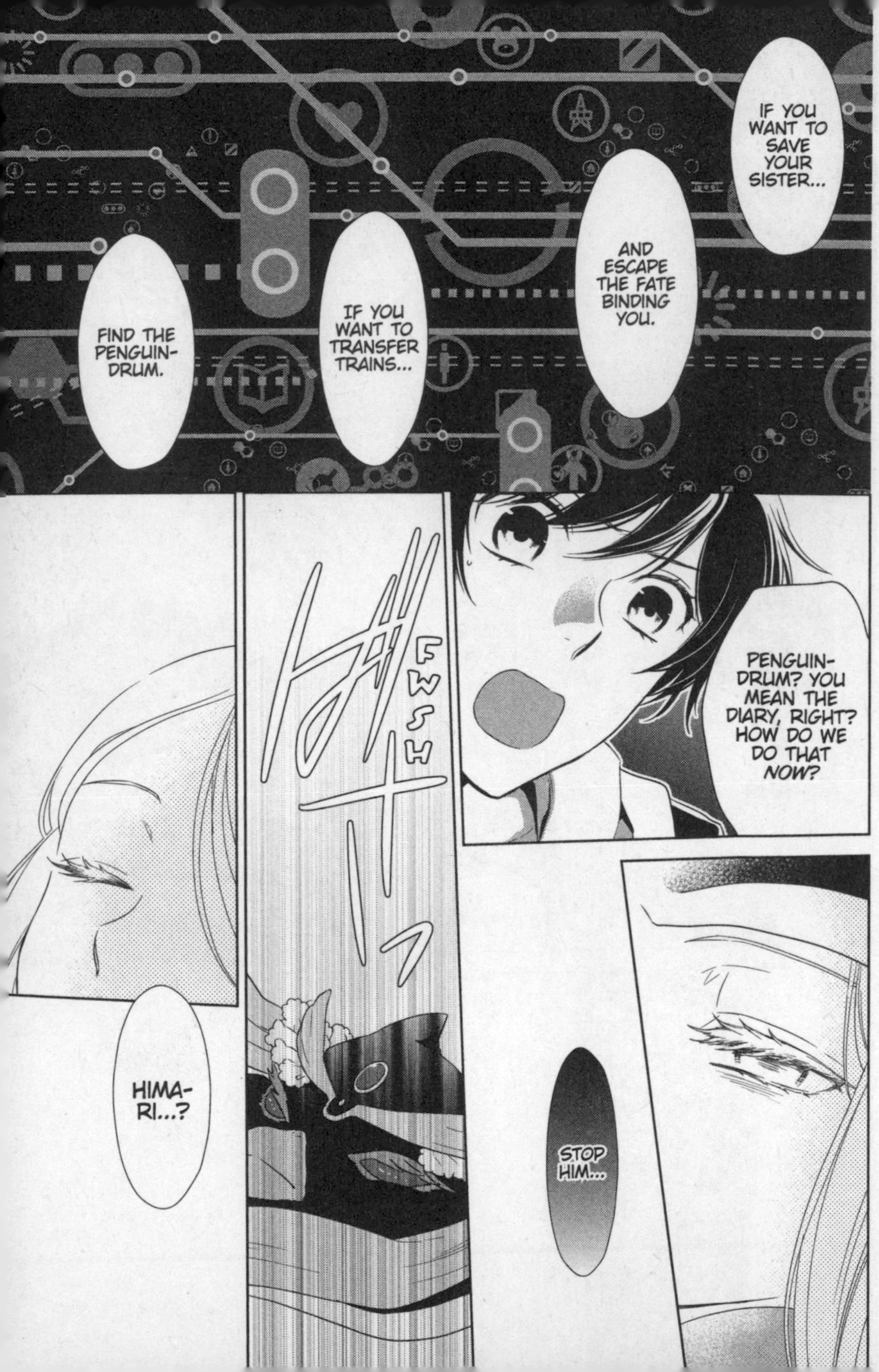
IF YOU WANT TO SAVE YOUR SISTER...
AND ESCAPE THE FATE BINDING YOU.
IF YOU WANT TO TRANSFER TRAINS...
FIND THE PENGUIN-DRUM.
PENGUIN-DRUM? YOU MEAN THE DIARY, RIGHT? HOW DO WE DO THAT NOW?
FWSH
STOP HIM...
HIMA-RI...?

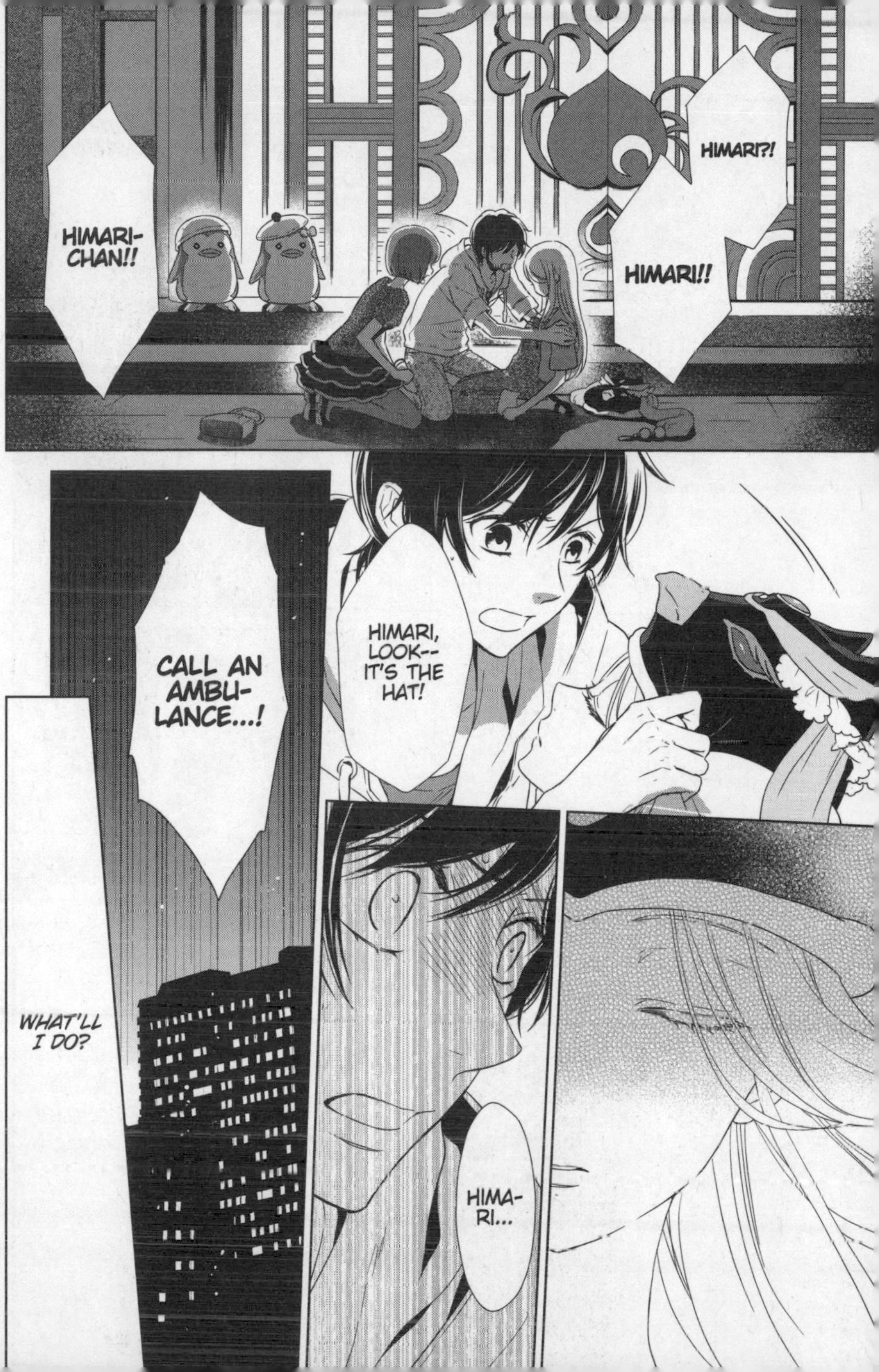
HIMARI?!
HIMARI!!
HIMARI-CHAN!!
HIMARI, LOOK--IT'S THE HAT!
CALL AN AMBULANCE...!
HIMA-RI...
WHAT'LL I DO?

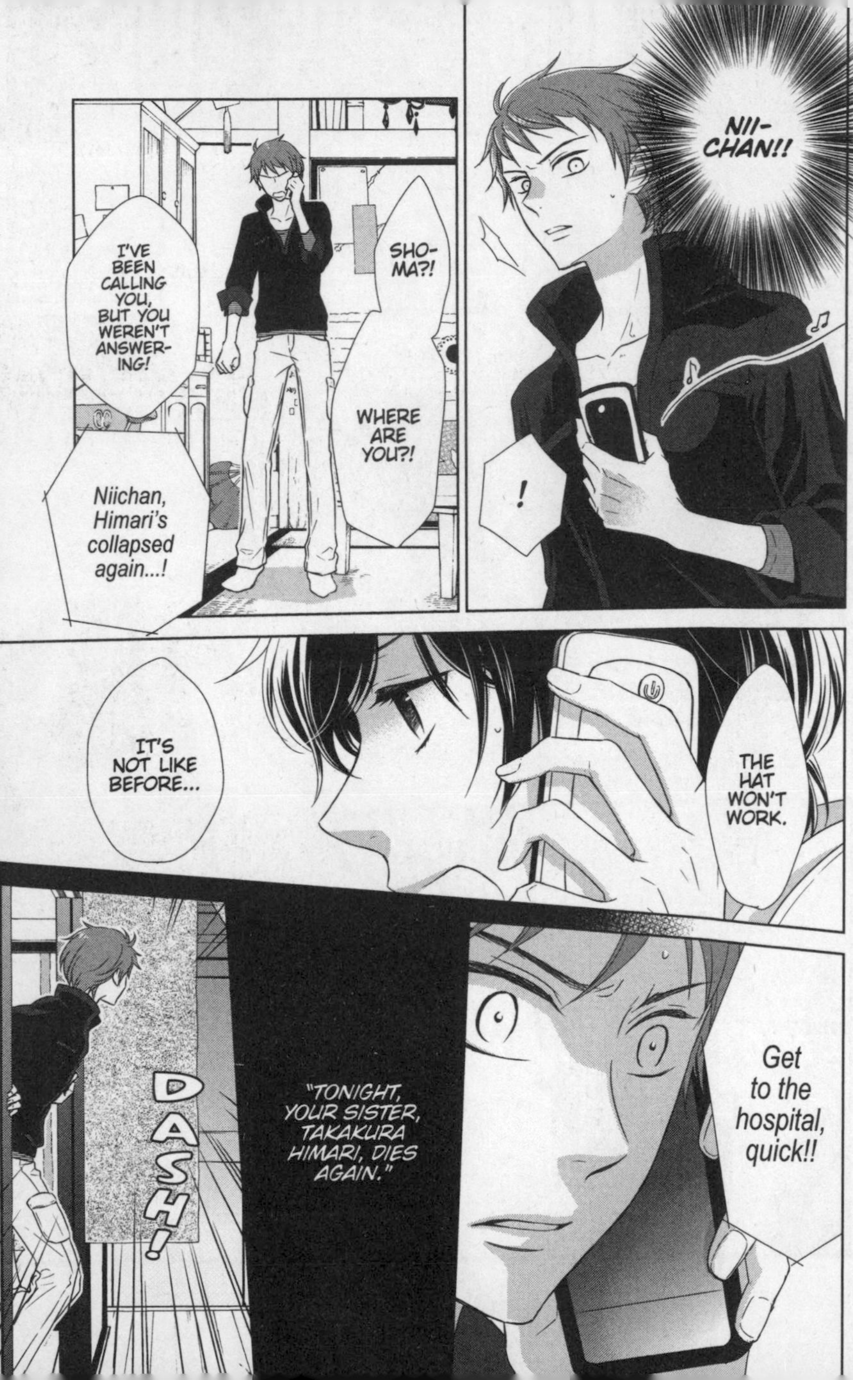
NII-CHAN!!
!
SHO-MA?!
WHERE ARE YOU?!
I'VE BEEN CALLING YOU, BUT YOU WEREN'T ANSWERING!
Niichan, Himari's collapsed again...!
THE HAT WON'T WORK.
IT'S NOT LIKE BEFORE...
Get to the hospital, quick!!
"TONIGHT, YOUR SISTER, TAKAKURA HIMARI, DIES AGAIN."
DASH!

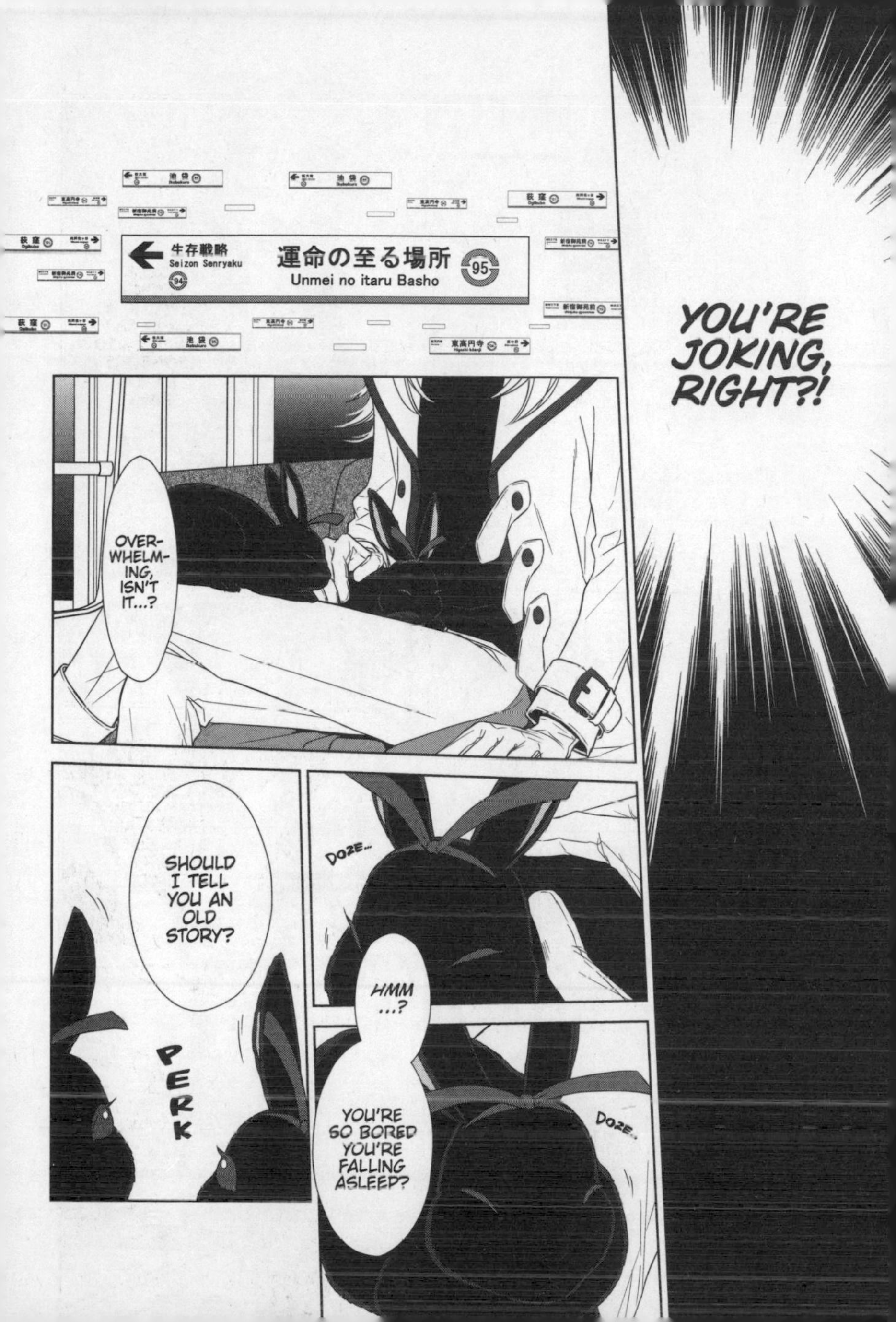
YOU'RE JOKING, RIGHT?!
牛存戦略
Seizon Senryaku
94
運命の至る場所
Unmei no itaru Basho
95
OVER-WHELMING, ISN'T IT...?
DOZE...
HMM ...?
YOU'RE SO BORED YOU'RE FALLING ASLEEP?
DOZE..
SHOULD I TELL YOU AN OLD STORY?
PERK

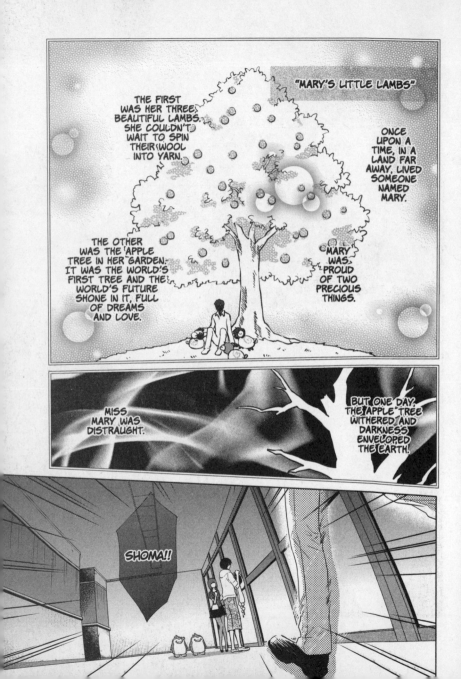

"MARY'S LITTLE LAMBS"

ONCE UPON A TIME, IN A LAND FAR AWAY, LIVED SOMEONE NAMED MARY.

MARY WAS PROUD OF TWO PRECIOUS THINGS.

THE FIRST WAS HER THREE BEAUTIFUL LAMBS. SHE COULDN'T WAIT TO SPIN THEIR WOOL INTO YARN.

THE OTHER WAS THE APPLE TREE IN HER GARDEN. IT WAS THE WORLD'S FIRST TREE AND THE WORLD'S FUTURE SHONE IN IT, FULL OF DREAMS AND LOVE.

BUT ONE DAY, THE APPLE TREE WITHERED AND DARKNESS ENVELOPED THE EARTH!

MISS MARY WAS DISTRAUGHT.

SHOMA!!

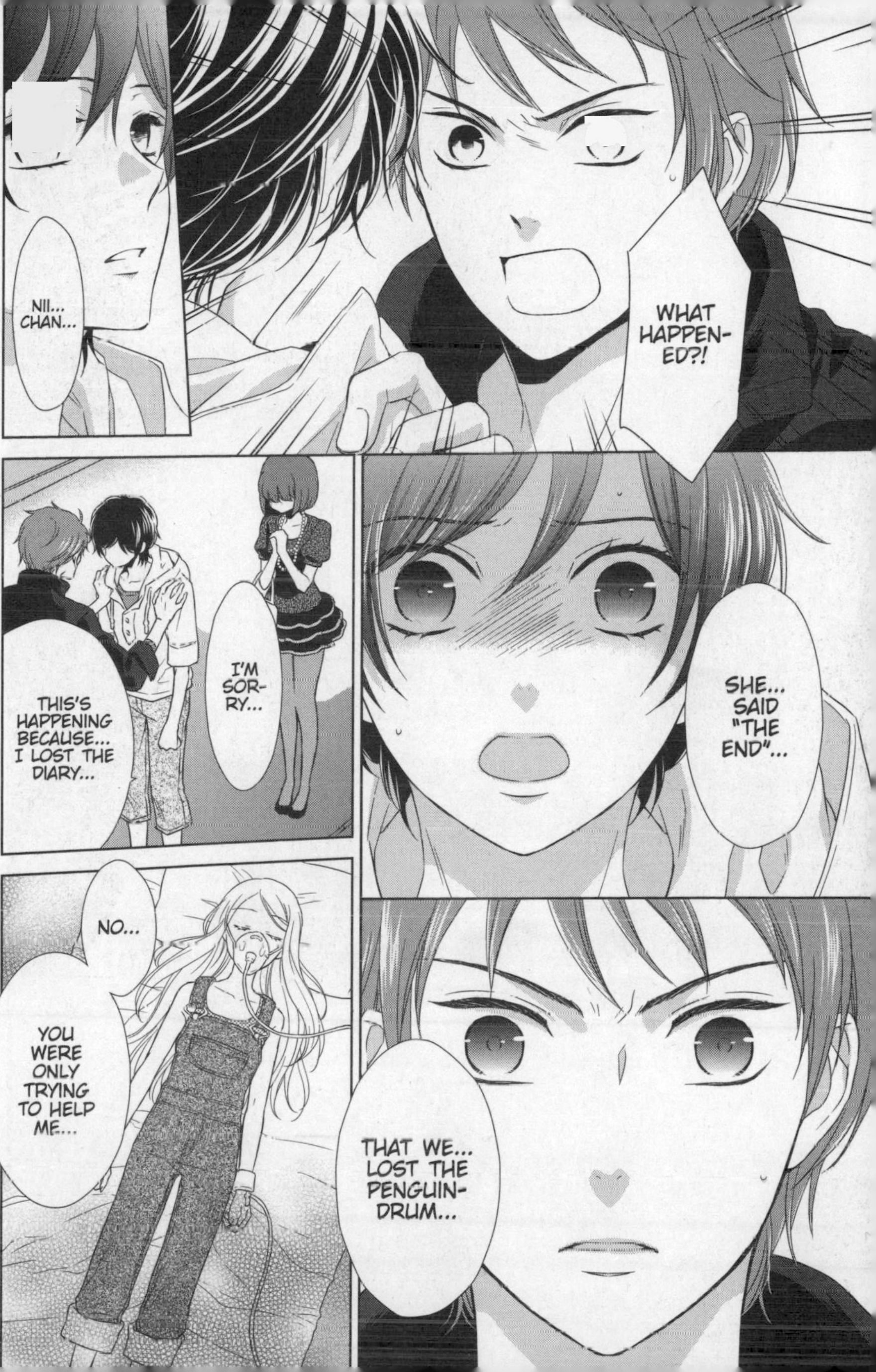
WHAT HAPPEN-ED?!
NII... CHAN...
SHE... SAID "THE END"...
I'M SOR-RY...
THIS'S HAPPENING BECAUSE... I LOST THE DIARY...
THAT WE... LOST THE PENGUIN-DRUM...
NO...
YOU WERE ONLY TRYING TO HELP ME...

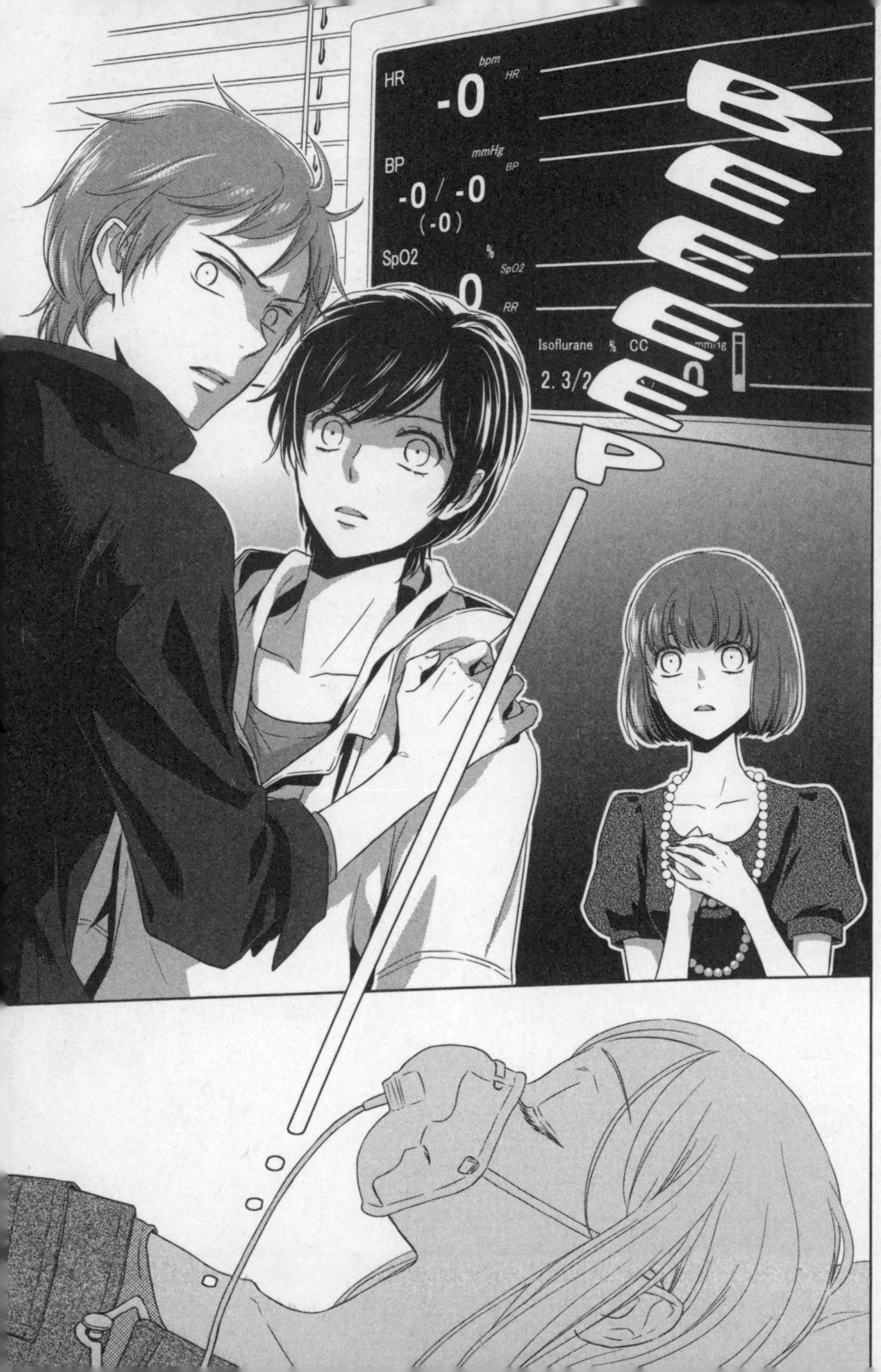
HR
bpm
-0
BP
mmHg
-0 / -0
(-0)
SpO2
%
RR
Isoflurane % CC
BEEEEEP

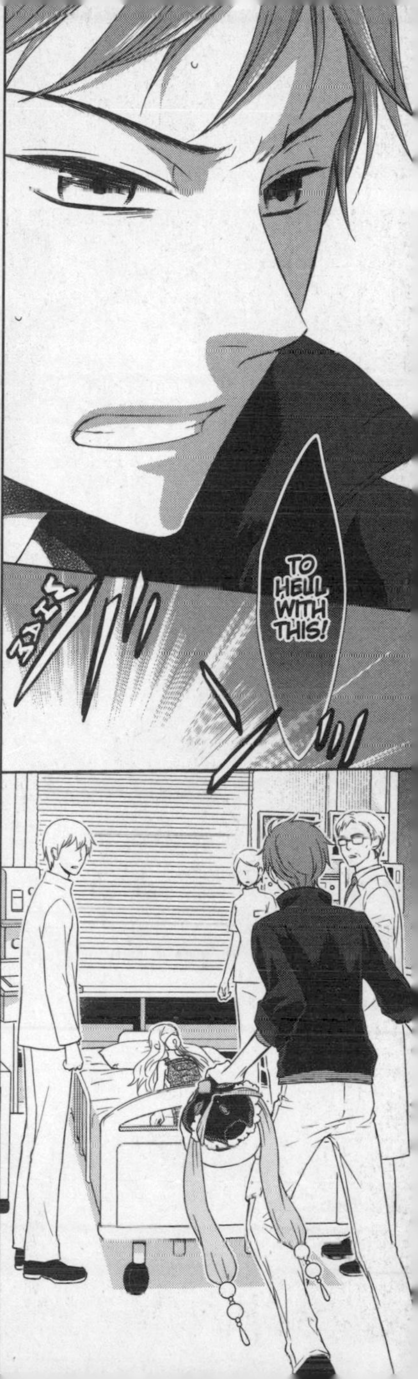
TO HELL WITH THIS!
WHAM
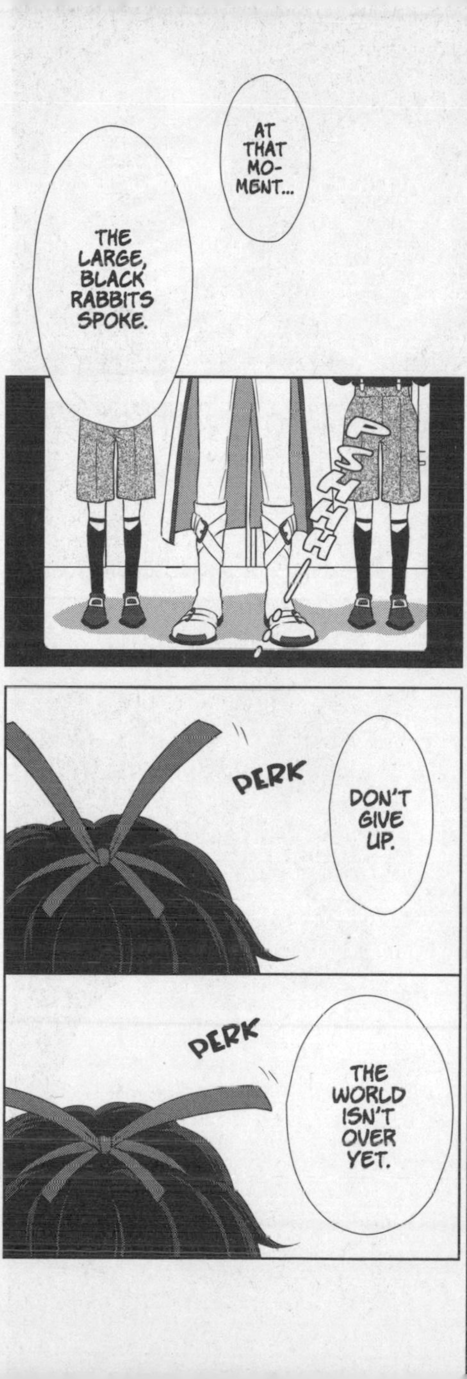
AT THAT MO-MENT...
THE LARGE, BLACK RABBITS SPOKE.
PSHHH
PERK
DON'T GIVE UP.
PERK
THE WORLD ISN'T OVER YET.

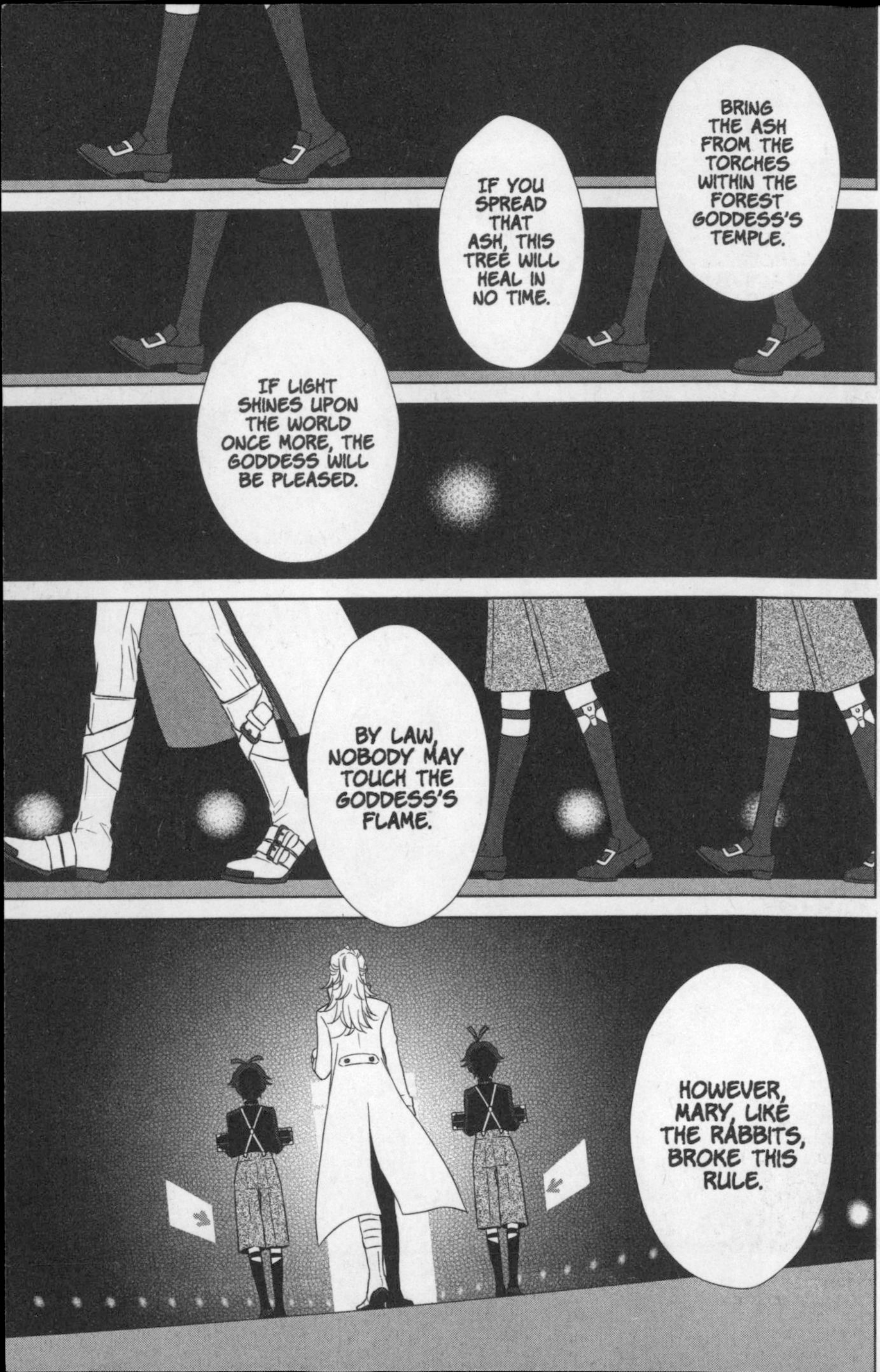
BRING THE ASH FROM THE TORCHES WITHIN THE FOREST GODDESS'S TEMPLE.
IF YOU SPREAD THAT ASH, THIS TREE WILL HEAL IN NO TIME.
IF LIGHT SHINES UPON THE WORLD ONCE MORE, THE GODDESS WILL BE PLEASED.
BY LAW, NOBODY MAY TOUCH THE GODDESS'S FLAME.
HOWEVER, MARY, LIKE THE RABBITS, BROKE THIS RULE.

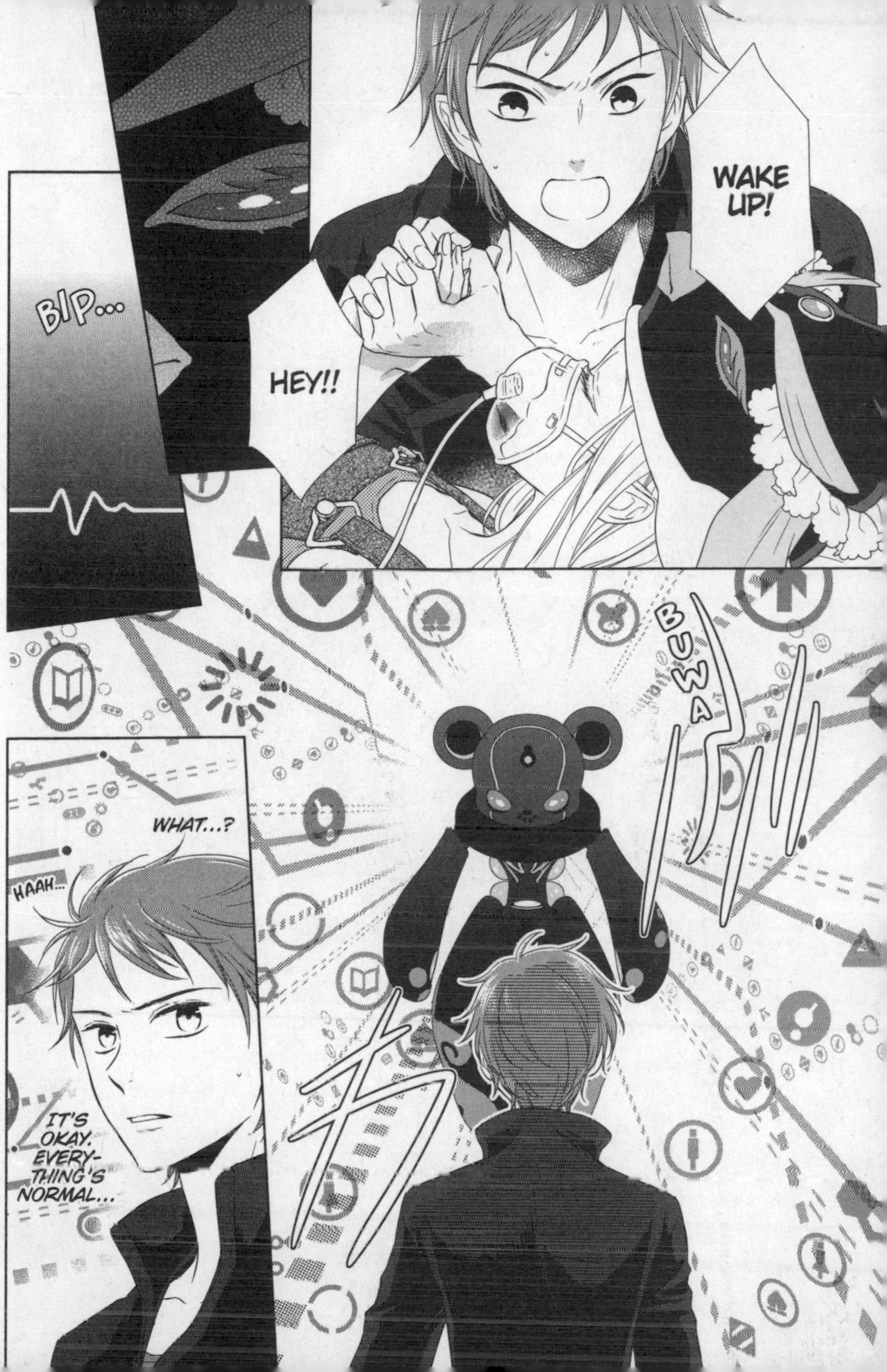
WAKE UP!
HEY!!
BIP...
BUWA
WHAT...?
HAAH...
IT'S OKAY. EVERYTHING'S NORMAL...

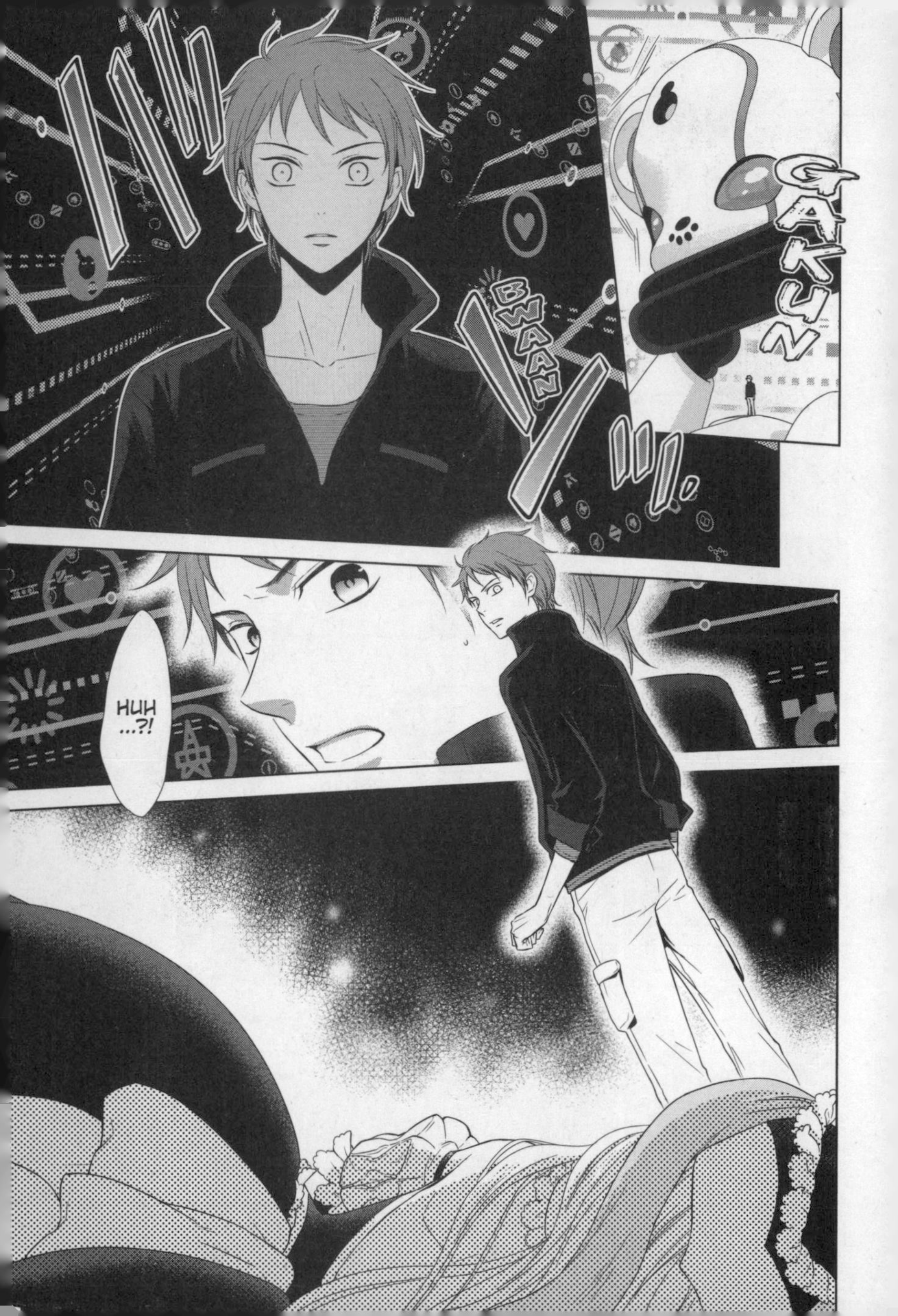
GAKUN
BWAAN
HUH ...?!

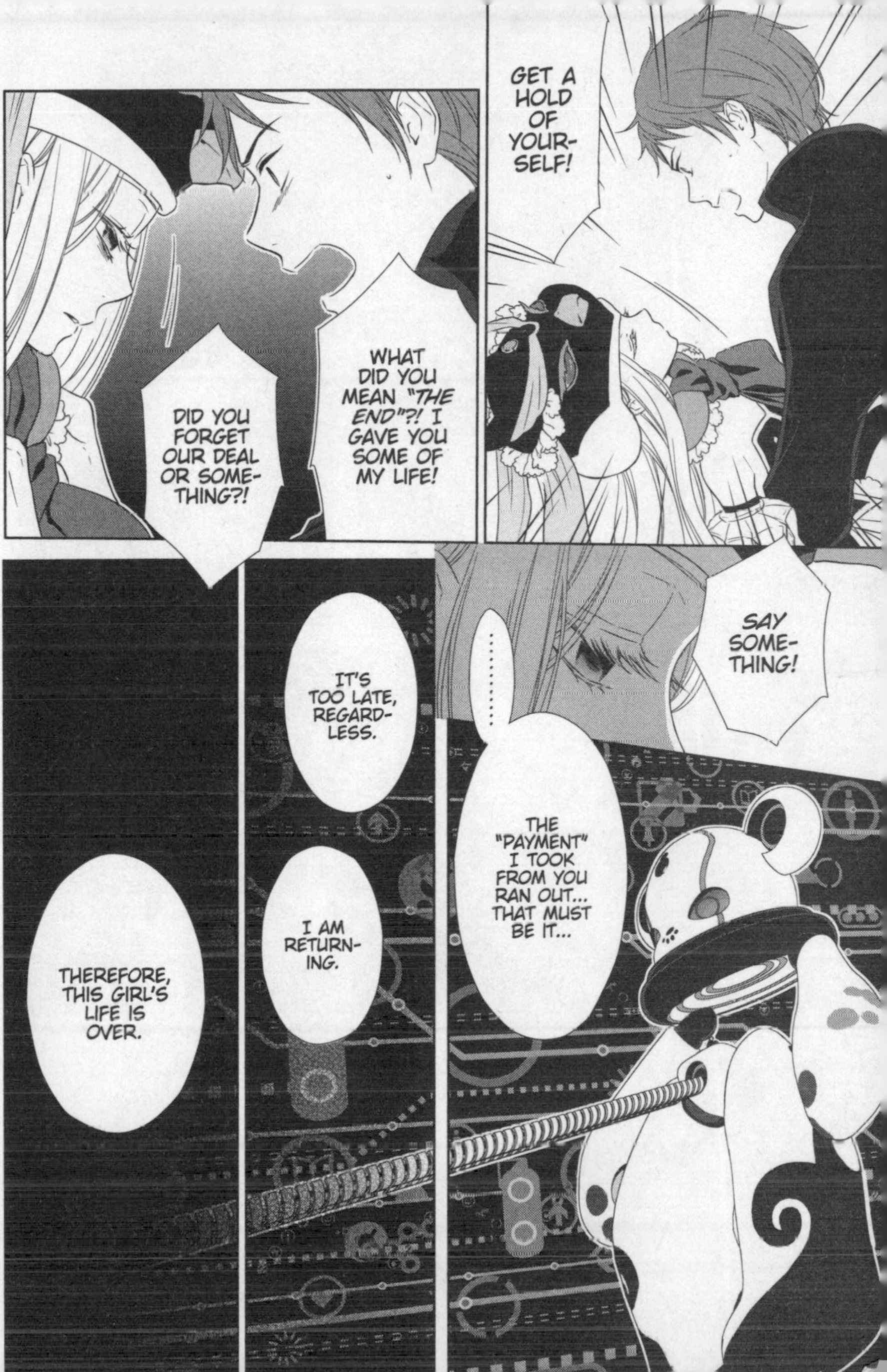
GET A HOLD OF YOURSELF!
WHAT DID YOU MEAN "THE END"?! I GAVE YOU SOME OF MY LIFE!
DID YOU FORGET OUR DEAL OR SOMETHING?!
SAY SOMETHING!
......
THE "PAYMENT" I TOOK FROM YOU RAN OUT... THAT MUST BE IT...
IT'S TOO LATE, REGARDLESS.
I AM RETURNING.
THEREFORE, THIS GIRL'S LIFE IS OVER.

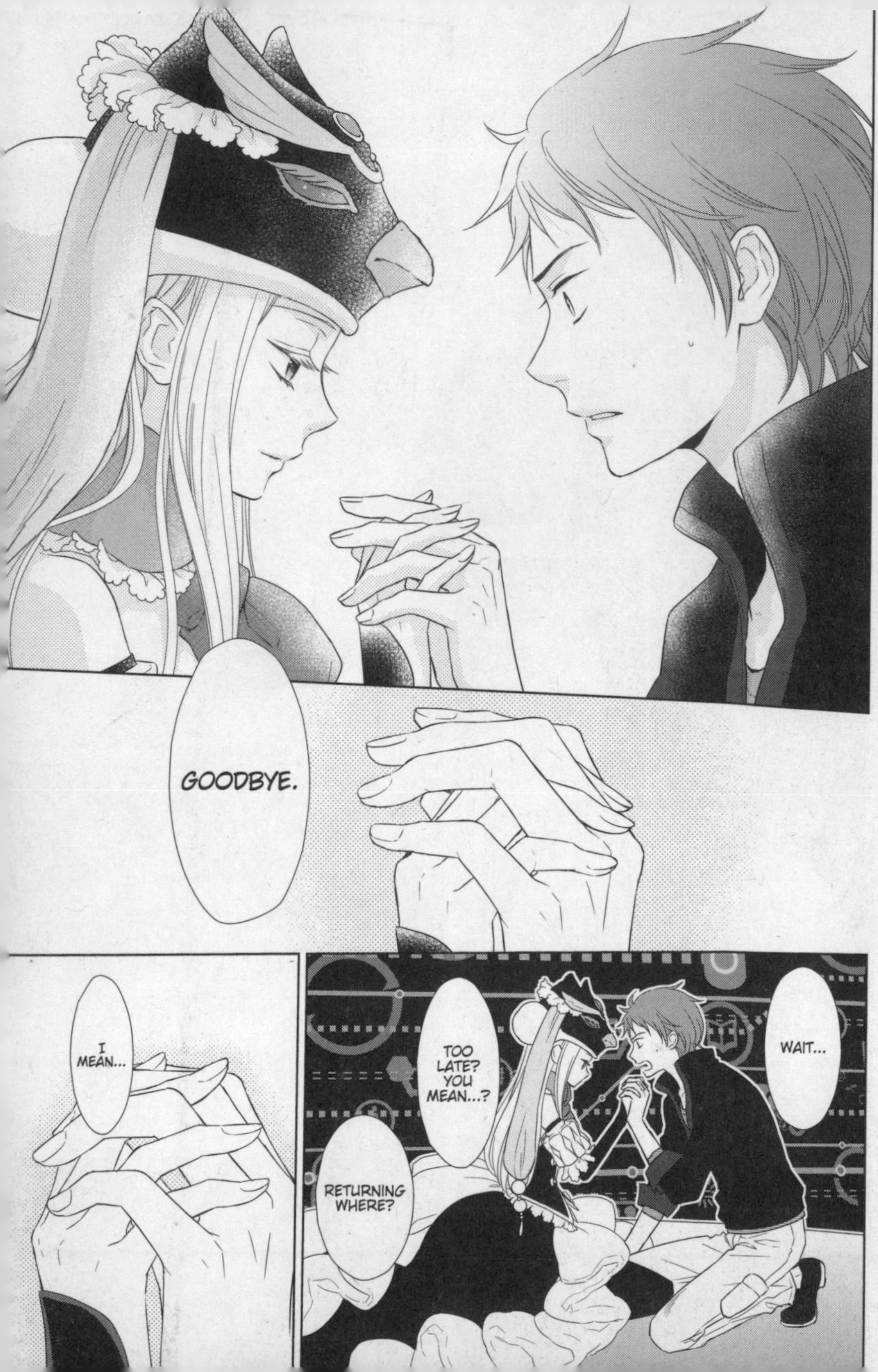
GOODBYE.
WAIT...
TOO LATE? YOU MEAN...?
RETURNING WHERE?
I MEAN...

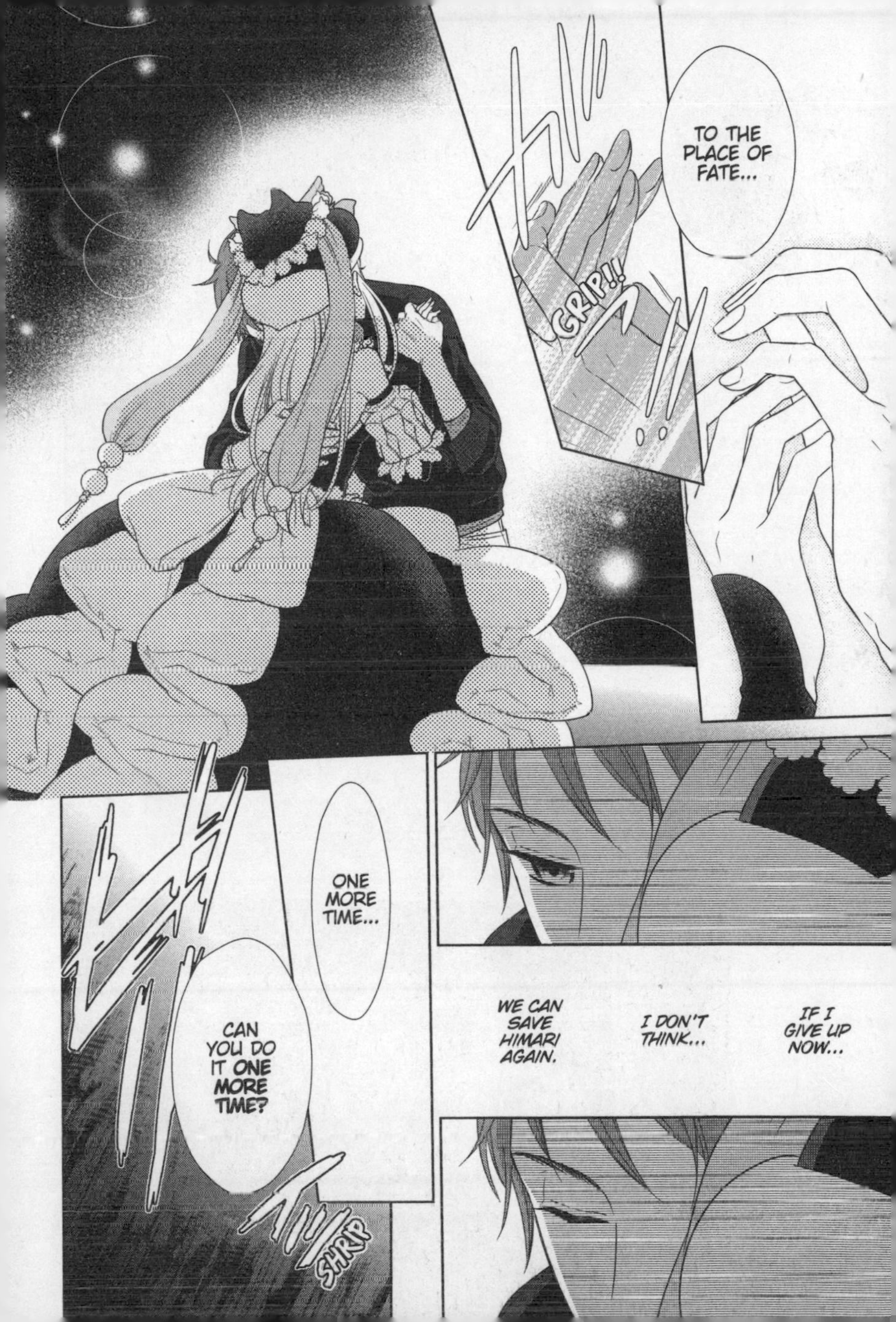
TO THE PLACE OF FATE...
GRIP!!
IF I GIVE UP NOW...
I DON'T THINK...
WE CAN SAVE HIMARI AGAIN.
ONE MORE TIME...
CAN YOU DO IT ONE MORE TIME?
SHRIP

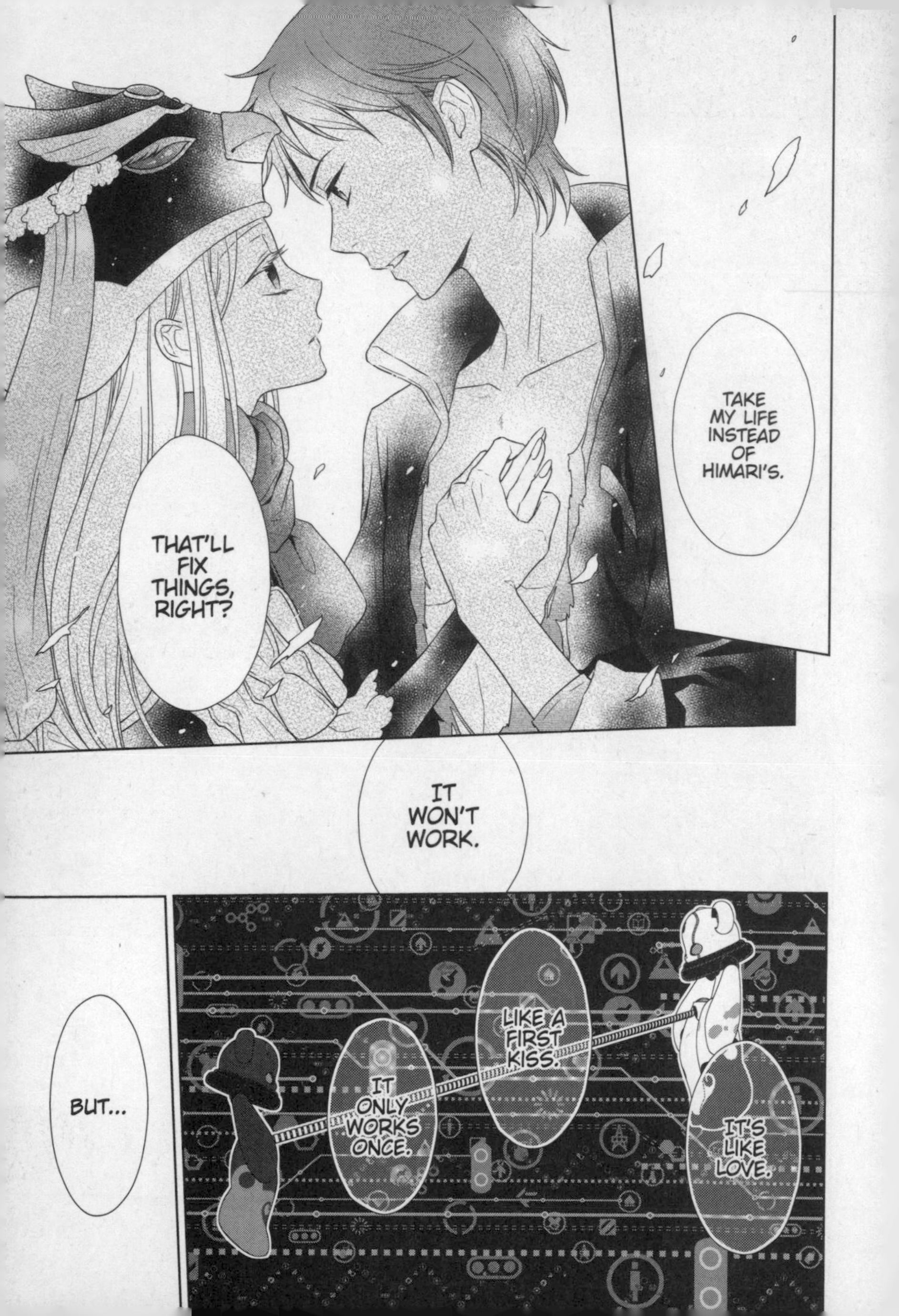
TAKE MY LIFE INSTEAD OF HIMARI'S.
THAT'LL FIX THINGS, RIGHT?
IT WON'T WORK.
IT'S LIKE LOVE.
LIKE A FIRST KISS.
IT ONLY WORKS ONCE.
BUT...

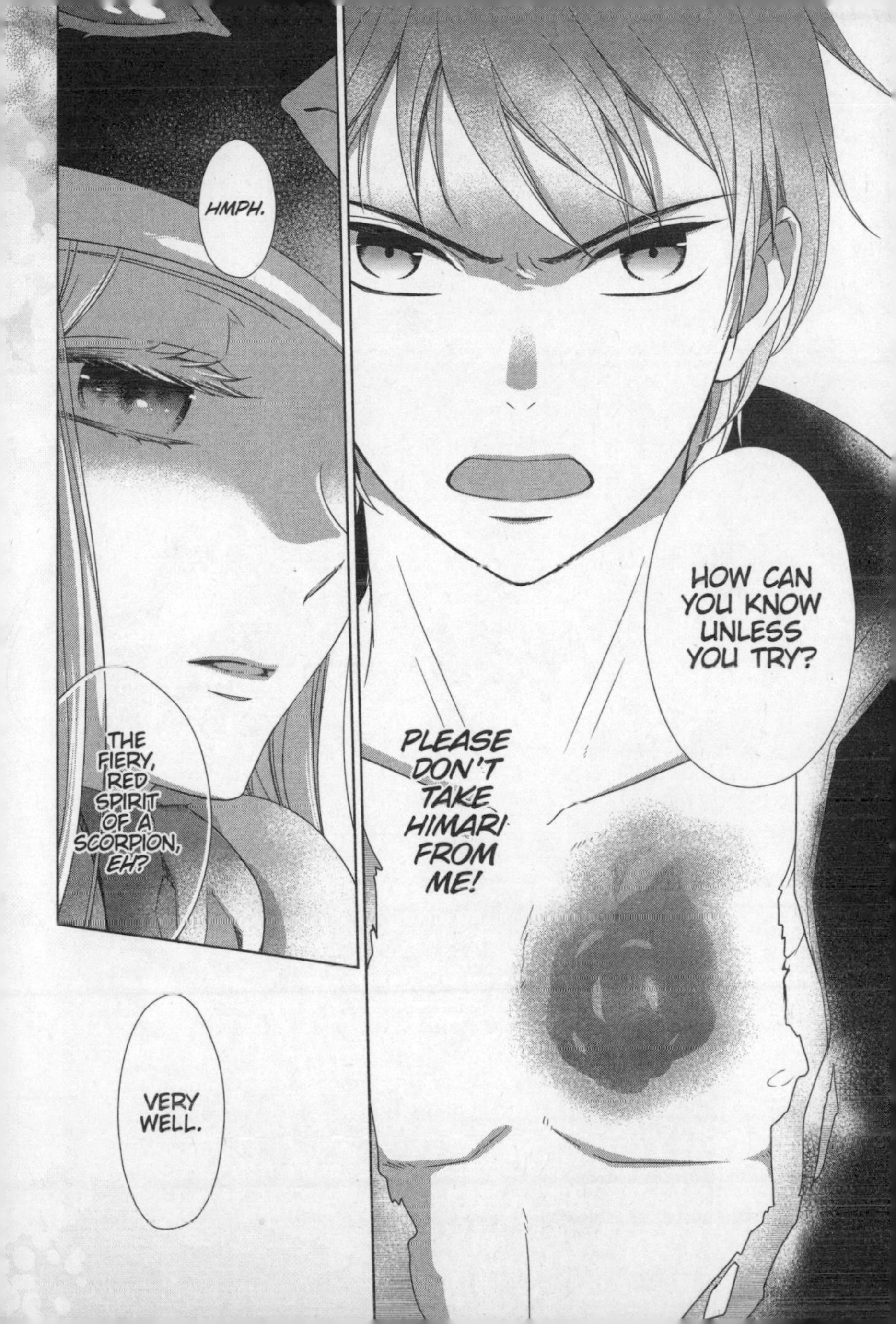
HOW CAN YOU KNOW UNLESS YOU TRY?
PLEASE DON'T TAKE HIMARI FROM ME!
HMPH.
THE FIERY, RED SPIRIT OF A SCORPION, EH?
VERY WELL.

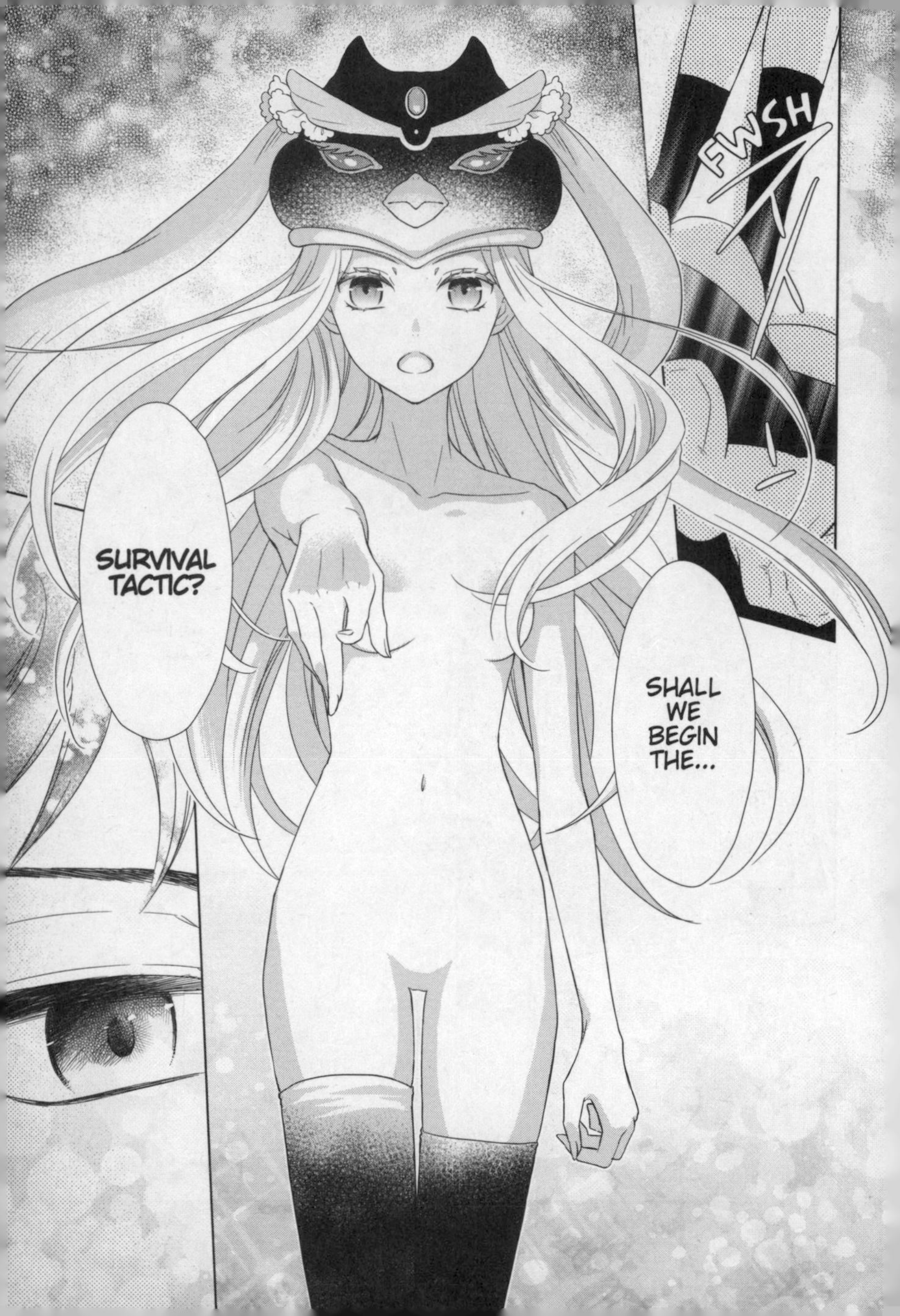
FWSH
SHALL WE BEGIN THE...
SURVIVAL TACTIC?

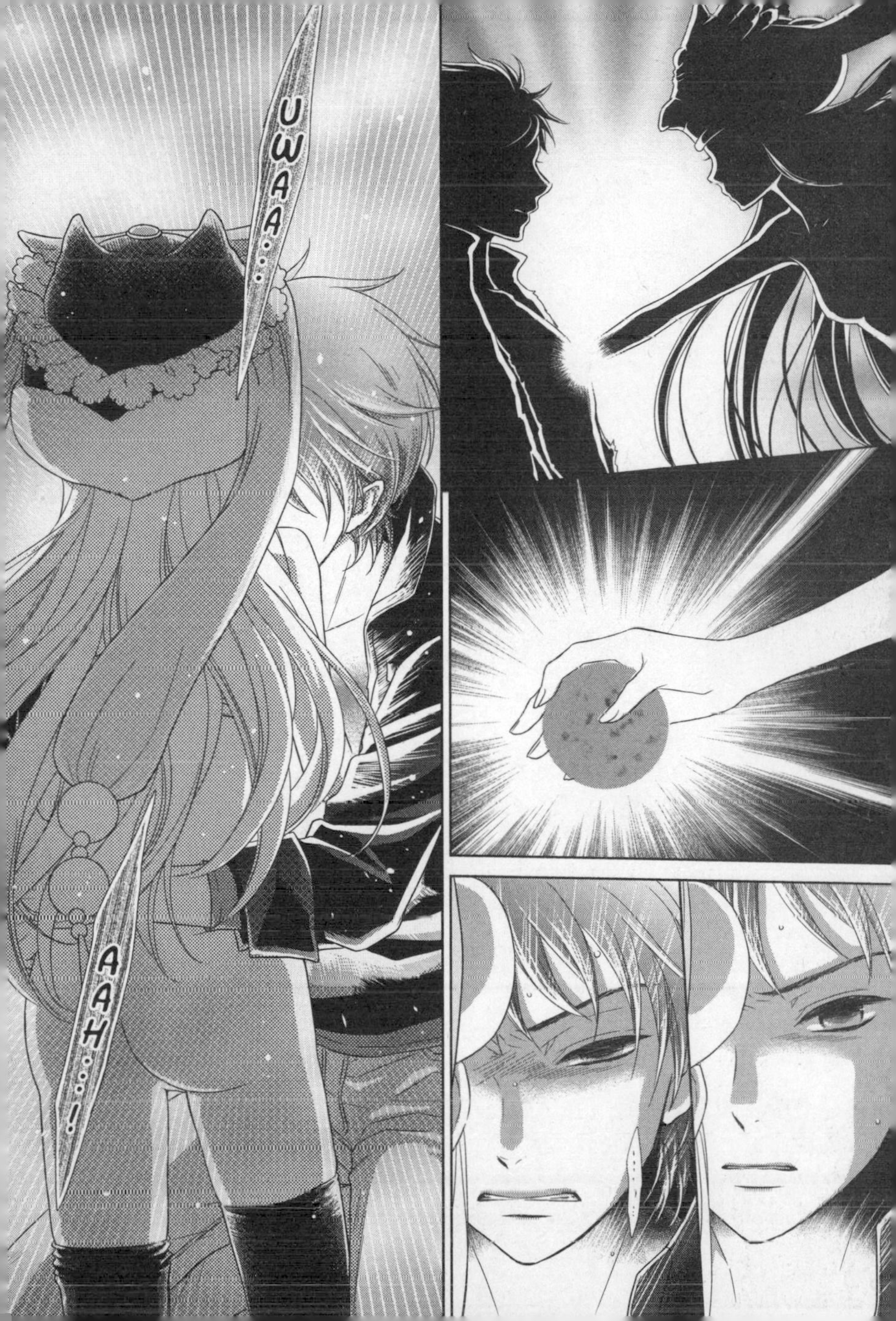
UWAAA...
AAAH...!

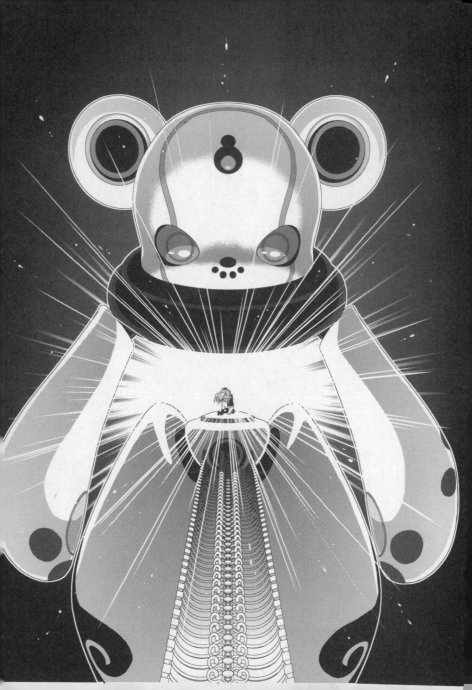

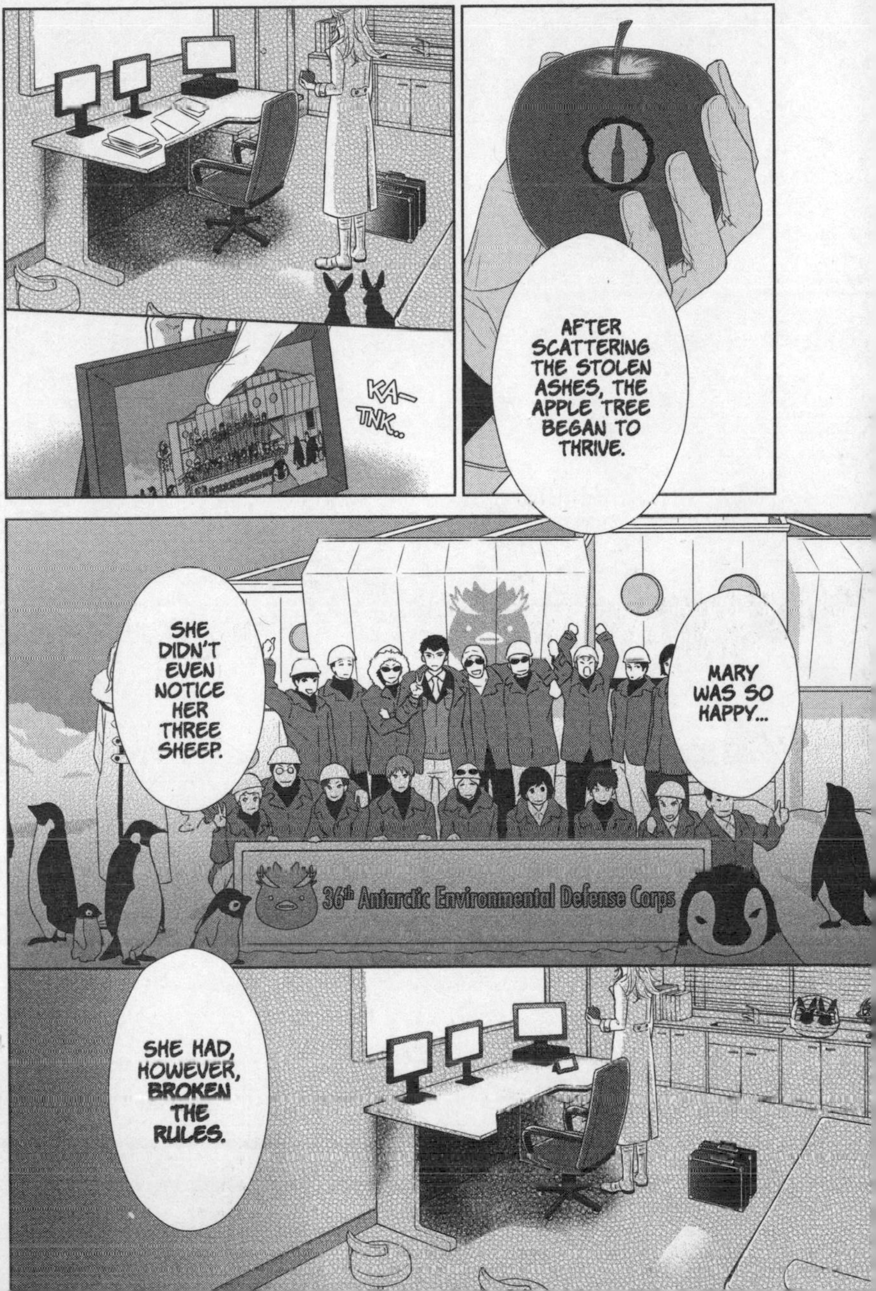
AFTER SCATTERING THE STOLEN ASHES, THE APPLE TREE BEGAN TO THRIVE.
KA-TNK...
MARY WAS SO HAPPY...
SHE DIDN'T EVEN NOTICE HER THREE SHEEP.
36th Antarctic Environmental Defense Corps
SHE HAD, HOWEVER, BROKEN THE RULES.

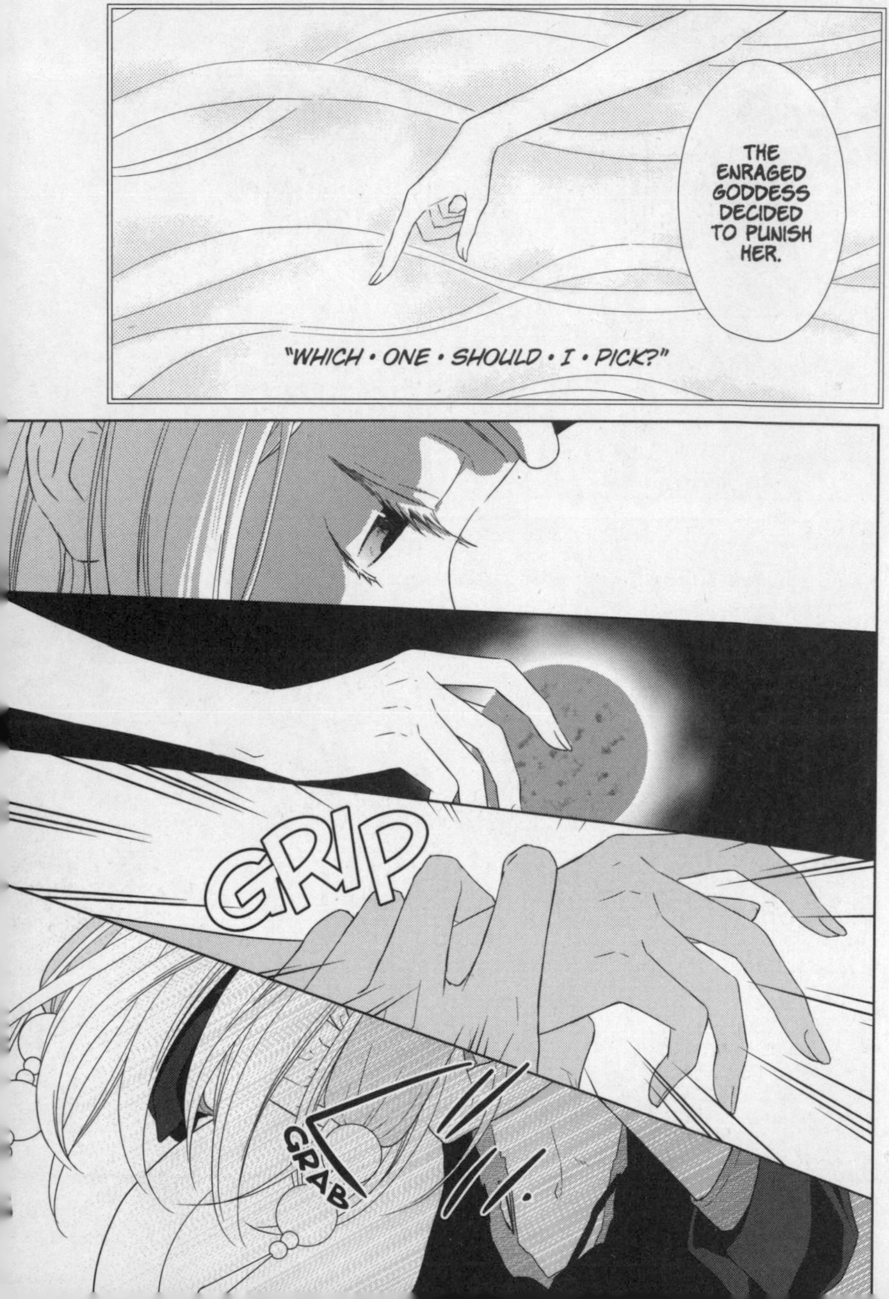
THE ENRAGED GODDESS DECIDED TO PUNISH HER.
"WHICH • ONE • SHOULD • I • PICK?"
GRIP
GRAB

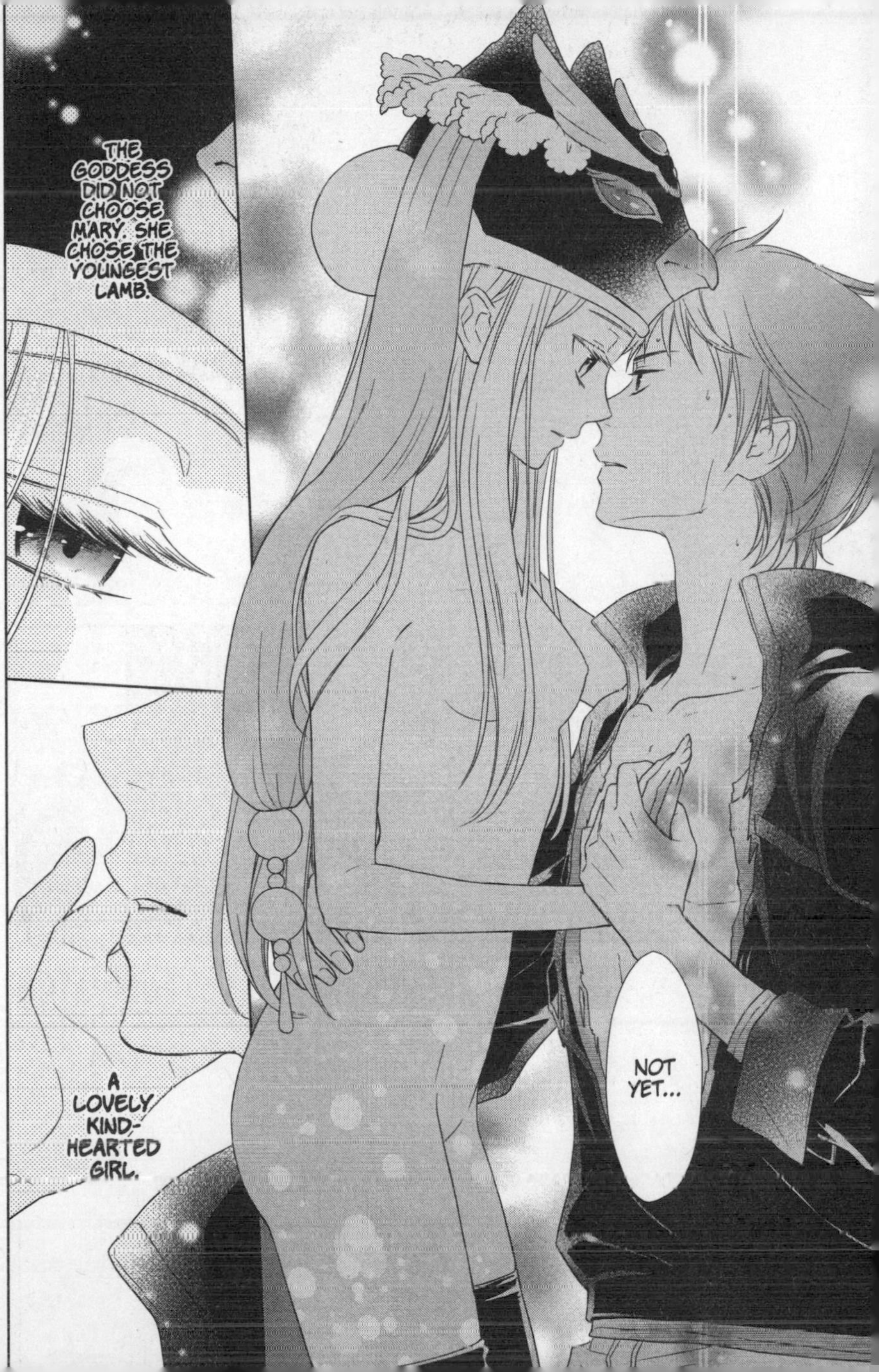
NOT YET...
THE GODDESS DID NOT CHOOSE MARY. SHE CHOSE THE YOUNGEST LAMB.
A LOVELY, KIND-HEARTED GIRL.

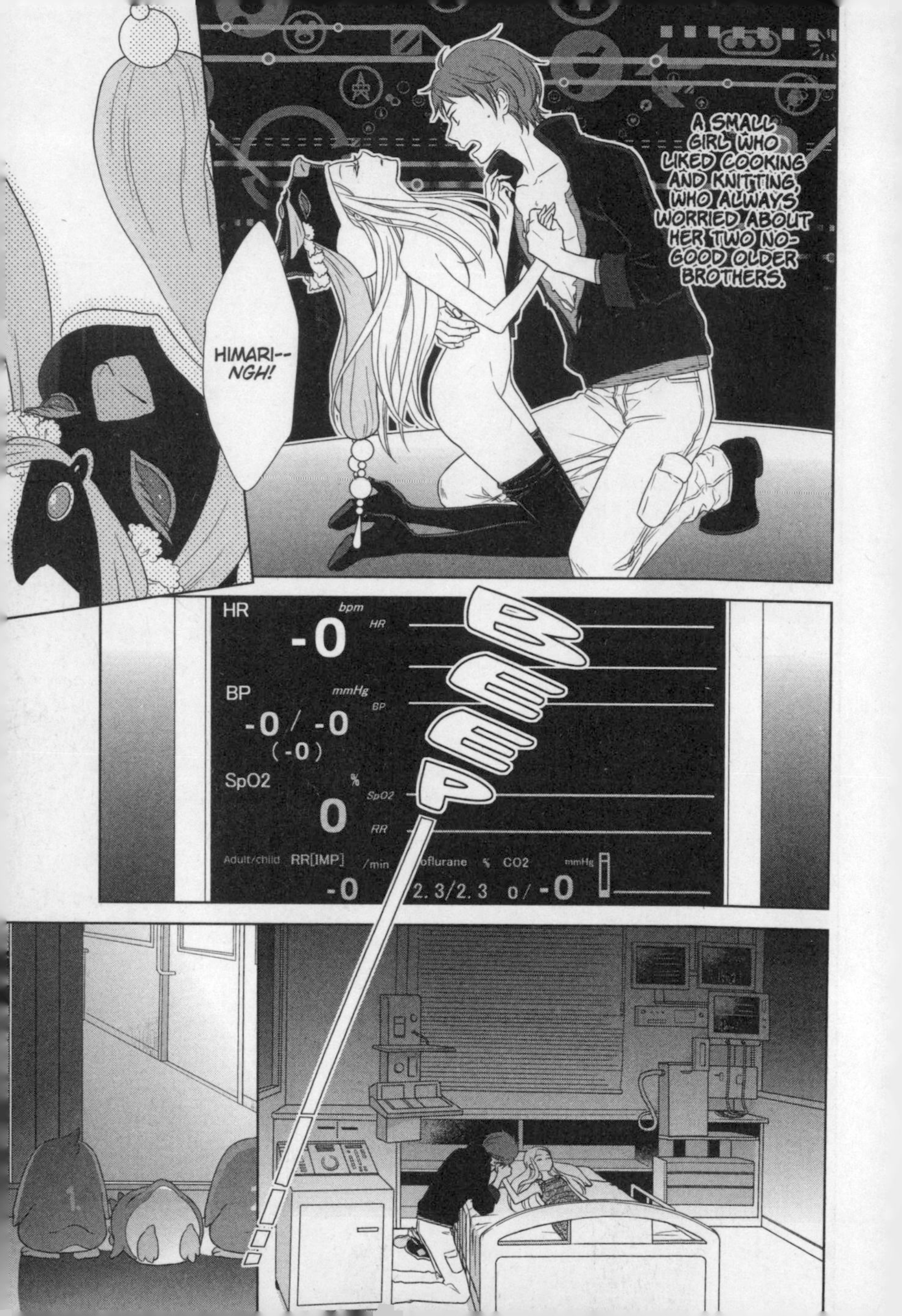
A SMALL GIRL WHO LIKED COOKING AND KNITTING, WHO ALWAYS WORRIED ABOUT HER TWO NO-GOOD OLDER BROTHERS.
HIMARI-- NGH!
HR bpm
HR
-0
BP mmHg
BP
-0 / -0
(-0)
SpO2 %
SpO2
0
RR
Adult/child RR[IMP] /min oflurane % CO2 mmHg
-0 2. 3/2. 3 o/ -0
BEEP

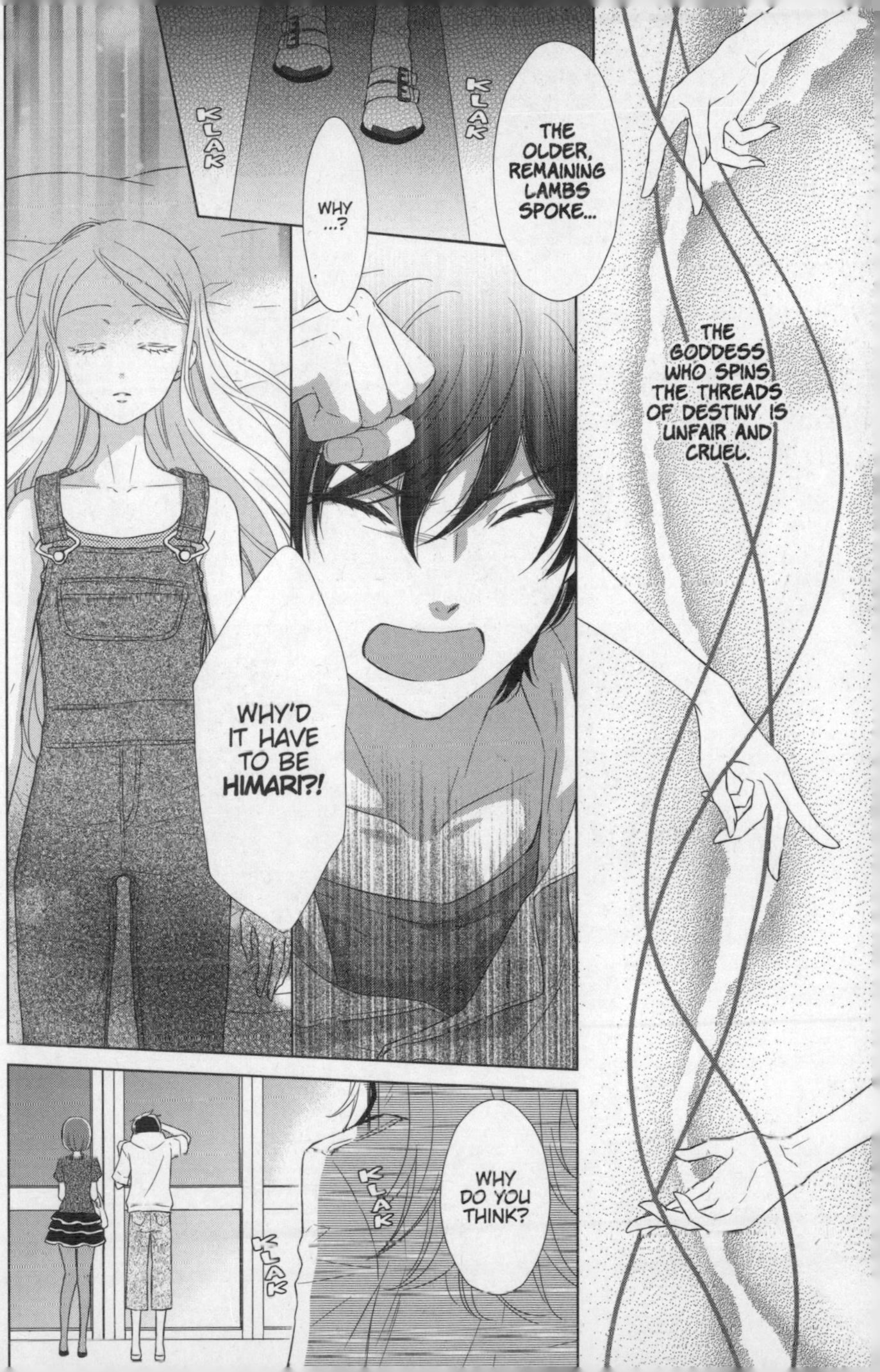
THE GODDESS WHO SPINS THE THREADS OF DESTINY IS UNFAIR AND CRUEL.
KLAK
THE OLDER, REMAINING LAMBS SPOKE...
KLAK
WHY ...?
WHY'D IT HAVE TO BE HIMARI?!
WHY DO YOU THINK?
KLAK
KLAK

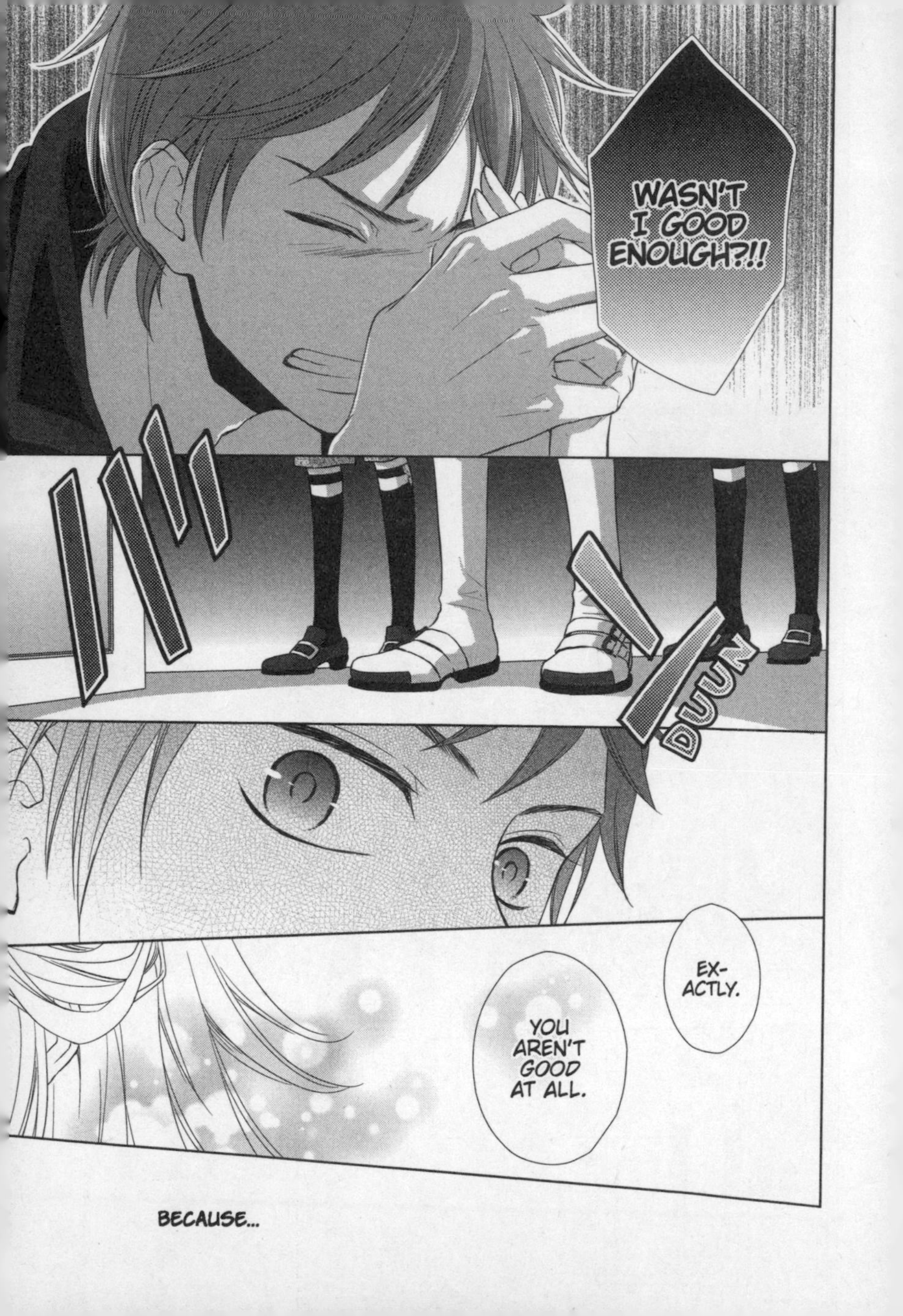
WASN'T I GOOD ENOUGH?!!
DUUN
EX-ACTLY.
YOU AREN'T GOOD AT ALL.
BECAUSE...

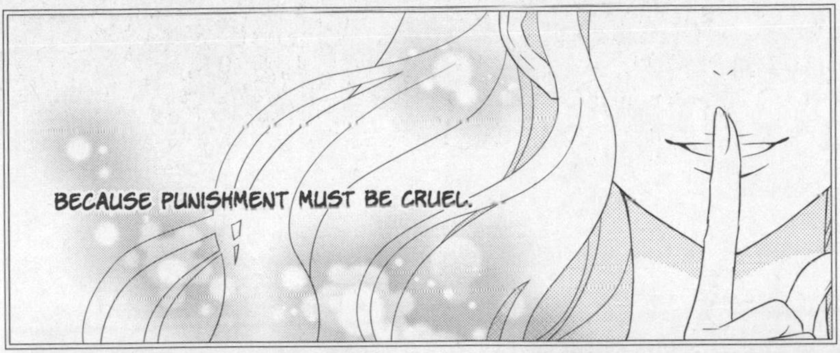
BECAUSE PUNISHMENT MUST BE CRUEL.
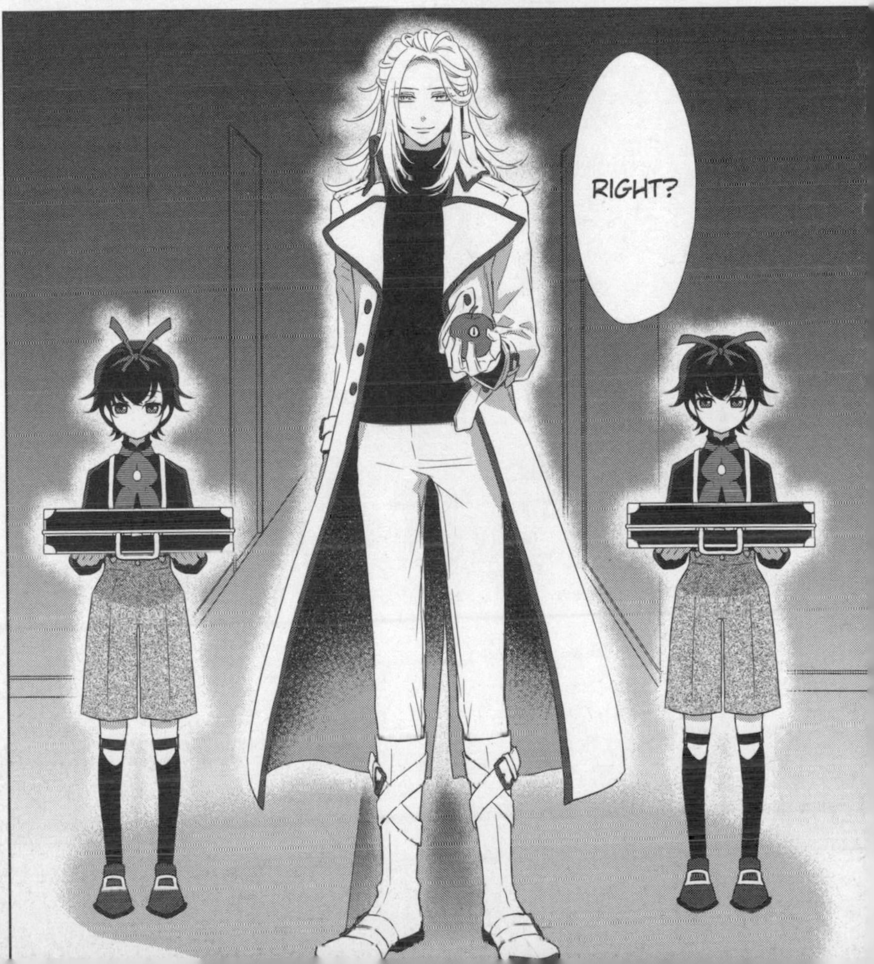
RIGHT?

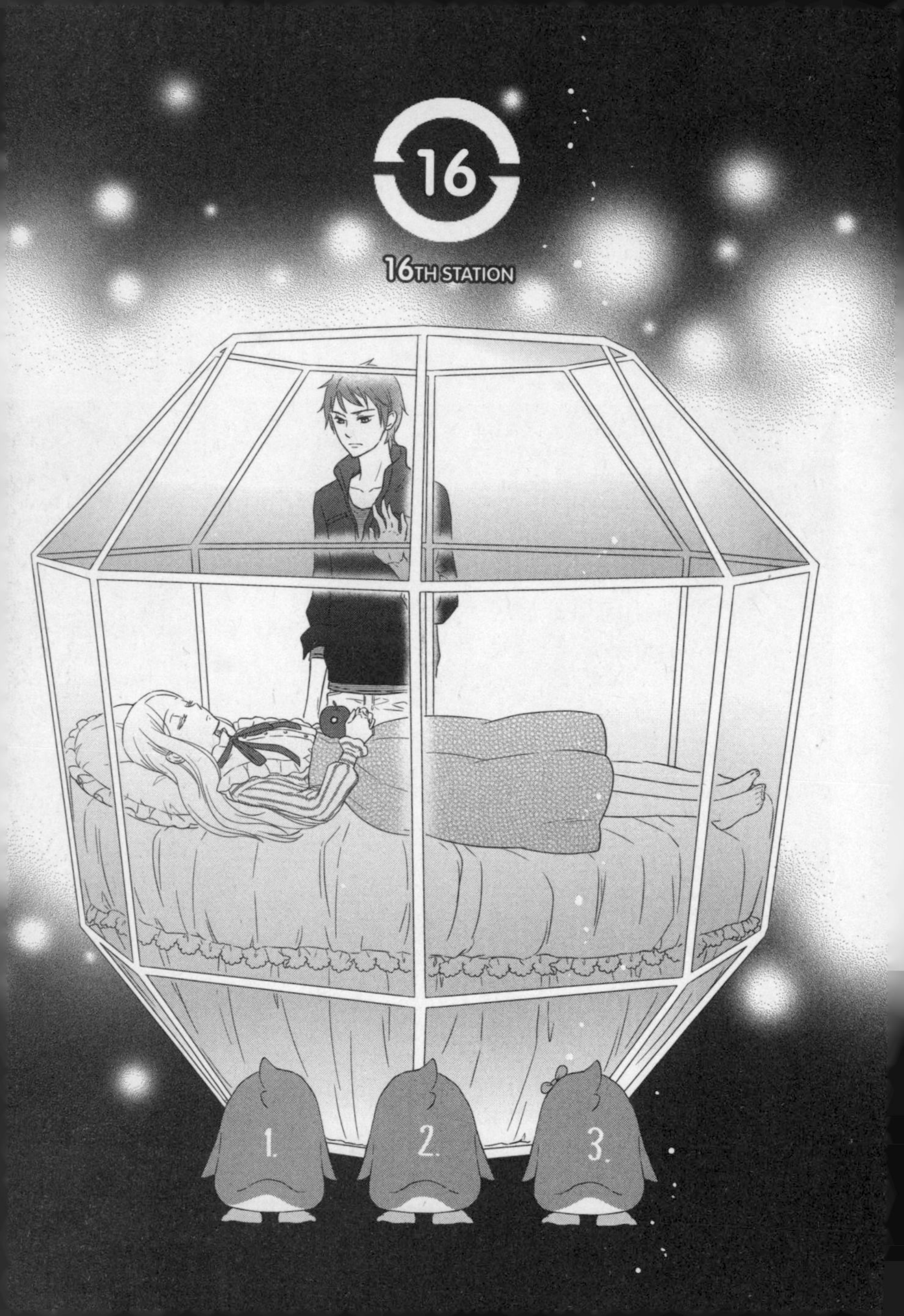
16
16TH STATION
1.
2.
3.

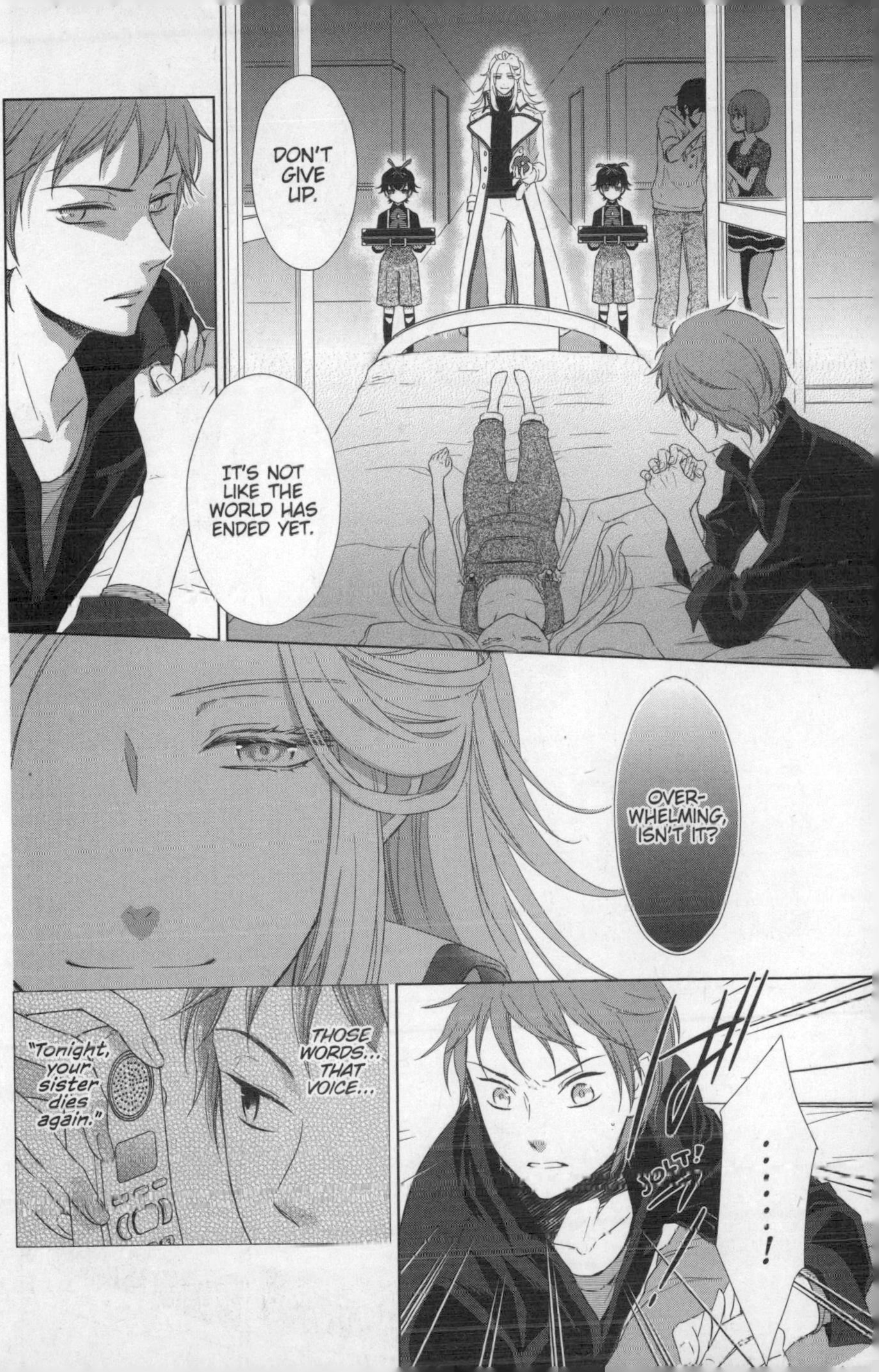
DON'T GIVE UP.
IT'S NOT LIKE THE WORLD HAS ENDED YET.
OVER-WHELMING, ISN'T IT?
JOLT!
......!
THOSE WORDS... THAT VOICE...
"Tonight, your sister dies again."

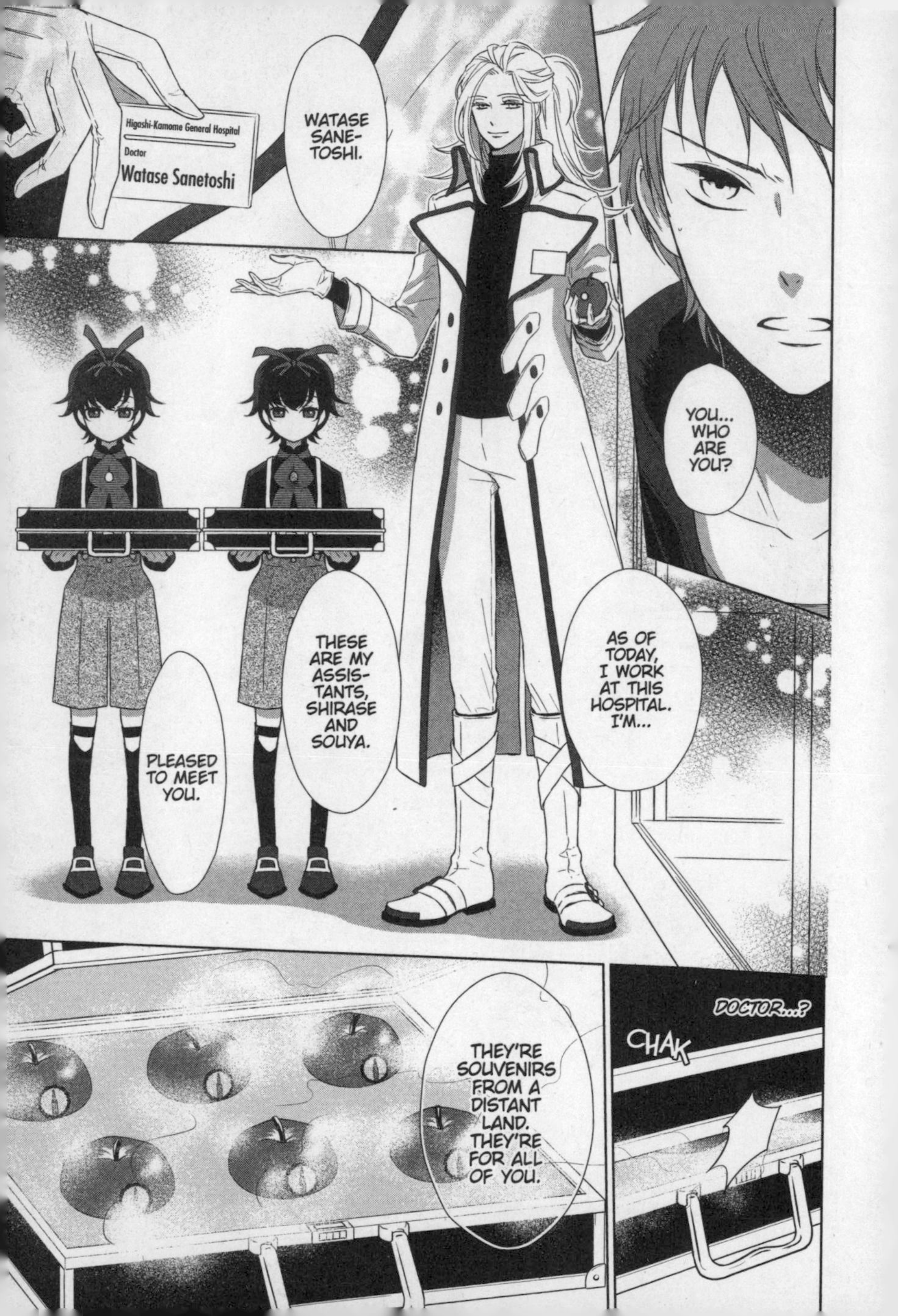
YOU... WHO ARE YOU?
AS OF TODAY, I WORK AT THIS HOSPITAL. I'M...
Higashi-Kamome General Hospital
Doctor
Watase Sanetoshi
WATASE SANE-TOSHI.
THESE ARE MY ASSIS-TANTS, SHIRASE AND SOUYA.
PLEASED TO MEET YOU.
CHAK
DOCTOR...?
THEY'RE SOUVENIRS FROM A DISTANT LAND. THEY'RE FOR ALL OF YOU.

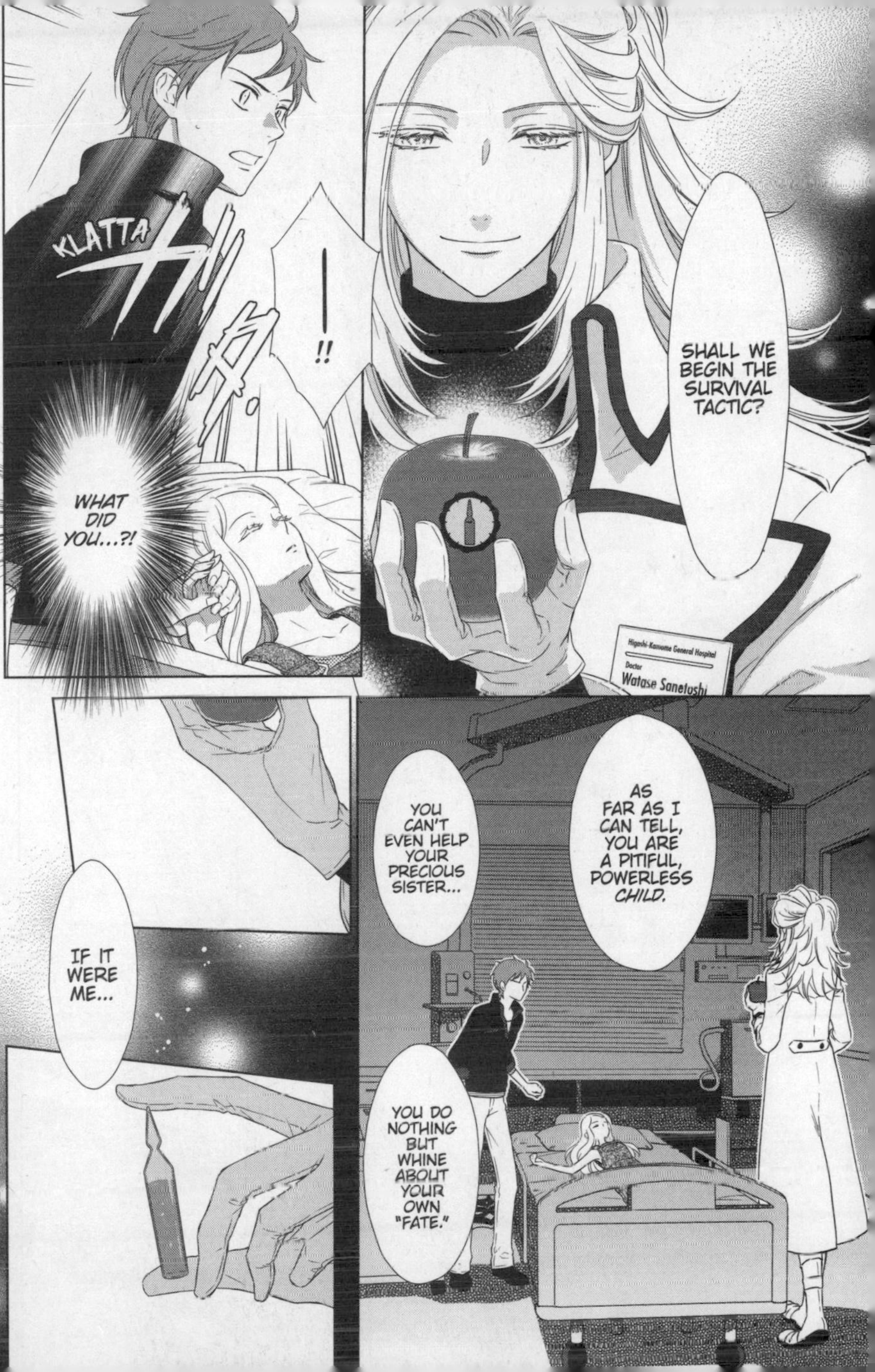
SHALL WE BEGIN THE SURVIVAL TACTIC?
Higashi-Kamome General Hospital
Doctor
Watase Sanetoshi
KLATTA
!!
WHAT DID YOU...?!
AS FAR AS I CAN TELL, YOU ARE A PITIFUL, POWERLESS *CHILD.*
YOU CAN'T EVEN HELP YOUR PRECIOUS SISTER...
YOU DO NOTHING BUT WHINE ABOUT YOUR OWN "FATE."
IF IT WERE ME...

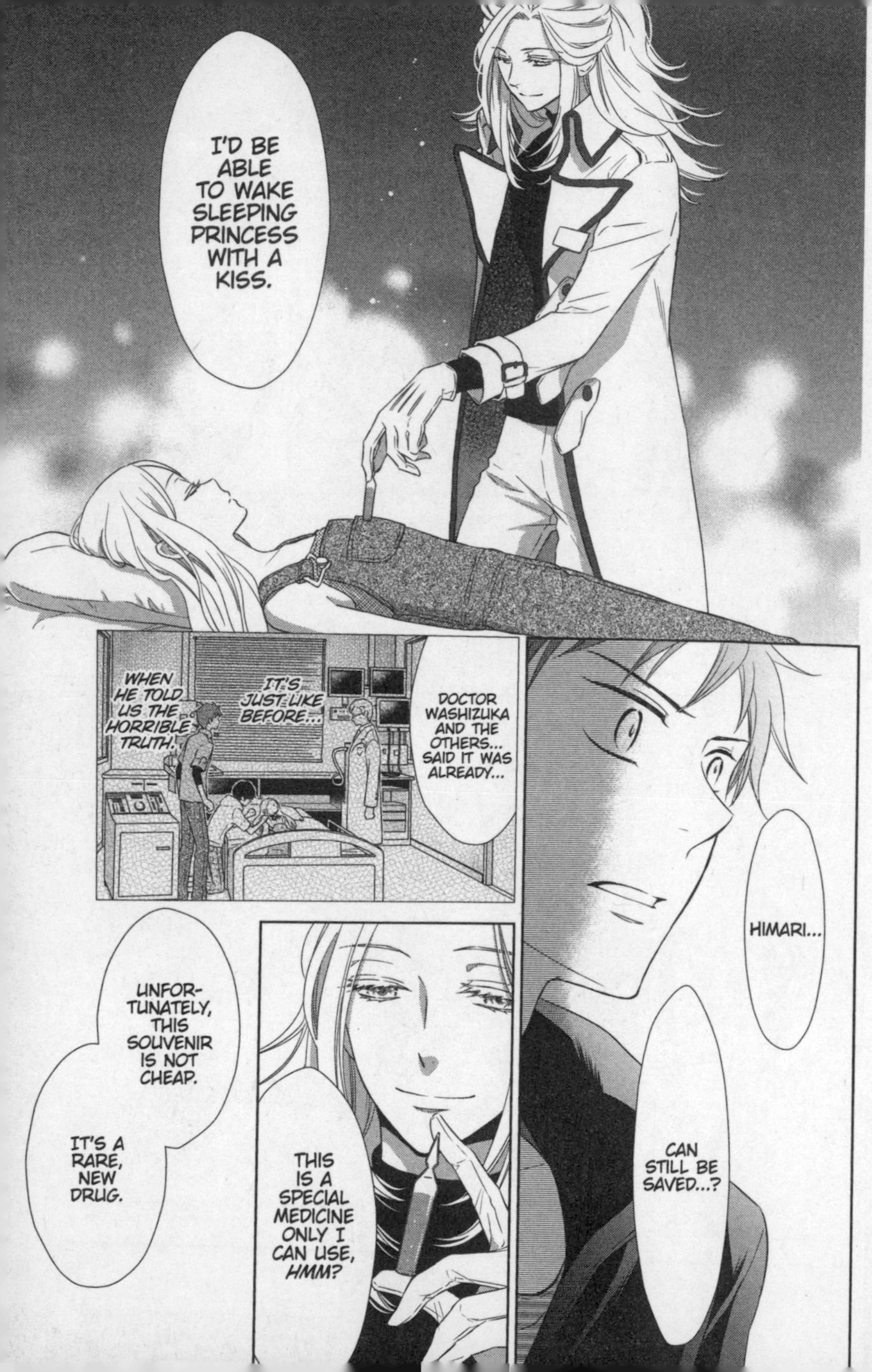
I'D BE ABLE TO WAKE SLEEPING PRINCESS WITH A KISS.
IT'S JUST LIKE BEFORE...
WHEN HE TOLD US THE HORRIBLE TRUTH.
DOCTOR WASHIZUKA AND THE OTHERS... SAID IT WAS ALREADY...
HIMARI...
CAN STILL BE SAVED...?
THIS IS A SPECIAL MEDICINE ONLY I CAN USE, HMM?
IT'S A RARE, NEW DRUG.
UNFORTUNATELY, THIS SOUVENIR IS NOT CHEAP.

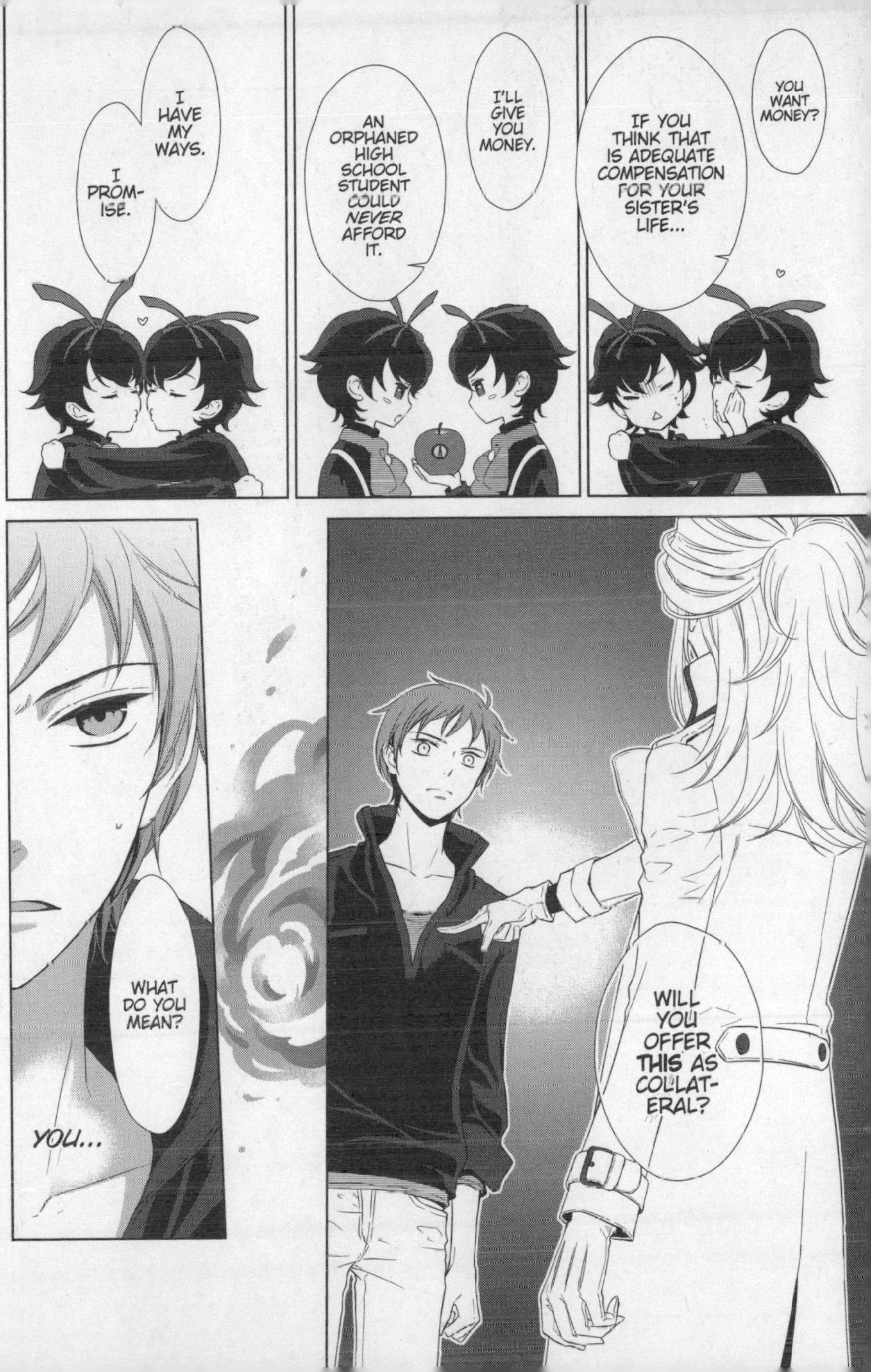
YOU WANT MONEY?
IF YOU THINK THAT IS ADEQUATE COMPENSATION FOR YOUR SISTER'S LIFE...
I'LL GIVE YOU MONEY.
AN ORPHANED HIGH SCHOOL STUDENT COULD *NEVER* AFFORD IT.
I HAVE MY WAYS.
I PROM-ISE.
WILL YOU OFFER THIS AS COLLAT-ERAL?
WHAT DO YOU MEAN?
YOU...

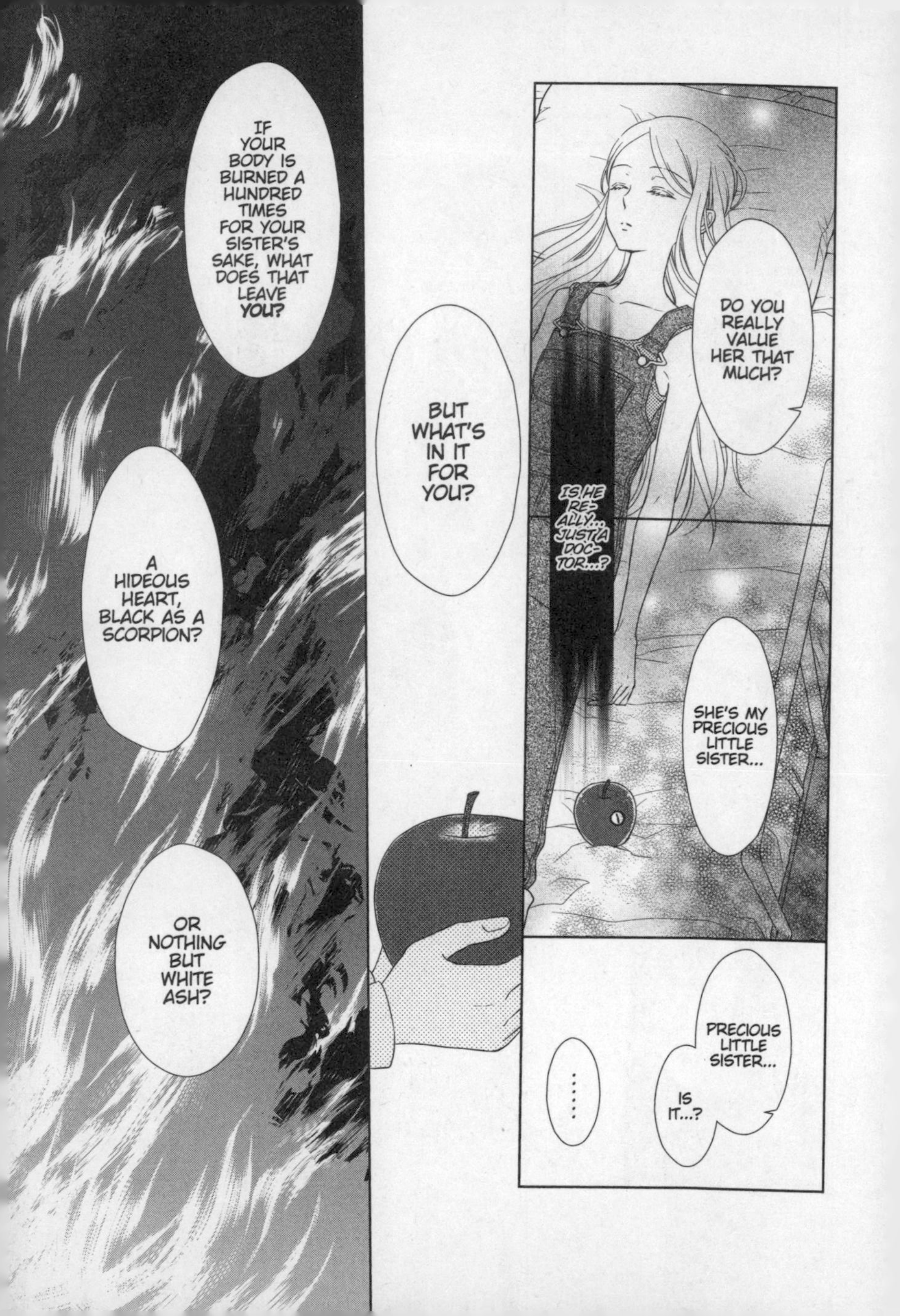
DO YOU REALLY VALUE HER THAT MUCH?
IS HE RE-ALLY... JUST A DOC-TOR...?
SHE'S MY PRECIOUS LITTLE SISTER...
PRECIOUS LITTLE SISTER...
IS IT...?
......
BUT WHAT'S IN IT FOR YOU?
IF YOUR BODY IS BURNED A HUNDRED TIMES FOR YOUR SISTER'S SAKE, WHAT DOES THAT LEAVE YOU?
A HIDEOUS HEART, BLACK AS A SCORPION?
OR NOTHING BUT WHITE ASH?

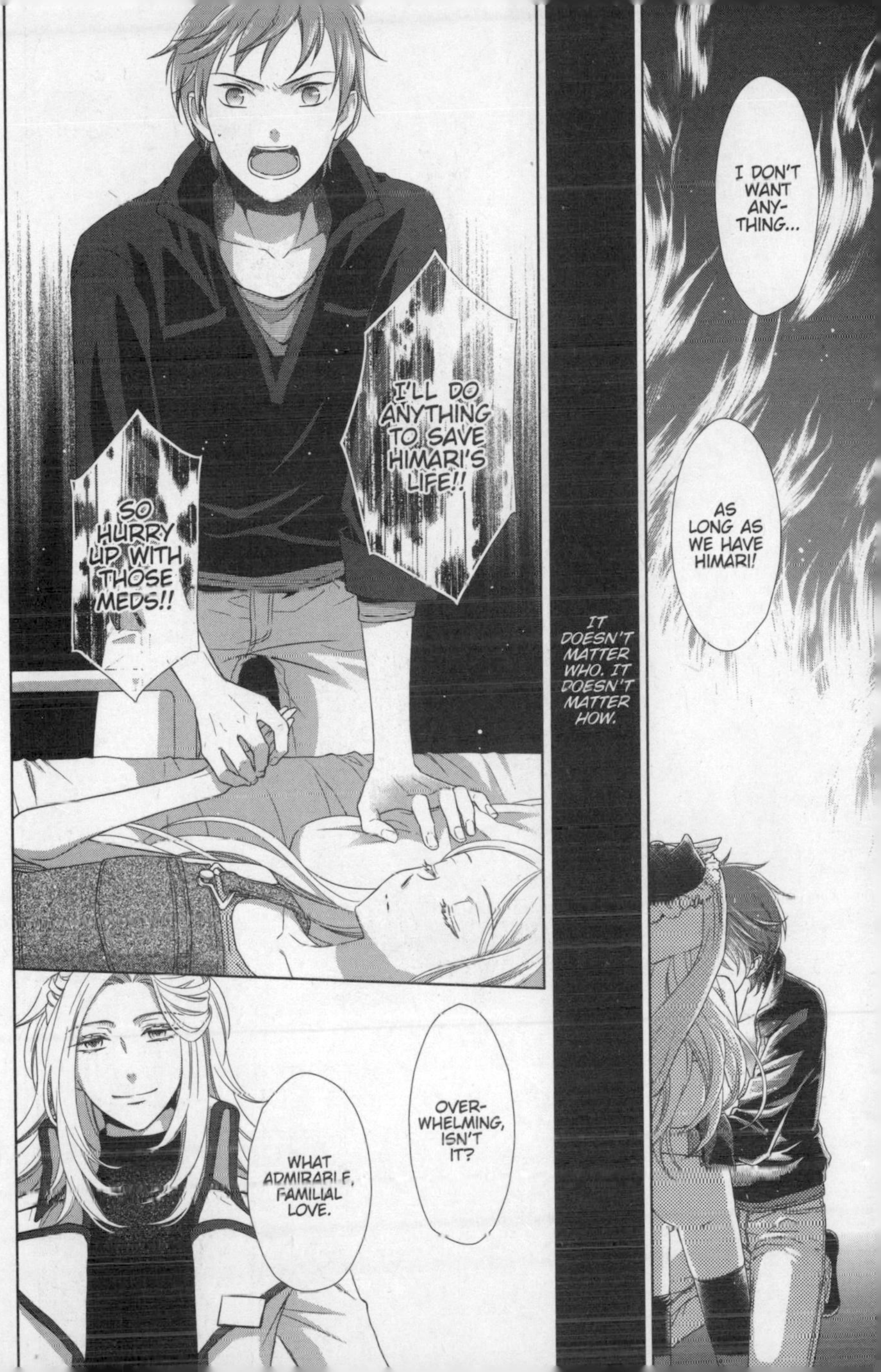
I DON'T WANT ANY-THING...
AS LONG AS WE HAVE HIMARI!
IT DOESN'T MATTER WHO. IT DOESN'T MATTER HOW.
I'LL DO ANYTHING TO SAVE HIMARI'S LIFE!!
SO HURRY UP WITH THOSE MEDS!!
OVER-WHELMING, ISN'T IT?
WHAT ADMIRABLE, FAMILIAL LOVE.

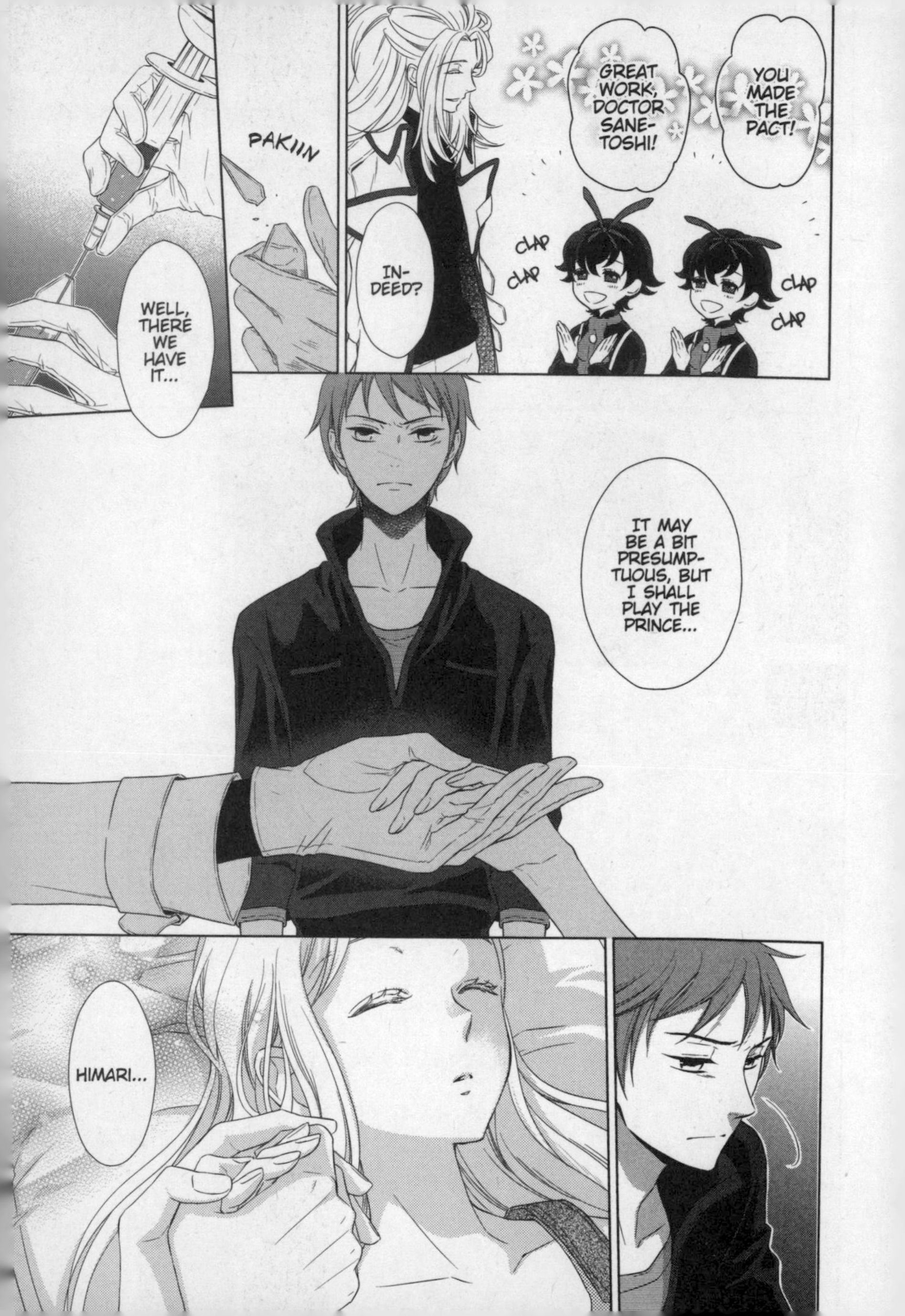
YOU MADE THE PACT!
GREAT WORK, DOCTOR SANE-TOSHI!
CLAP
CLAP
CLAP
CLAP
IN-DEED?
PAKIIN
WELL, THERE WE HAVE IT...
IT MAY BE A BIT PRESUMP-TUOUS, BUT I SHALL PLAY THE PRINCE...
HIMARI...

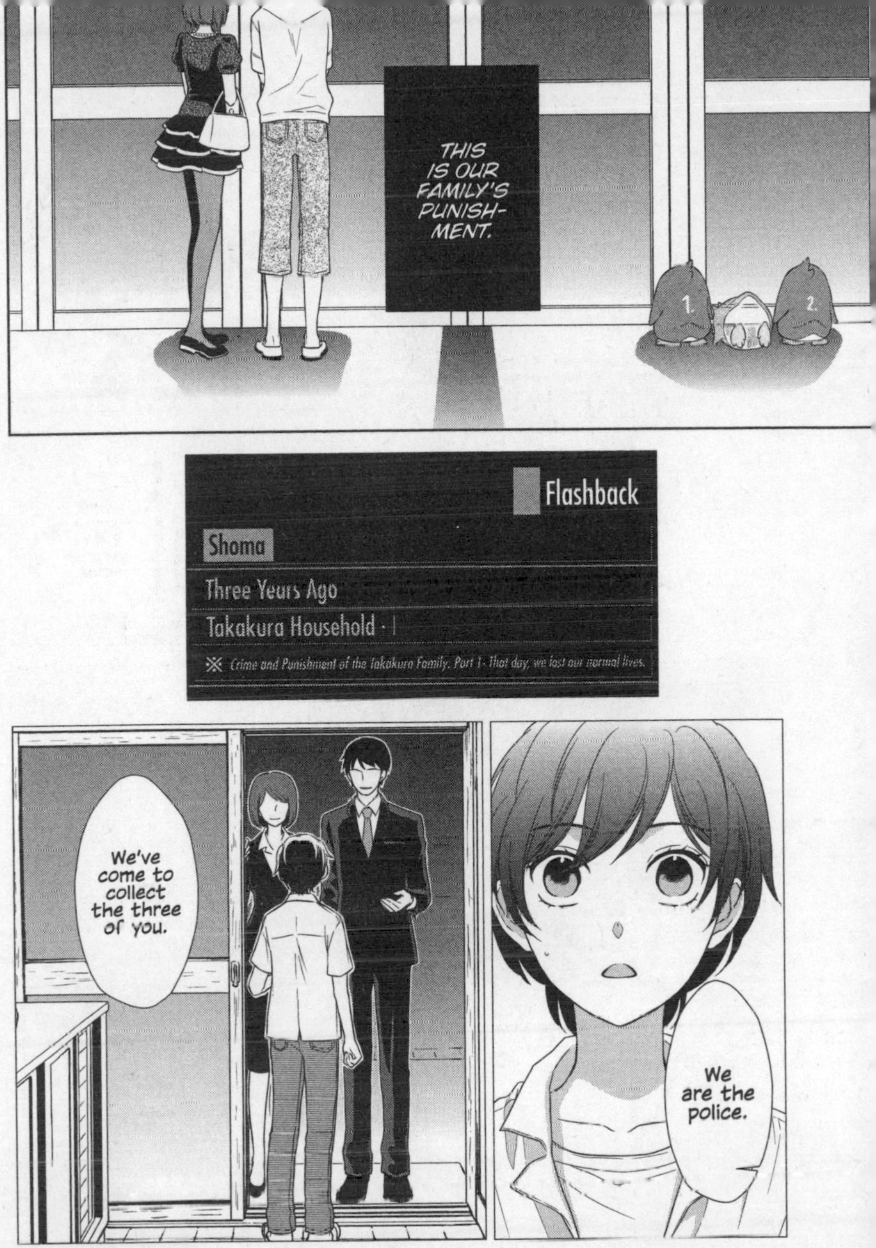
THIS IS OUR FAMILY'S PUNISHMENT.
Flashback
Shoma
Three Years Ago
Takakura Household ·
※ Crime and Punishment of the Takakura Family. Part 1 - That day, we lost our normal lives.
We are the police.
We've come to collect the three of you.

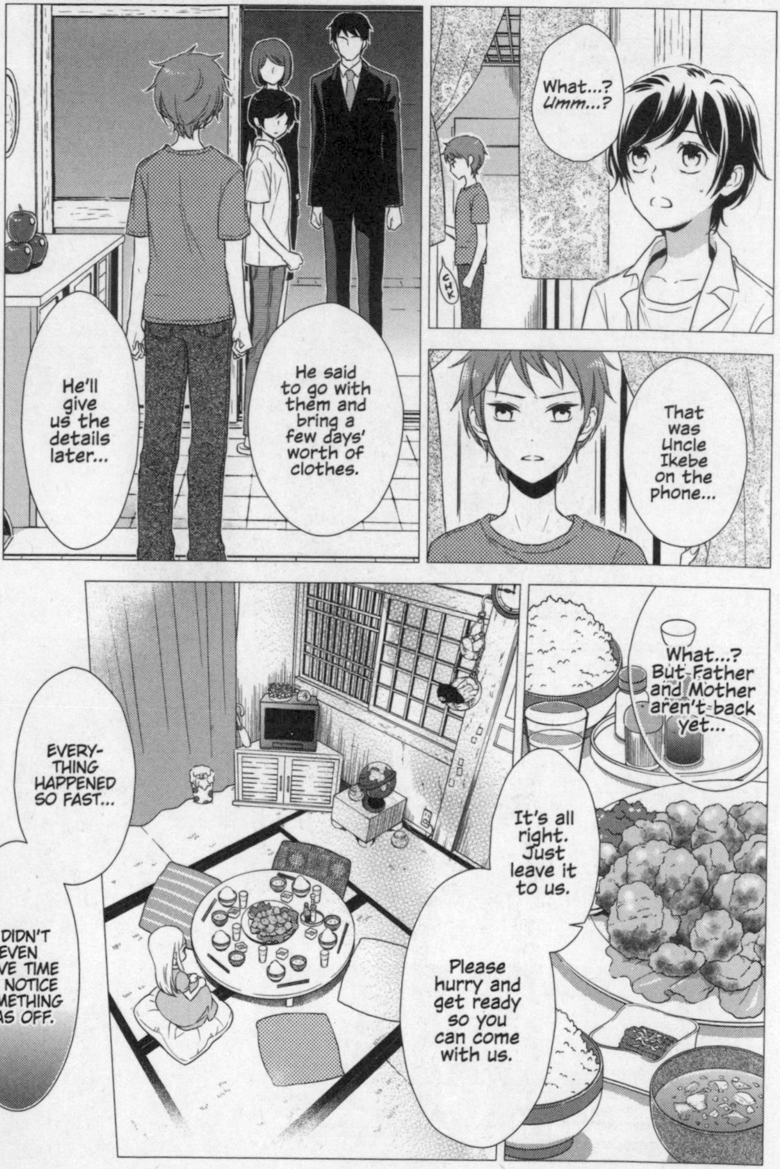
What...? Umm...?
UHK
That was Uncle Ikebe on the phone...
He said to go with them and bring a few days' worth of clothes.
He'll give us the details later...
What...? But Father and Mother aren't back yet...
It's all right. Just leave it to us.
Please hurry and get ready so you can come with us.
EVERYTHING HAPPENED SO FAST...
I DIDN'T EVEN HAVE TIME TO NOTICE SOMETHING WAS OFF.

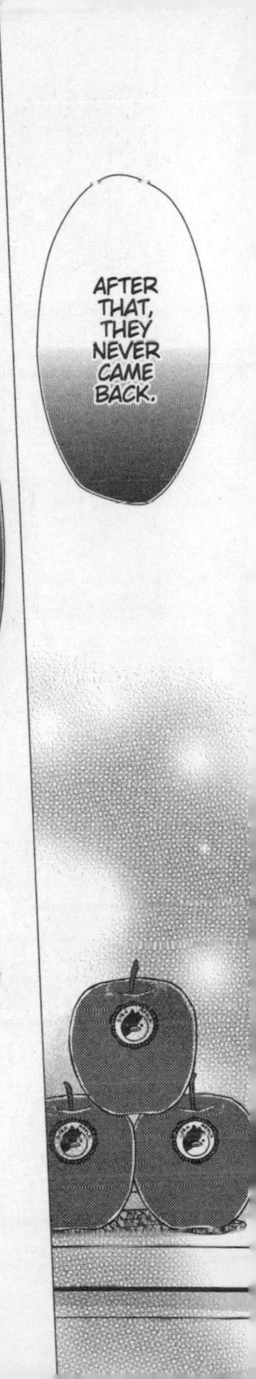
AFTER THAT, THEY NEVER CAME BACK.
IT WAS THE END.

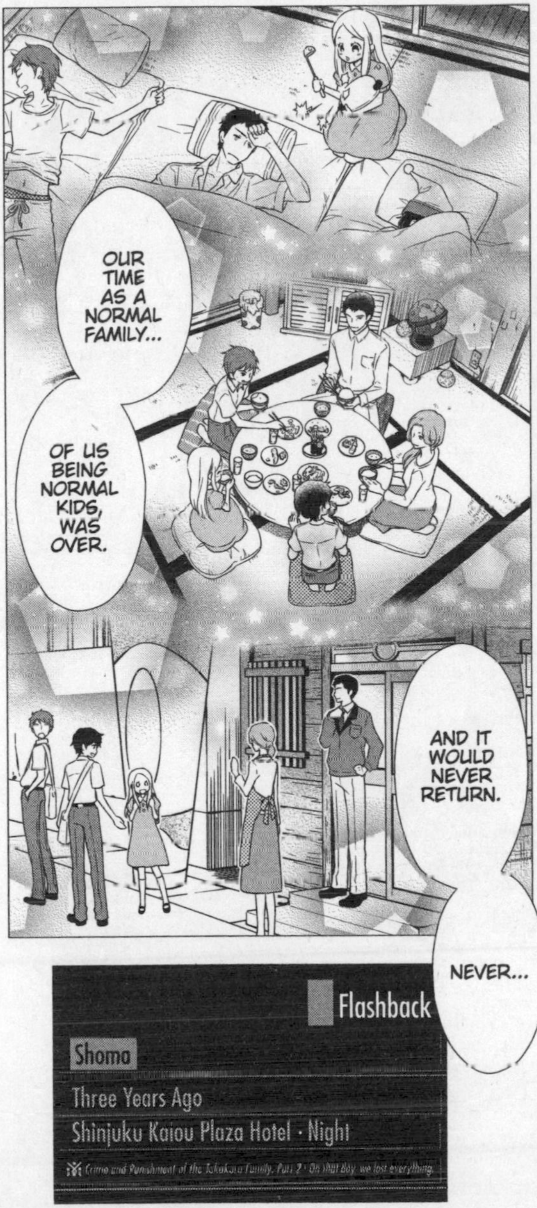
OUR TIME AS A NORMAL FAMILY...
OF US BEING NORMAL KIDS, WAS OVER.
AND IT WOULD NEVER RETURN.
NEVER...
Flashback
Shoma
Three Years Ago
Shinjuku Kaiou Plaza Hotel · Night
Crime and Punishment of the Takakura Family, Part 2: On that day, we lost everything.

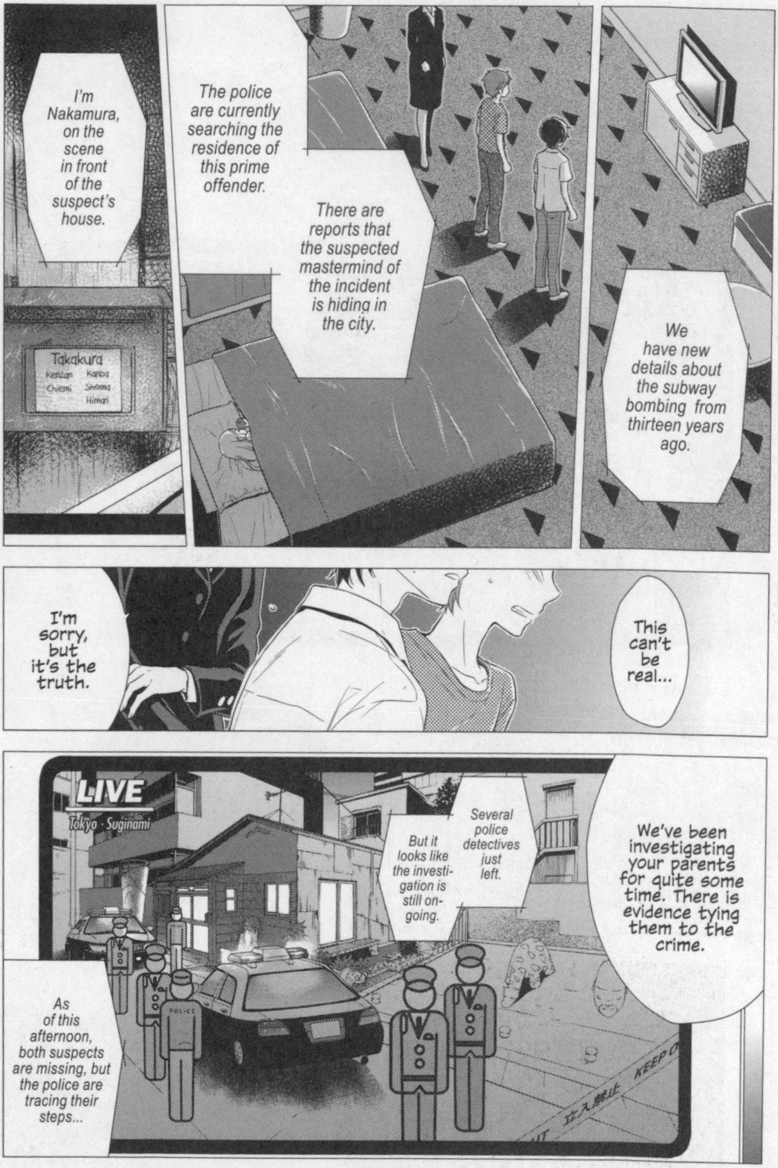
We have new details about the subway bombing from thirteen years ago.
The police are currently searching the residence of this prime offender.
There are reports that the suspected mastermind of the incident is hiding in the city.
I'm Nakamura, on the scene in front of the suspect's house.
Takakura
Kenzan Kanba
Chiemi Shoma
Himari
This can't be real...
I'm sorry, but it's the truth.
We've been investigating your parents for quite some time. There is evidence tying them to the crime.
LIVE
Tokyo・Suginami
Several police detectives just left.
But it looks like the investigation is still on-going.
As of this afternoon, both suspects are missing, but the police are tracing their steps...

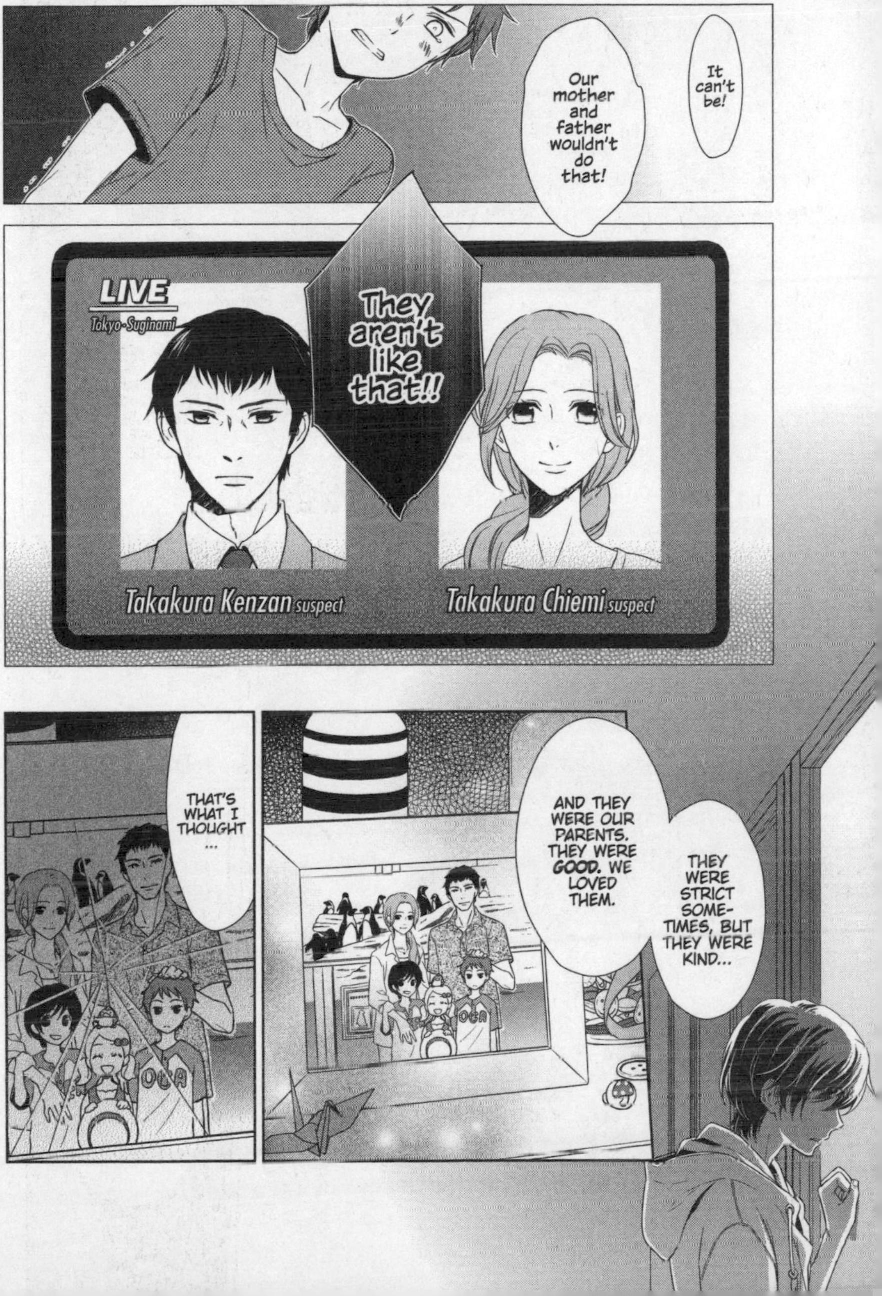
It can't be!
Our mother and father wouldn't do that!
They aren't like that!!
LIVE
Tokyo-Suginami
Takakura Chiemi suspect
Takakura Kenzan suspect
THEY WERE STRICT SOME-TIMES, BUT THEY WERE KIND...
AND THEY WERE OUR PARENTS. THEY WERE GOOD. WE LOVED THEM.
THAT'S WHAT I THOUGHT ...

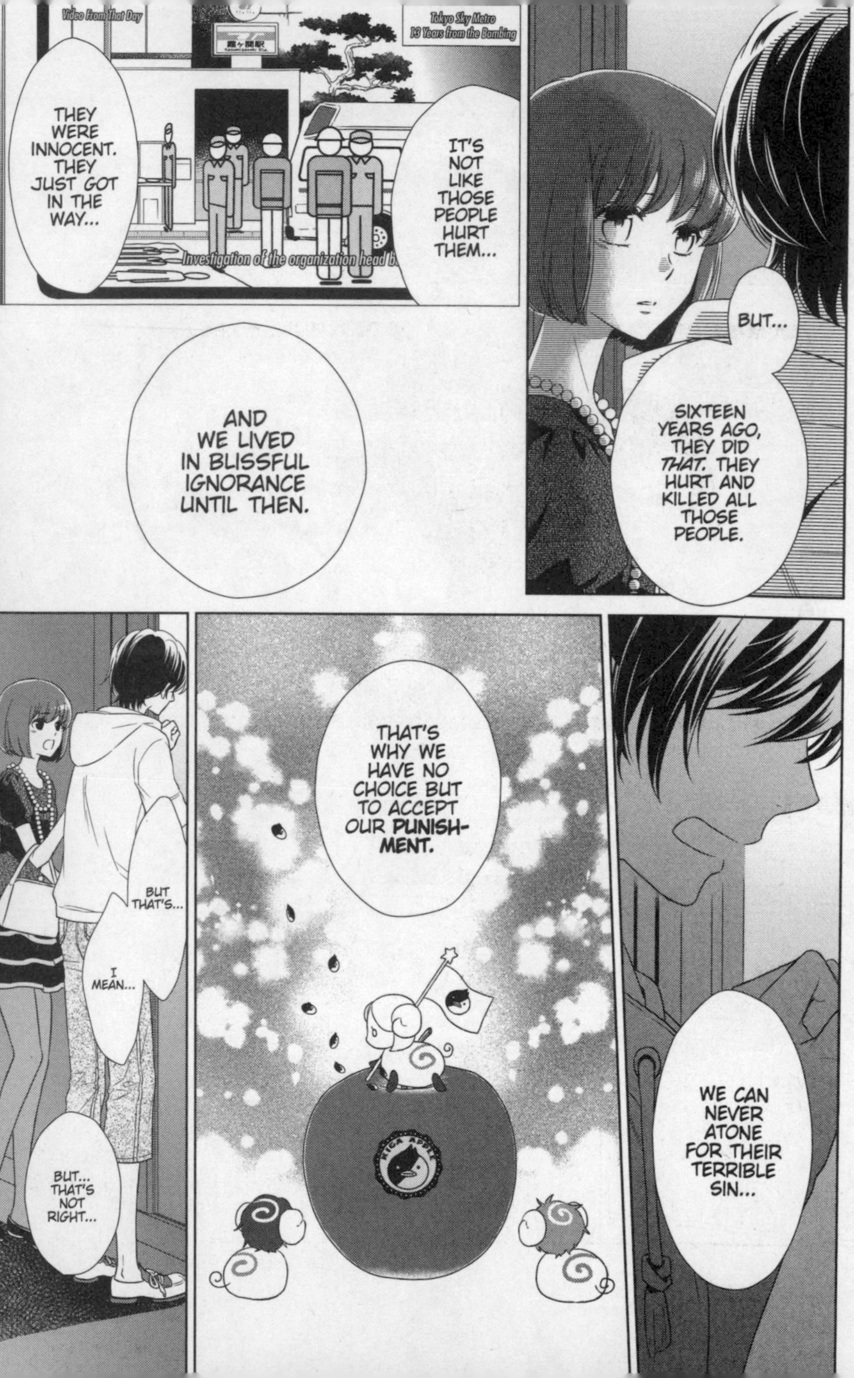

BUT...
SIXTEEN YEARS AGO, THEY DID *THAT*. THEY HURT AND KILLED ALL THOSE PEOPLE.
Tokyo Sky Metro 13 Years from the Bombing
Video From That Day
IT'S NOT LIKE THOSE PEOPLE HURT THEM...
THEY WERE INNOCENT. THEY JUST GOT IN THE WAY...
Investigation of the organization head b
AND WE LIVED IN BLISSFUL IGNORANCE UNTIL THEN.
WE CAN NEVER ATONE FOR THEIR TERRIBLE SIN...
THAT'S WHY WE HAVE NO CHOICE BUT TO ACCEPT OUR **PUNISHMENT.**
BUT THAT'S...
I MEAN...
BUT... THAT'S NOT RIGHT...

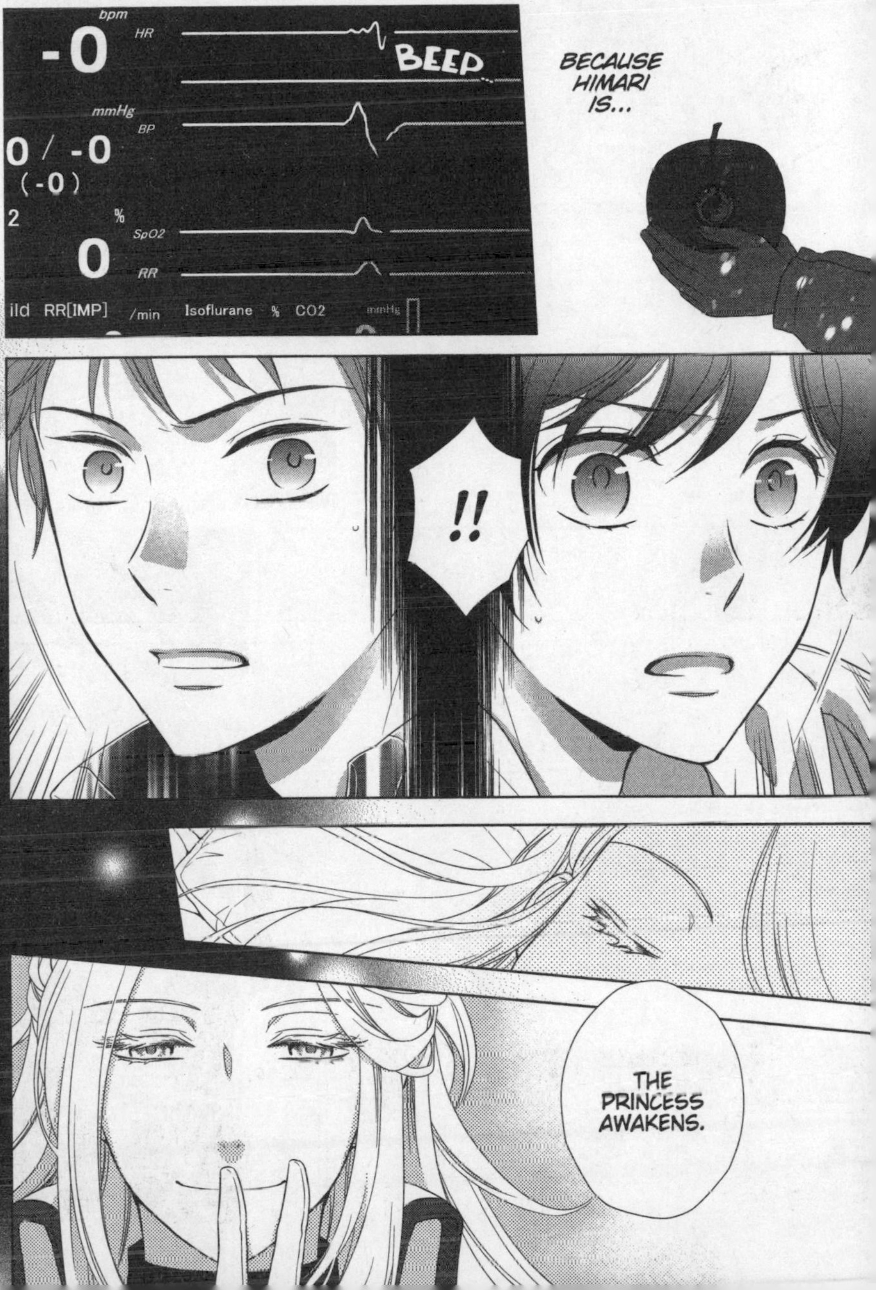
BECAUSE HIMARI IS...
bpm
-0
HR
BEEP
mmHg
BP
0 / -0
(-0)
2
%
SpO2
0
RR
ild RR[IMP] /min Isoflurane % CO2 mmHg
!!
THE PRINCESS AWAKENS.

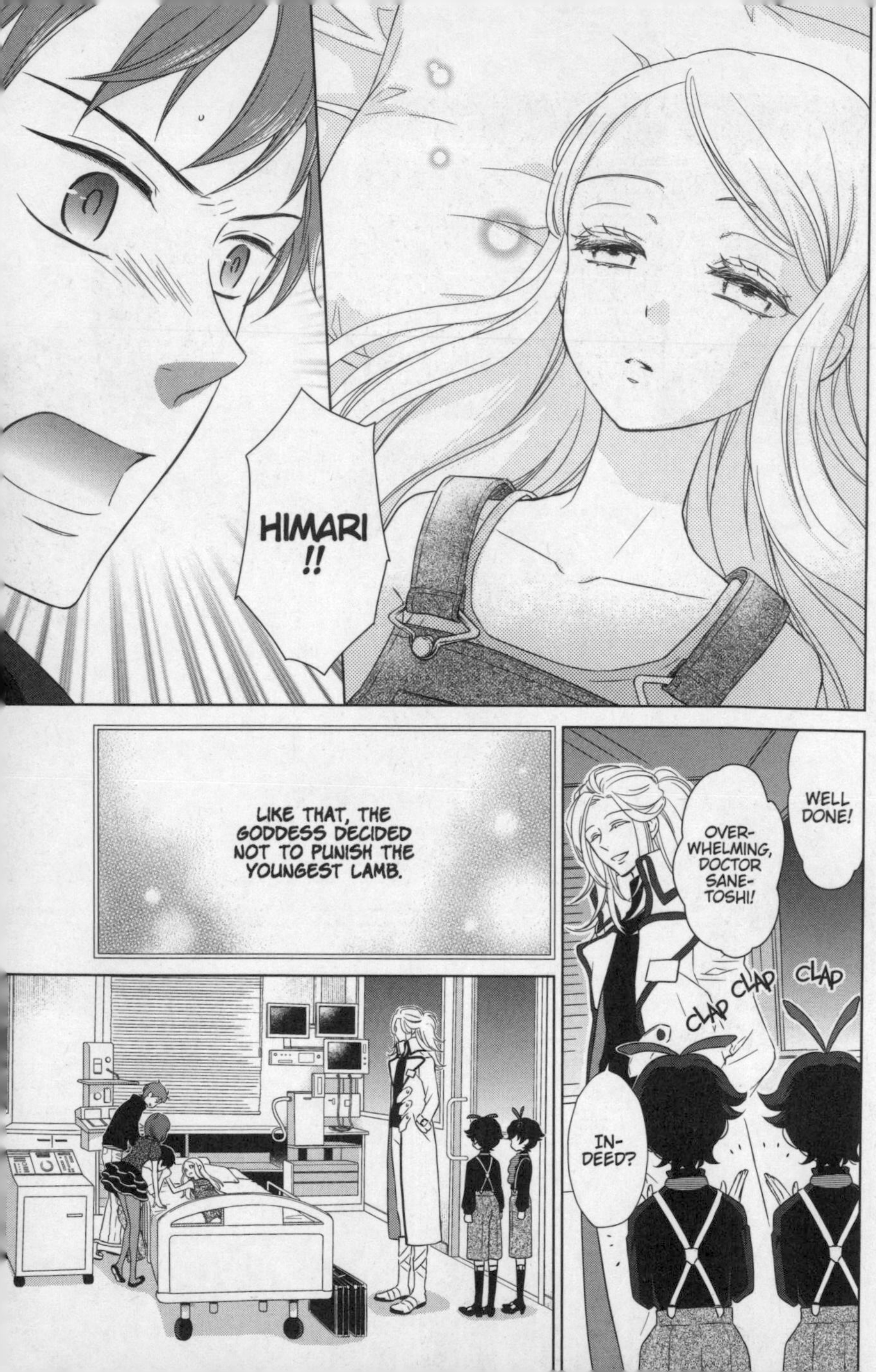
HIMARI !!
WELL DONE!
OVER-WHELMING, DOCTOR SANE-TOSHI!
CLAP CLAP CLAP
IN-DEED?
LIKE THAT, THE GODDESS DECIDED NOT TO PUNISH THE YOUNGEST LAMB.

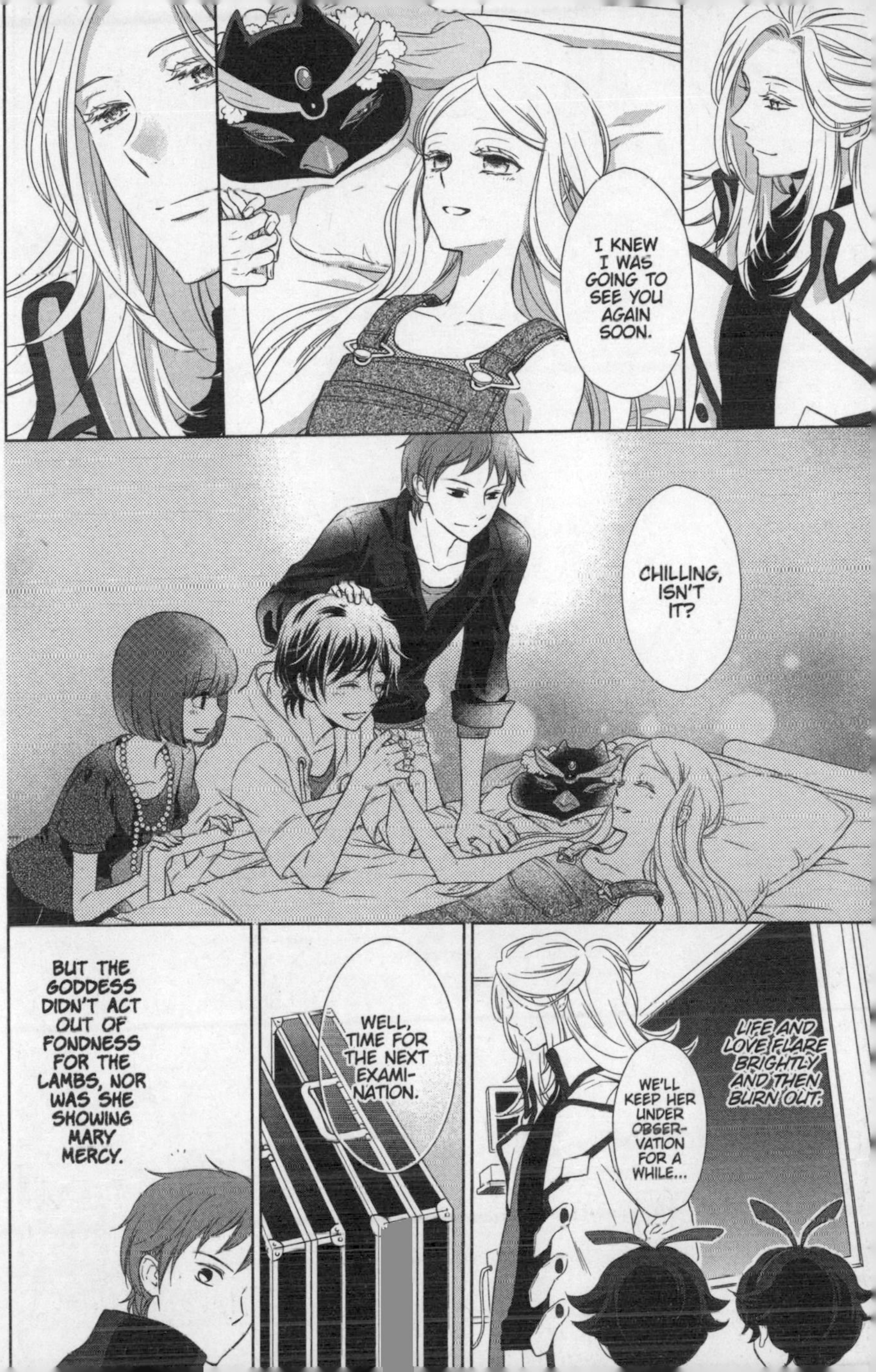
I KNEW I WAS GOING TO SEE YOU AGAIN SOON.
CHILLING, ISN'T IT?
LIFE AND LOVE FLARE BRIGHTLY AND THEN BURN OUT.
WE'LL KEEP HER UNDER OBSERVATION FOR A WHILE...
WELL, TIME FOR THE NEXT EXAMINATION.
BUT THE GODDESS DIDN'T ACT OUT OF FONDNESS FOR THE LAMBS, NOR WAS SHE SHOWING MARY MERCY.

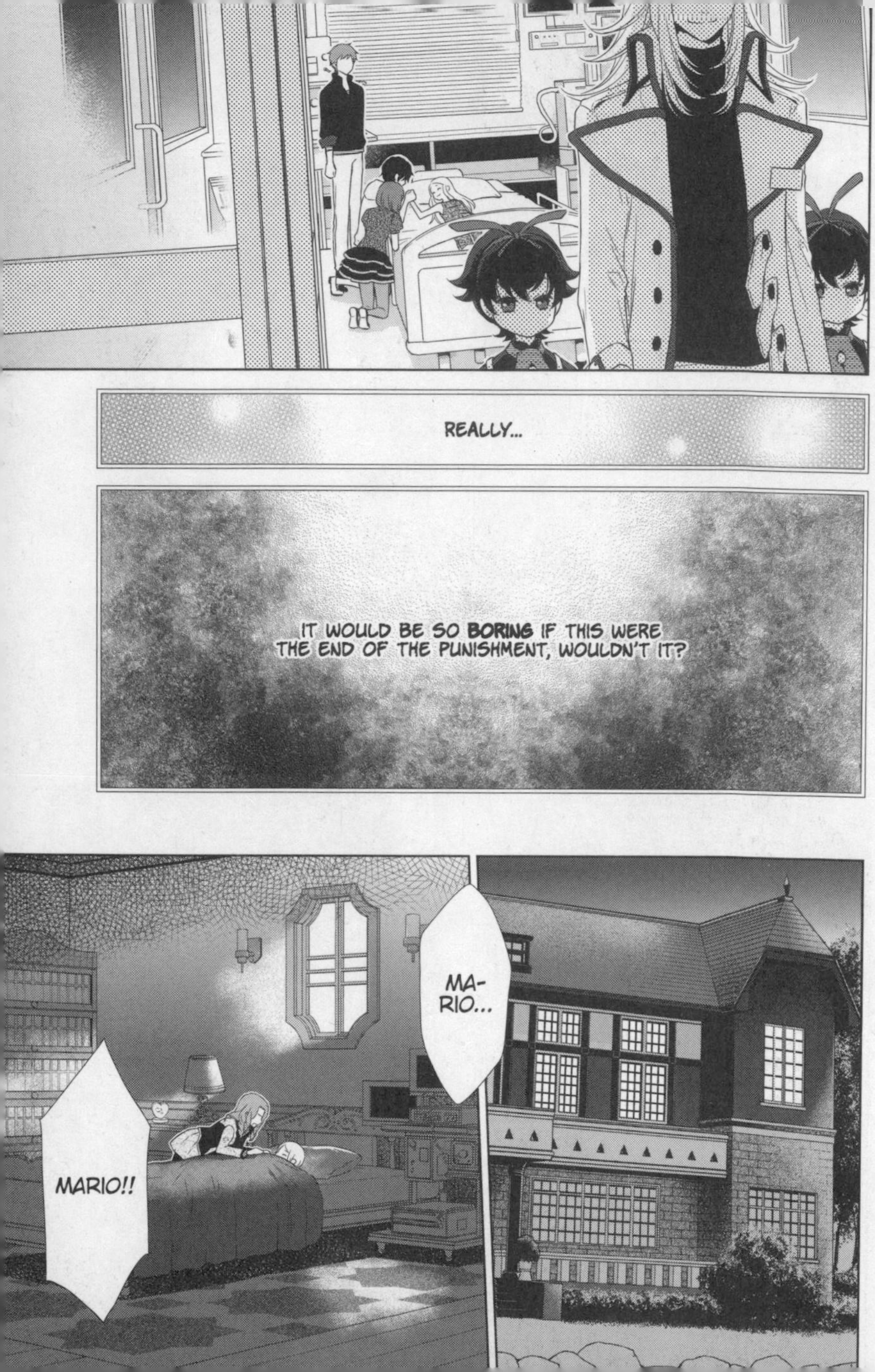
REALLY...
IT WOULD BE SO BORING IF THIS WERE THE END OF THE PUNISHMENT, WOULDN'T IT?
MA-RIO...
MARIO!!

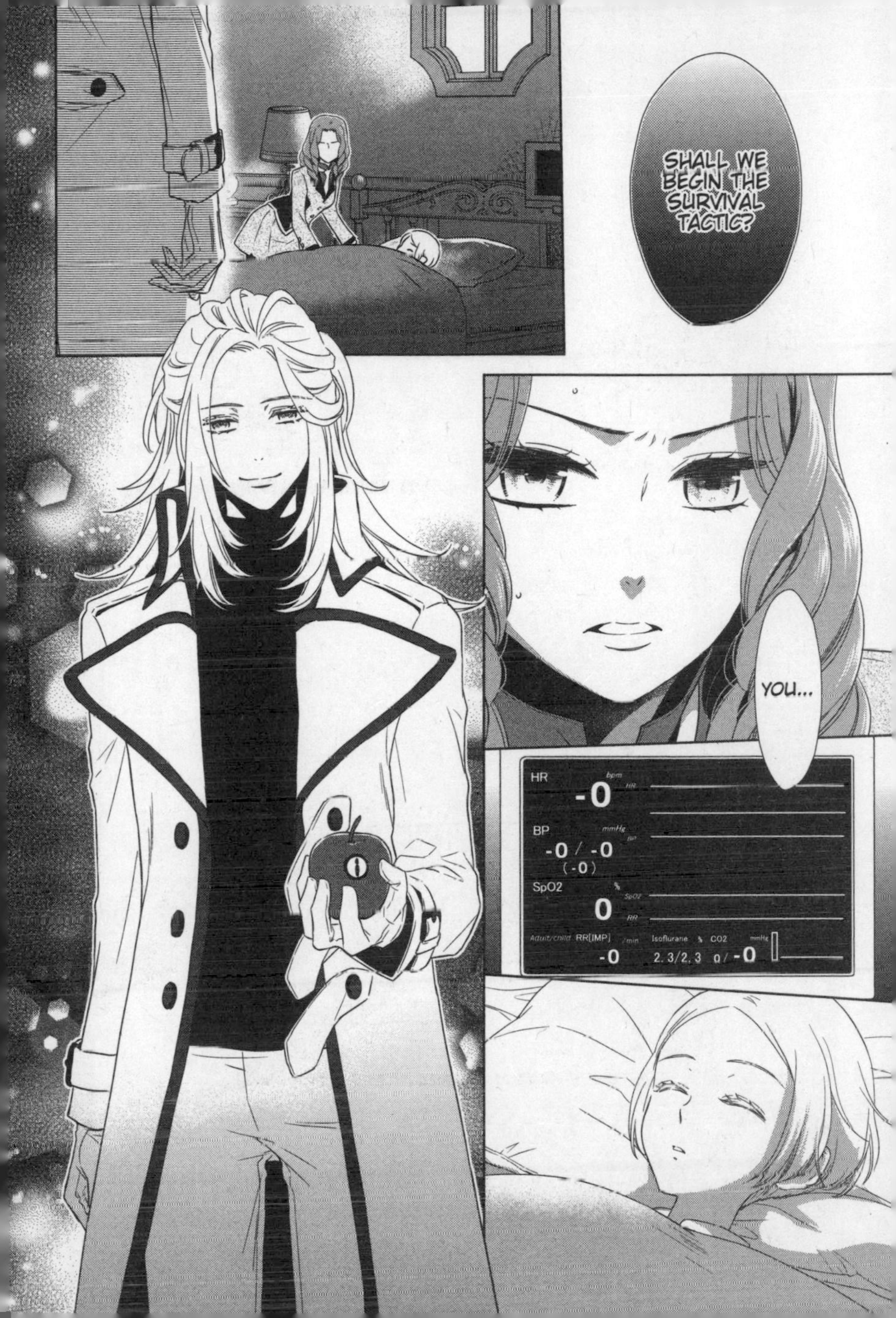
SHALL WE BEGIN THE SURVIVAL TACTIC?
YOU...
HR bpm -0
BP mmHg -0 / -0 (-0)
SpO2 % 0
Adult/child RR[IMP] /min -0
Isoflurane % 2.3/2.3
CO2 mmHg 0/-0

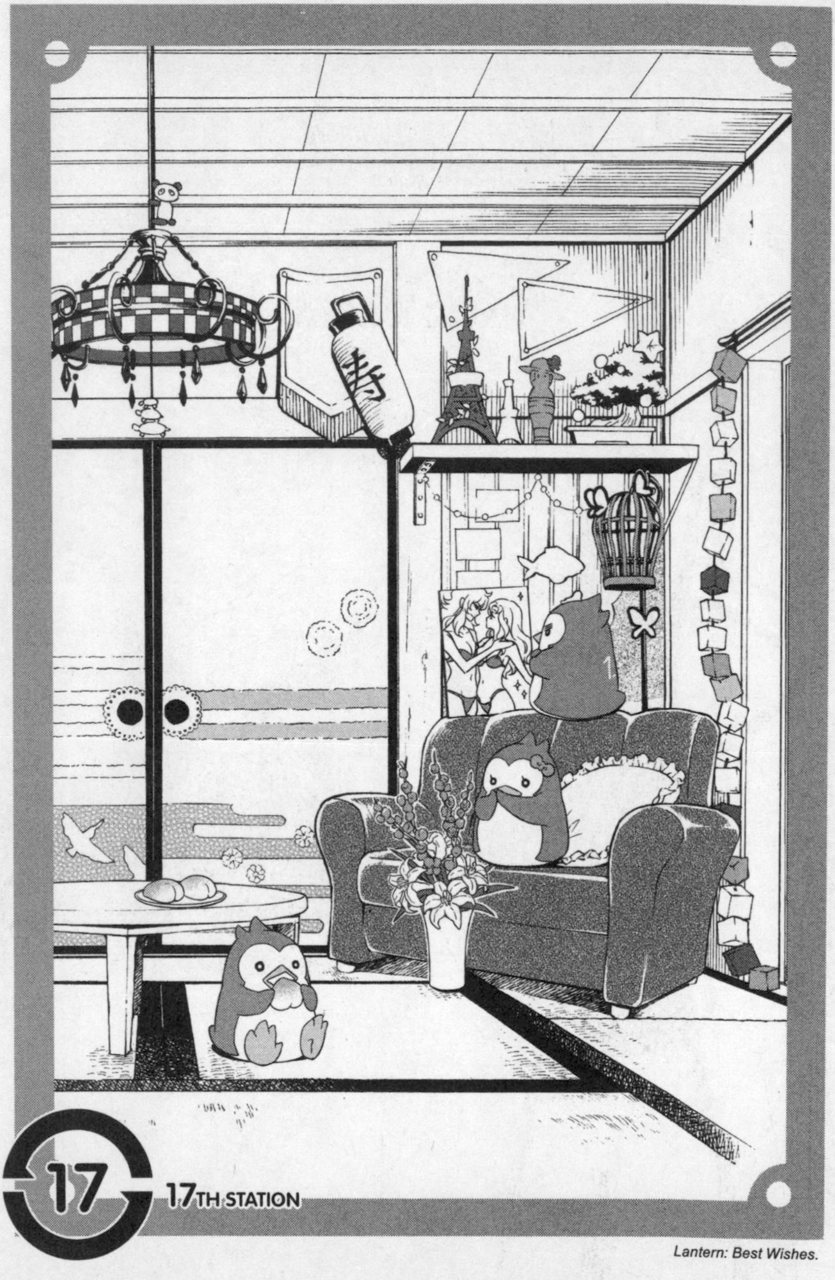
寿
17
17TH STATION

Lantern: Best Wishes.

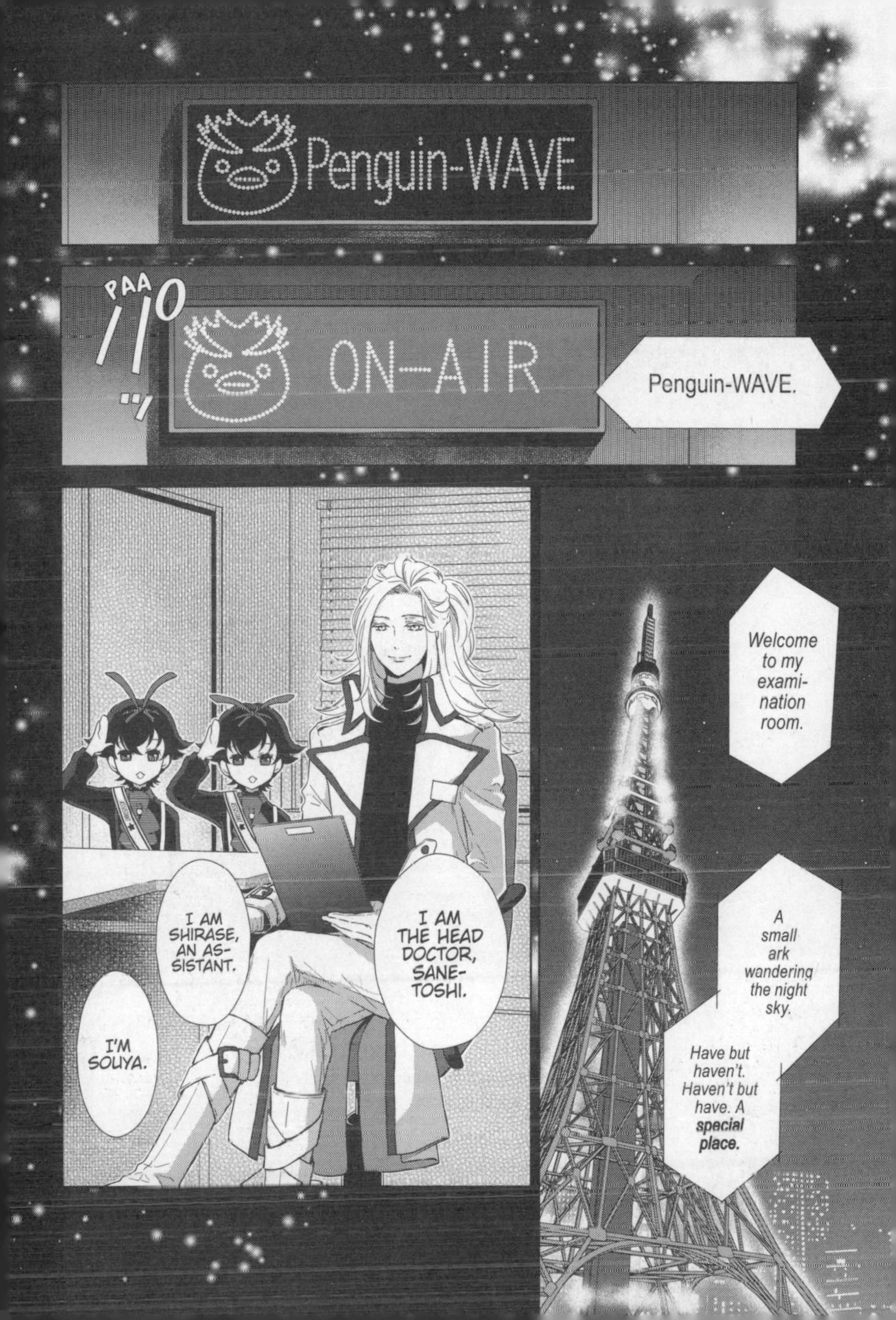
Penguin-WAVE
PAA
ON-AIR
Penguin-WAVE.
Welcome to my examination room.
A small ark wandering the night sky.
Have but haven't. Haven't but have. A **special place.**
I AM THE HEAD DOCTOR, SANETOSHI.
I AM SHIRASE, AN ASSISTANT.
I'M SOUYA.

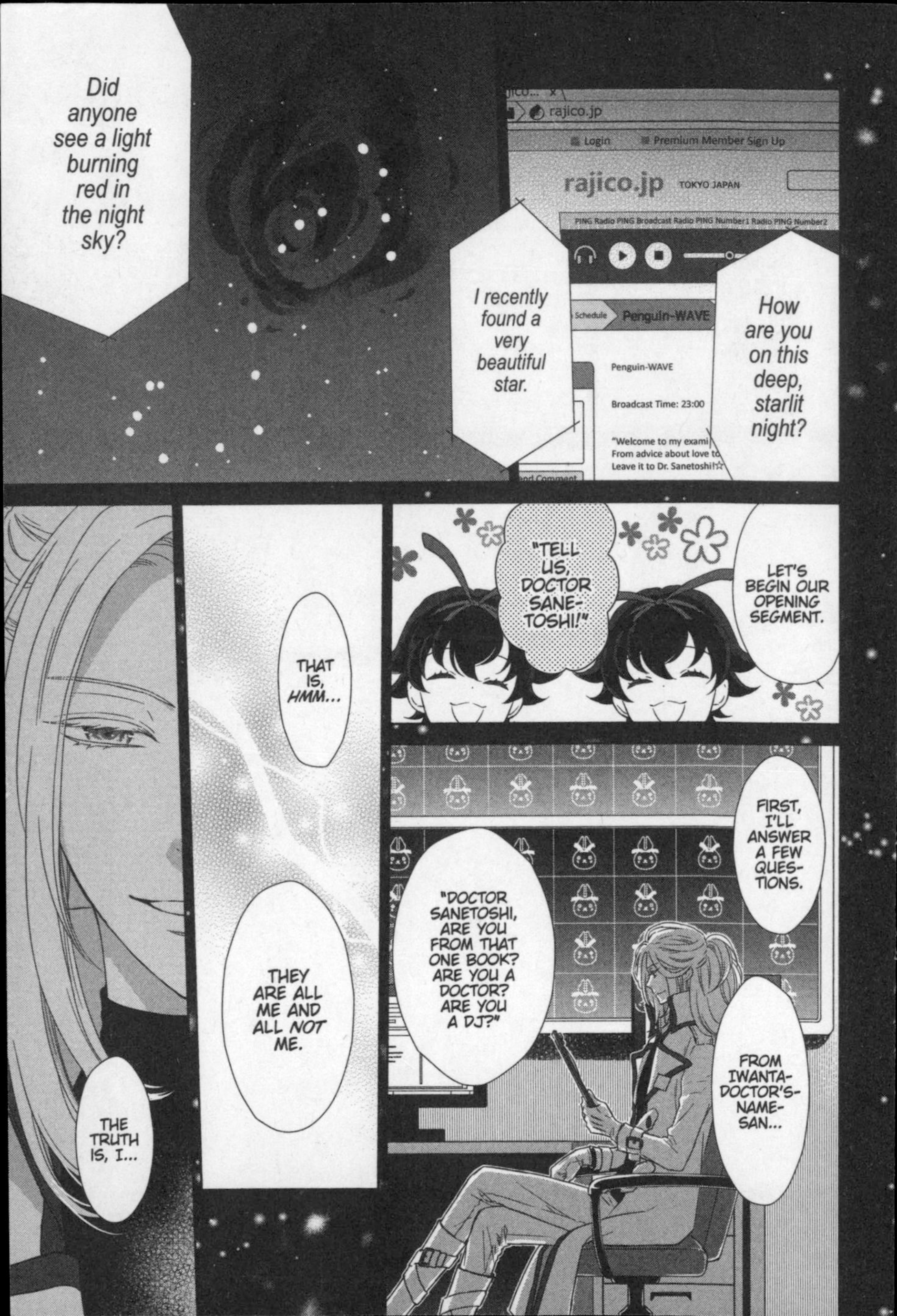
How are you on this deep, starlit night?
rajico.jp
Login
Premium Member Sign Up
rajico.jp TOKYO JAPAN
PING Radio PING Broadcast Radio PING Number1 Radio PING Number2
Schedule
Penguin-WAVE
Penguin-WAVE
Broadcast Time: 23:00
"Welcome to my exami
From advice about love to
Leave it to Dr. Sanetoshi!☆
I recently found a very beautiful star.
Did anyone see a light burning red in the night sky?
LET'S BEGIN OUR OPENING SEGMENT.
"TELL US, DOCTOR SANETOSHI!"
FIRST, I'LL ANSWER A FEW QUESTIONS.
FROM IWANTA-DOCTOR'S-NAME-SAN...
"DOCTOR SANETOSHI, ARE YOU FROM THAT ONE BOOK? ARE YOU A DOCTOR? ARE YOU A DJ?"
THAT IS, HMM...
THEY ARE ALL ME AND ALL *NOT* ME.
THE TRUTH IS, I...

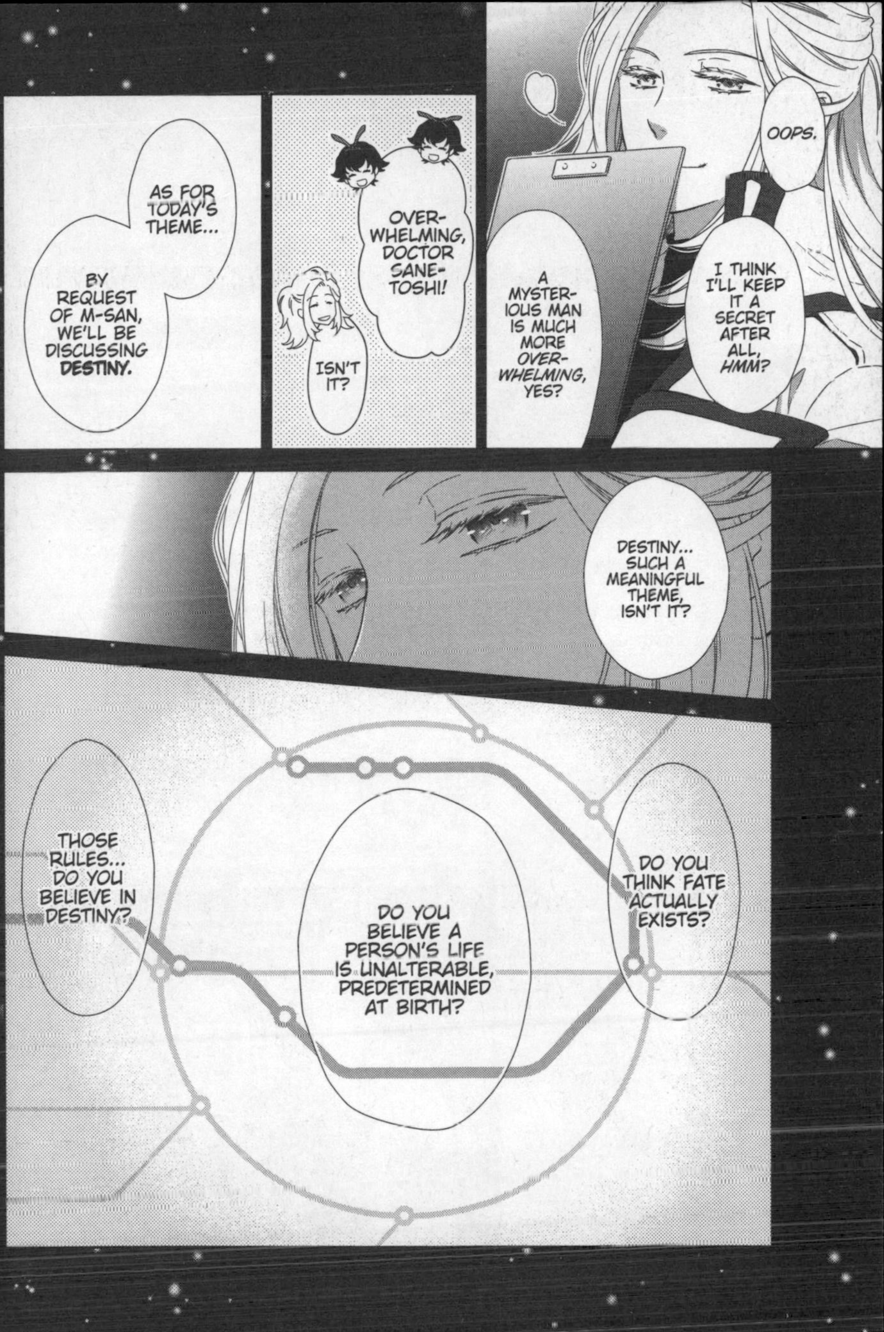
OOPS.
I THINK I'LL KEEP IT A SECRET AFTER ALL, HMM?
A MYSTERIOUS MAN IS MUCH MORE OVERWHELMING, YES?
OVERWHELMING, DOCTOR SANETOSHI!
ISN'T IT?
AS FOR TODAY'S THEME...
BY REQUEST OF M-SAN, WE'LL BE DISCUSSING DESTINY.
DESTINY... SUCH A MEANINGFUL THEME, ISN'T IT?
DO YOU THINK FATE ACTUALLY EXISTS?
DO YOU BELIEVE A PERSON'S LIFE IS UNALTERABLE, PREDETERMINED AT BIRTH?
THOSE RULES... DO YOU BELIEVE IN DESTINY?

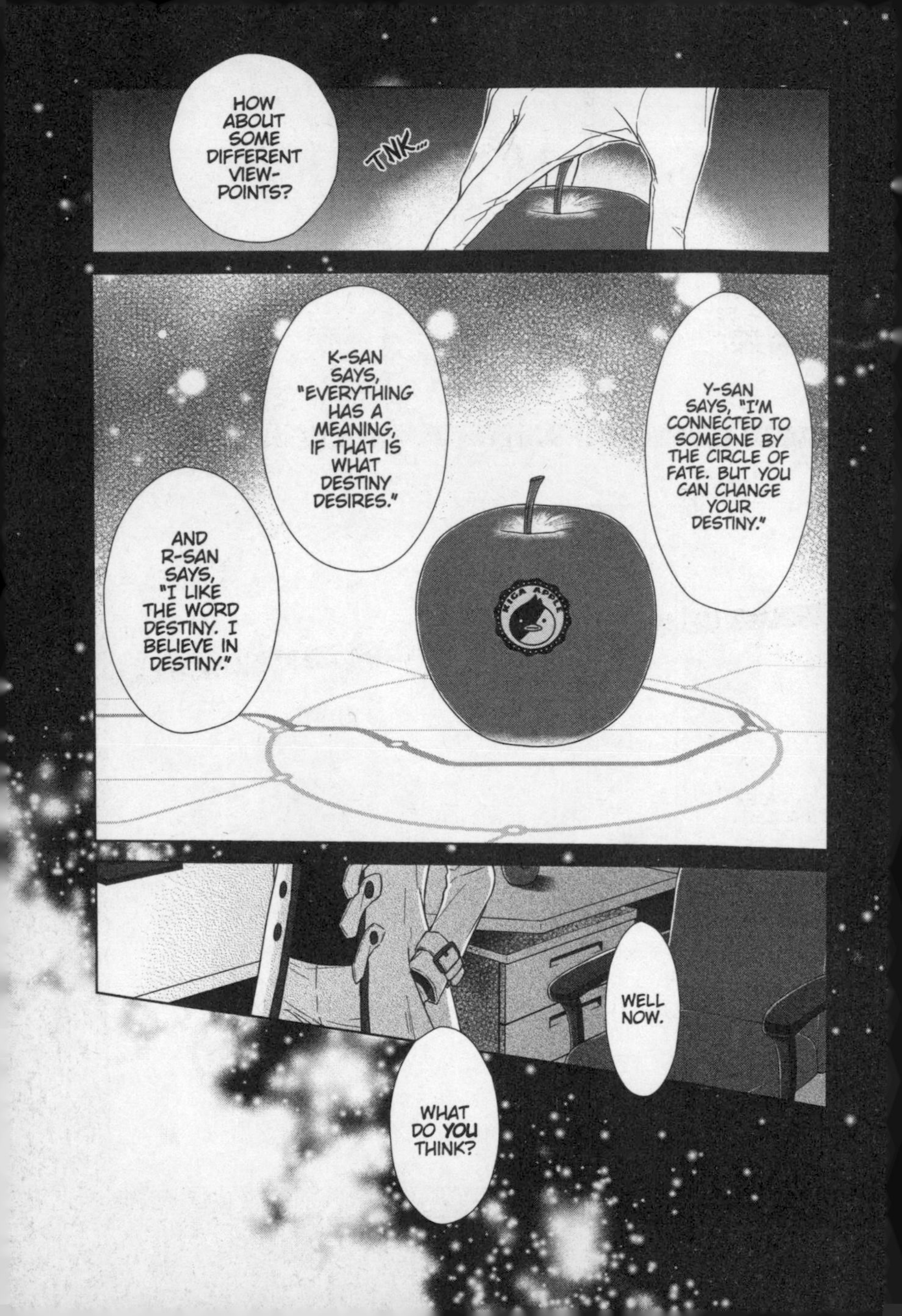
TNK...
HOW ABOUT SOME DIFFERENT VIEW-POINTS?
Y-SAN SAYS, "I'M CONNECTED TO SOMEONE BY THE CIRCLE OF FATE. BUT YOU CAN CHANGE YOUR DESTINY."
K-SAN SAYS, "EVERYTHING HAS A MEANING, IF THAT IS WHAT DESTINY DESIRES."
AND R-SAN SAYS, "I LIKE THE WORD DESTINY. I BELIEVE IN DESTINY."
WELL NOW.
WHAT DO YOU THINK?

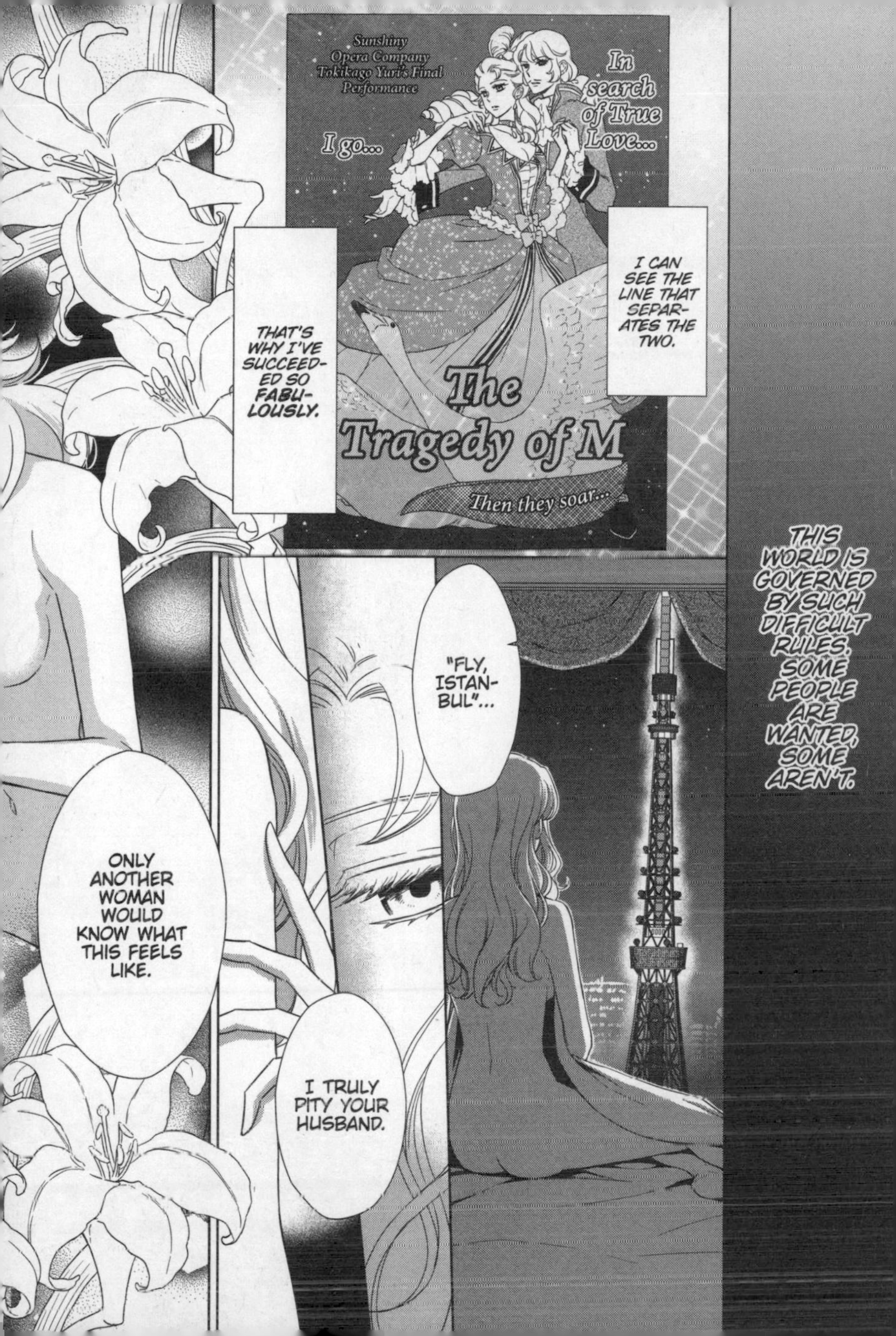
THIS WORLD IS GOVERNED BY SUCH DIFFICULT RULES. SOME PEOPLE ARE WANTED, SOME AREN'T.
In search of True Love...
I go...
Sunshiny Opera Company Tokikago Yuri's Final Performance
The Tragedy of M
Then they soar...
I CAN SEE THE LINE THAT SEPAR-ATES THE TWO.
THAT'S WHY I'VE SUCCEED-ED SO FABU-LOUSLY.
"FLY, ISTAN-BUL"...
I TRULY PITY YOUR HUSBAND.
ONLY ANOTHER WOMAN WOULD KNOW WHAT THIS FEELS LIKE.

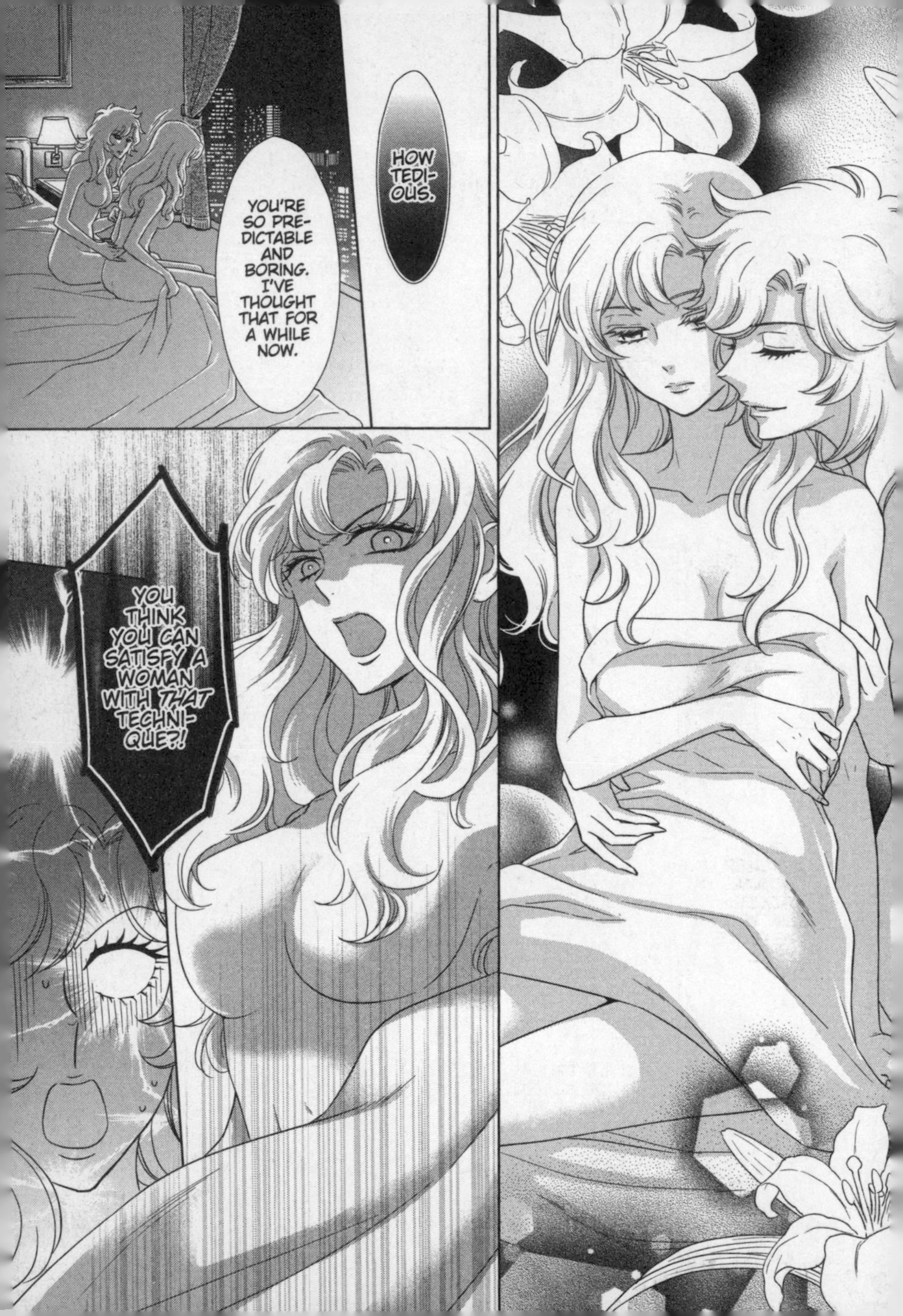
HOW TEDI-OUS.
YOU'RE SO PRE-DICTABLE AND BORING. I'VE THOUGHT THAT FOR A WHILE NOW.
YOU THINK YOU CAN SATISFY A WOMAN WITH THAT TECHNI-QUE?!

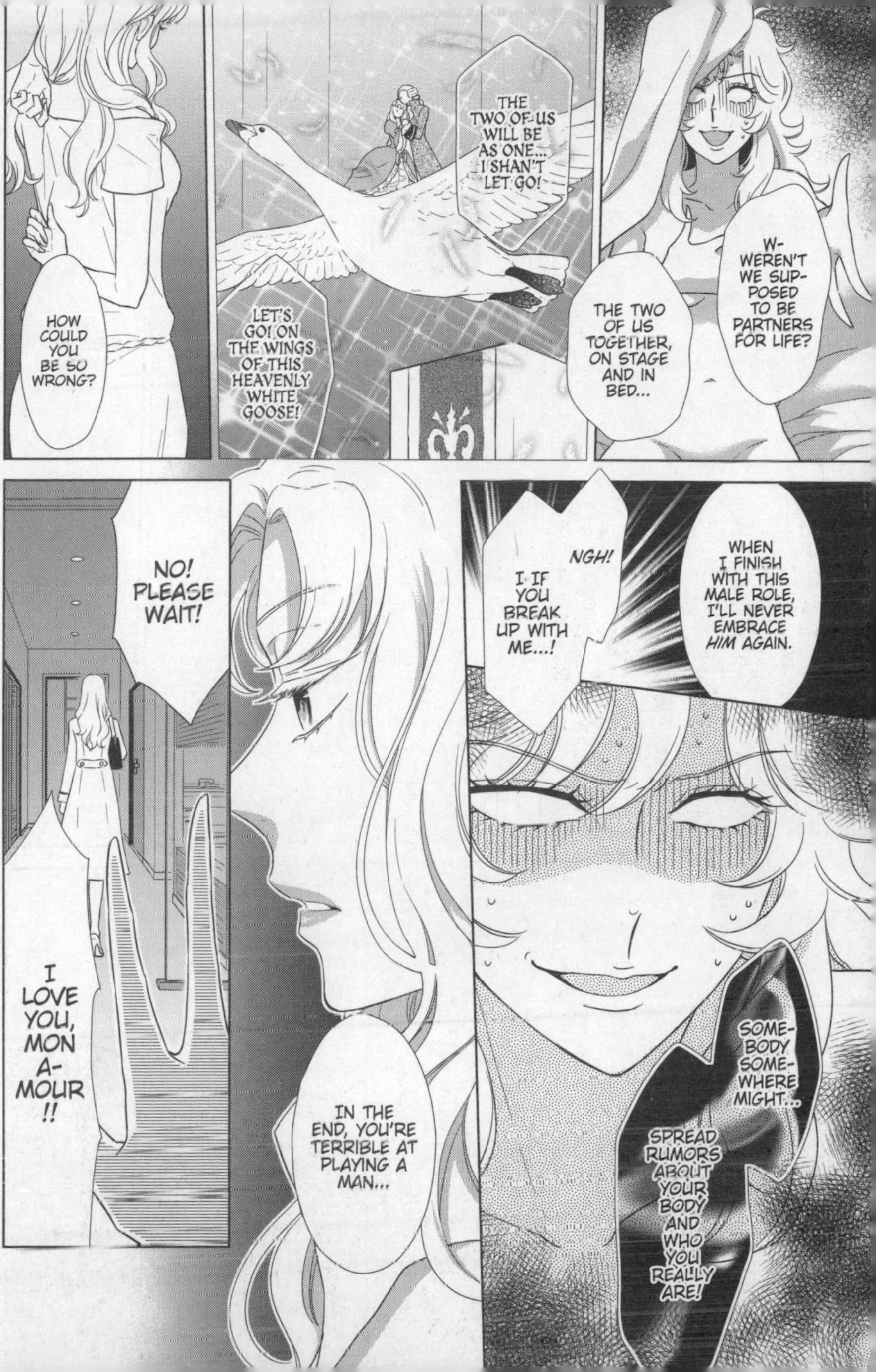
W-WEREN'T WE SUPPOSED TO BE PARTNERS FOR LIFE?
THE TWO OF US TOGETHER, ON STAGE AND IN BED...
THE TWO OF US WILL BE AS ONE... I SHAN'T LET GO!
LET'S GO! ON THE WINGS OF THIS HEAVENLY WHITE GOOSE!
HOW COULD YOU BE SO WRONG?
WHEN I FINISH WITH THIS MALE ROLE, I'LL NEVER EMBRACE *HIM* AGAIN.
NGH!
I IF YOU BREAK UP WITH ME...!
SOMEBODY SOMEWHERE MIGHT...
SPREAD RUMORS ABOUT YOUR BODY AND WHO YOU REALLY ARE!
IN THE END, YOU'RE TERRIBLE AT PLAYING A MAN...
NO! PLEASE WAIT!
I LOVE YOU, MON AMOUR!!

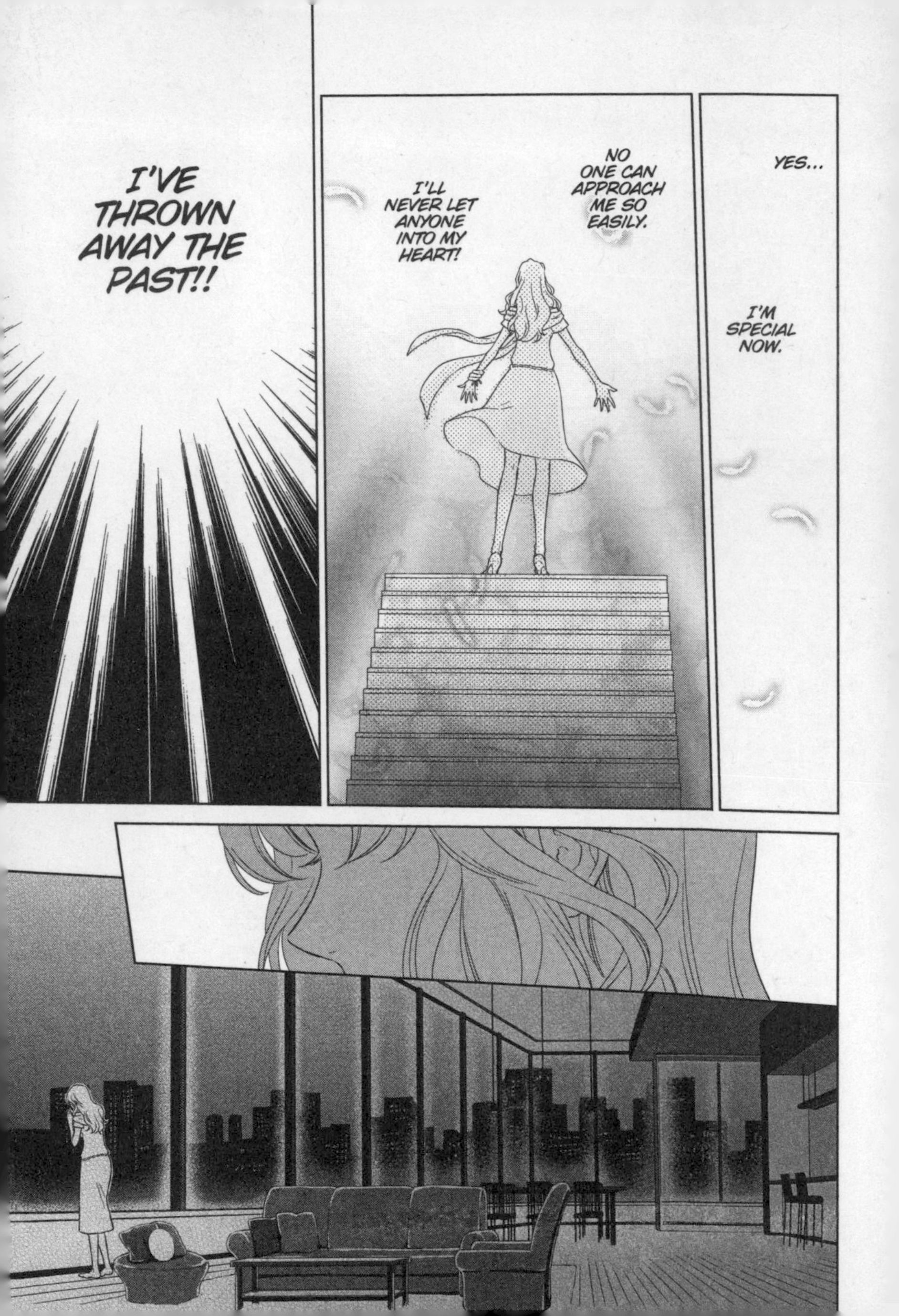
YES...
I'M SPECIAL NOW.
NO ONE CAN APPROACH ME SO EASILY.
I'LL NEVER LET ANYONE INTO MY HEART!
I'VE THROWN AWAY THE PAST!!

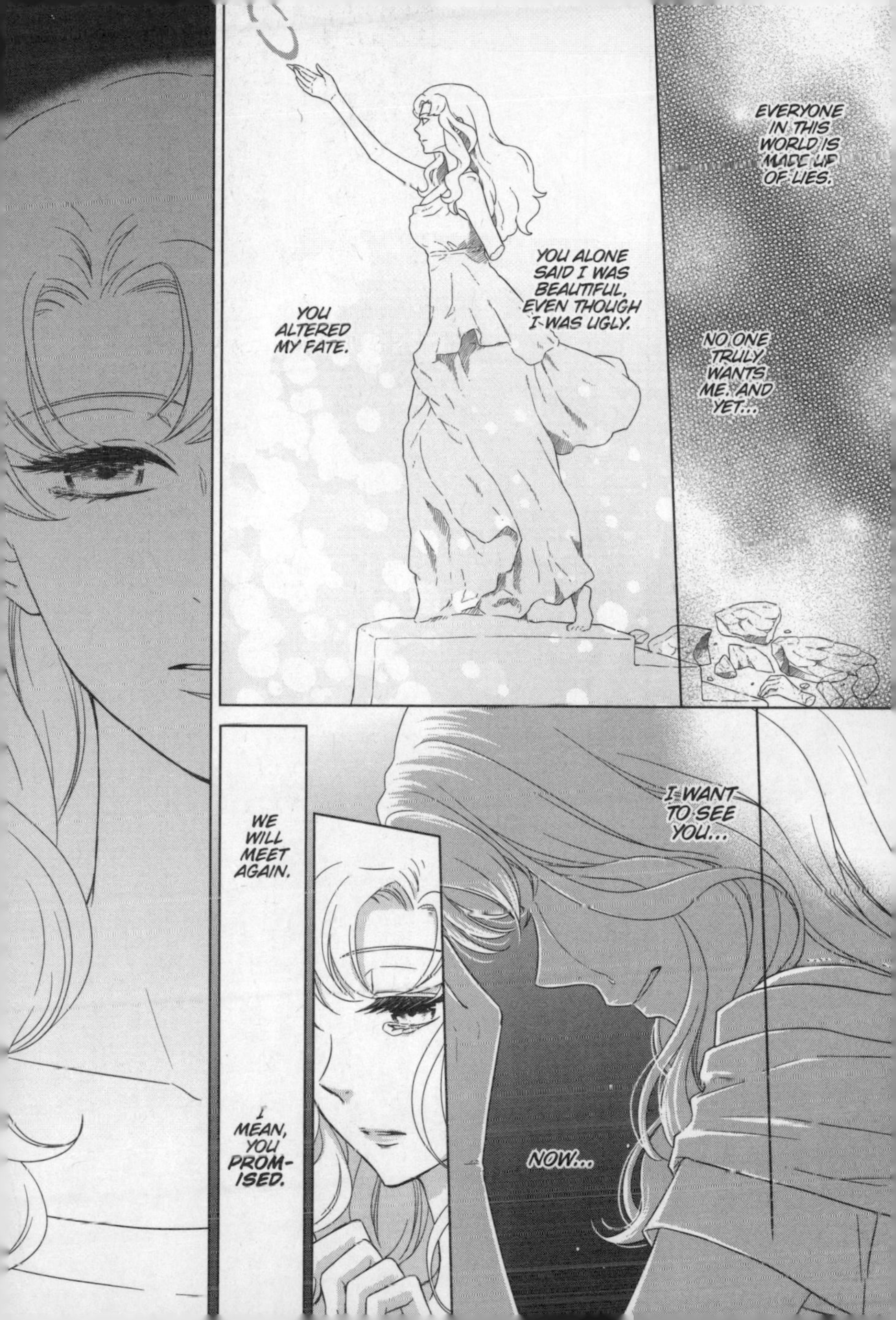
EVERYONE IN THIS WORLD IS MADE UP OF LIES.
NO ONE TRULY WANTS ME. AND YET...
YOU ALONE SAID I WAS BEAUTIFUL, EVEN THOUGH I WAS UGLY.
YOU ALTERED MY FATE.
I WANT TO SEE YOU...
NOW...
WE WILL MEET AGAIN.
I MEAN, YOU PROMISED.

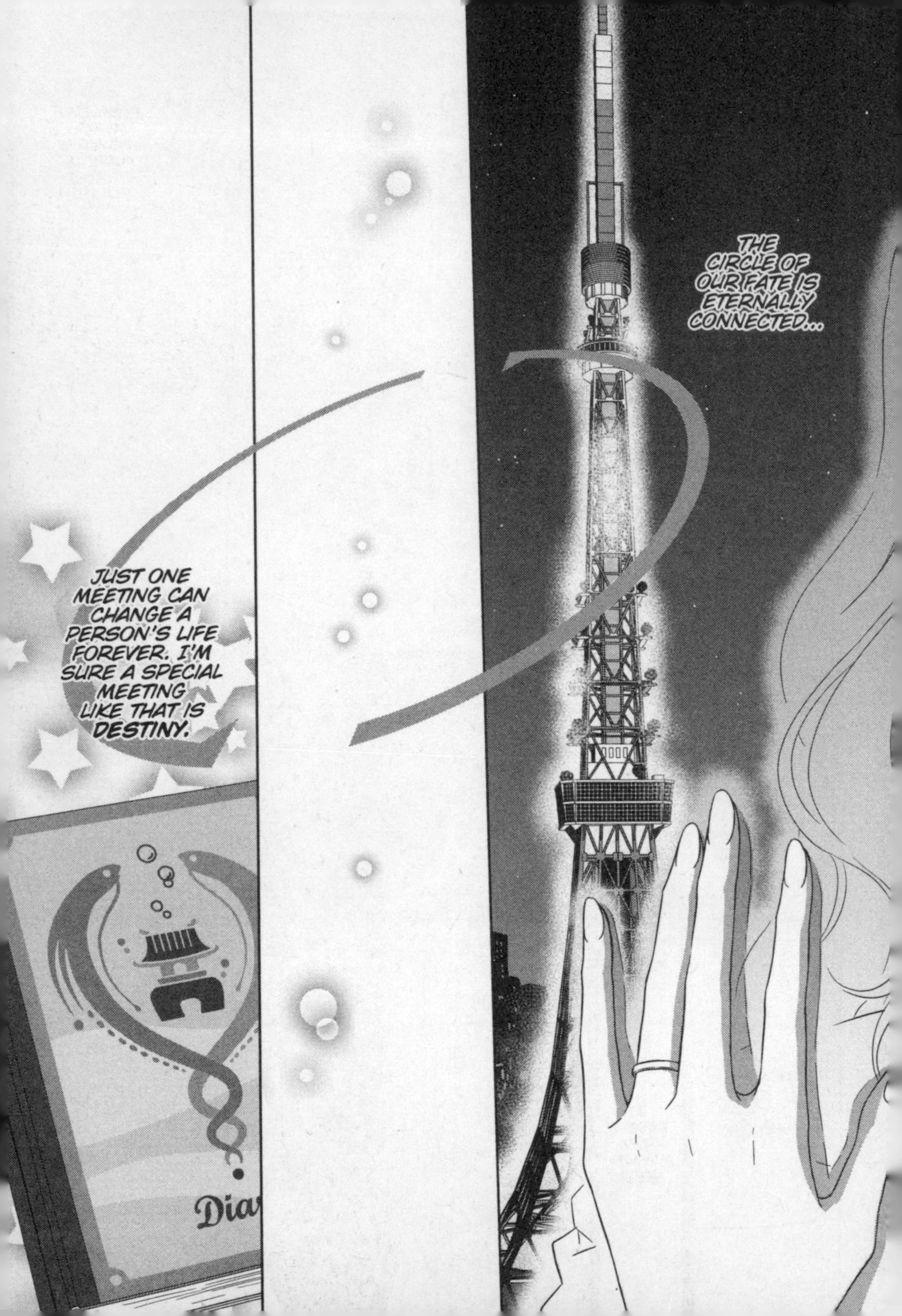
THE CIRCLE OF OUR FATE IS ETERNALLY CONNECTED...
JUST ONE MEETING CAN CHANGE A PERSON'S LIFE FOREVER. I'M SURE A SPECIAL MEETING LIKE THAT IS DESTINY.

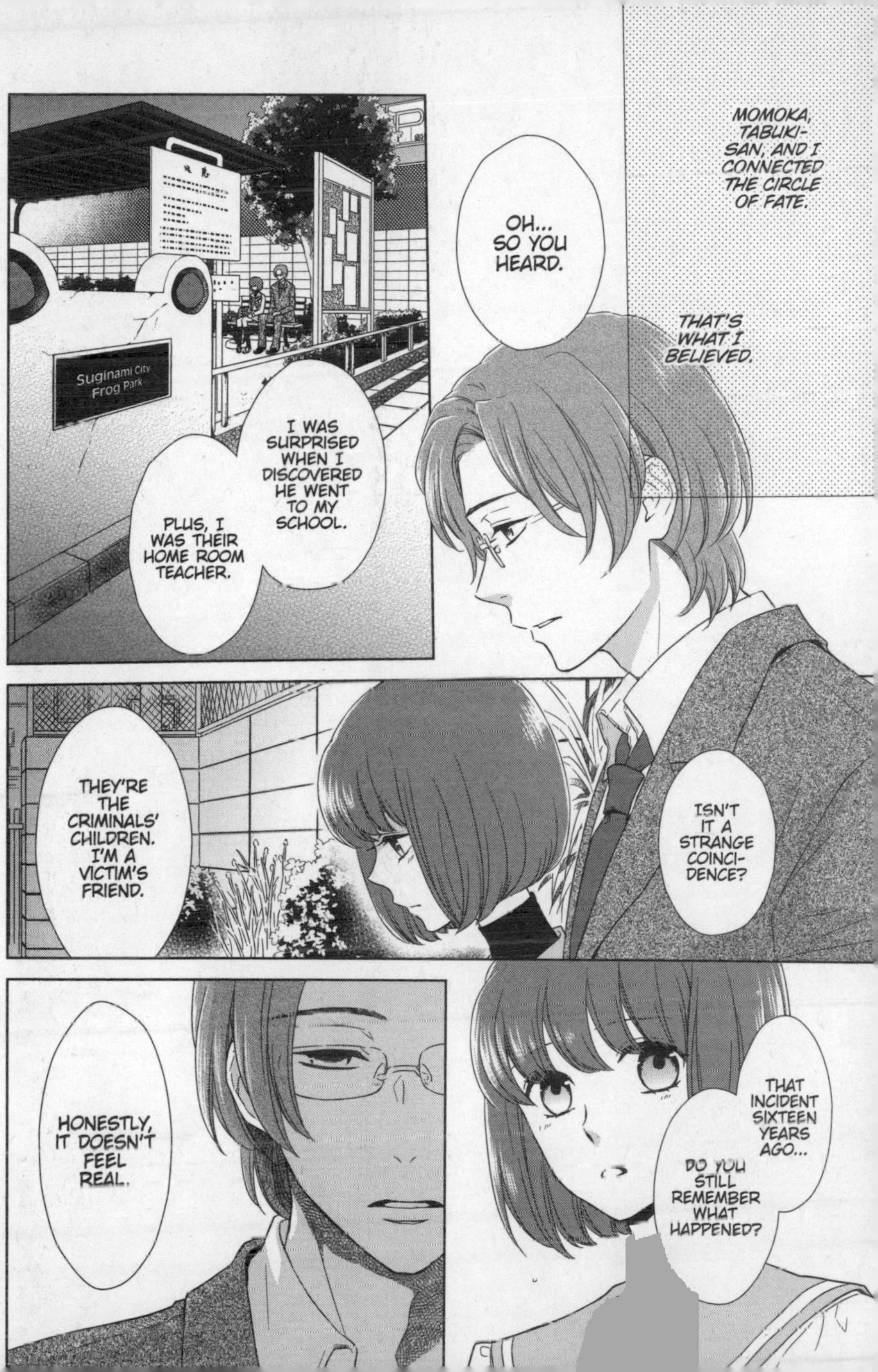
MOMOKA, TABUKI-SAN, AND I CONNECTED THE CIRCLE OF FATE.
THAT'S WHAT I BELIEVED.
OH... SO YOU HEARD.
I WAS SURPRISED WHEN I DISCOVERED HE WENT TO MY SCHOOL.
PLUS, I WAS THEIR HOME ROOM TEACHER.
Suginami City Frog Park
ISN'T IT A STRANGE COINCIDENCE?
THEY'RE THE CRIMINALS' CHILDREN. I'M A VICTIM'S FRIEND.
THAT INCIDENT SIXTEEN YEARS AGO...
DO YOU STILL REMEMBER WHAT HAPPENED?
HONESTLY, IT DOESN'T FEEL REAL.

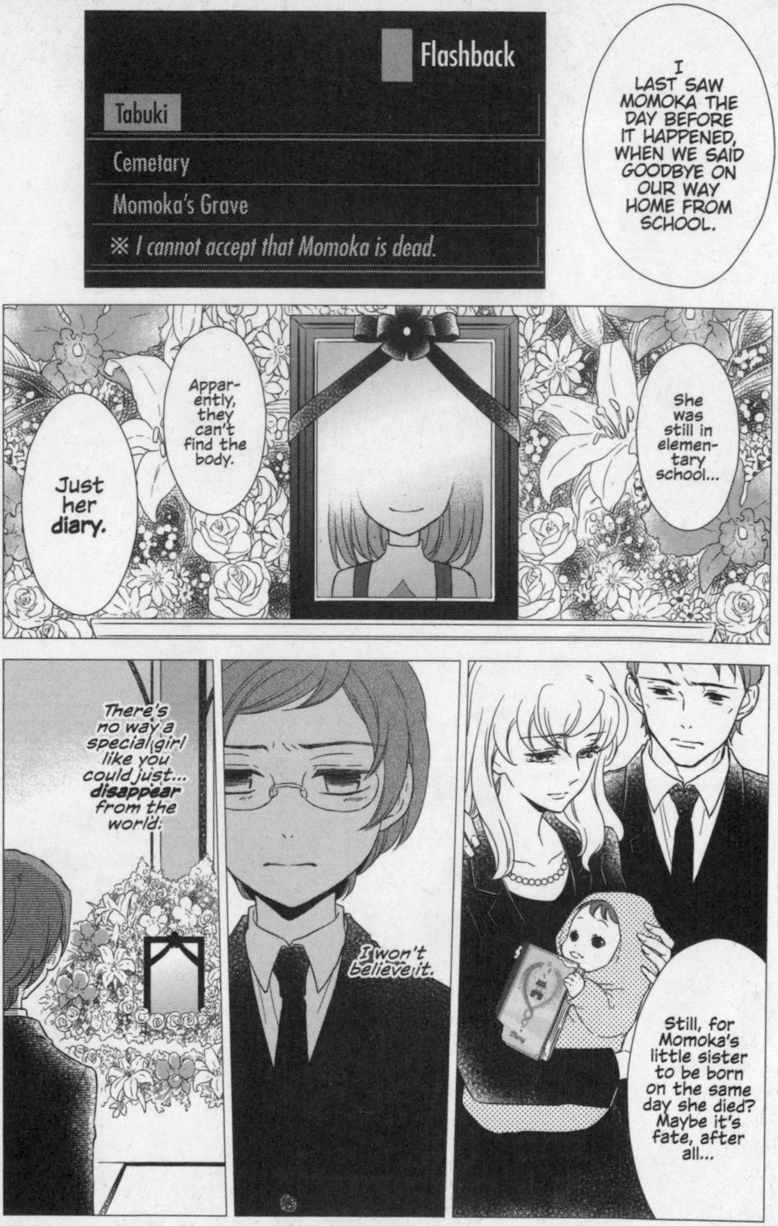
I LAST SAW MOMOKA THE DAY BEFORE IT HAPPENED, WHEN WE SAID GOODBYE ON OUR WAY HOME FROM SCHOOL.
Flashback
Tabuki
Cemetary
Momoka's Grave
※ I cannot accept that Momoka is dead.
She was still in elementary school...
Apparently, they can't find the body.
Just her diary.
Still, for Momoka's little sister to be born on the same day she died? Maybe it's fate, after all...
I won't believe it.
There's no way a special girl like you could just... disappear from the world.

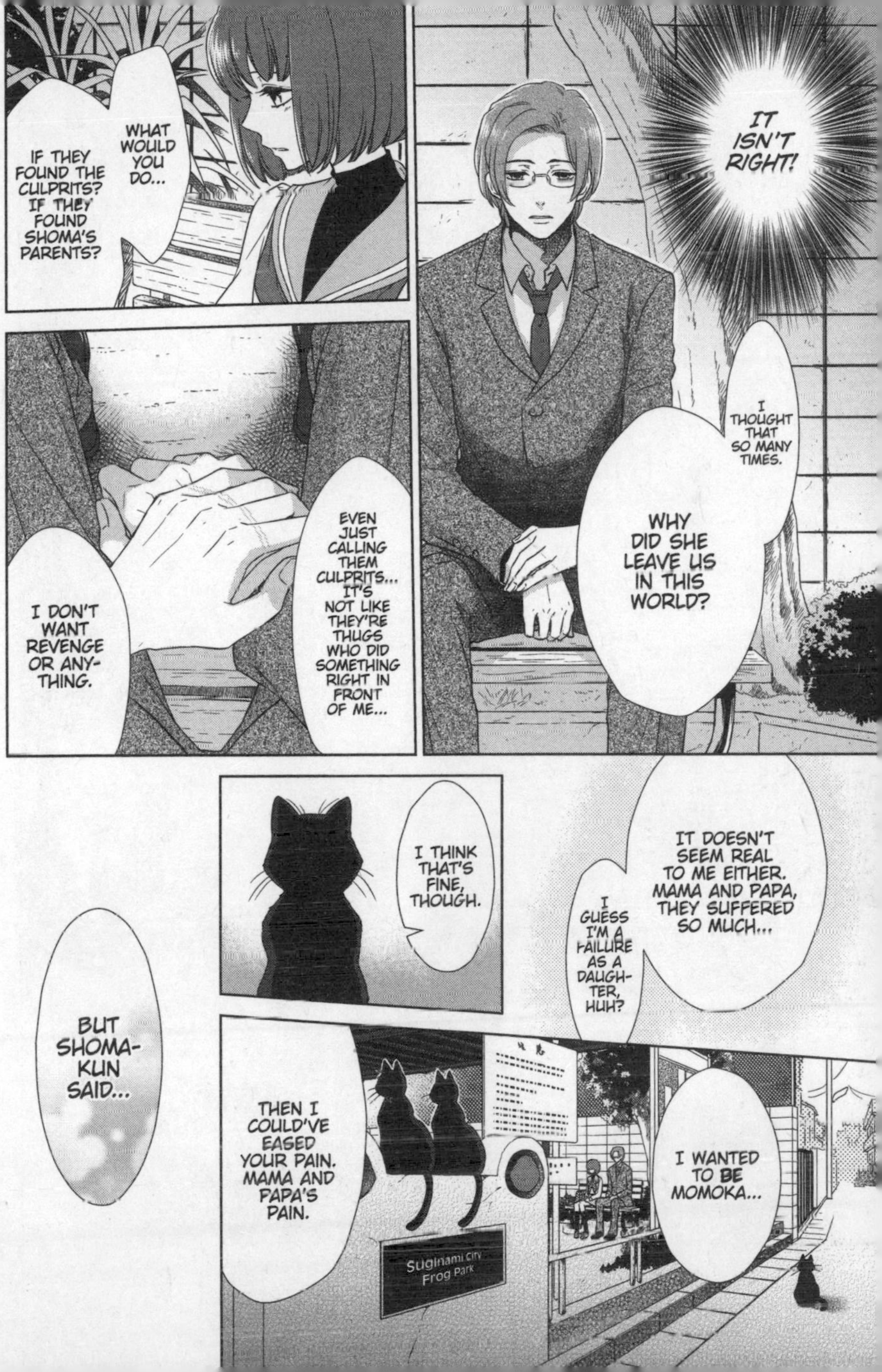
IT ISN'T RIGHT!
I THOUGHT THAT SO MANY TIMES.
WHY DID SHE LEAVE US IN THIS WORLD?
WHAT WOULD YOU DO...
IF THEY FOUND THE CULPRITS? IF THEY FOUND SHOMA'S PARENTS?
EVEN JUST CALLING THEM CULPRITS... IT'S NOT LIKE THEY'RE THUGS WHO DID SOMETHING RIGHT IN FRONT OF ME...
I DON'T WANT REVENGE OR ANY-THING.
IT DOESN'T SEEM REAL TO ME EITHER. MAMA AND PAPA, THEY SUFFERED SO MUCH...
I GUESS I'M A FAILURE AS A DAUGH-TER, HUH?
I THINK THAT'S FINE, THOUGH.
BUT SHOMA-KUN SAID...
I WANTED TO BE MOMOKA...
THEN I COULD'VE EASED YOUR PAIN. MAMA AND PAPA'S PAIN.
Suginami City
Frog Park

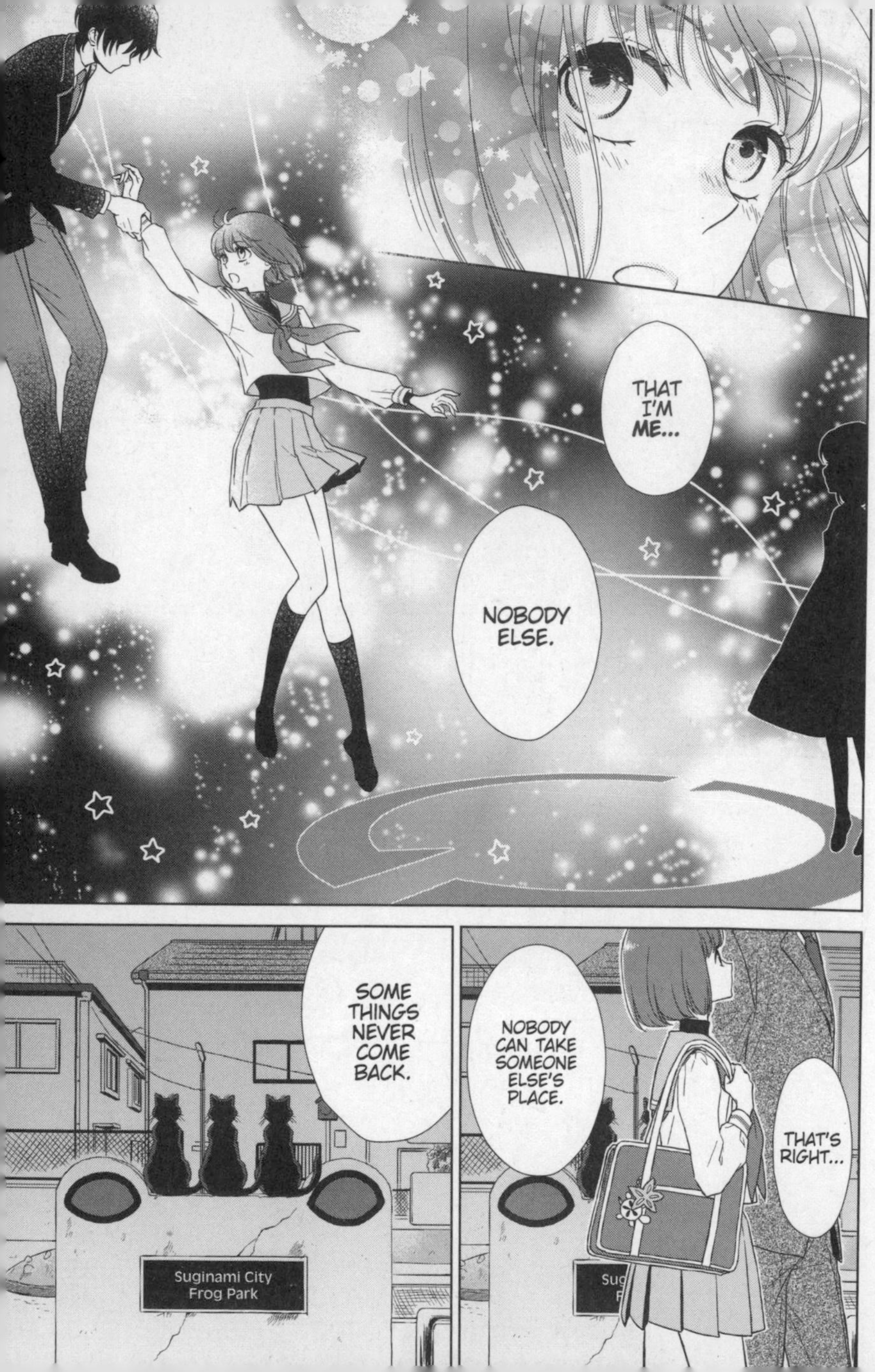
THAT I'M ME...
NOBODY ELSE.
NOBODY CAN TAKE SOMEONE ELSE'S PLACE.
THAT'S RIGHT...
SOME THINGS NEVER COME BACK.
Suginami City Frog Park

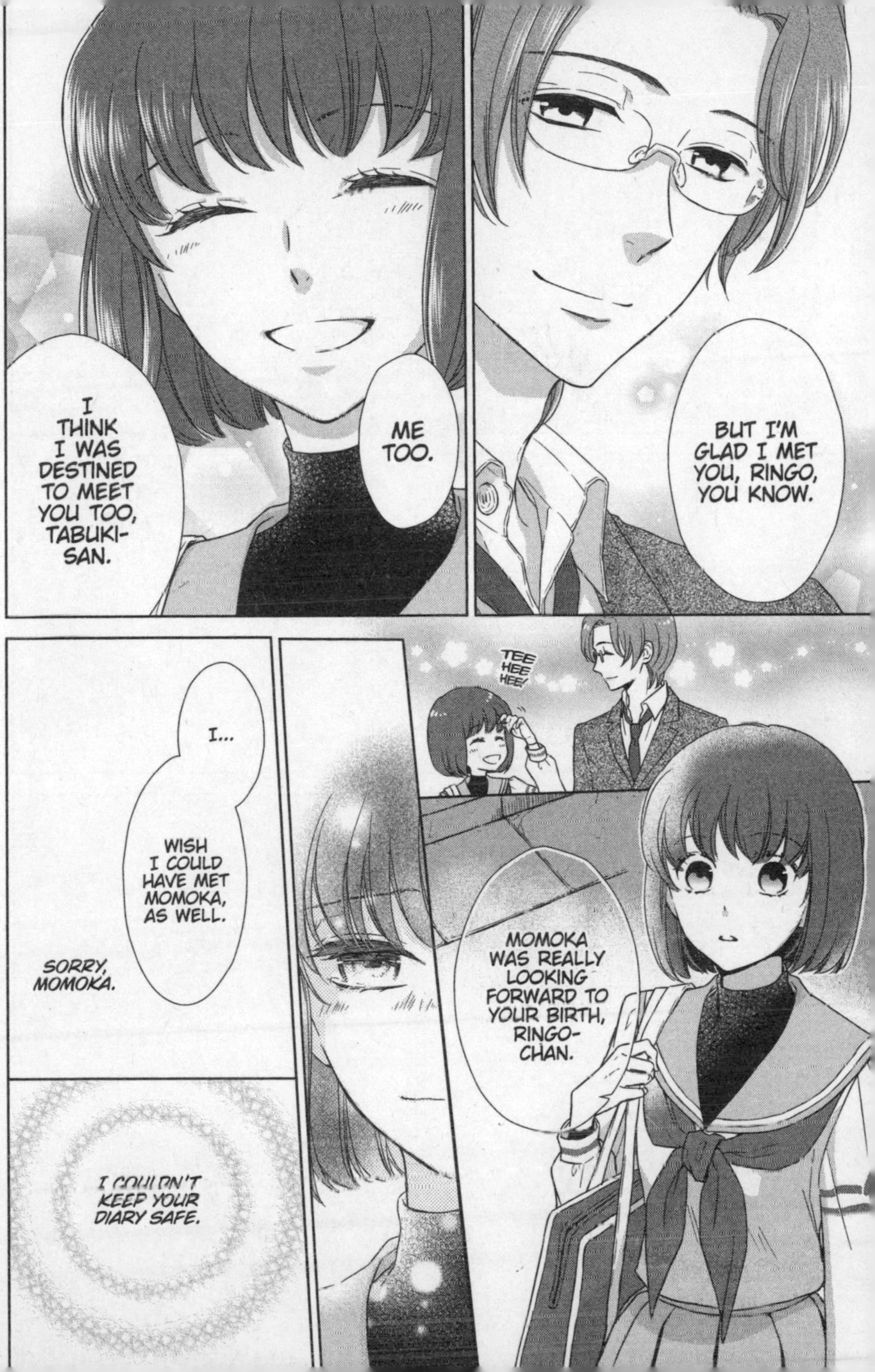
BUT I'M GLAD I MET YOU, RINGO, YOU KNOW.
ME TOO.
I THINK I WAS DESTINED TO MEET YOU TOO, TABUKI-SAN.
TEE HEE HEE!
MOMOKA WAS REALLY LOOKING FORWARD TO YOUR BIRTH, RINGO-CHAN.
I...
WISH I COULD HAVE MET MOMOKA, AS WELL.
SORRY, MOMOKA.
I COULDN'T KEEP YOUR DIARY SAFE.

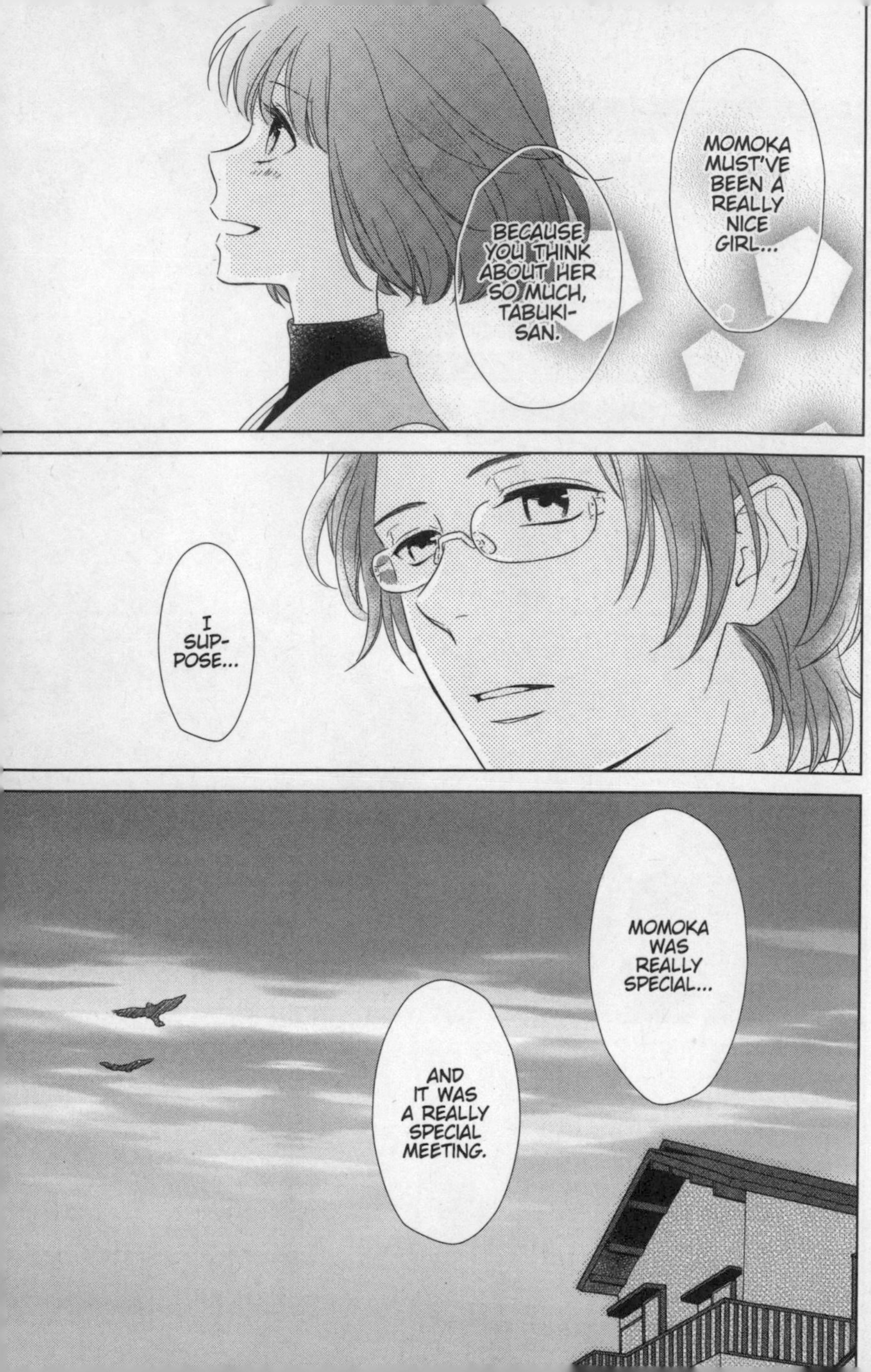
MOMOKA MUST'VE BEEN A REALLY NICE GIRL...
BECAUSE YOU THINK ABOUT HER SO MUCH, TABUKI-SAN.
I SUP-POSE...
MOMOKA WAS REALLY SPECIAL...
AND IT WAS A REALLY SPECIAL MEETING.

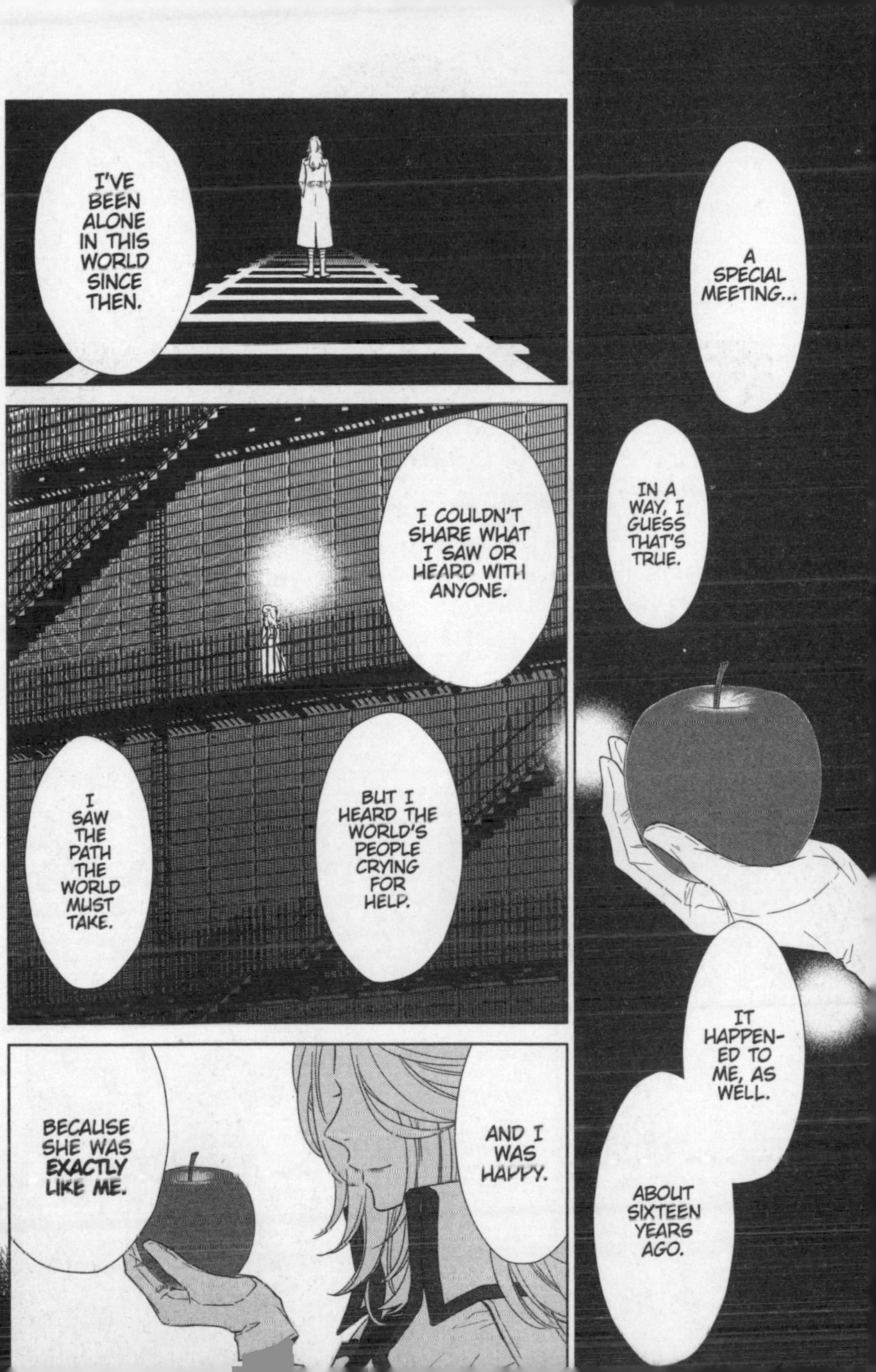
A SPECIAL MEETING...
IN A WAY, I GUESS THAT'S TRUE.
IT HAPPENED TO ME, AS WELL.
ABOUT SIXTEEN YEARS AGO.
I'VE BEEN ALONE IN THIS WORLD SINCE THEN.
I COULDN'T SHARE WHAT I SAW OR HEARD WITH ANYONE.
BUT I HEARD THE WORLD'S PEOPLE CRYING FOR HELP.
I SAW THE PATH THE WORLD MUST TAKE.
AND I WAS HAPPY.
BECAUSE SHE WAS **EXACTLY LIKE ME.**

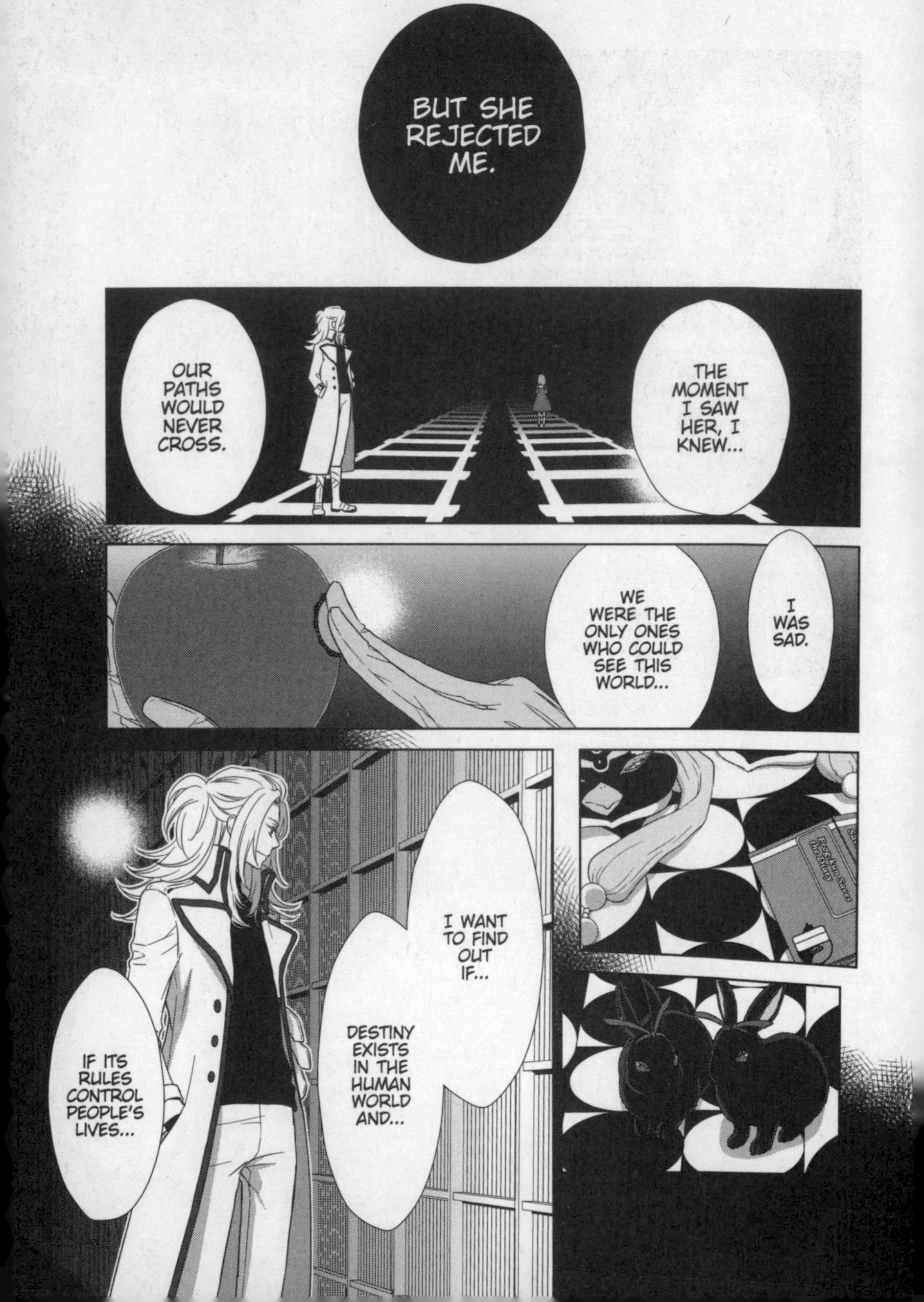
BUT SHE REJECTED ME.
THE MOMENT I SAW HER, I KNEW...
OUR PATHS WOULD NEVER CROSS.
I WAS SAD.
WE WERE THE ONLY ONES WHO COULD SEE THIS WORLD...
I WANT TO FIND OUT IF...
DESTINY EXISTS IN THE HUMAN WORLD AND...
IF ITS RULES CONTROL PEOPLE'S LIVES...

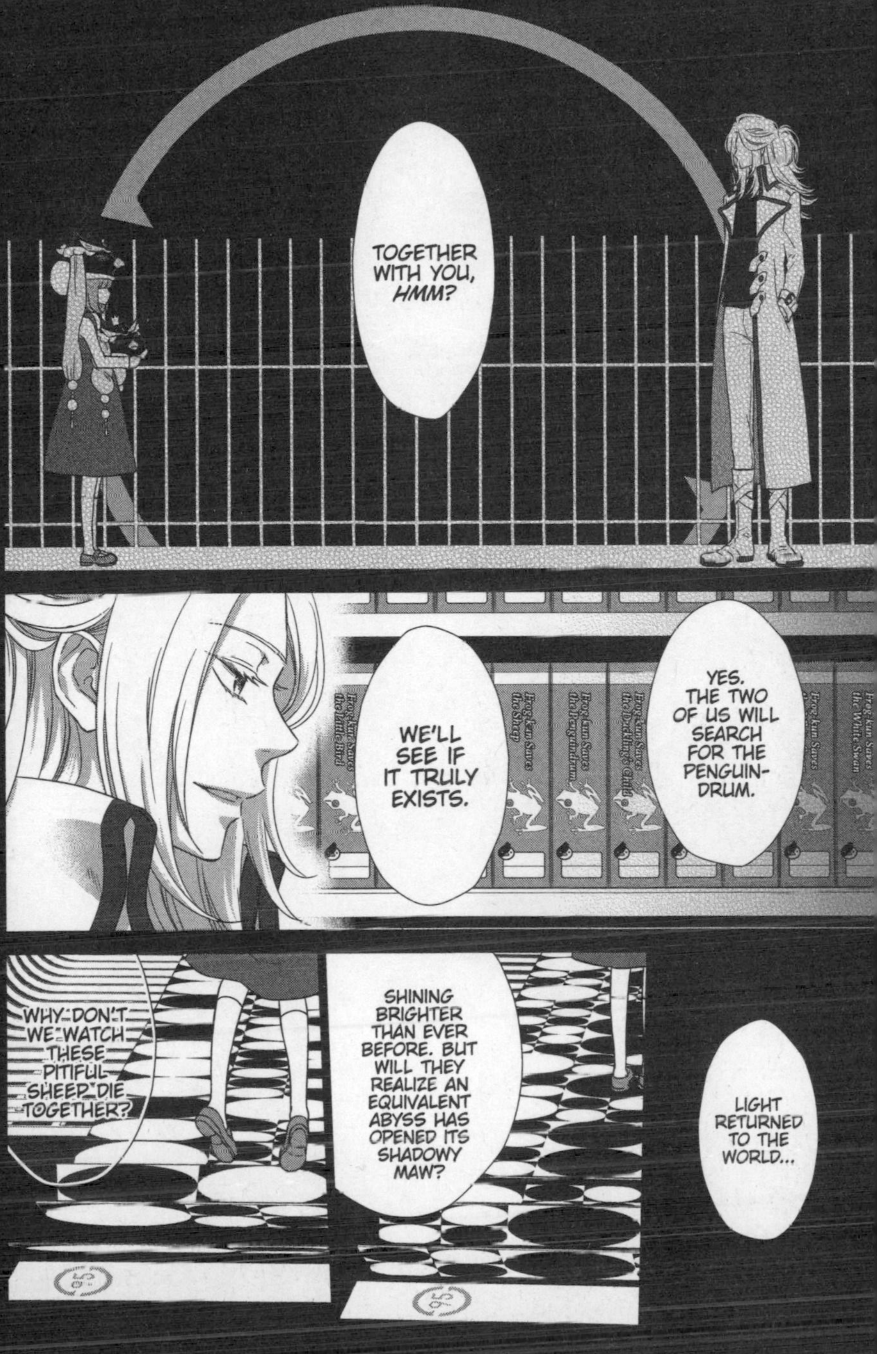
TOGETHER WITH YOU, *HMM?*
YES. THE TWO OF US WILL SEARCH FOR THE PENGUINDRUM.
WE'LL SEE IF IT TRULY EXISTS.
LIGHT RETURNED TO THE WORLD...
SHINING BRIGHTER THAN EVER BEFORE. BUT WILL THEY REALIZE AN EQUIVALENT ABYSS HAS OPENED ITS SHADOWY MAW?
WHY DON'T WE WATCH THESE PITIFUL SHEEP DIE TOGETHER?

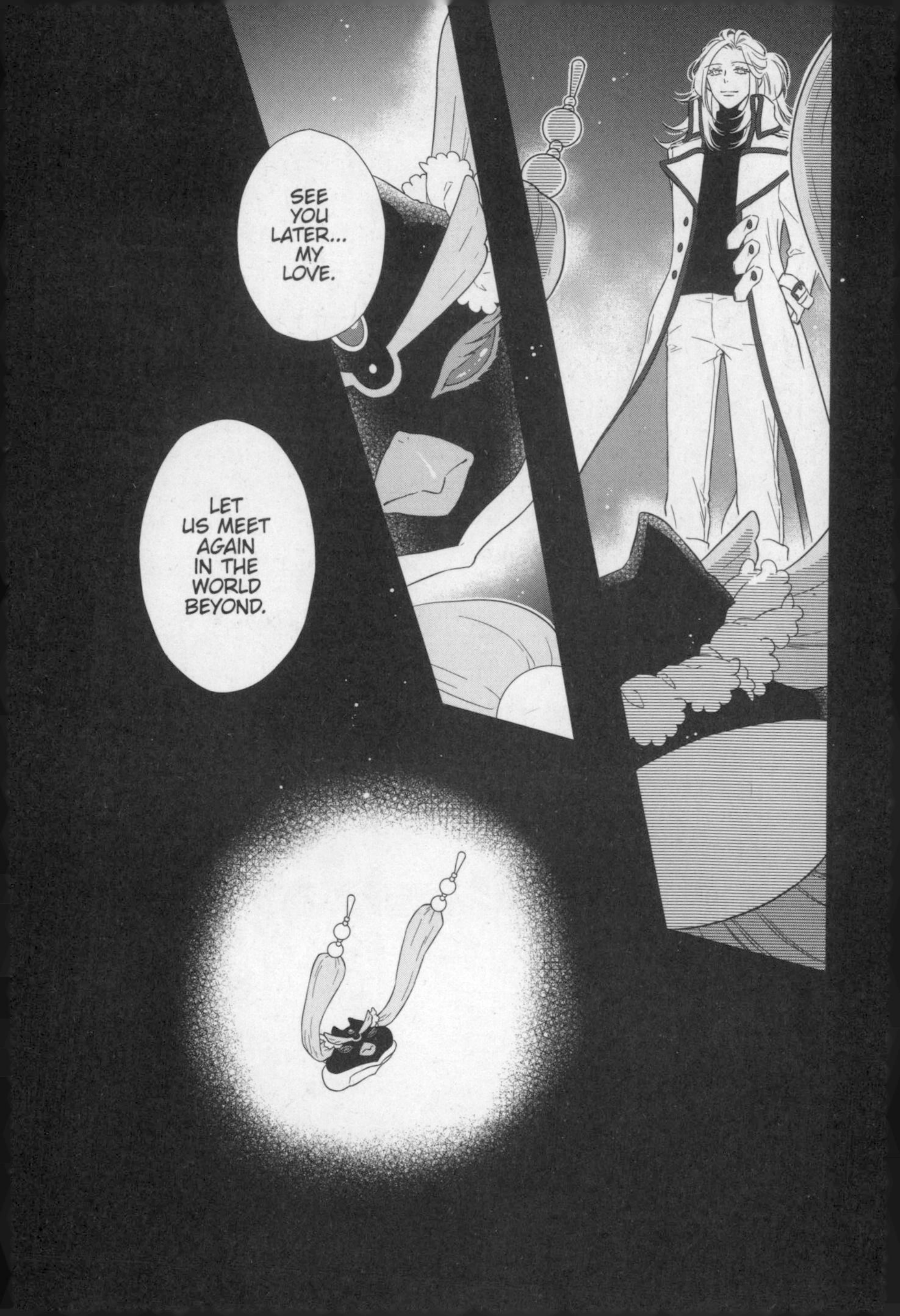
SEE YOU LATER... MY LOVE.
LET US MEET AGAIN IN THE WORLD BEYOND.

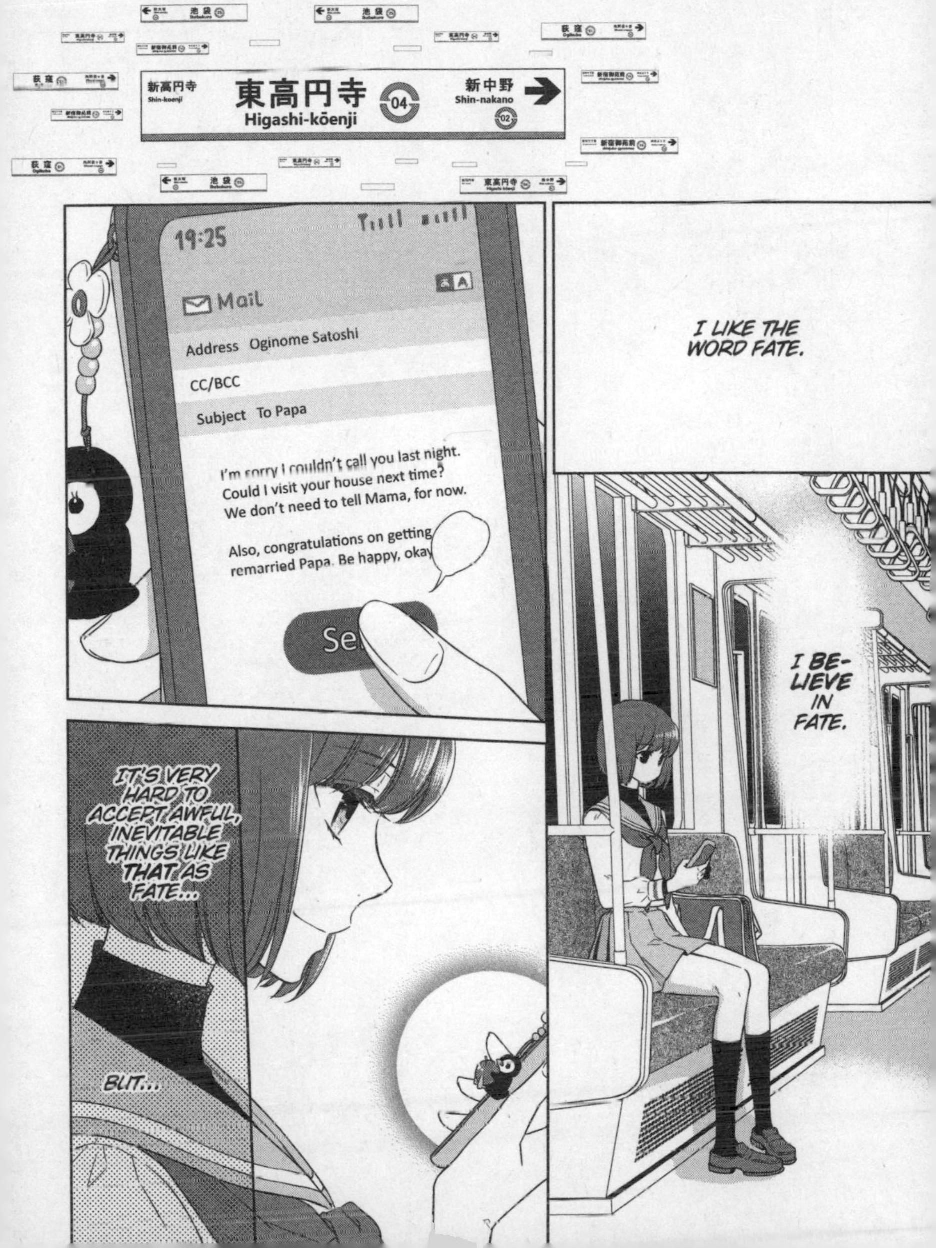
新高円寺
Shin-koenji
東高円寺
Higashi-kōenji
04
新中野
Shin-nakano
02
I LIKE THE WORD FATE.
I BE-LIEVE IN FATE.
19:25
Mail
Address Oginome Satoshi
CC/BCC
Subject To Papa
I'm sorry I couldn't call you last night.
Could I visit your house next time?
We don't need to tell Mama, for now.
Also, congratulations on getting remarried Papa. Be happy, okay
IT'S VERY HARD TO ACCEPT AWFUL, INEVITABLE THINGS LIKE THAT AS FATE...
BUT...

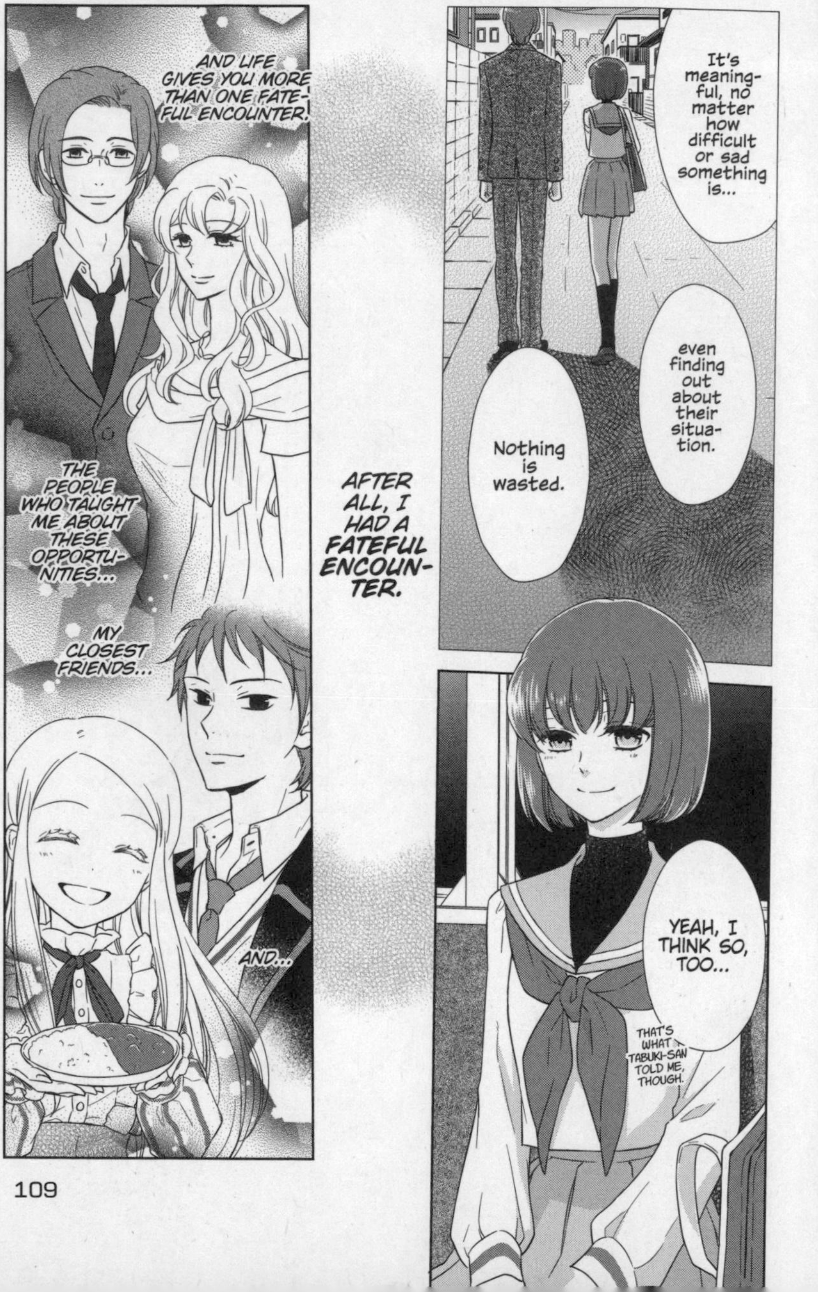
It's meaningful, no matter how difficult or sad something is...
even finding out about their situation.
Nothing is wasted.
YEAH, I THINK SO, TOO...
THAT'S WHAT TABUKI-SAN TOLD ME, THOUGH.
AFTER ALL, I HAD A FATEFUL ENCOUNTER.
AND LIFE GIVES YOU MORE THAN ONE FATEFUL ENCOUNTER!
THE PEOPLE WHO TAUGHT ME ABOUT THESE OPPORTUNITIES...
MY CLOSEST FRIENDS...
AND...

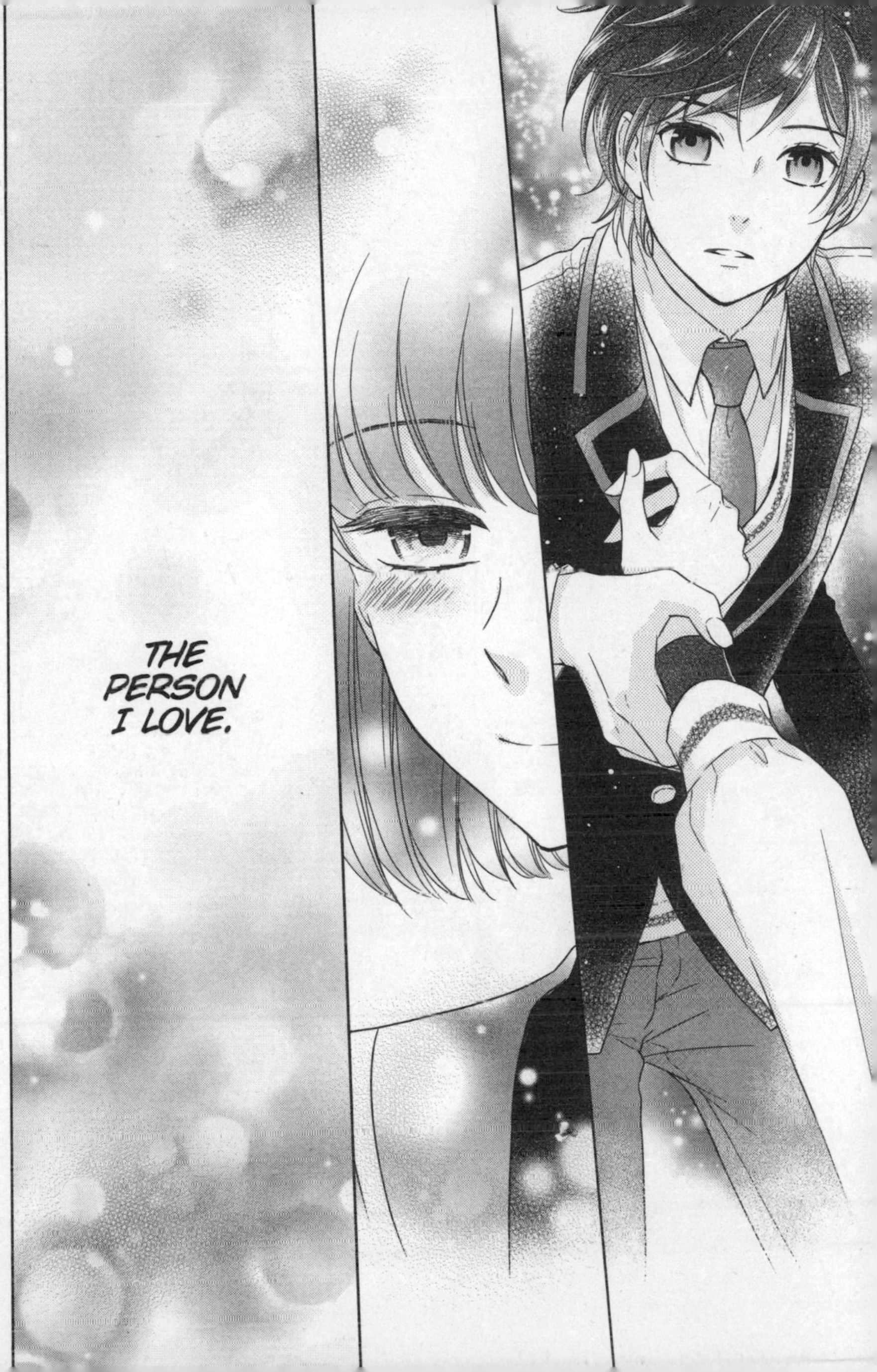
THE PERSON I LOVE.

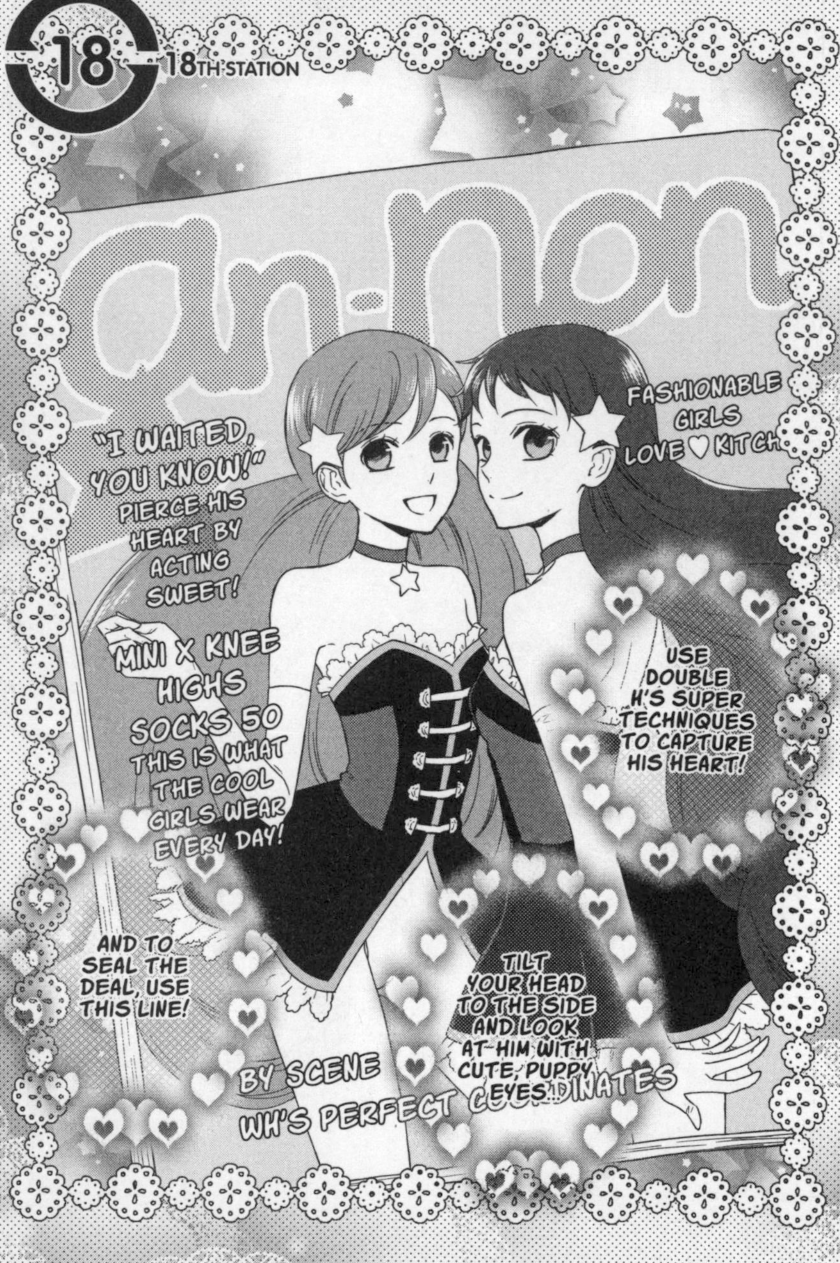
18
18TH STATION
an-non
FASHIONABLE GIRLS LOVE ♥ KITCH
"I WAITED, YOU KNOW!" PIERCE HIS HEART BY ACTING SWEET!
USE DOUBLE H'S SUPER TECHNIQUES TO CAPTURE HIS HEART!
MINI X KNEE HIGHS SOCKS 50 THIS IS WHAT THE COOL GIRLS WEAR EVERY DAY!
TILT YOUR HEAD TO THE SIDE AND LOOK AT HIM WITH CUTE, PUPPY EYES...
AND TO SEAL THE DEAL, USE THIS LINE!
BY SCENE
WH'S PERFECT

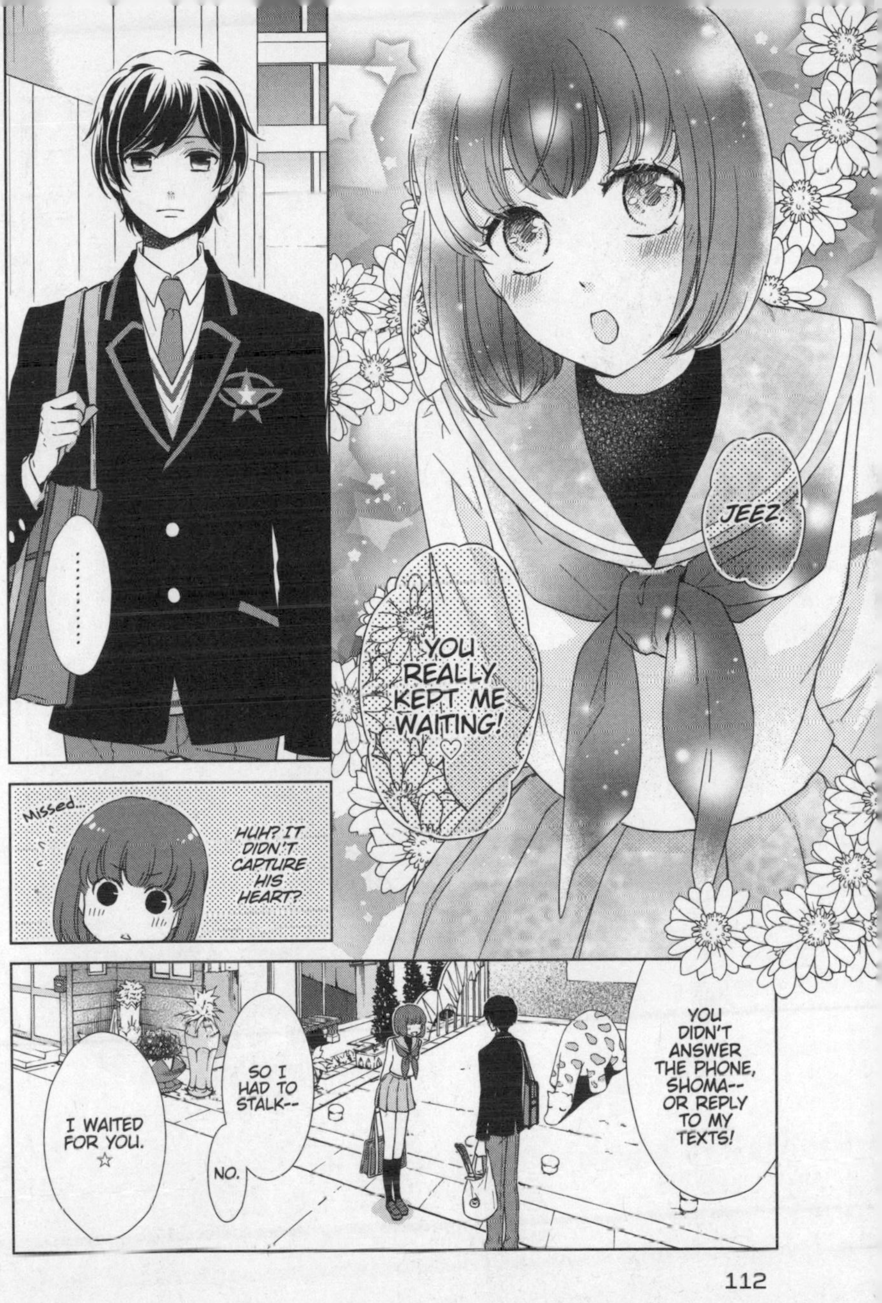
JEEZ.
YOU REALLY KEPT ME WAITING! ♡
......
Missed...
HUH? IT DIDN'T CAPTURE HIS HEART?
YOU DIDN'T ANSWER THE PHONE, SHOMA-- OR REPLY TO MY TEXTS!
SO I HAD TO STALK--
NO.
I WAITED FOR YOU. ☆

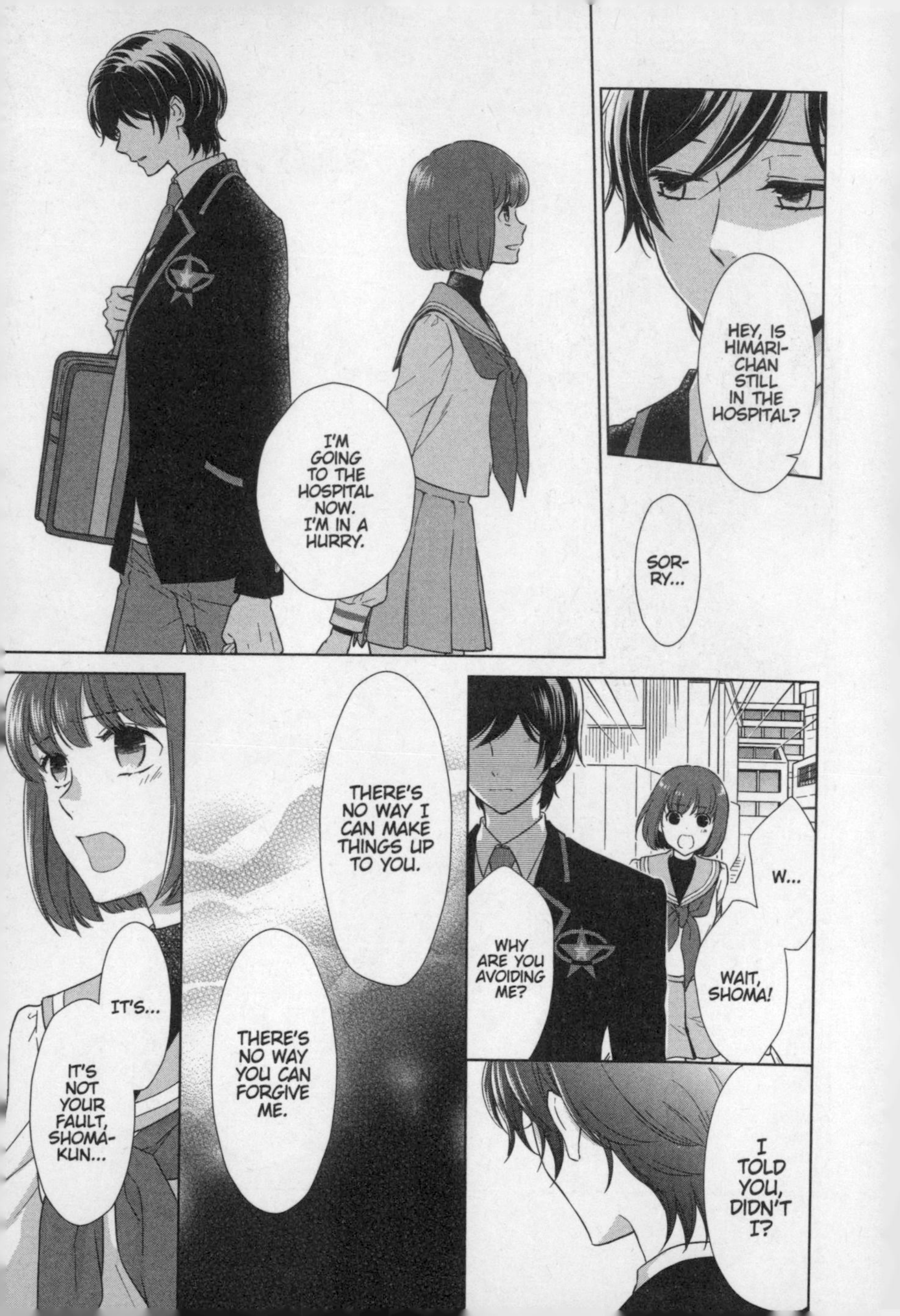
HEY, IS HIMARI-CHAN STILL IN THE HOSPITAL?
SORRY...
I'M GOING TO THE HOSPITAL NOW. I'M IN A HURRY.
W...
WAIT, SHOMA!
WHY ARE YOU AVOIDING ME?
I TOLD YOU, DIDN'T I?
THERE'S NO WAY I CAN MAKE THINGS UP TO YOU.
THERE'S NO WAY YOU CAN FORGIVE ME.
IT'S...
IT'S NOT YOUR FAULT, SHOMA-KUN...

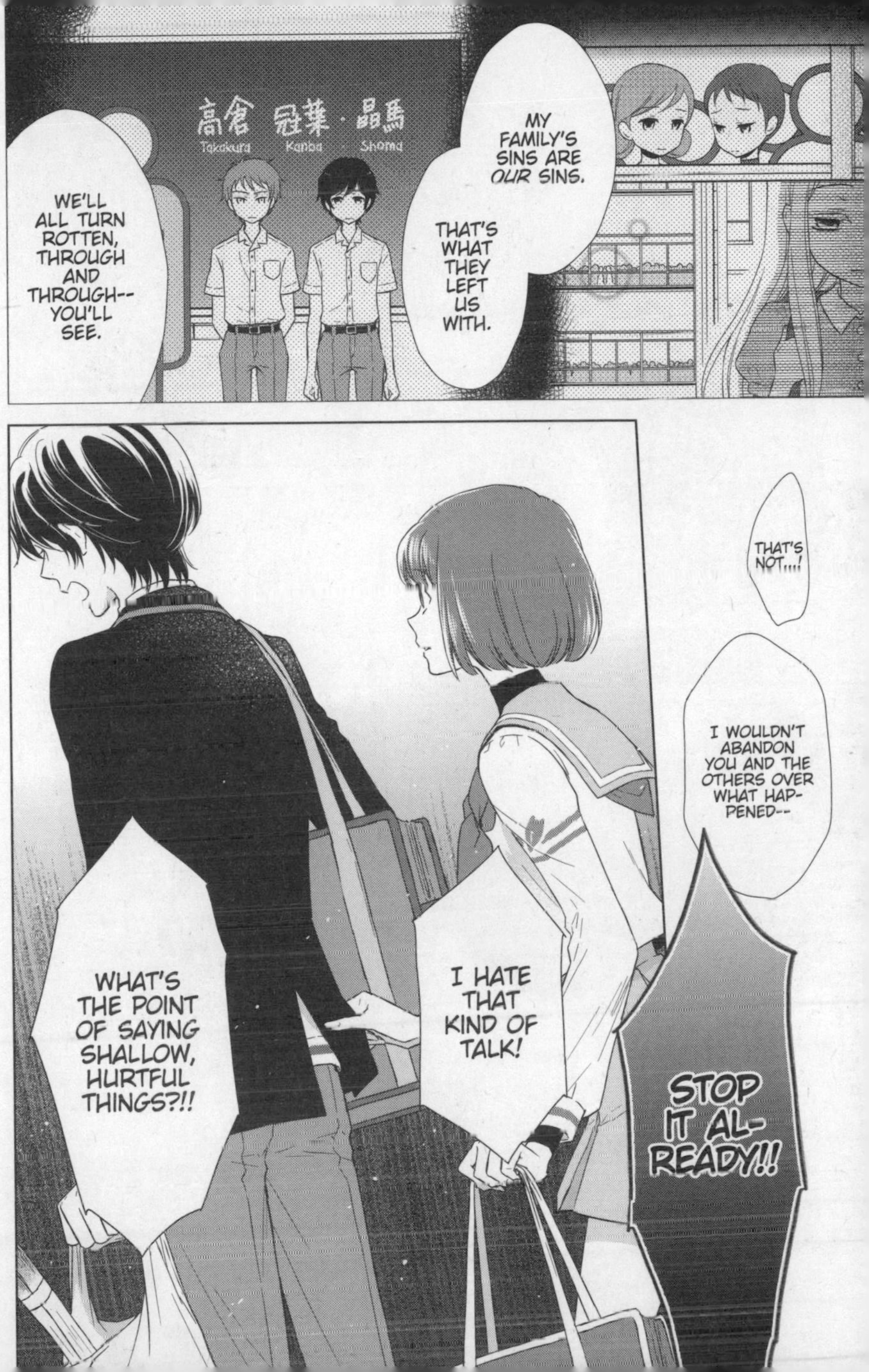

高倉 冠葉・晶馬
Takakura Kanba Shoma
MY FAMILY'S SINS ARE *OUR* SINS.
THAT'S WHAT THEY LEFT US WITH.
WE'LL ALL TURN ROTTEN, THROUGH AND THROUGH--YOU'LL SEE.
THAT'S NOT...!
I WOULDN'T ABANDON YOU AND THE OTHERS OVER WHAT HAP-PENED--
STOP IT AL-READY!!
I HATE THAT KIND OF TALK!
WHAT'S THE POINT OF SAYING SHALLOW, HURTFUL THINGS?!!

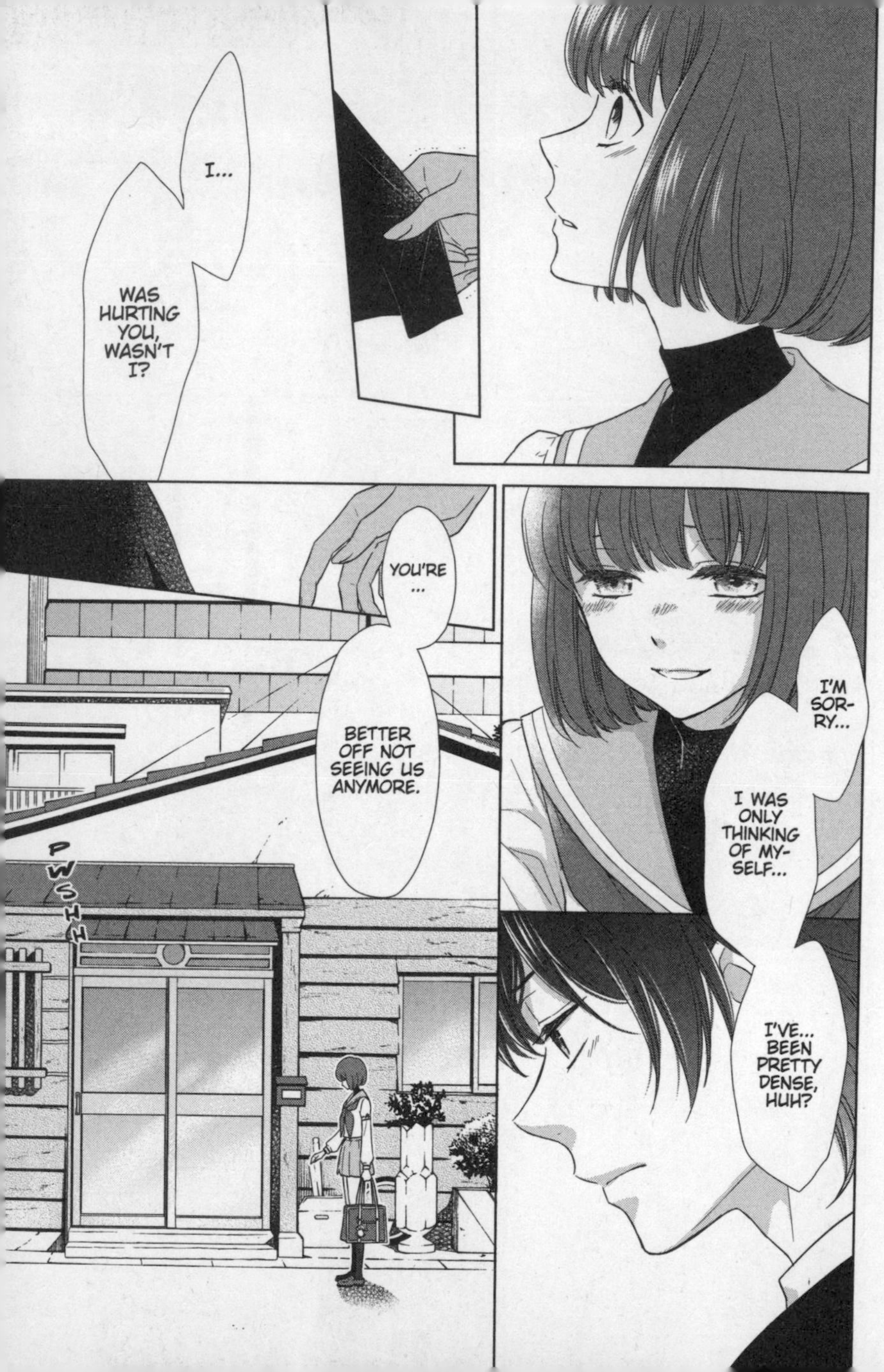
I...
WAS HURTING YOU, WASN'T I?
I'M SORRY...
I WAS ONLY THINKING OF MYSELF...
I'VE... BEEN PRETTY DENSE, HUH?
YOU'RE ...
BETTER OFF NOT SEEING US ANYMORE.
PWSHH

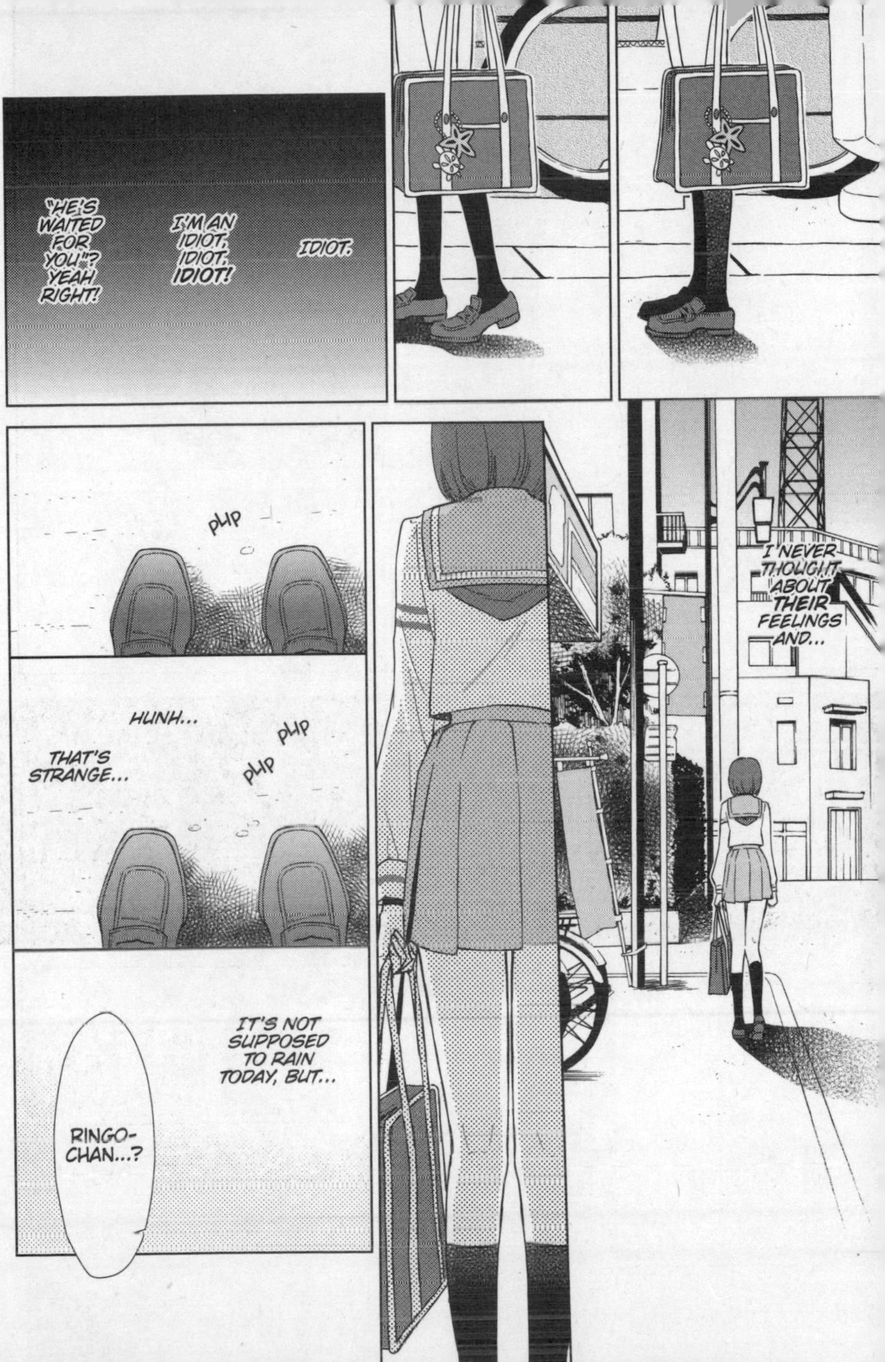
IDIOT.
I'M AN IDIOT, IDIOT, IDIOT!
"HE'S WAITED FOR YOU"? YEAH RIGHT!
I NEVER THOUGHT ABOUT THEIR FEELINGS AND...
PLIP
PLIP
HUNH...
THAT'S STRANGE...
PLIP
IT'S NOT SUPPOSED TO RAIN TODAY, BUT...
RINGO-CHAN...?

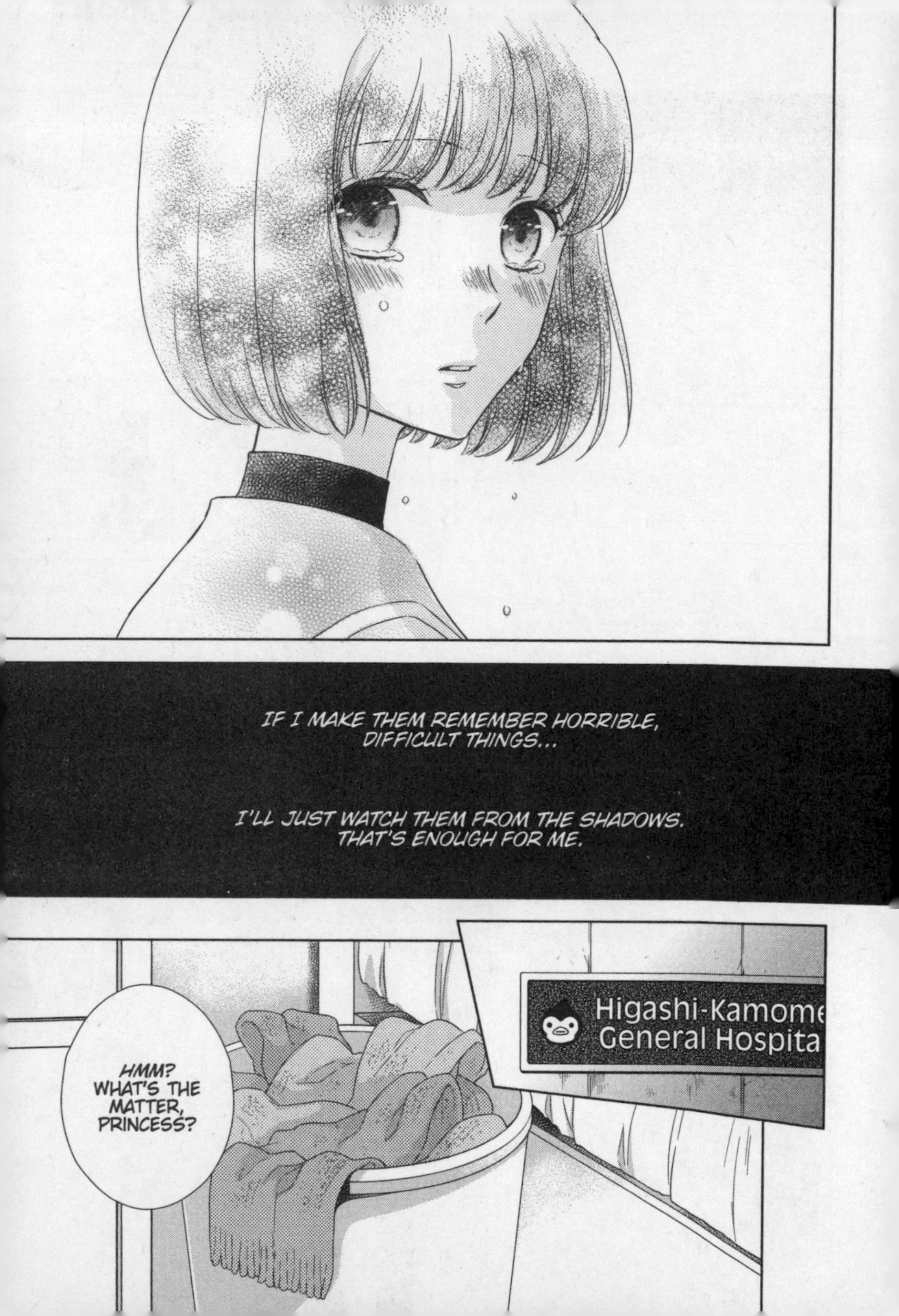
IF I MAKE THEM REMEMBER HORRIBLE, DIFFICULT THINGS...
I'LL JUST WATCH THEM FROM THE SHADOWS. THAT'S ENOUGH FOR ME.
Higashi-Kamome General Hospita
HMM? WHAT'S THE MATTER, PRINCESS?

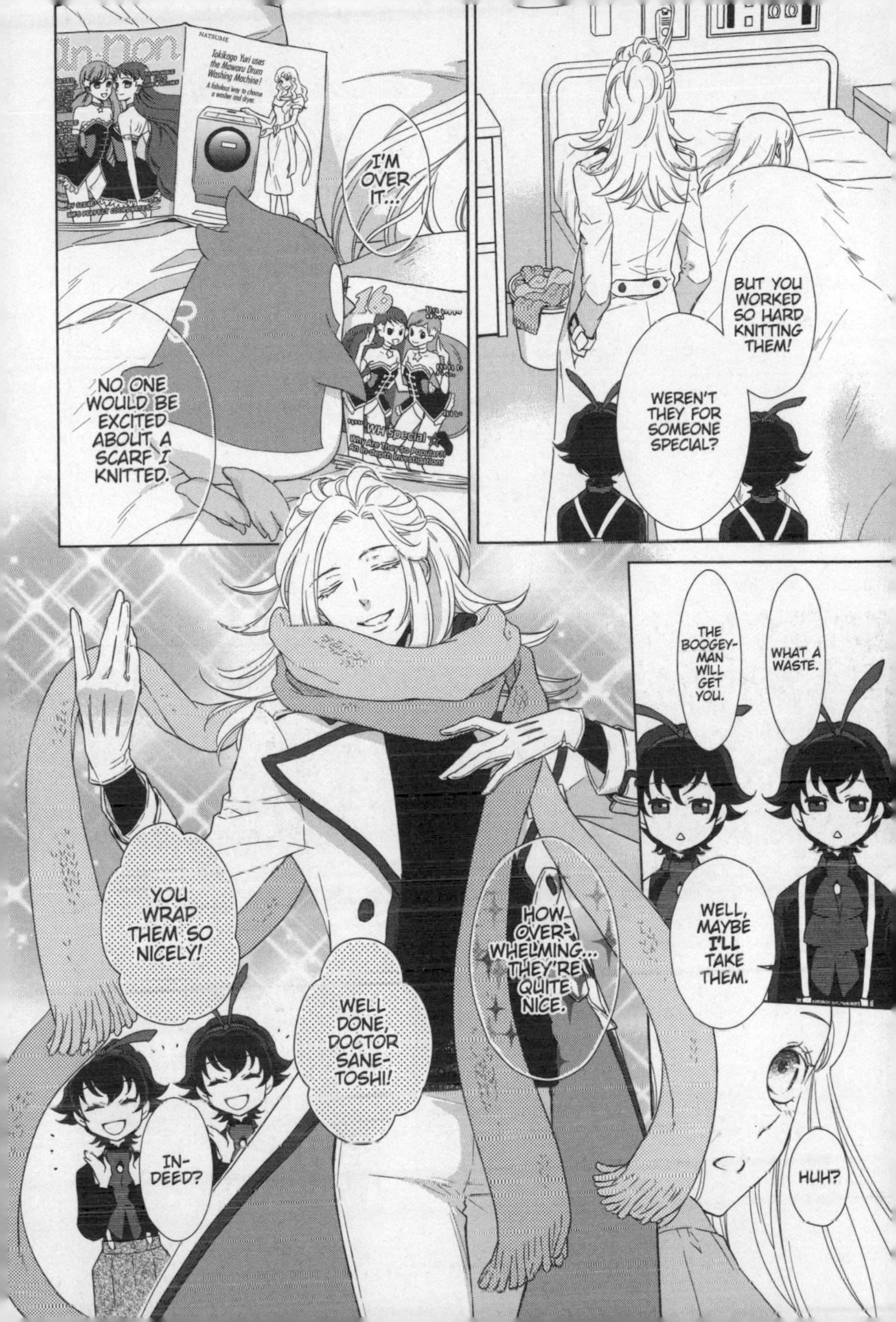
BUT YOU WORKED SO HARD KNITTING THEM!
WEREN'T THEY FOR SOMEONE SPECIAL?
NATSUME
Tokikago Yuri uses the Mowaru Drum Washing Machine!
A fabulous way to choose a washer and dryer.
I'M OVER IT...
WH Special
Why Are They So Popular?? An In-depth Investigation!
NO ONE WOULD BE EXCITED ABOUT A SCARF I KNITTED.
WHAT A WASTE.
THE BOOGEY-MAN WILL GET YOU.
WELL, MAYBE I'LL TAKE THEM.
HOW OVER-WHELMING... THEY'RE QUITE NICE.
YOU WRAP THEM SO NICELY!
WELL DONE, DOCTOR SANE-TOSHI!
IN-DEED?
HUH?

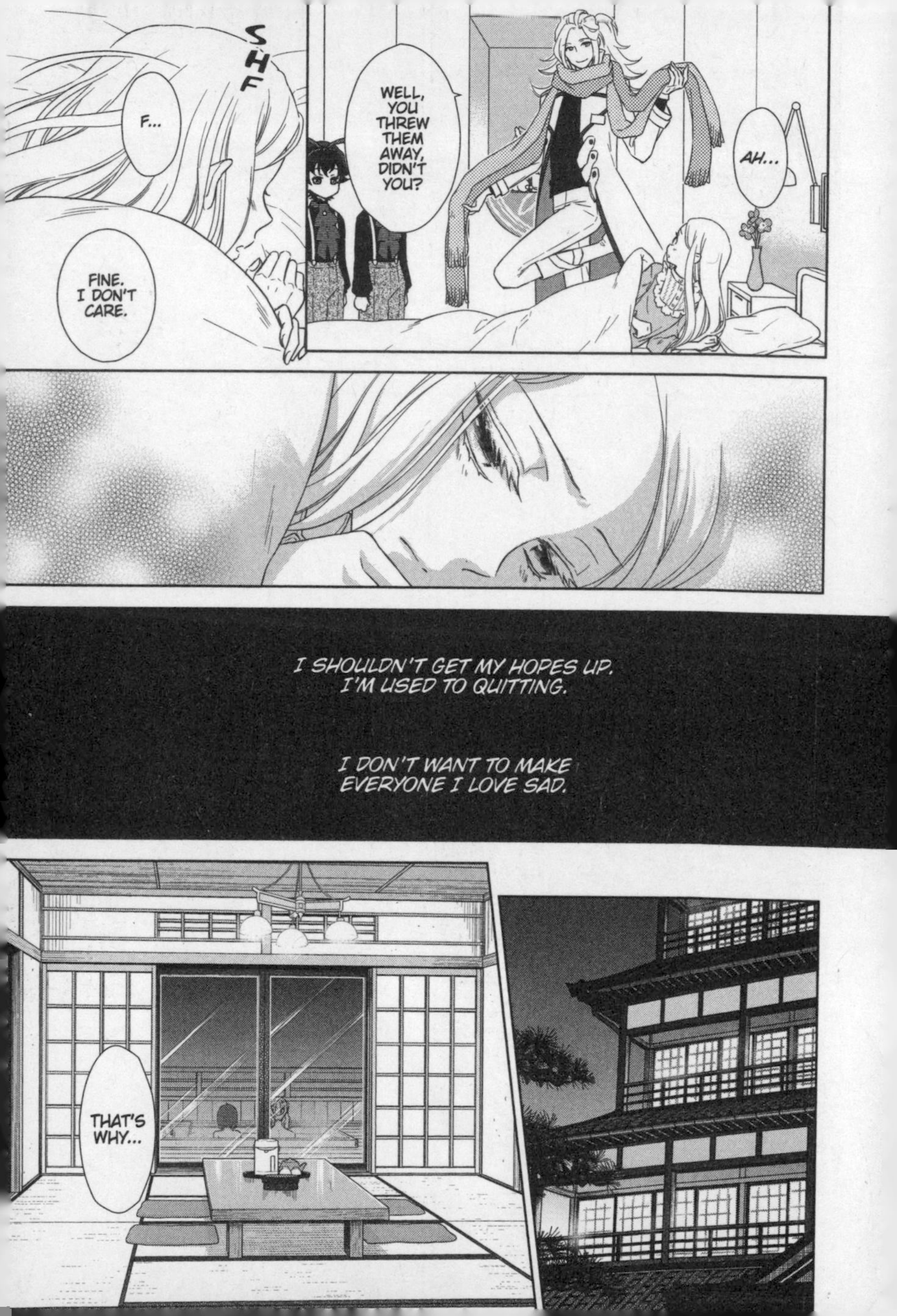
AH...
WELL, YOU THREW THEM AWAY, DIDN'T YOU?
SHF
F...
FINE. I DON'T CARE.
I SHOULDN'T GET MY HOPES UP. I'M USED TO QUITTING.
I DON'T WANT TO MAKE EVERYONE I LOVE SAD.
THAT'S WHY...

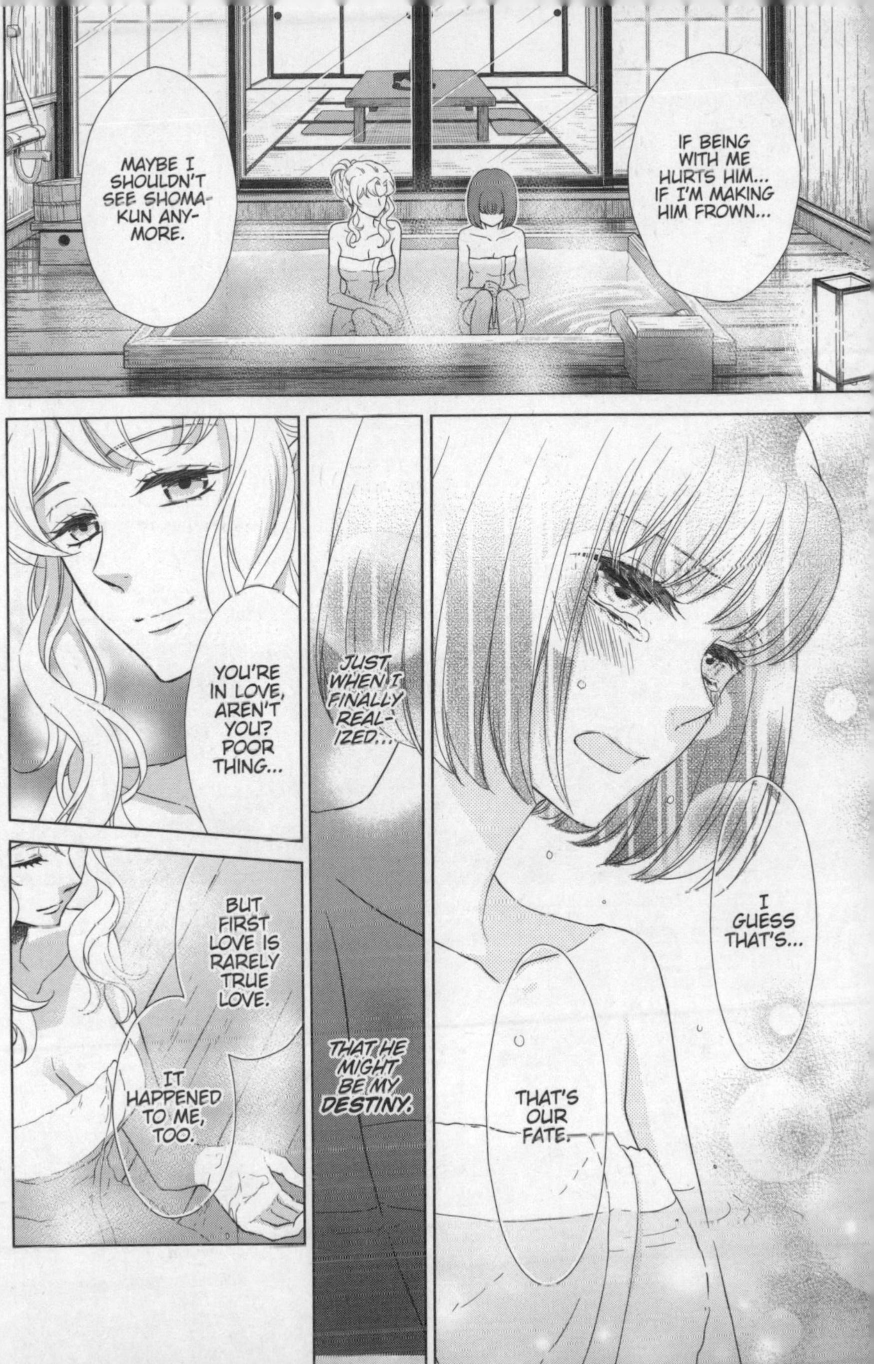
IF BEING WITH ME HURTS HIM... IF I'M MAKING HIM FROWN...
MAYBE I SHOULDN'T SEE SHOMA-KUN ANYMORE.
I GUESS THAT'S...
THAT'S OUR FATE.
JUST WHEN I FINALLY REALIZED...
THAT HE MIGHT BE MY DESTINY.
YOU'RE IN LOVE, AREN'T YOU? POOR THING...
BUT FIRST LOVE IS RARELY TRUE LOVE.
IT HAPPENED TO ME, TOO.

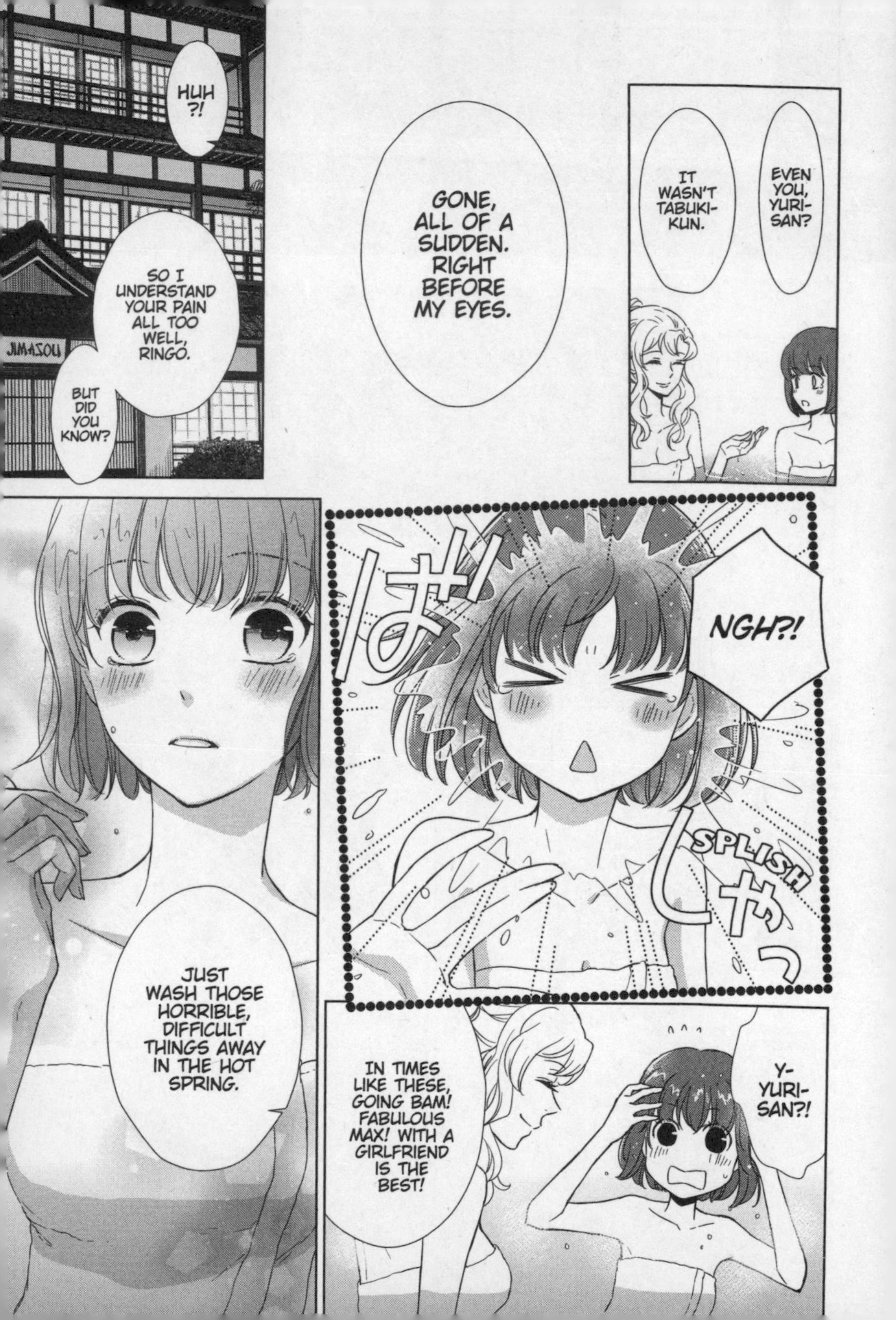
EVEN YOU, YURI-SAN?
IT WASN'T TABUKI-KUN.
GONE, ALL OF A SUDDEN. RIGHT BEFORE MY EYES.
HUH ?!
SO I UNDERSTAND YOUR PAIN ALL TOO WELL, RINGO.
BUT DID YOU KNOW?
ばっ
NGH?!
SPLISH
しゃっ
Y-YURI-SAN?!
IN TIMES LIKE THESE, GOING BAM! FABULOUS MAX! WITH A GIRLFRIEND IS THE BEST!
JUST WASH THOSE HORRIBLE, DIFFICULT THINGS AWAY IN THE HOT SPRING.

I FEEL HELPLESS...

I WANT THE PEOPLE I LOVE TO BE HAPPY, BUT I CAN'T DO ANYTHING FOR THEM.

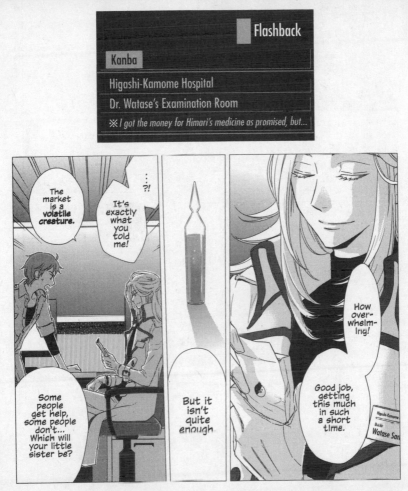

Flashback

Kanba

Higashi-Kamome Hospital

Dr. Watase's Examination Room

※*I got the money for Himari's medicine as promised, but...*

How overwhelming!
Good job, getting this much in such a short time.
But it isn't quite enough.
...?!
It's exactly what you told me!
The market is a **volatile creature.**
Some people get help, some people don't... Which will your little sister be?

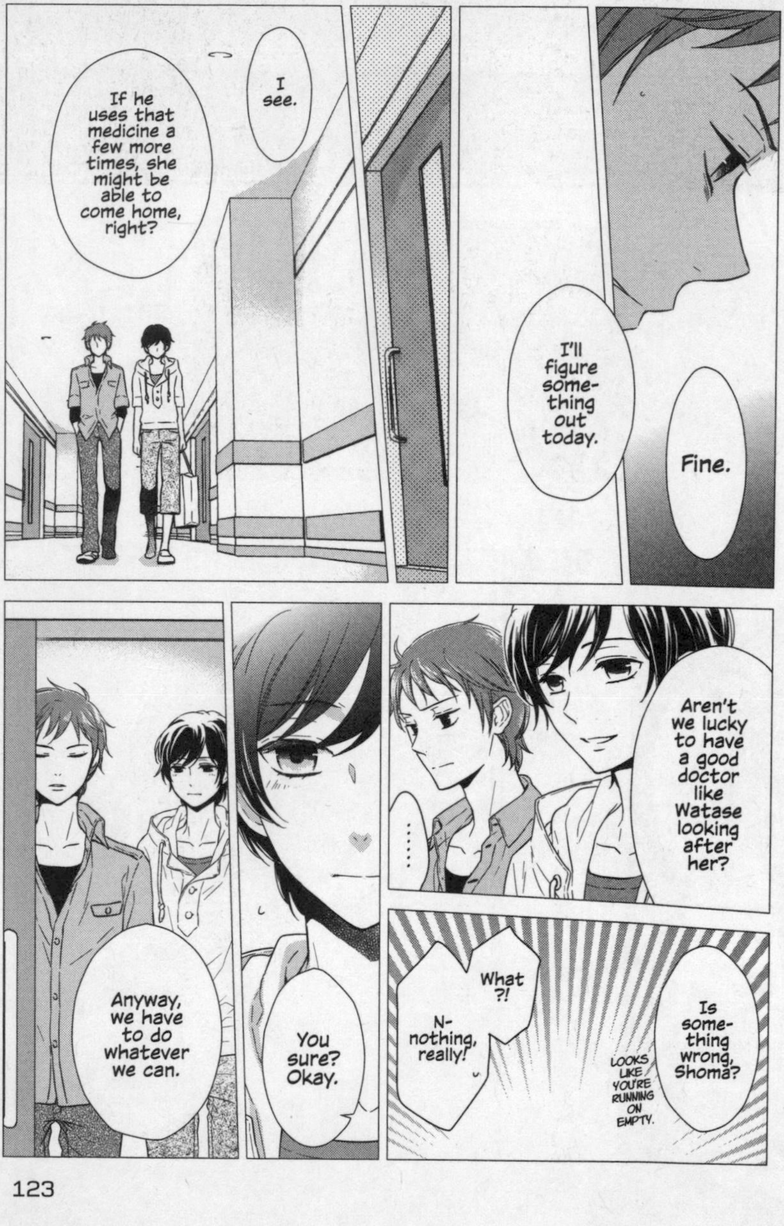

Fine.
I'll figure something out today.
I see.
If he uses that medicine a few more times, she might be able to come home, right?
Aren't we lucky to have a good doctor like Watase looking after her?
......
Is something wrong, Shoma?
LOOKS LIKE YOU'RE RUNNING ON EMPTY.
What?!
N-nothing, really!
You sure? Okay.
Anyway, we have to do whatever we can.

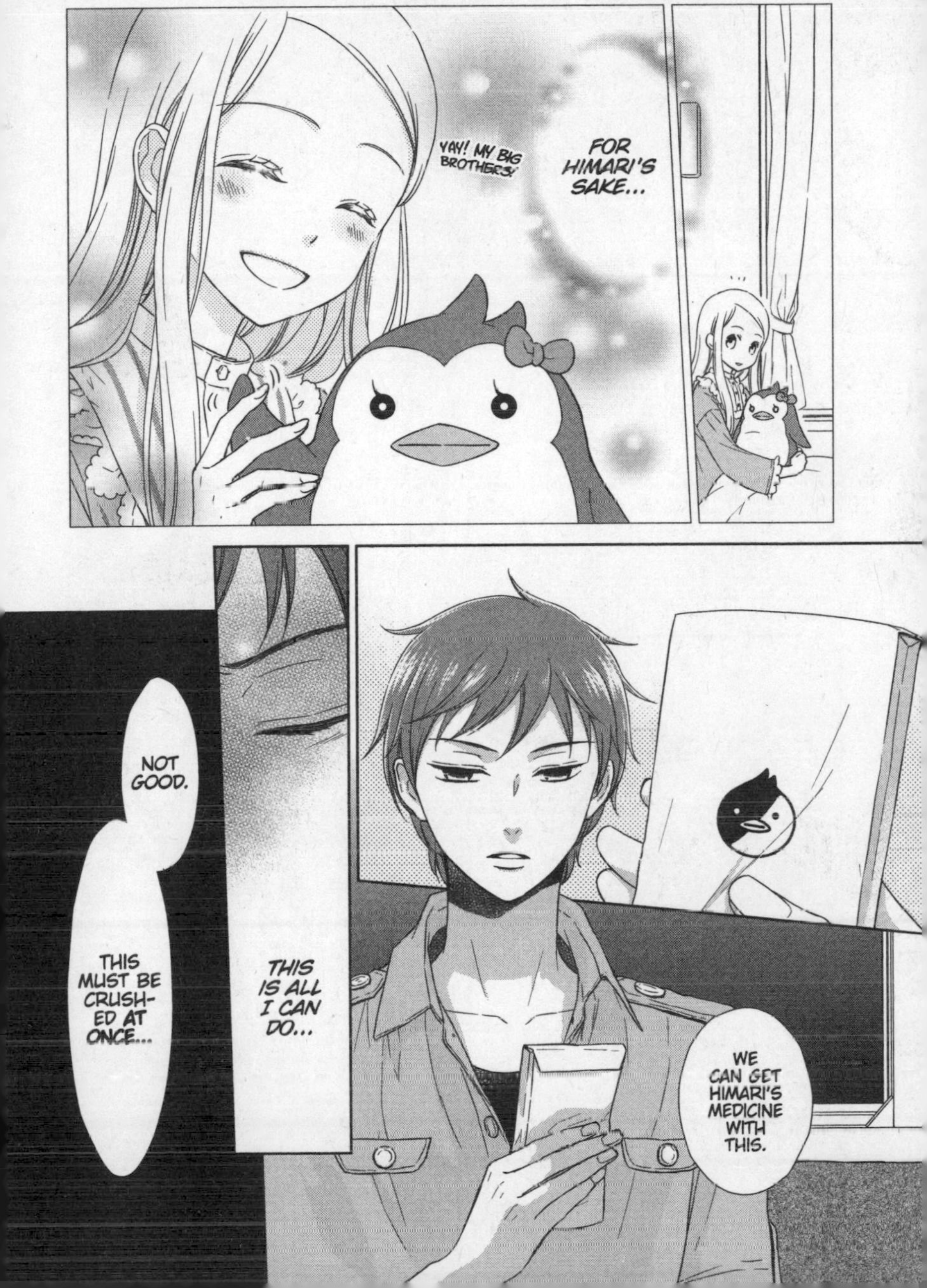
...
FOR HIMARI'S SAKE...
YAY! MY BIG BROTHERS!
WE CAN GET HIMARI'S MEDICINE WITH THIS.
THIS IS ALL I CAN DO...
NOT GOOD.
THIS MUST BE CRUSH-ED AT ONCE...

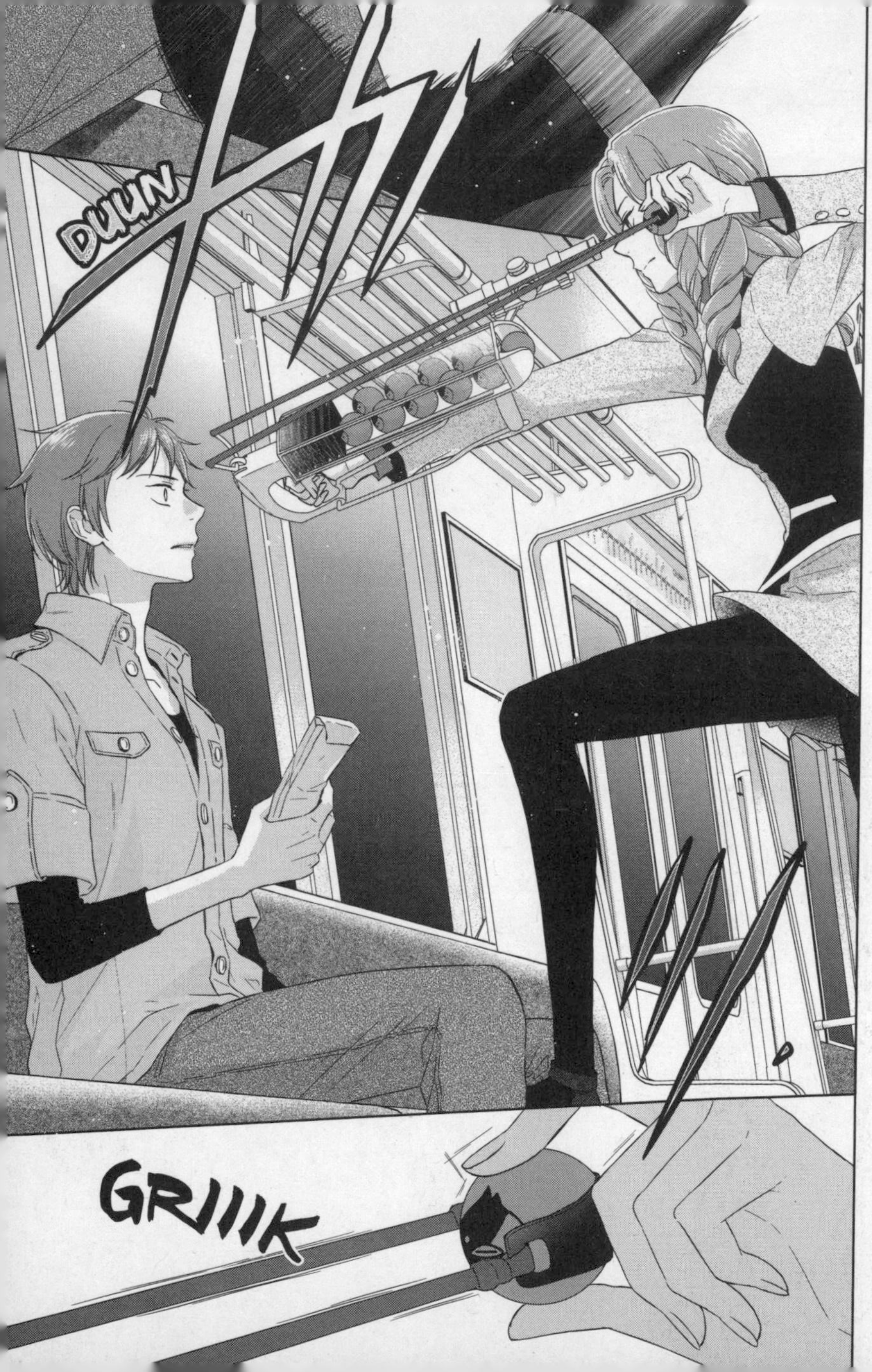
DUUN
GRIIIK

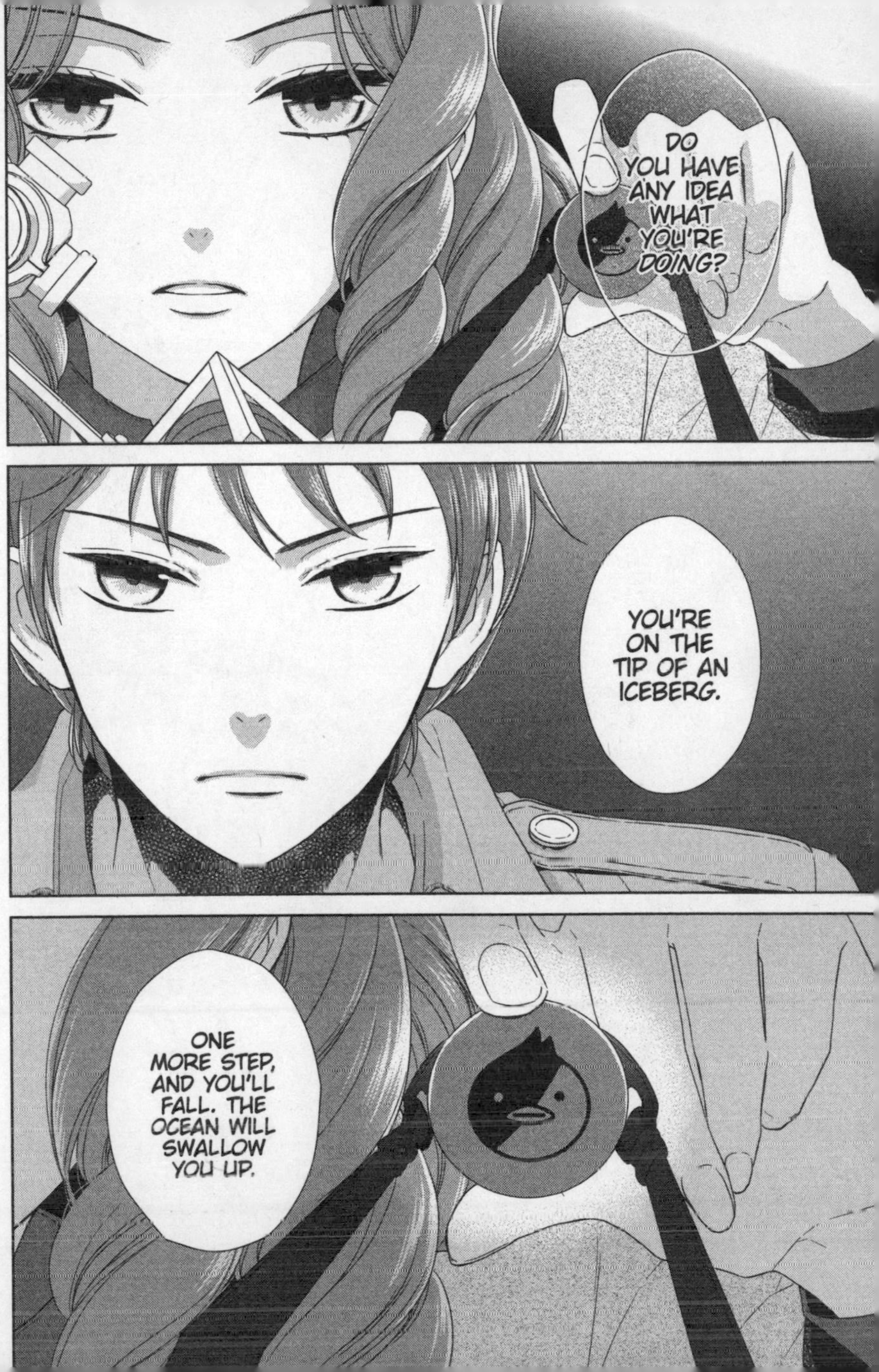
DO YOU HAVE ANY IDEA WHAT YOU'RE DOING?
YOU'RE ON THE TIP OF AN ICEBERG.
ONE MORE STEP, AND YOU'LL FALL. THE OCEAN WILL SWALLOW YOU UP.

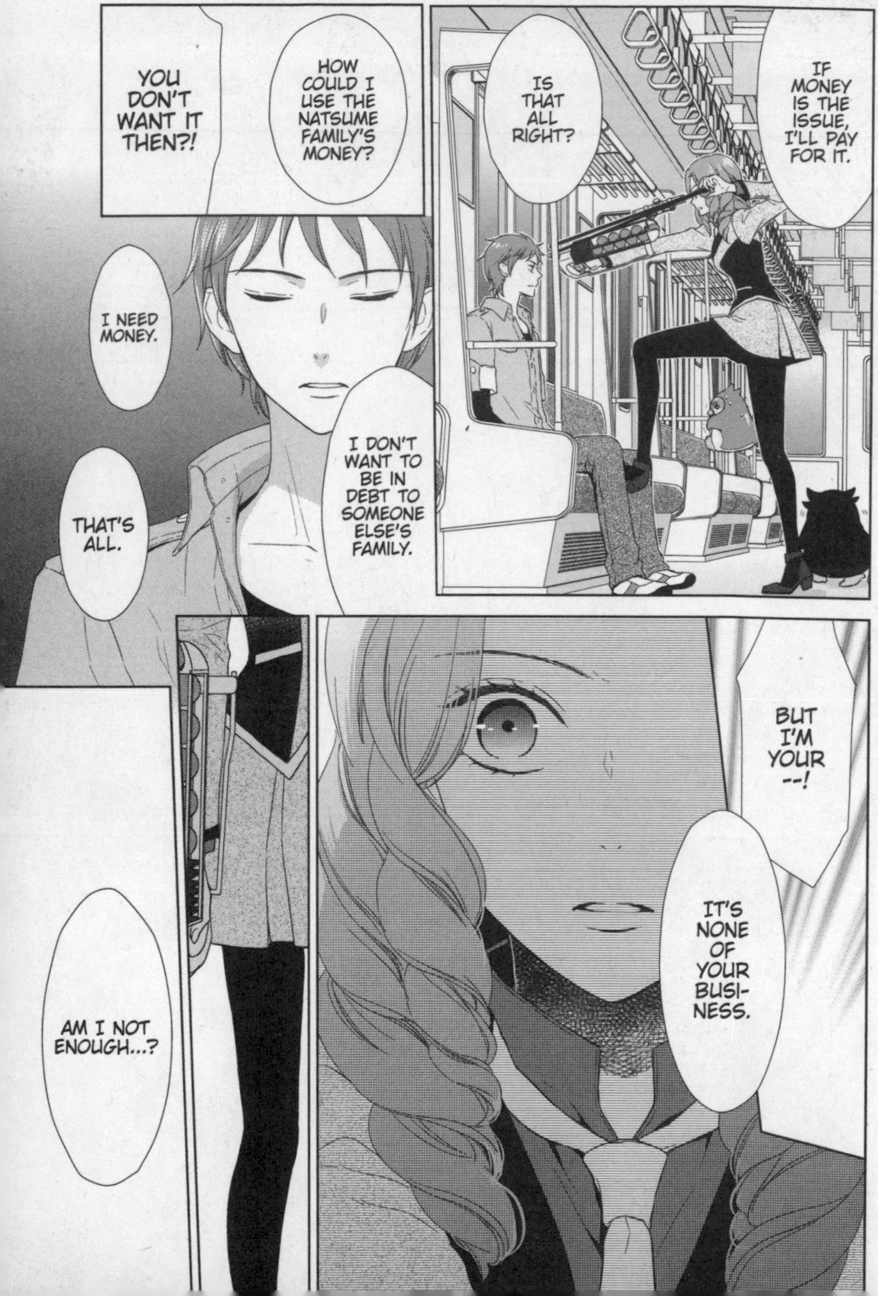
IF MONEY IS THE ISSUE, I'LL PAY FOR IT.
IS THAT ALL RIGHT?
HOW COULD I USE THE NATSUME FAMILY'S MONEY?
YOU DON'T WANT IT THEN?!
I NEED MONEY.
I DON'T WANT TO BE IN DEBT TO SOMEONE ELSE'S FAMILY.
THAT'S ALL.
BUT I'M YOUR --!
IT'S NONE OF YOUR BUSI-NESS.
AM I NOT ENOUGH...?

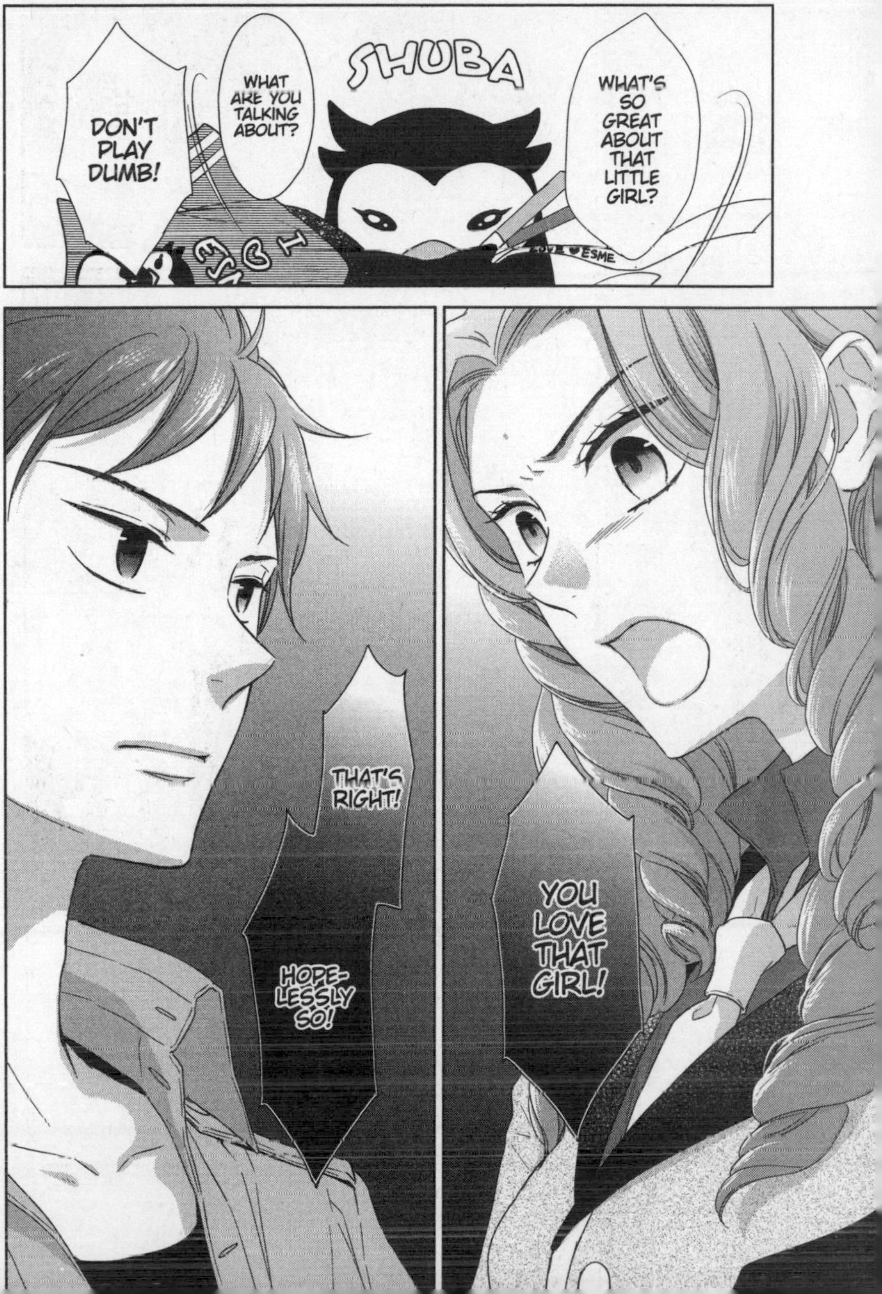
WHAT'S SO GREAT ABOUT THAT LITTLE GIRL?
SHUBA
WHAT ARE YOU TALKING ABOUT?
DON'T PLAY DUMB!
YOU LOVE THAT GIRL!
THAT'S RIGHT!
HOPE-LESSLY SO!

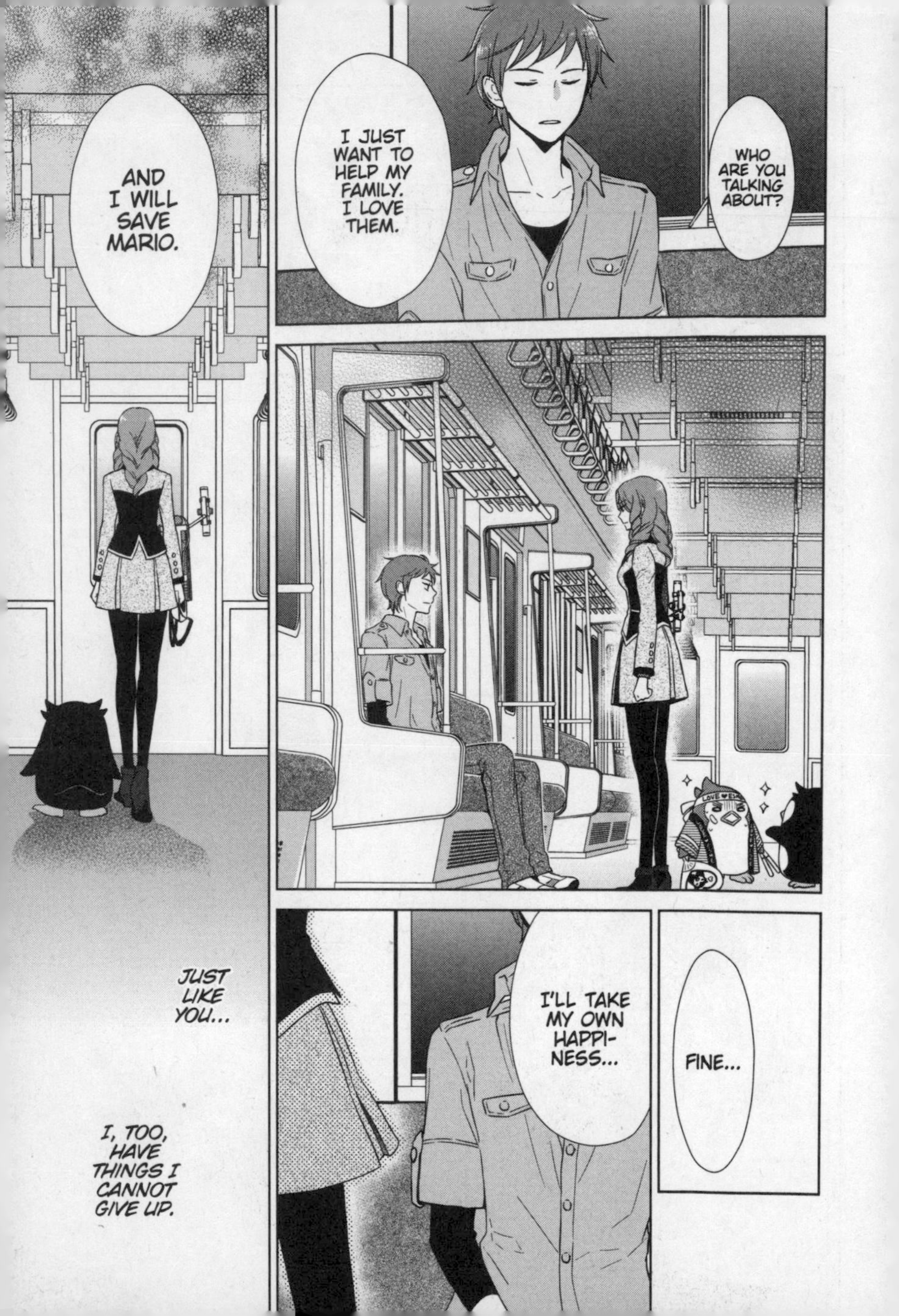
WHO ARE YOU TALKING ABOUT?
I JUST WANT TO HELP MY FAMILY. I LOVE THEM.
FINE...
I'LL TAKE MY OWN HAPPI-NESS...
AND I WILL SAVE MARIO.
JUST LIKE YOU...
I, TOO, HAVE THINGS I CANNOT GIVE UP.

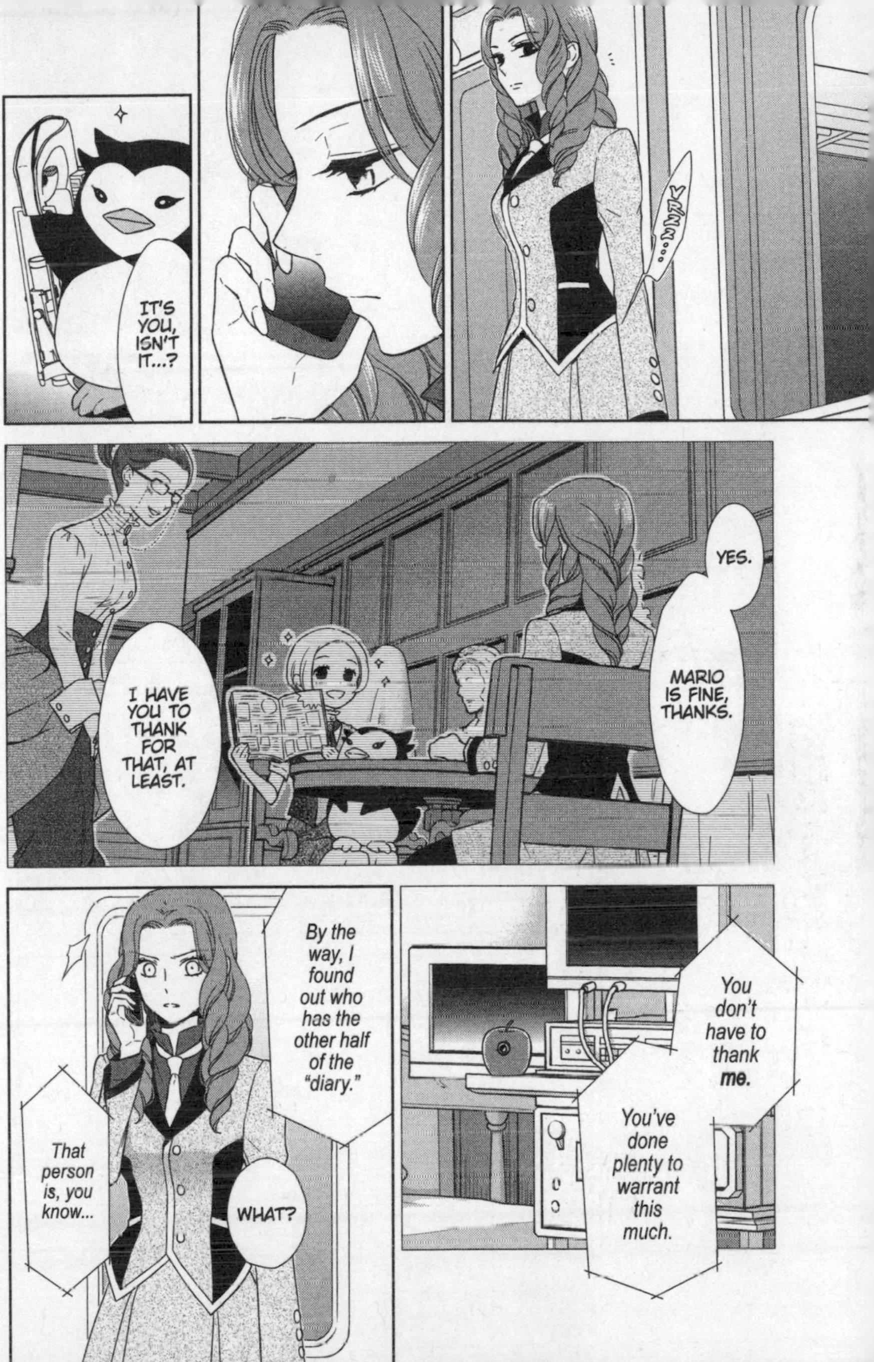
VRNN...
IT'S YOU, ISN'T IT...?
YES.
MARIO IS FINE, THANKS.
I HAVE YOU TO THANK FOR THAT, AT LEAST.
You don't have to thank **me.**
You've done plenty to warrant this much.
By the way, I found out who has the other half of the "diary."
WHAT?
That person is, you know...

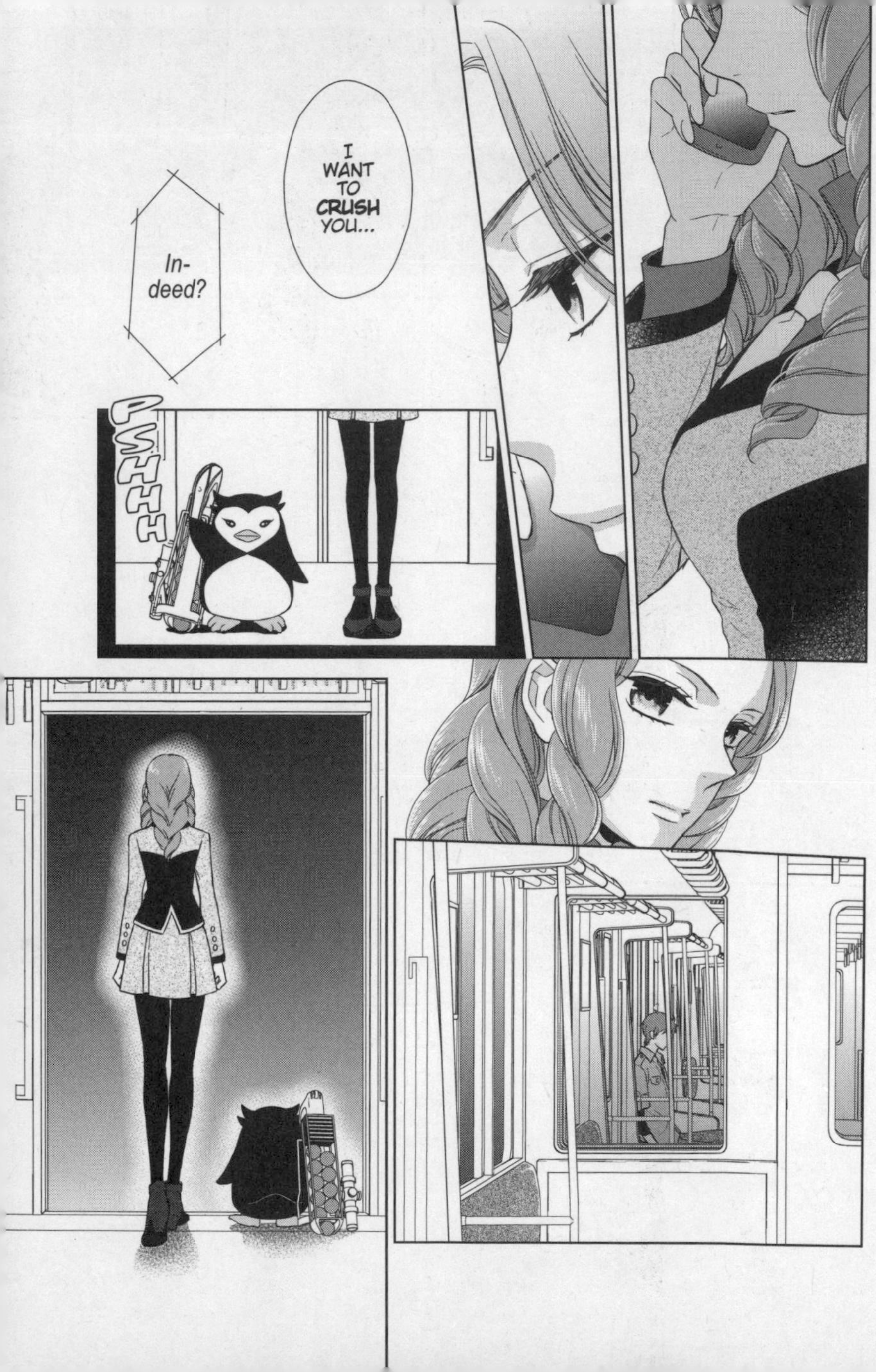
I WANT TO CRUSH YOU...
In-deed?
PSHHH

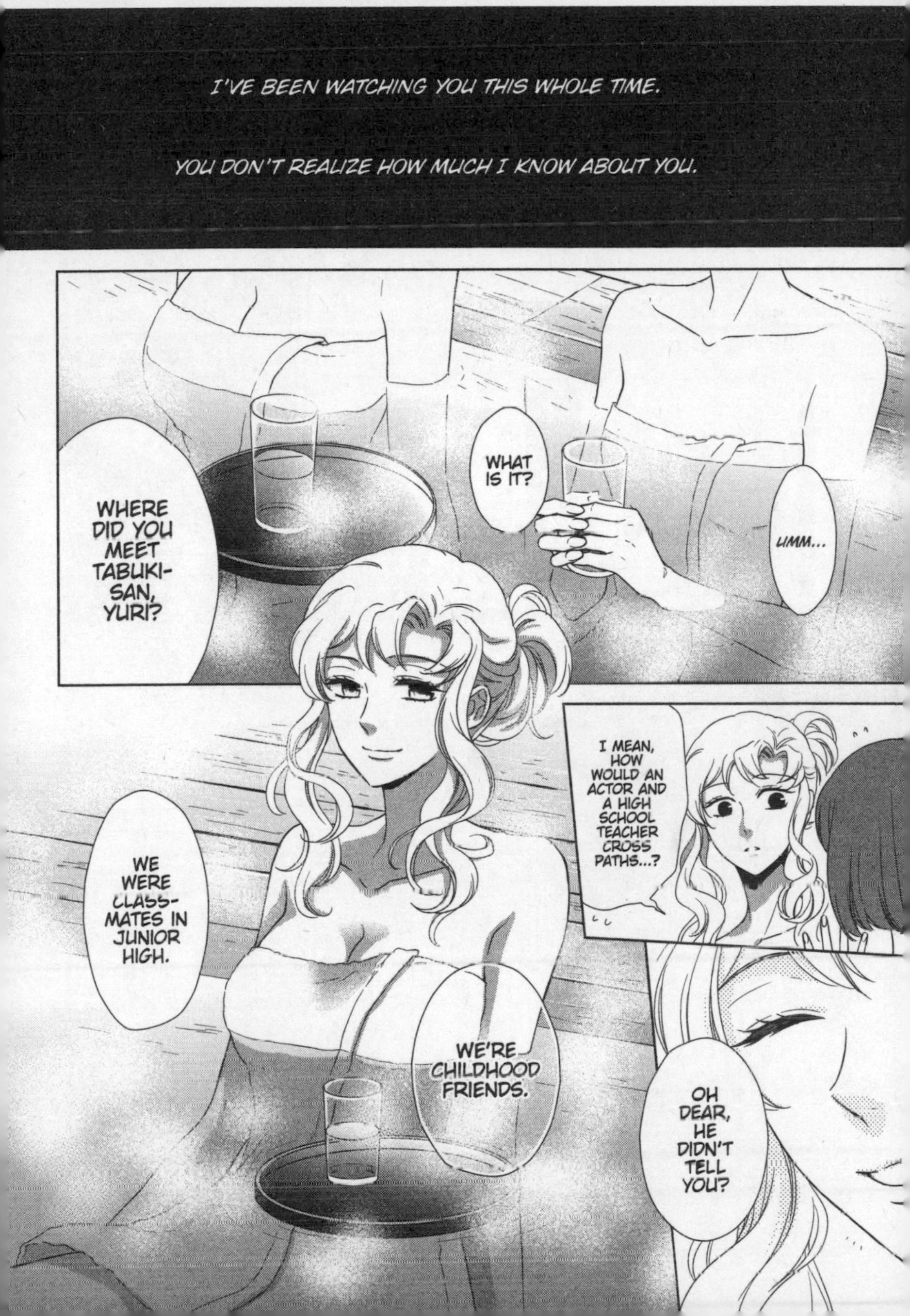
I'VE BEEN WATCHING YOU THIS WHOLE TIME.
YOU DON'T REALIZE HOW MUCH I KNOW ABOUT YOU.
UMM...
WHAT IS IT?
WHERE DID YOU MEET TABUKI-SAN, YURI?
I MEAN, HOW WOULD AN ACTOR AND A HIGH SCHOOL TEACHER CROSS PATHS...?
OH DEAR, HE DIDN'T TELL YOU?
WE'RE CHILDHOOD FRIENDS.
WE WERE CLASSMATES IN JUNIOR HIGH.

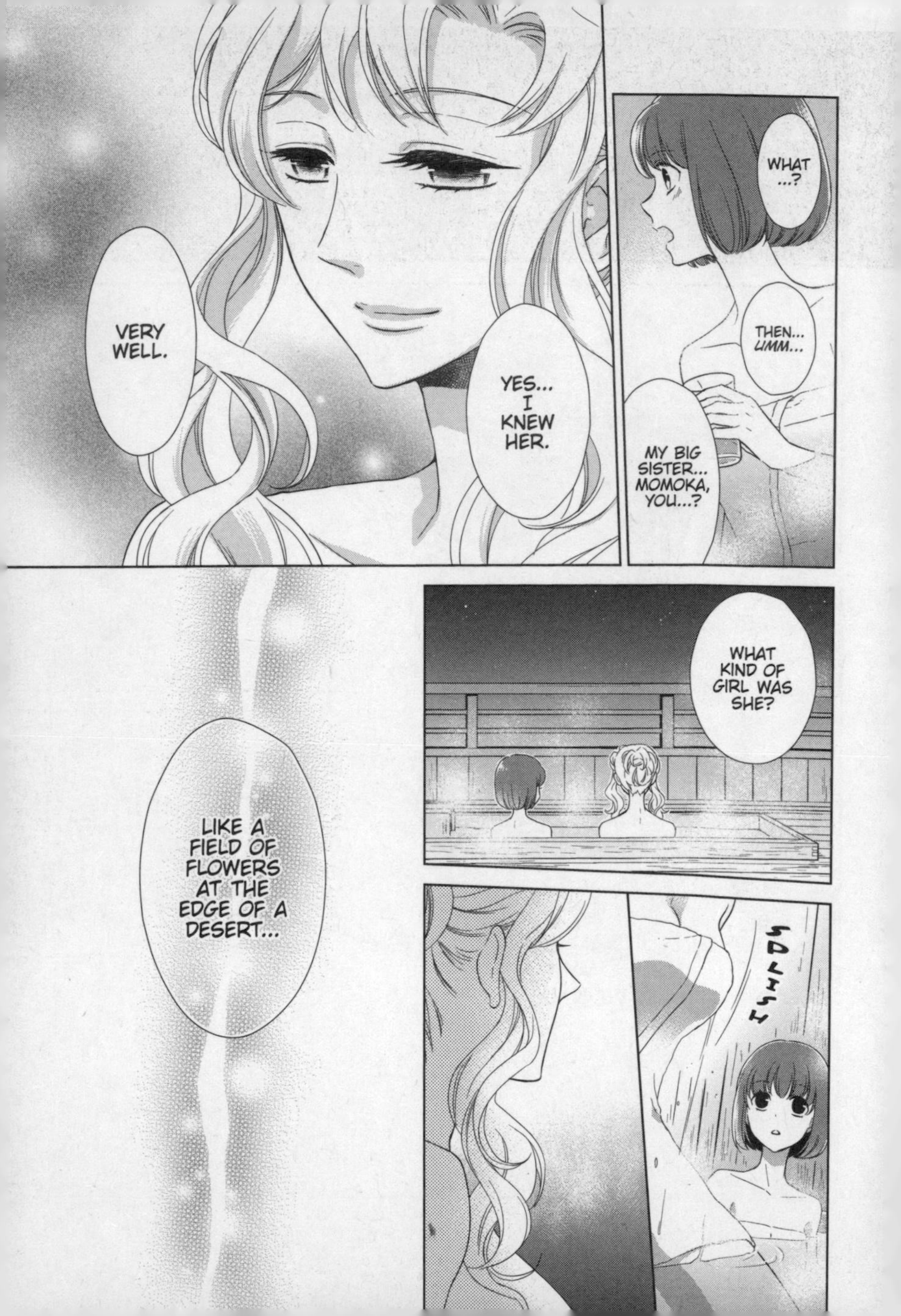
WHAT ...?
THEN... UMM...
MY BIG SISTER... MOMOKA, YOU...?
YES... I KNEW HER.
VERY WELL.
WHAT KIND OF GIRL WAS SHE?
SPLISH
LIKE A FIELD OF FLOWERS AT THE EDGE OF A DESERT...

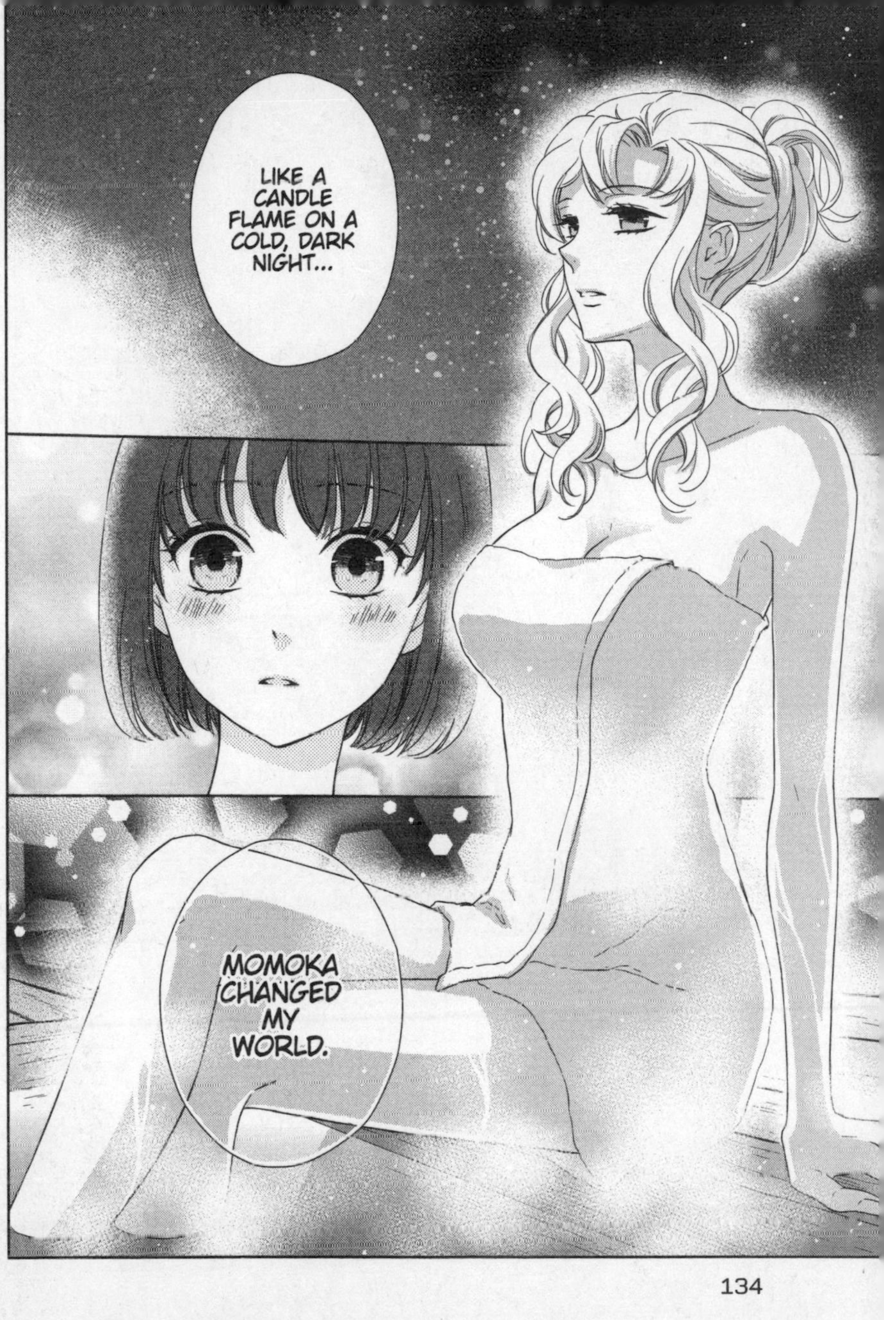
LIKE A CANDLE FLAME ON A COLD, DARK NIGHT...
MOMOKA CHANGED MY WORLD.

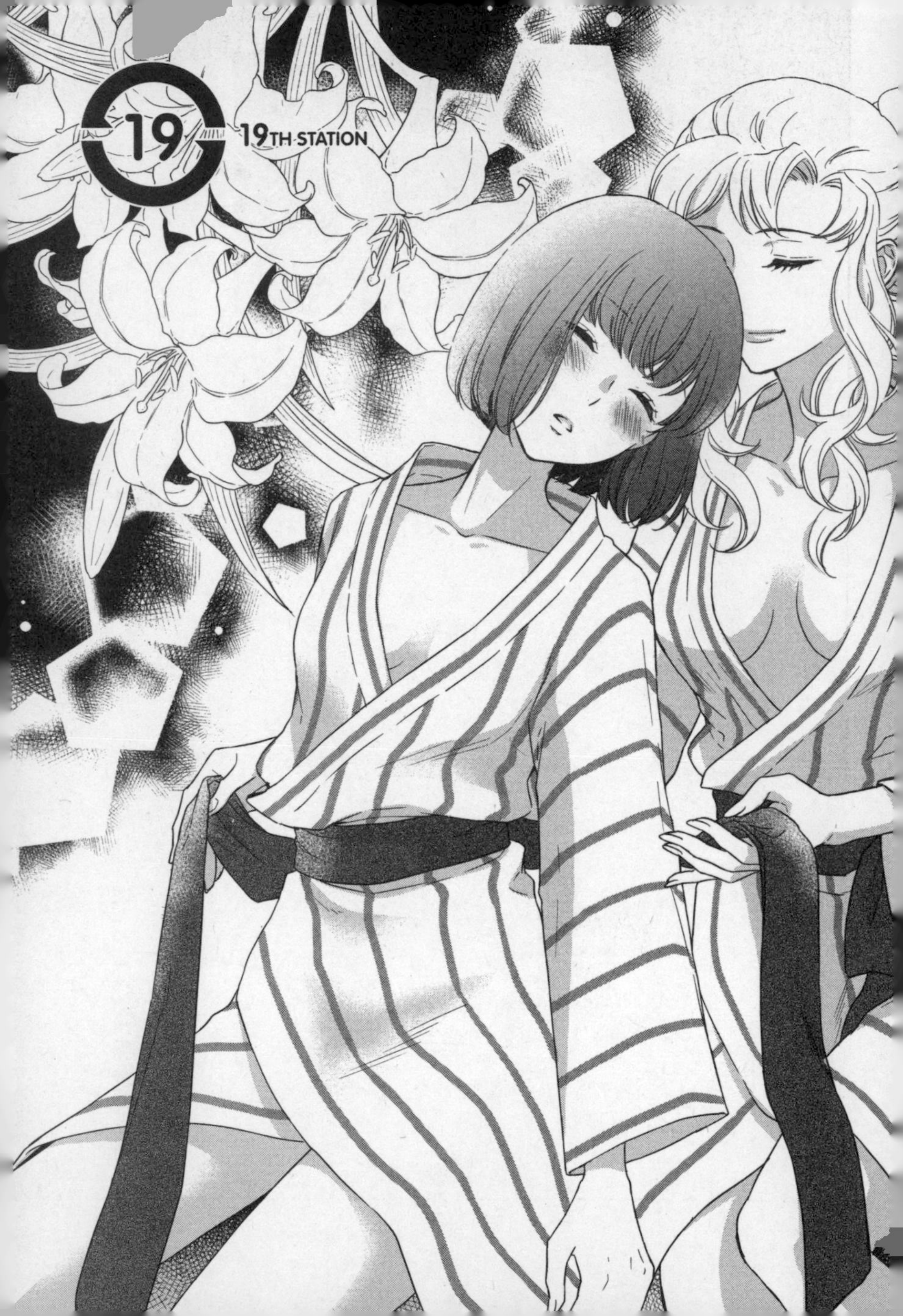
19
19TH STATION

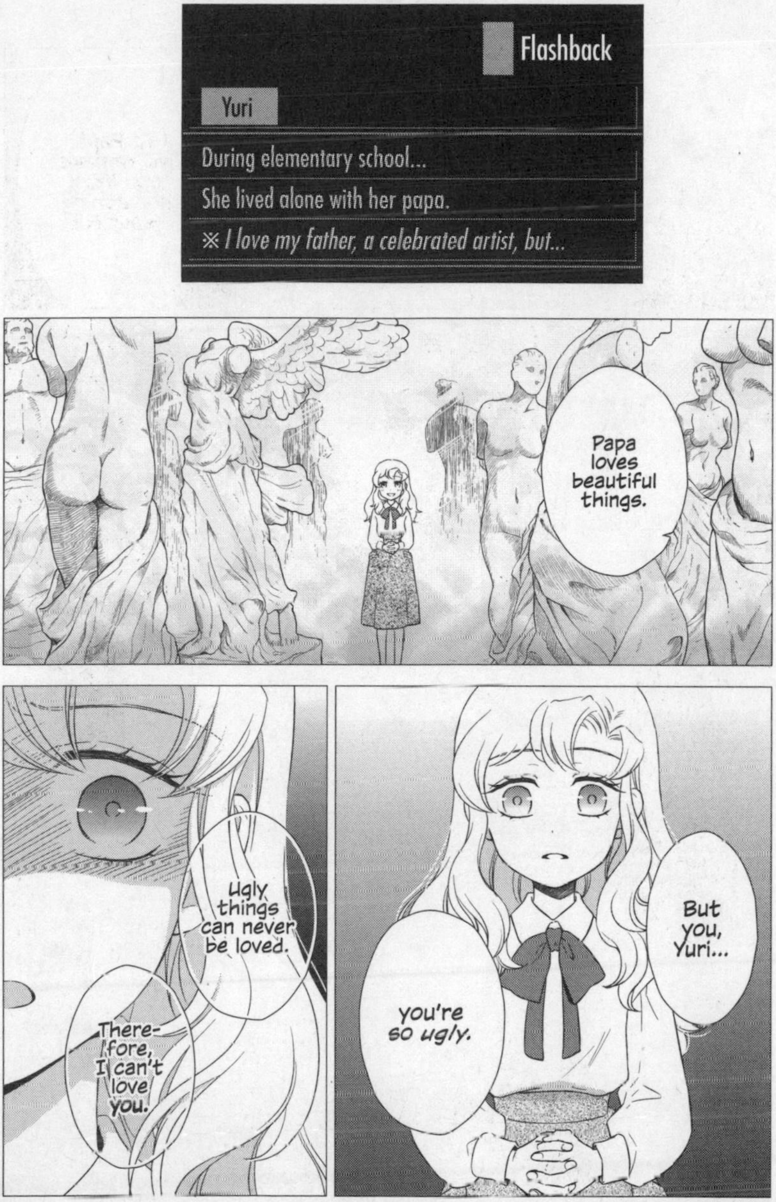
Flashback
Yuri
During elementary school...
She lived alone with her papa.
※ I love my father, a celebrated artist, but...
Papa loves beautiful things.
But you, Yuri...
you're so ugly.
Ugly things can never be loved.
Therefore, I can't love you.

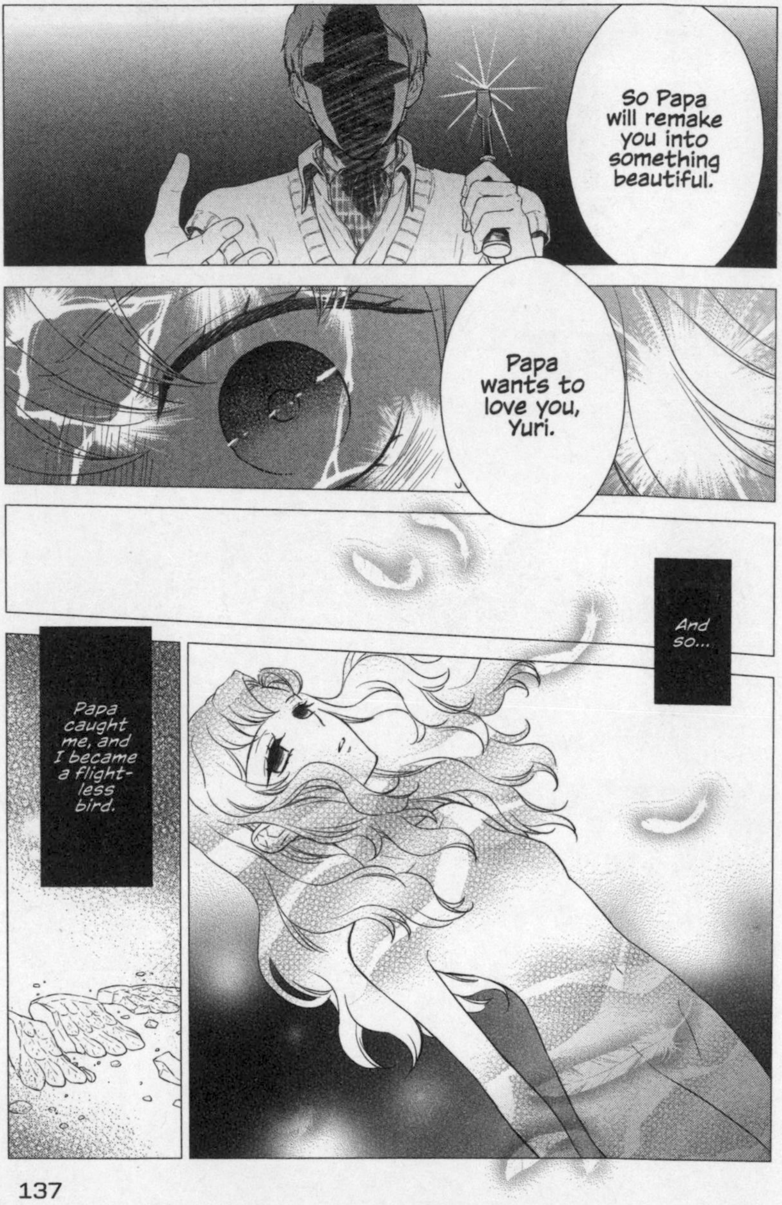
So Papa will remake you into something beautiful.
Papa wants to love you, Yuri.
And so...
Papa caught me, and I became a flight-less bird.

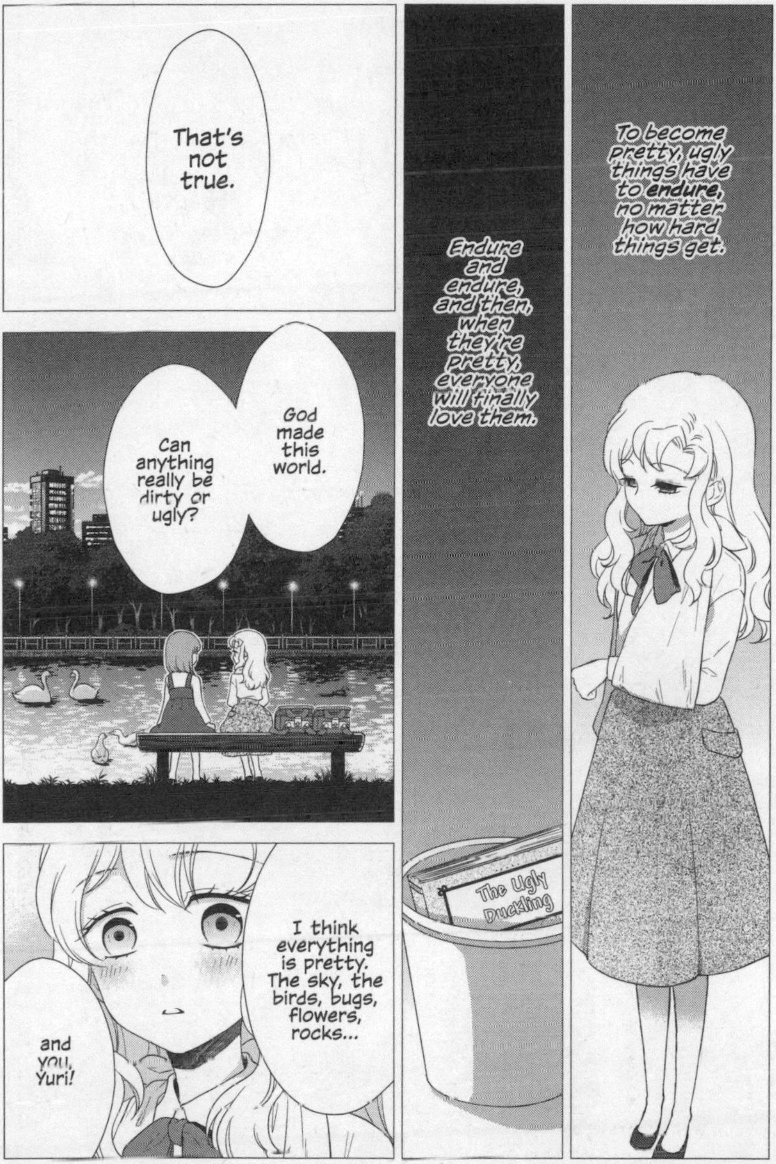
To become pretty, ugly things have to **endure**, no matter how hard things get.
Endure and endure, and then, when they're pretty, everyone will finally love them.
The Ugly Duckling
That's not true.
God made this world.
Can anything really be dirty or ugly?
I think everything is pretty. The sky, the birds, bugs, flowers, rocks...
and you, Yuri!

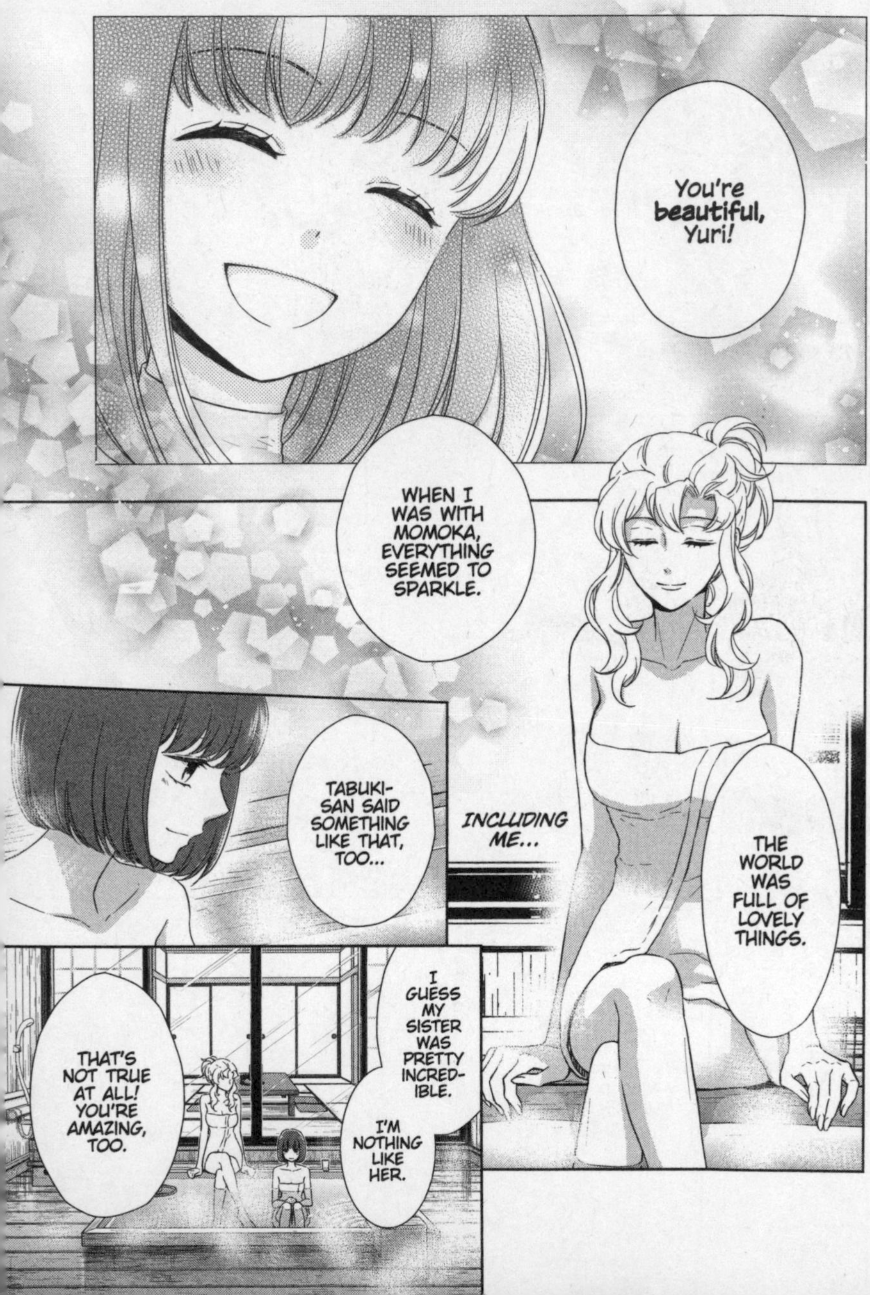
You're beautiful, Yuri!
WHEN I WAS WITH MOMOKA, EVERYTHING SEEMED TO SPARKLE.
THE WORLD WAS FULL OF LOVELY THINGS.
INCLUDING ME...
TABUKI-SAN SAID SOMETHING LIKE THAT, TOO...
I GUESS MY SISTER WAS PRETTY INCREDIBLE.
I'M NOTHING LIKE HER.
THAT'S NOT TRUE AT ALL! YOU'RE AMAZING, TOO.

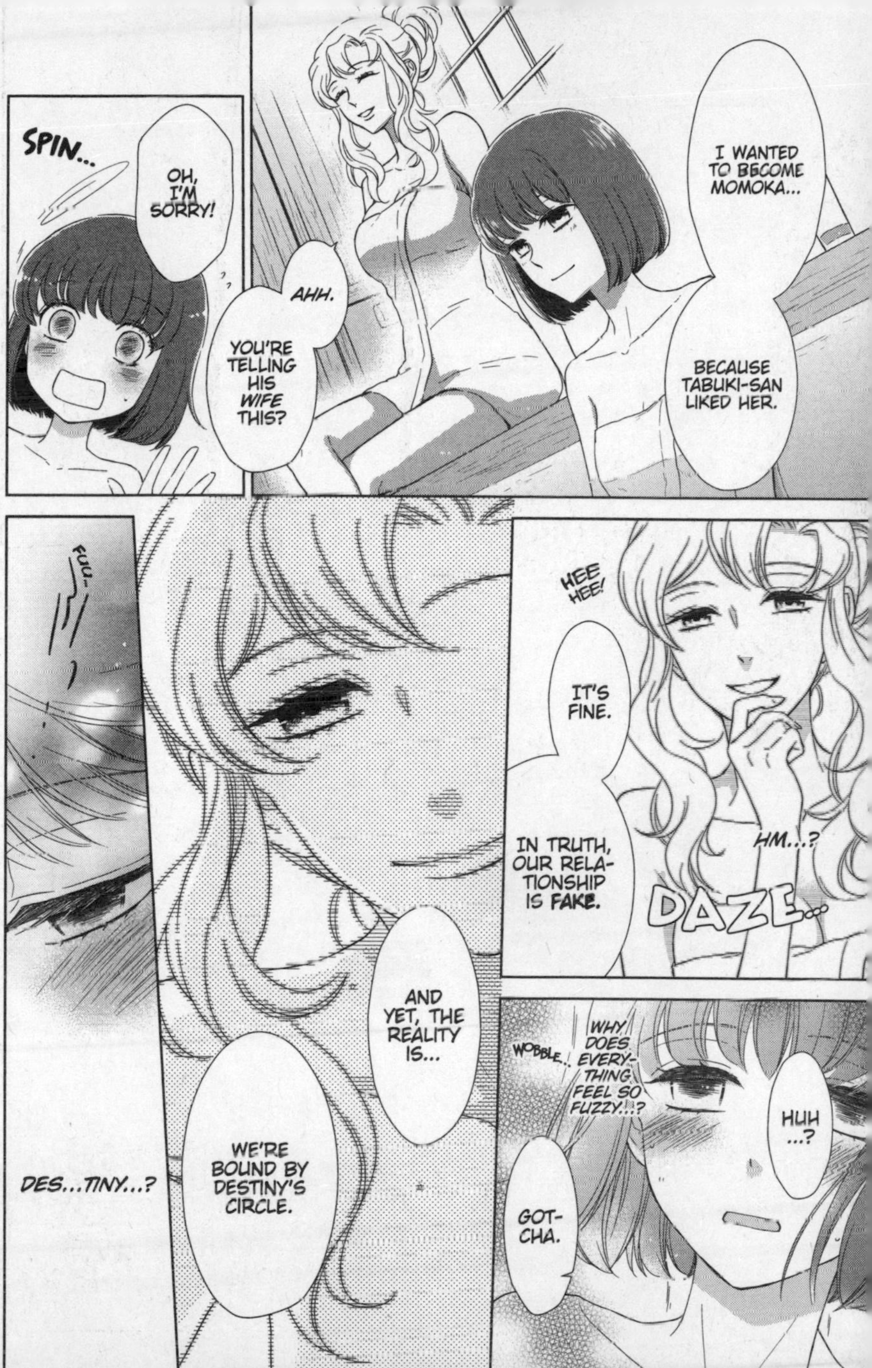
I WANTED TO BECOME MOMOKA...
BECAUSE TABUKI-SAN LIKED HER.
AHH.
YOU'RE TELLING HIS *WIFE* THIS?
SPIN...
OH, I'M SORRY!
HEE HEE!
IT'S FINE.
HM...?
IN TRUTH, OUR RELATIONSHIP IS **FAKE**.
DAZE...
HUH ...?
WHY DOES EVERYTHING FEEL SO FUZZY...?
WOBBLE..
GOT-CHA.
AND YET, THE REALITY IS...
WE'RE BOUND BY DESTINY'S CIRCLE.
FUU-
DES...TINY...?

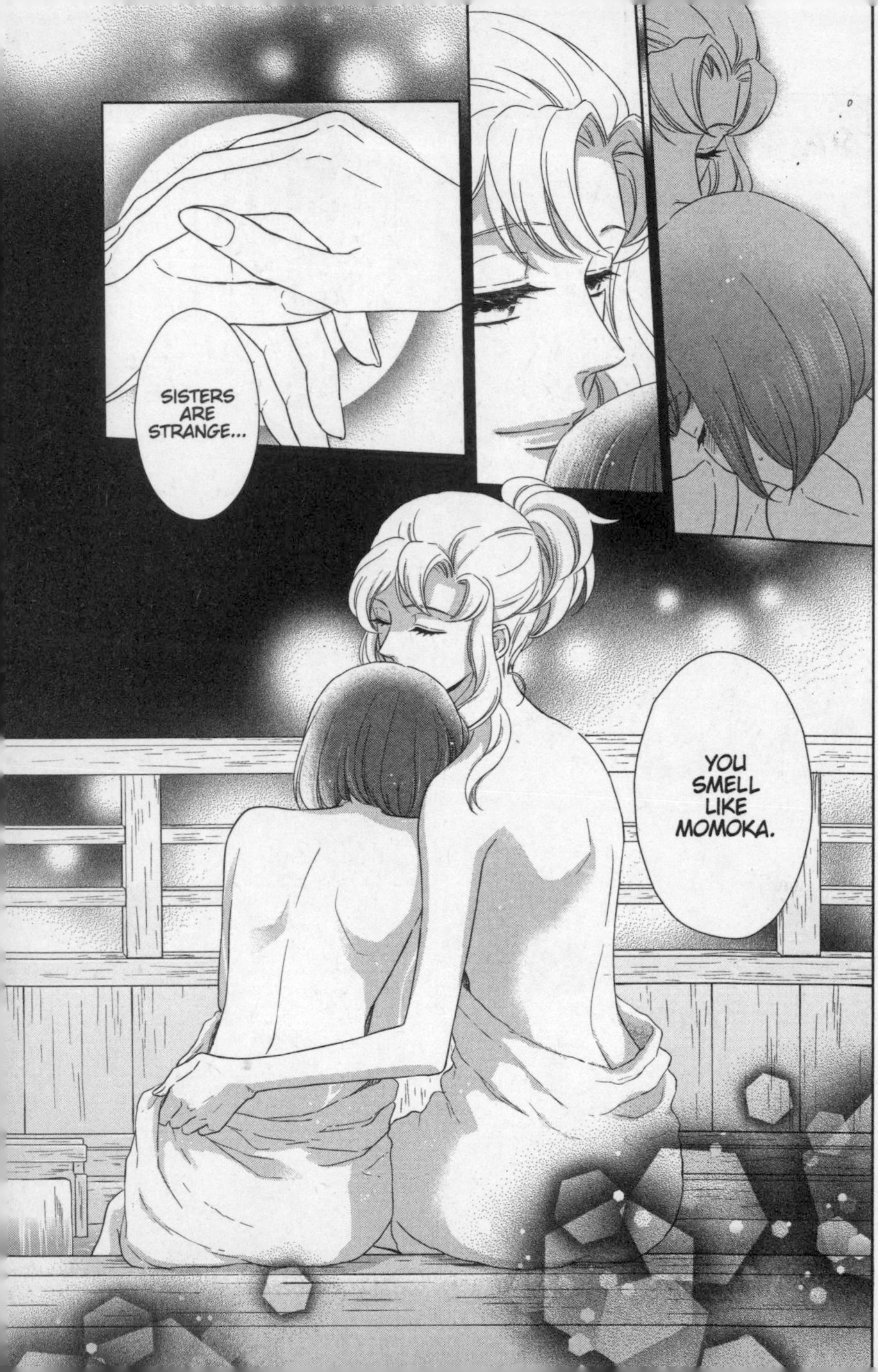
SISTERS ARE STRANGE...
YOU SMELL LIKE MOMOKA.

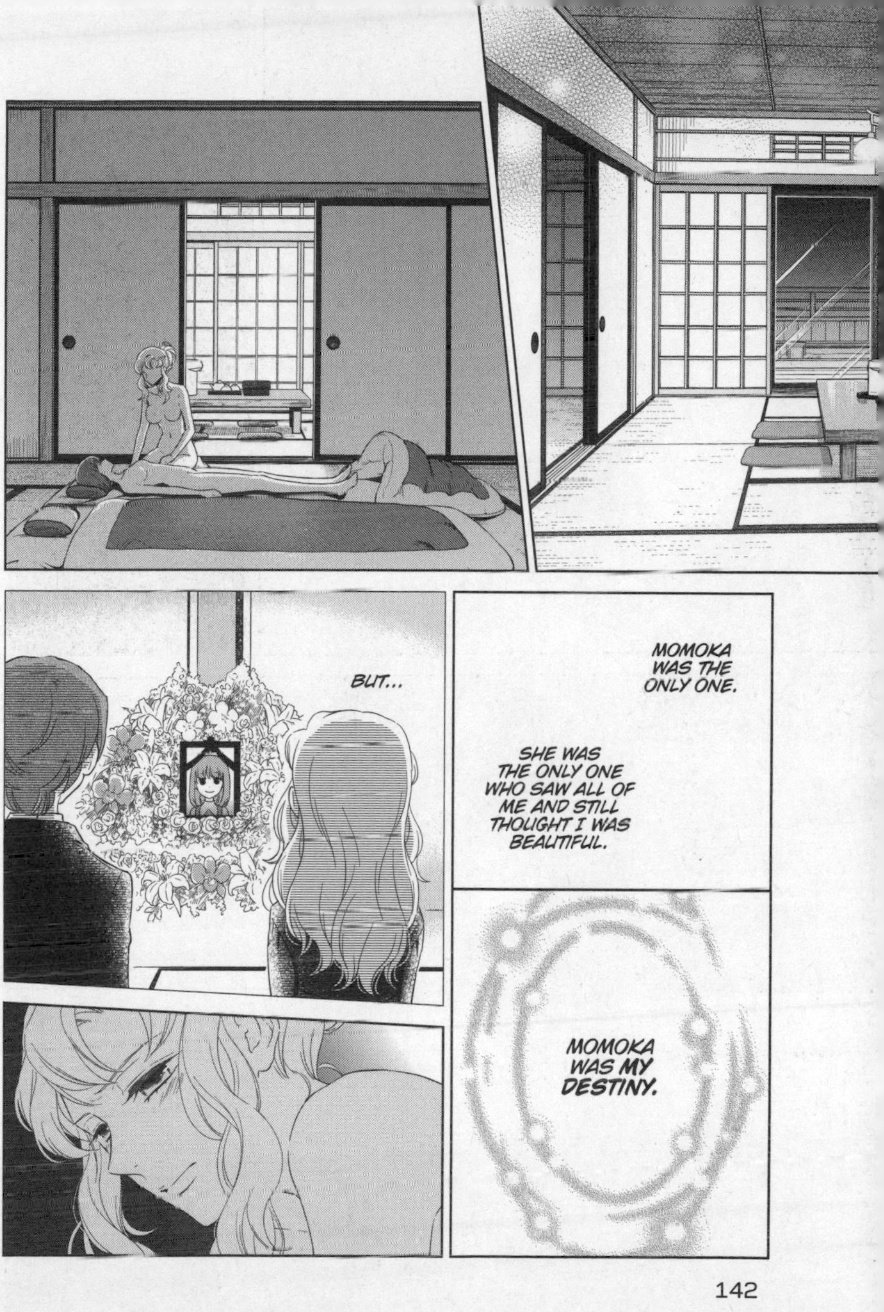
MOMOKA WAS THE ONLY ONE.
SHE WAS THE ONLY ONE WHO SAW ALL OF ME AND STILL THOUGHT I WAS BEAUTIFUL.
MOMOKA WAS MY DESTINY.
BUT...

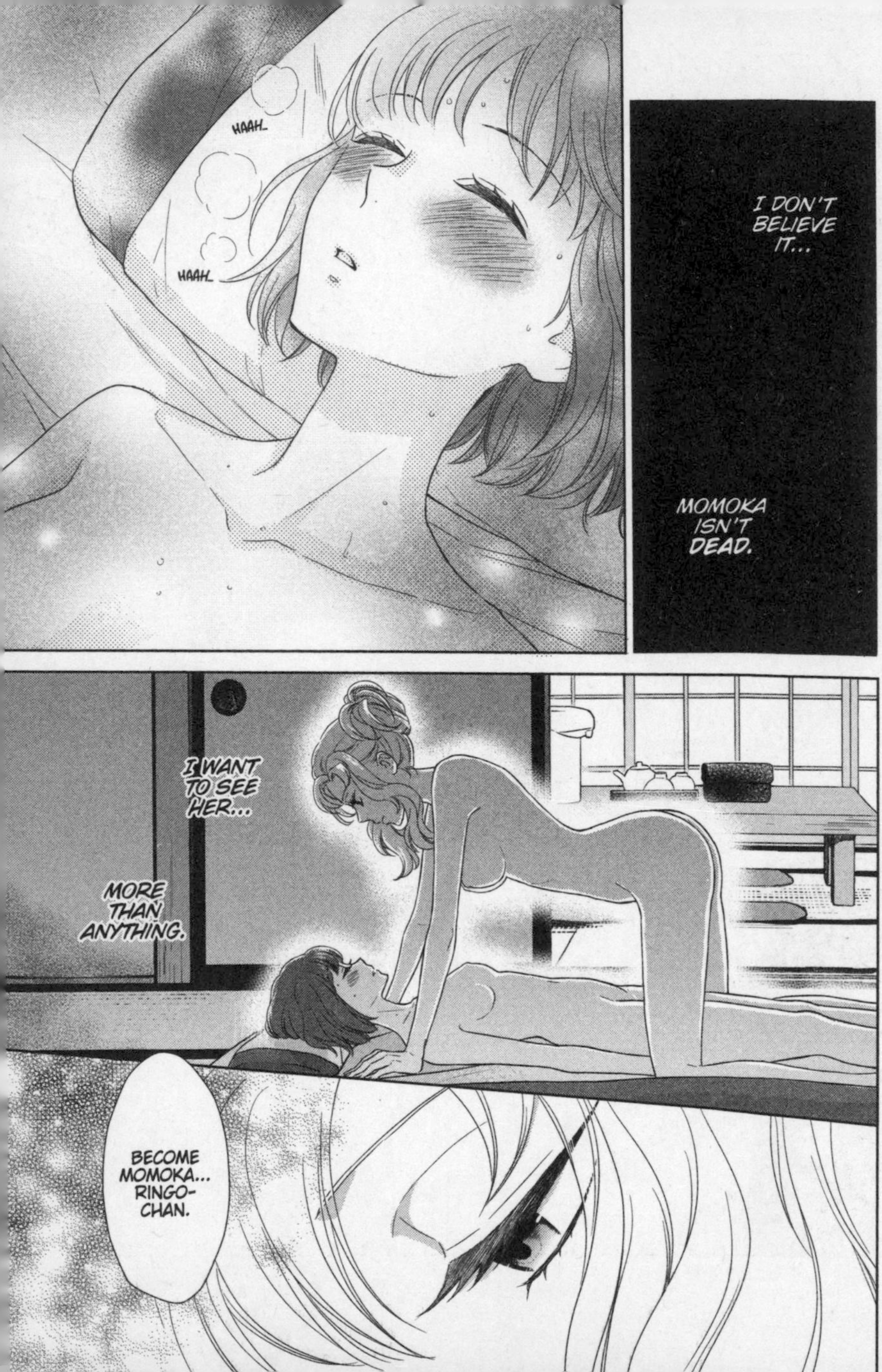
I DON'T BELIEVE IT...
MOMOKA ISN'T DEAD.
HAAH_
HAAH_
I WANT TO SEE HER...
MORE THAN ANYTHING.
BECOME MOMOKA... RINGO-CHAN.

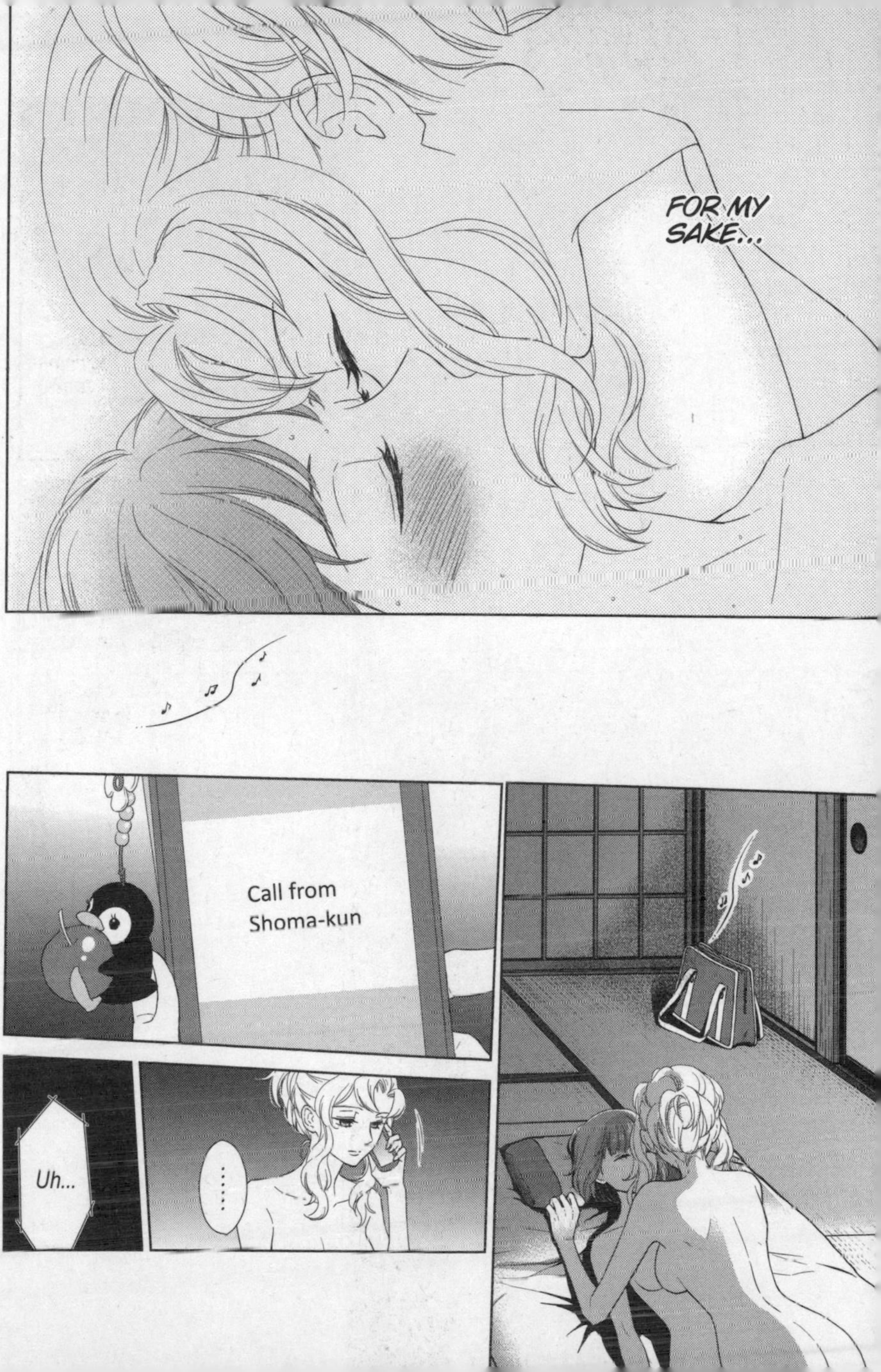
FOR MY SAKE...
Call from
Shoma-kun
......
Uh...

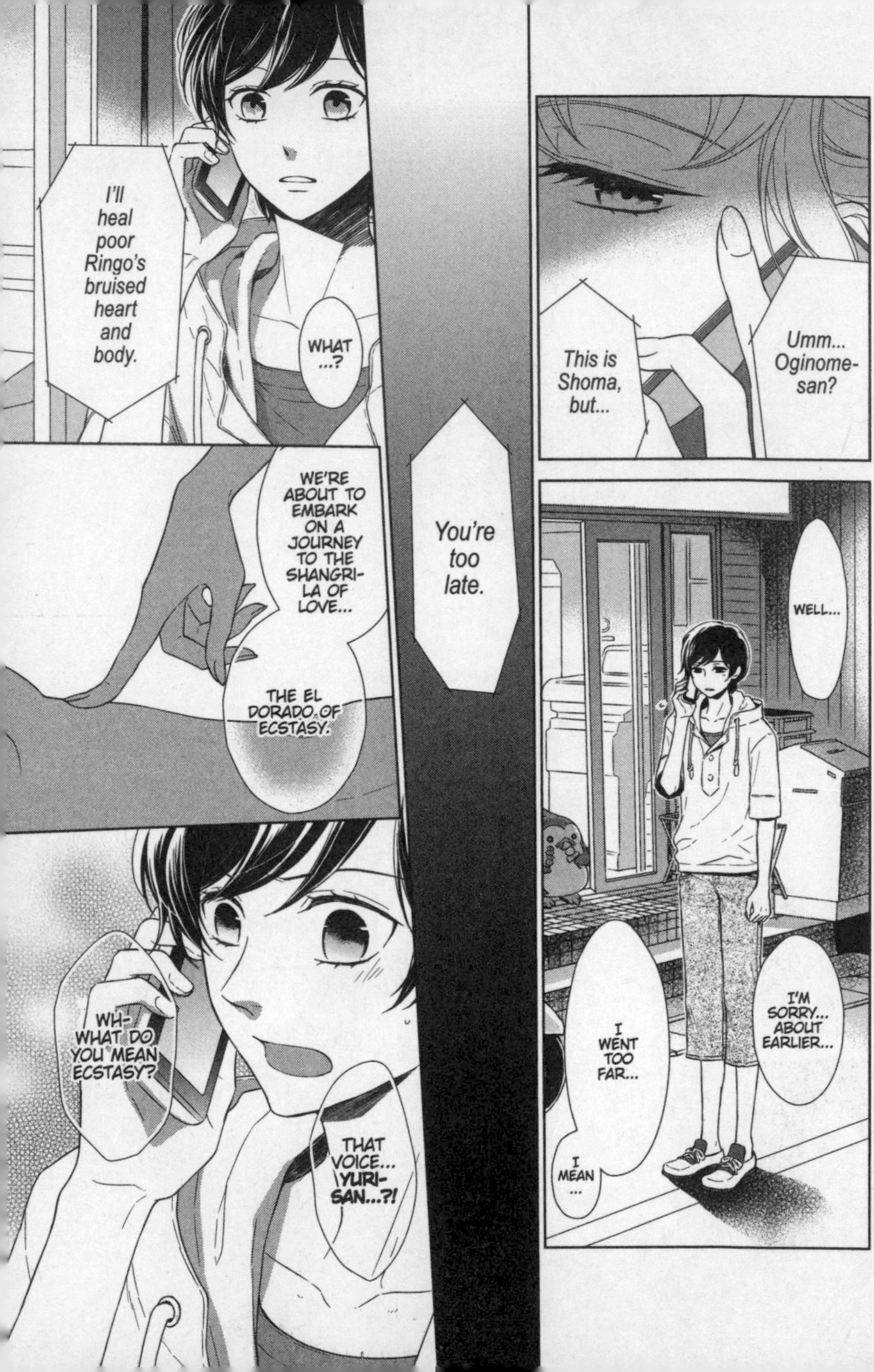
Umm... Oginome-san?
This is Shoma, but...
WELL...
I'M SORRY... ABOUT EARLIER...
I WENT TOO FAR...
I MEAN ...
You're too late.
I'll heal poor Ringo's bruised heart and body.
WHAT ...?
WE'RE ABOUT TO EMBARK ON A JOURNEY TO THE SHANGRI-LA OF LOVE...
THE EL DORADO OF ECSTASY.
WH-WHAT DO YOU MEAN ECSTASY?
THAT VOICE... YURI-SAN...?!

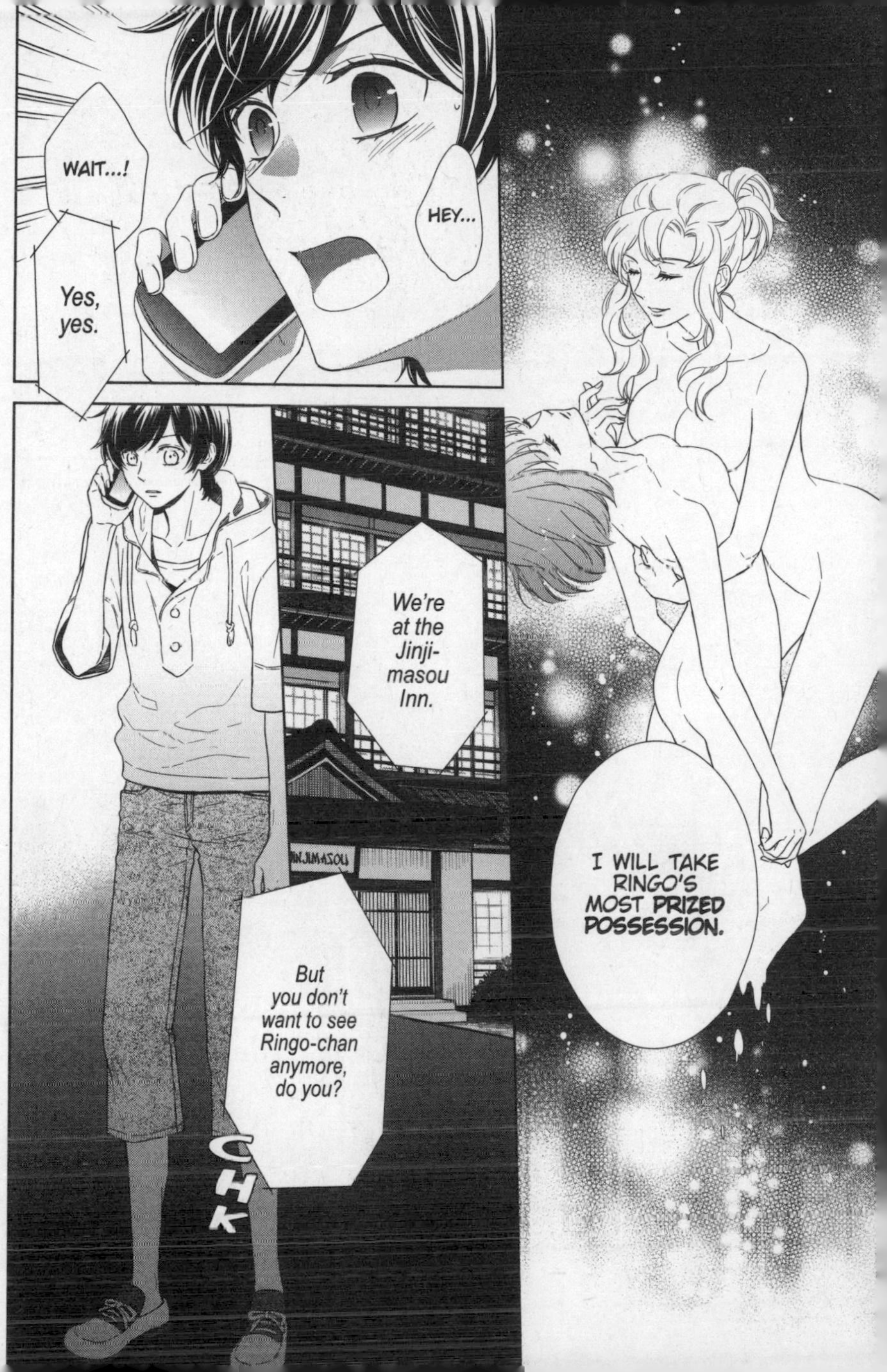
I WILL TAKE RINGO'S MOST PRIZED POSSESSION.
HEY...
WAIT...!
Yes, yes.
We're at the Jinji-masou Inn.
JINJIMASOU
But you don't want to see Ringo-chan anymore, do you?
CHK

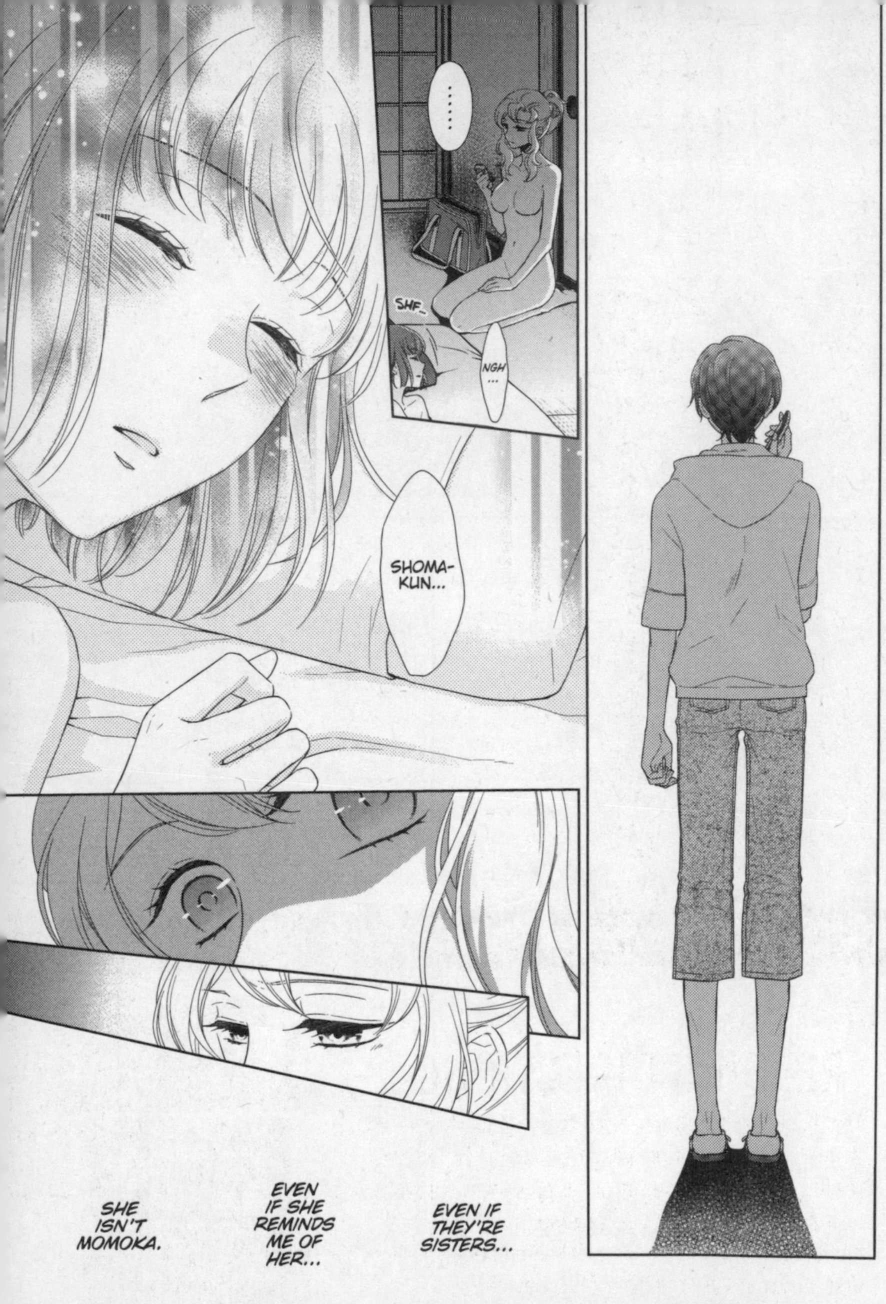
......
SHF..
NGH...
SHOMA-KUN...
EVEN IF THEY'RE SISTERS...
EVEN IF SHE REMINDS ME OF HER...
SHE ISN'T MOMOKA.

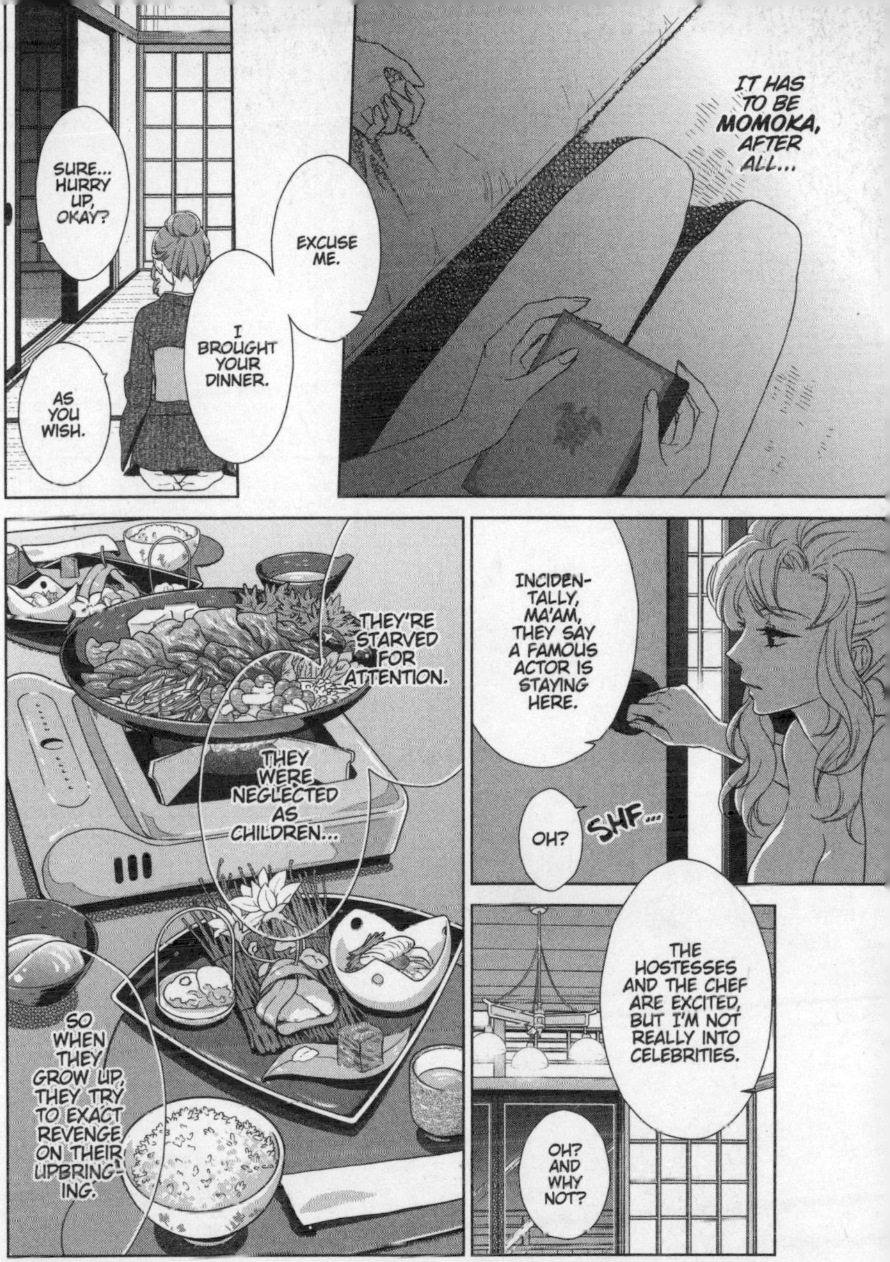
IT HAS TO BE MOMOKA, AFTER ALL...
EXCUSE ME.
I BROUGHT YOUR DINNER.
SURE... HURRY UP, OKAY?
AS YOU WISH.
INCIDENTALLY, MA'AM, THEY SAY A FAMOUS ACTOR IS STAYING HERE.
OH?
SHF...
THE HOSTESSES AND THE CHEF ARE EXCITED, BUT I'M NOT REALLY INTO CELEBRITIES.
OH? AND WHY NOT?
THEY'RE STARVED FOR ATTENTION.
THEY WERE NEGLECTED AS CHILDREN...
SO WHEN THEY GROW UP, THEY TRY TO EXACT REVENGE ON THEIR UPBRINGING.

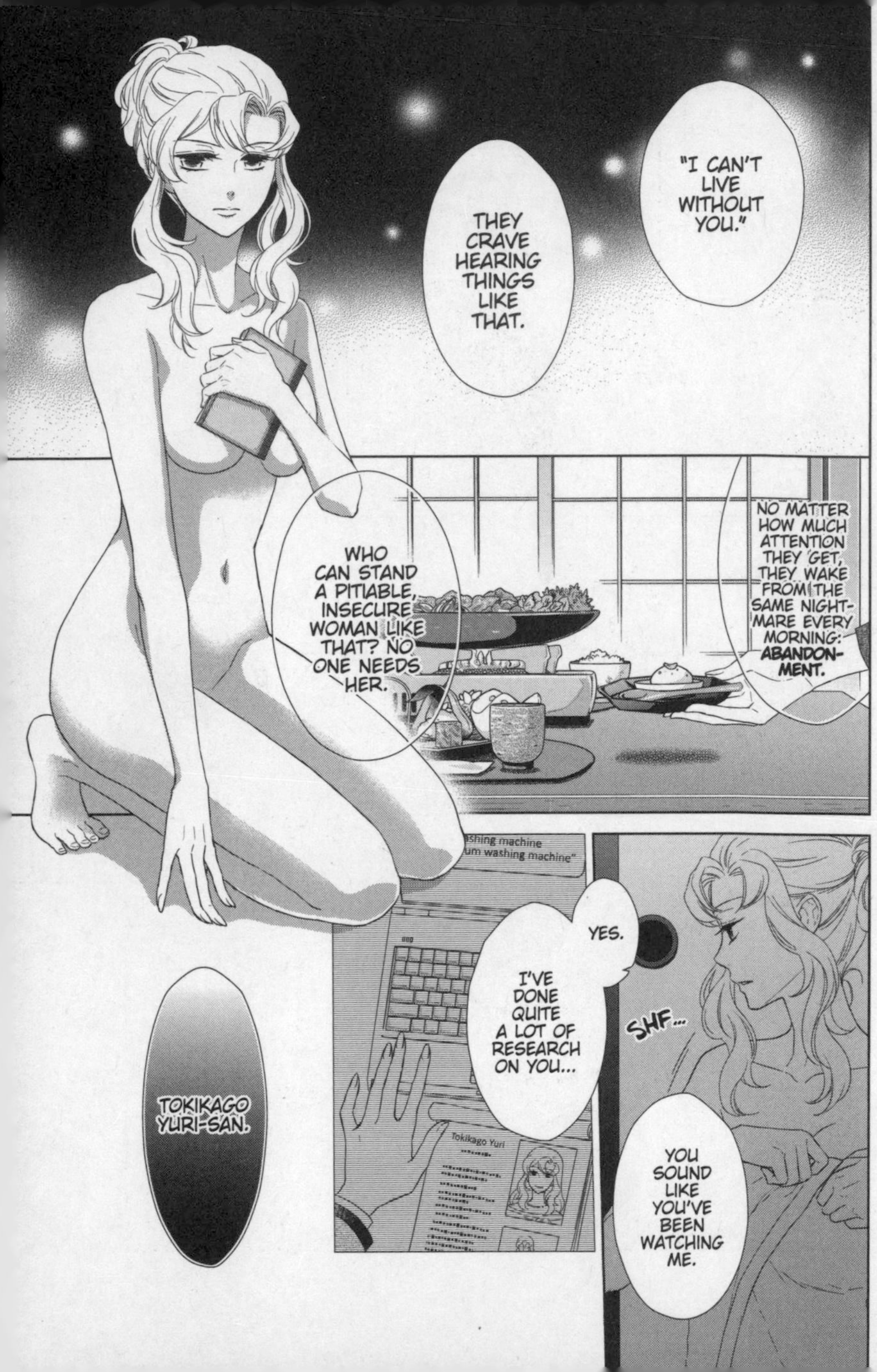
"I CAN'T LIVE WITHOUT YOU."
THEY CRAVE HEARING THINGS LIKE THAT.
NO MATTER HOW MUCH ATTENTION THEY GET, THEY WAKE FROM THE SAME NIGHT-MARE EVERY MORNING: **ABANDONMENT.**
WHO CAN STAND A PITIABLE, INSECURE WOMAN LIKE THAT? NO ONE NEEDS HER.
YES.
I'VE DONE QUITE A LOT OF RESEARCH ON YOU...
SHF...
YOU SOUND LIKE YOU'VE BEEN WATCHING ME.
Tokikago Yuri
TOKIKAGO YURI-SAN.

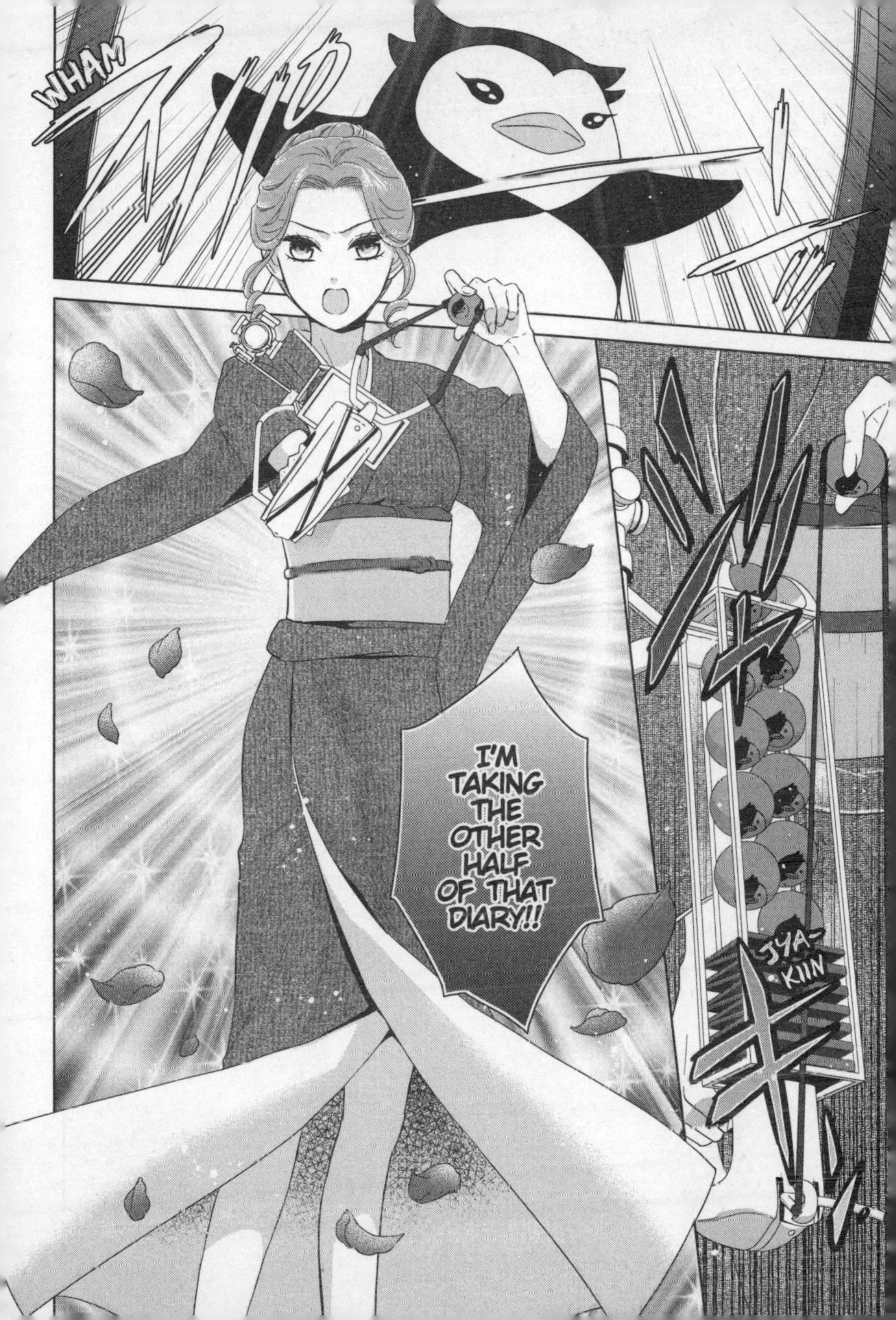
WHAM
JYA-KIIN
I'M TAKING THE OTHER HALF OF THAT DIARY!!

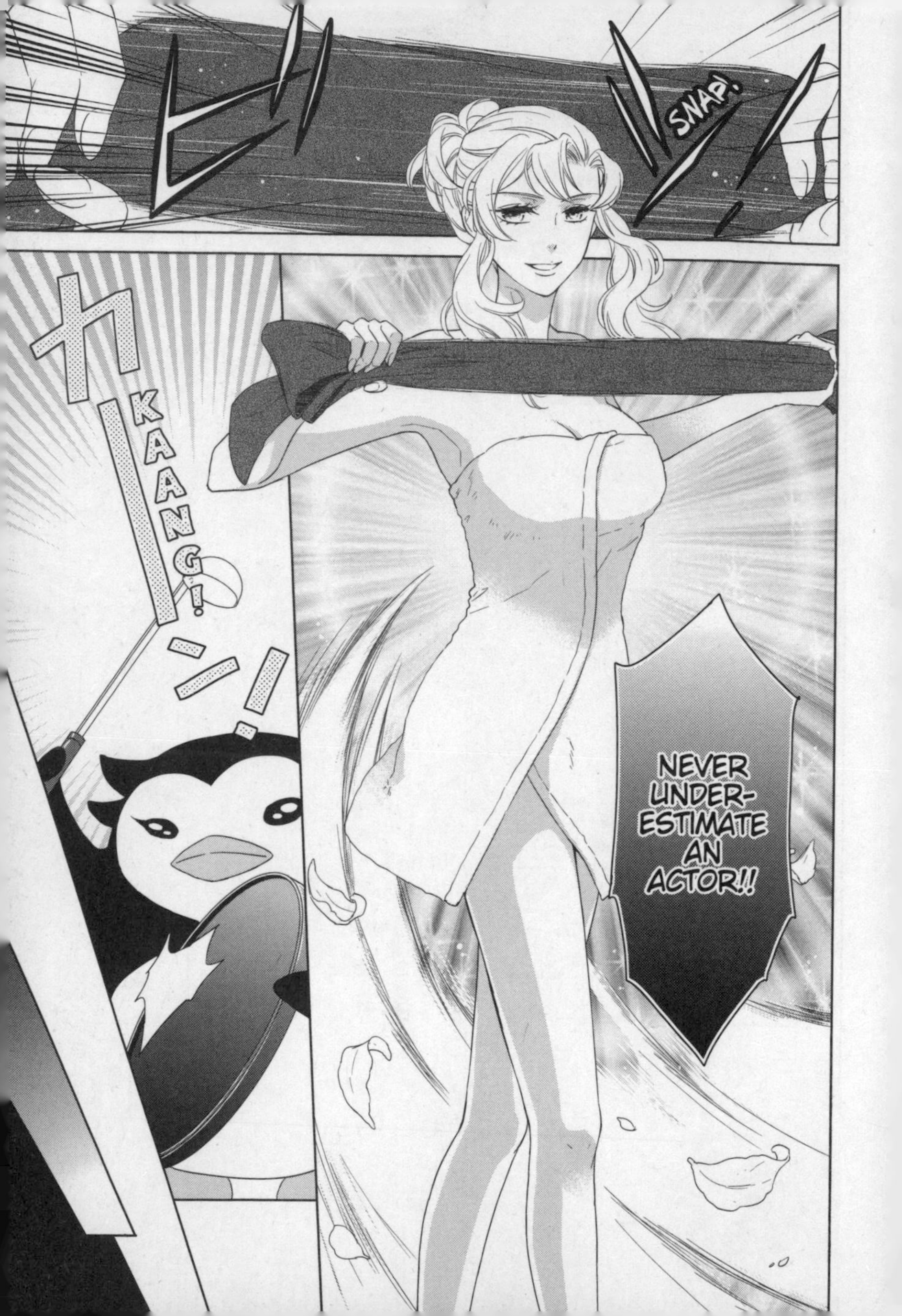
SNAP!
KAANG!
NEVER UNDER-ESTIMATE AN ACTOR!!

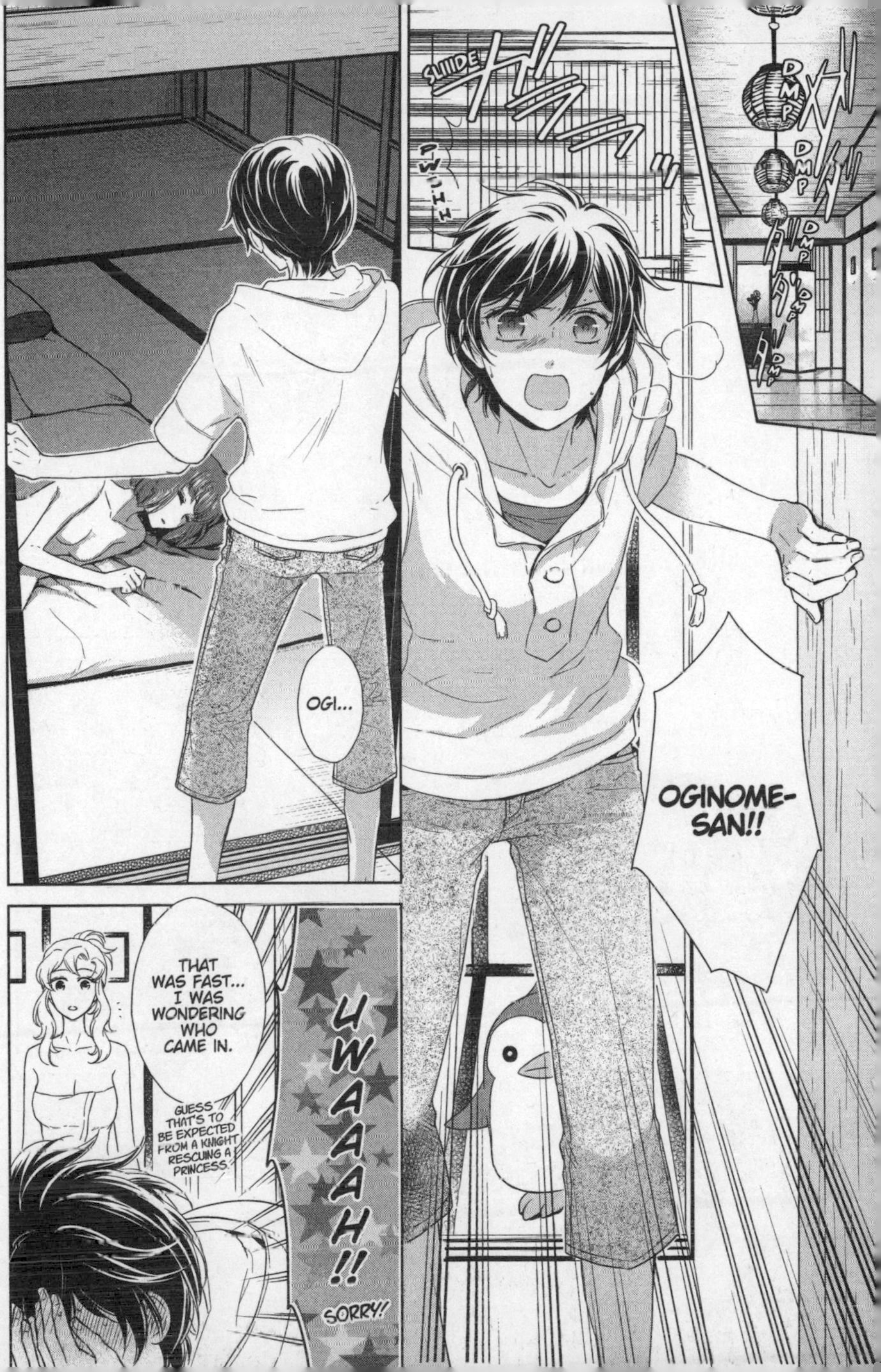
DMP DMP DMP DMP DMP DMP
SLIIDE
PWUHH
OGINOME-SAN!!
OGI...
UWAAAAH!!
SORRY!
THAT WAS FAST... I WAS WONDERING WHO CAME IN.
GUESS THAT'S TO BE EXPECTED FROM A KNIGHT RESCUING A PRINCESS.

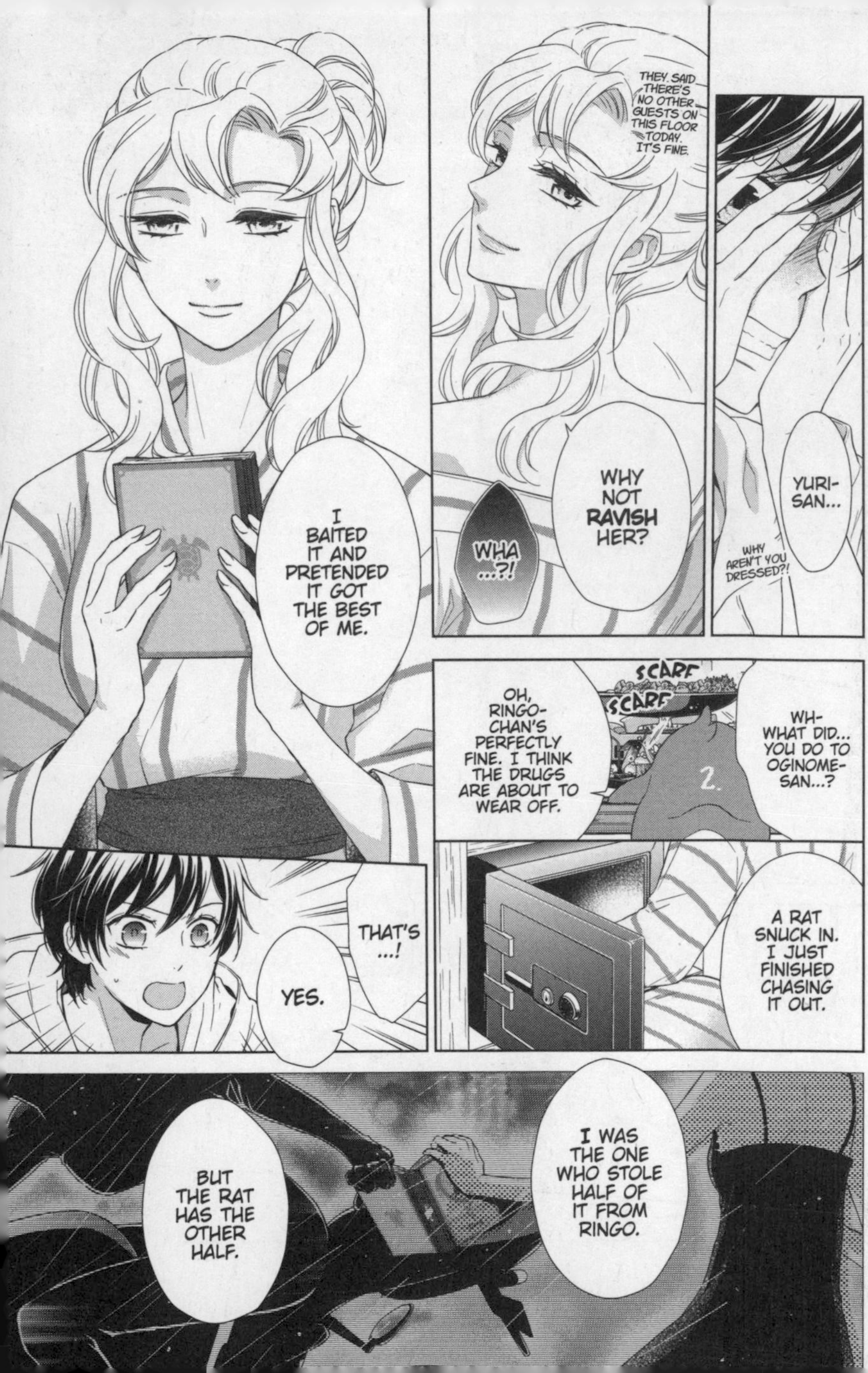
YURI-SAN...
WHY AREN'T YOU DRESSED?!
THEY. SAID THERE'S NO OTHER GUESTS ON THIS FLOOR TODAY. IT'S FINE.
WHY NOT RAVISH HER?
WHA...?!
WH- WHAT DID... YOU DO TO OGINOME-SAN...?
SCARF
SCARF
OH, RINGO-CHAN'S PERFECTLY FINE. I THINK THE DRUGS ARE ABOUT TO WEAR OFF.
A RAT SNUCK IN. I JUST FINISHED CHASING IT OUT.
I BAITED IT AND PRETENDED IT GOT THE BEST OF ME.
THAT'S ...!
YES.
I WAS THE ONE WHO STOLE HALF OF IT FROM RINGO.
BUT THE RAT HAS THE OTHER HALF.

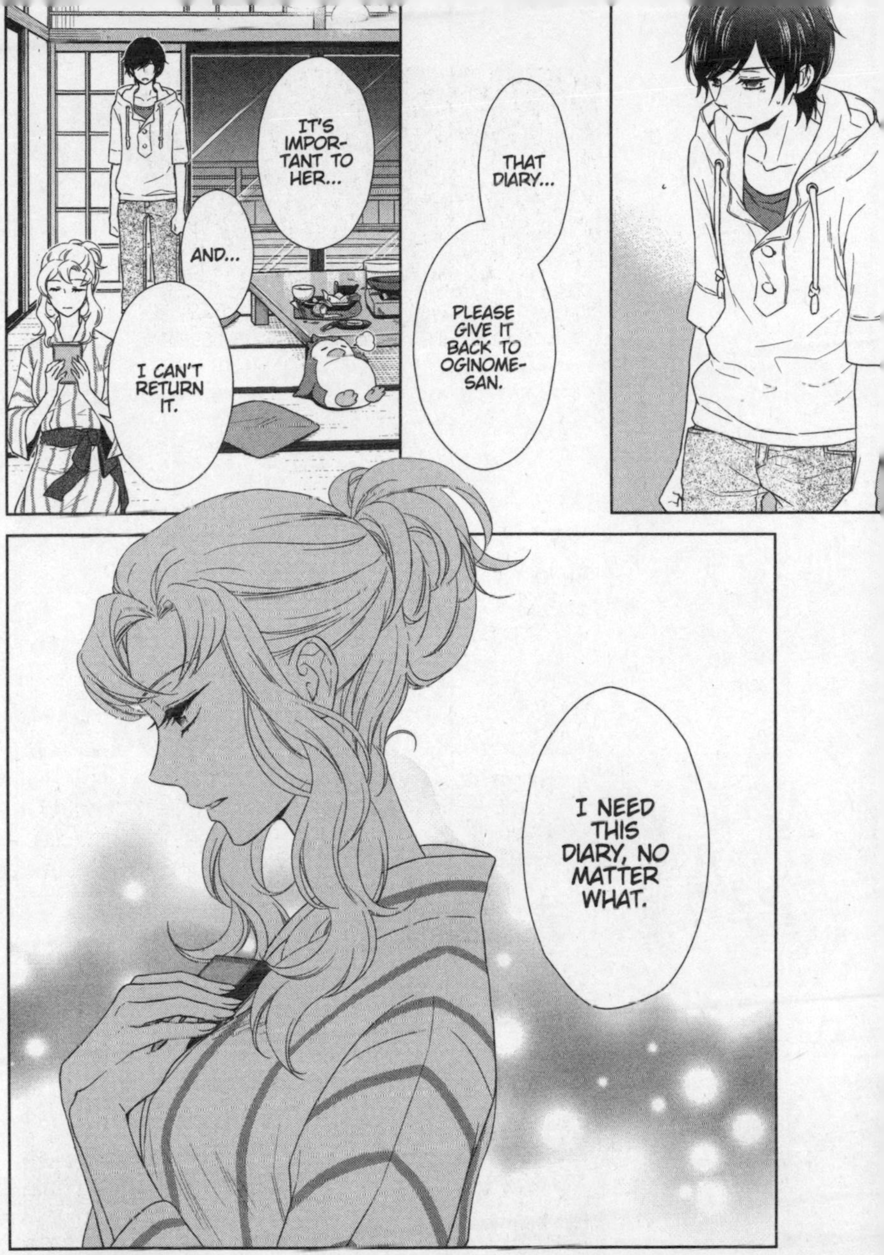
THAT DIARY...
PLEASE GIVE IT BACK TO OGINOME-SAN.
IT'S IMPORTANT TO HER...
AND...
I CAN'T RETURN IT.
I NEED THIS DIARY, NO MATTER WHAT.

Flashback

Yuri

On the way home from school...

Her Papa's Absolute Words

※ *I didn't believe Momoka. After all, Papa...*

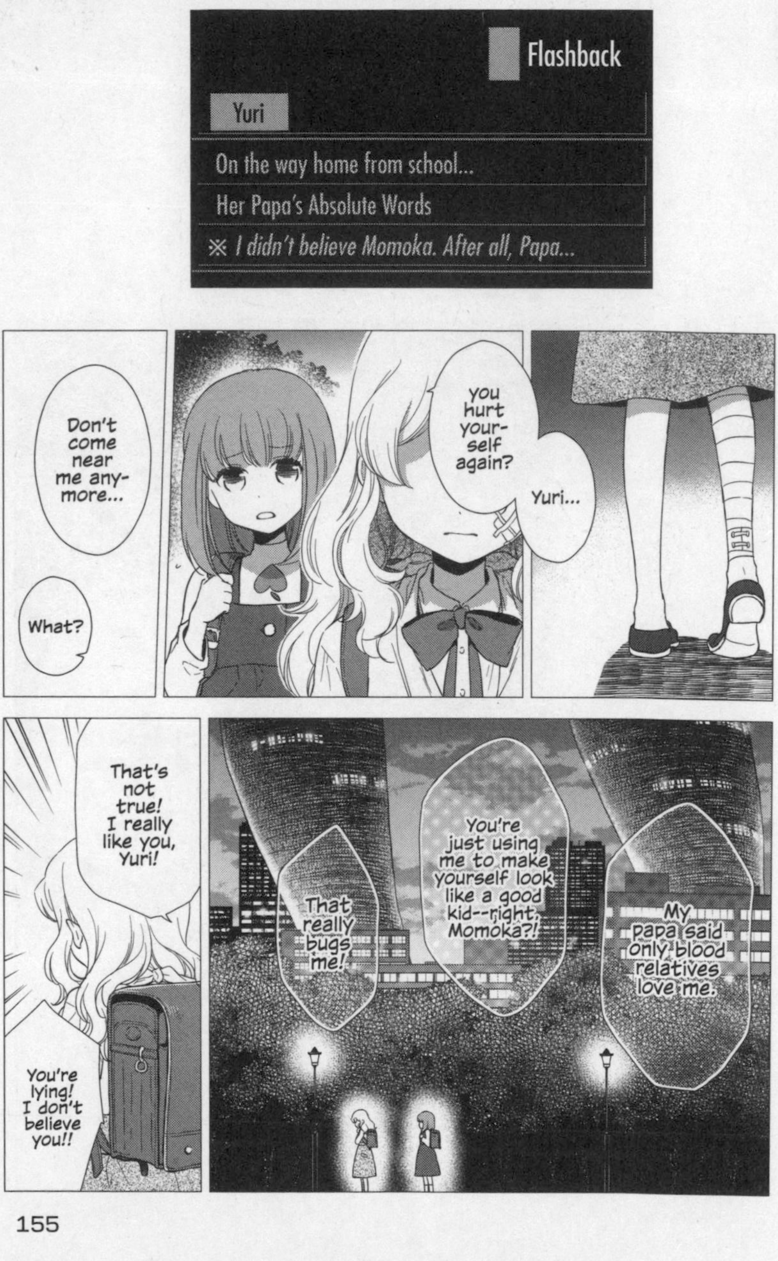
Yuri...
you hurt your-self again?
Don't come near me any-more...
What?
My papa said only blood relatives love me.
You're just using me to make yourself look like a good kid--right, Momoka?!
That really bugs me!
That's not true! I really like you, Yuri!
You're lying! I don't believe you!!

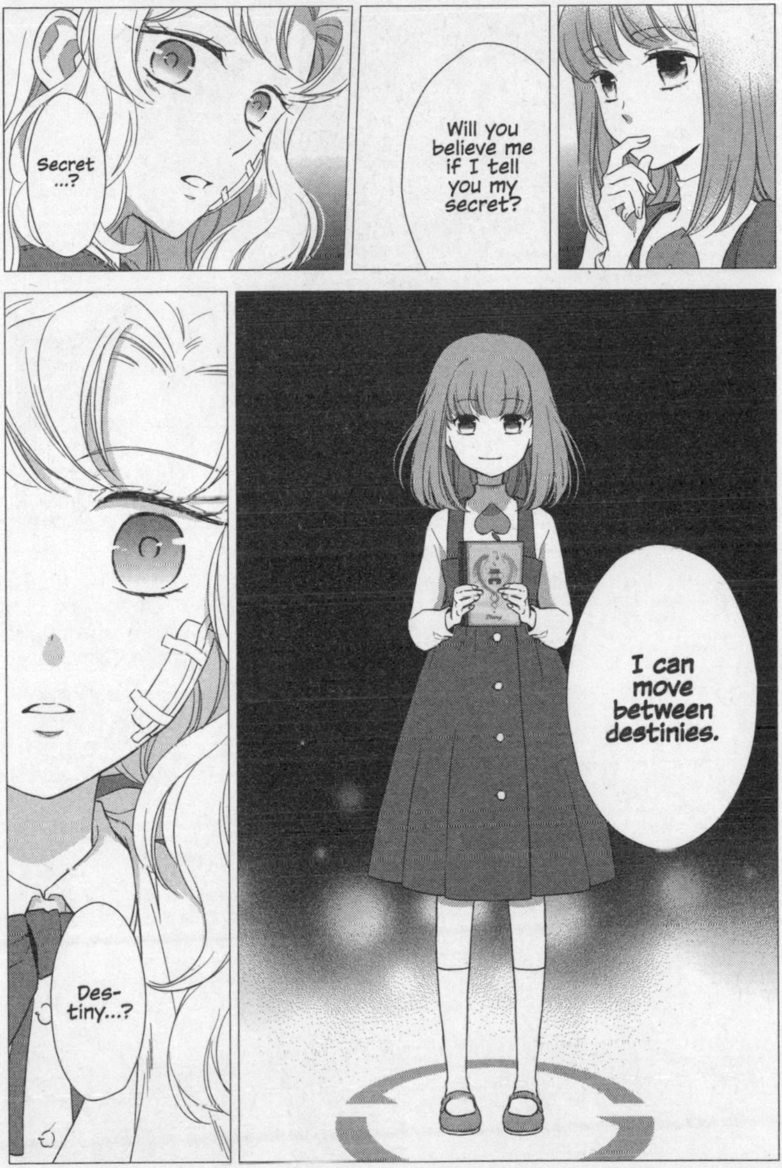
Will you believe me if I tell you my secret?
Secret ...?
I can move between destinies.
Des-tiny...?

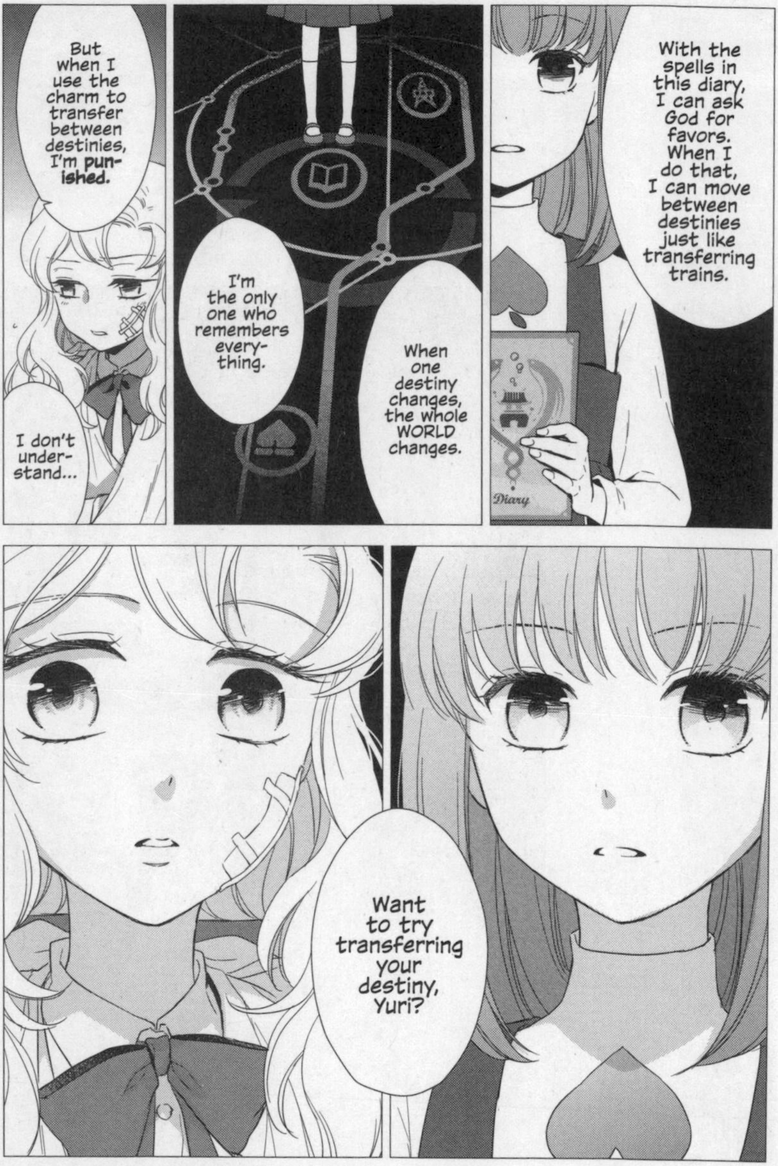
With the spells in this diary, I can ask God for favors. When I do that, I can move between destinies just like transferring trains.
When one destiny changes, the whole WORLD changes.
I'm the only one who remembers every-thing.
But when I use the charm to transfer between destinies, I'm **pun-ished.**
I don't under-stand...
Want to try transferring your destiny, Yuri?

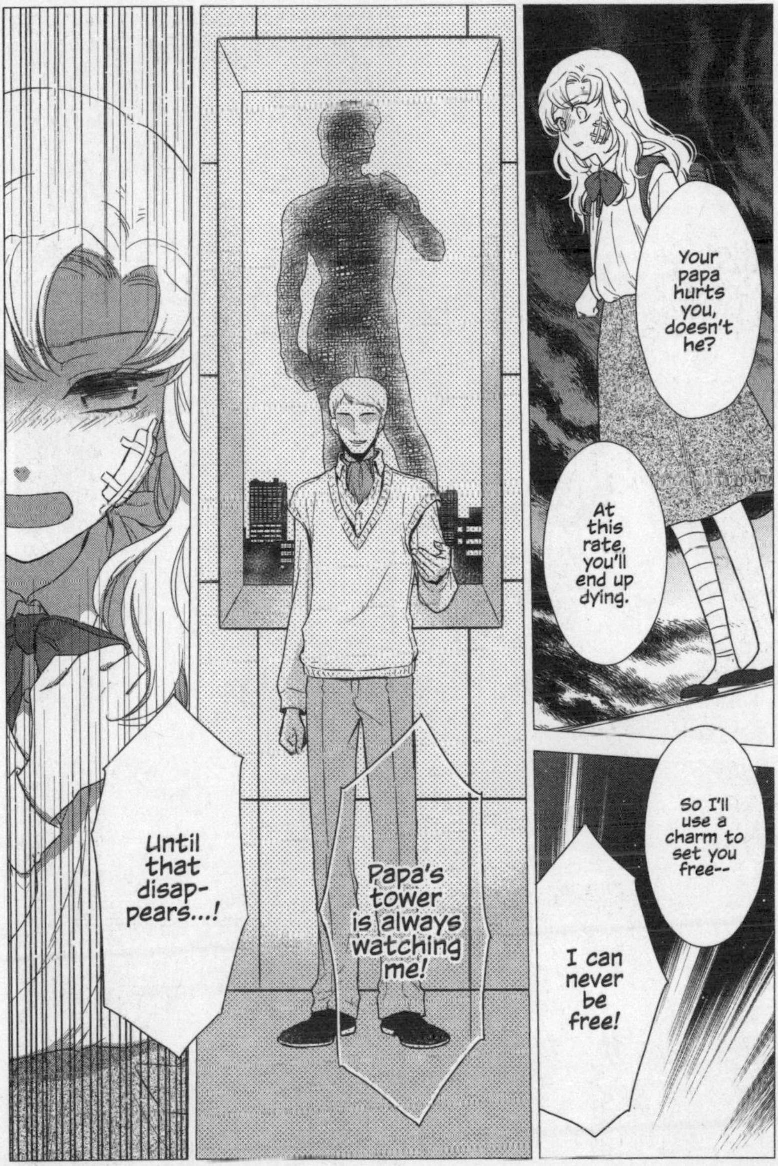
Your papa hurts you, doesn't he?
At this rate, you'll end up dying.
So I'll use a charm to set you free--
I can never be free!
Papa's tower is always watching me!
Until that disap-pears...!

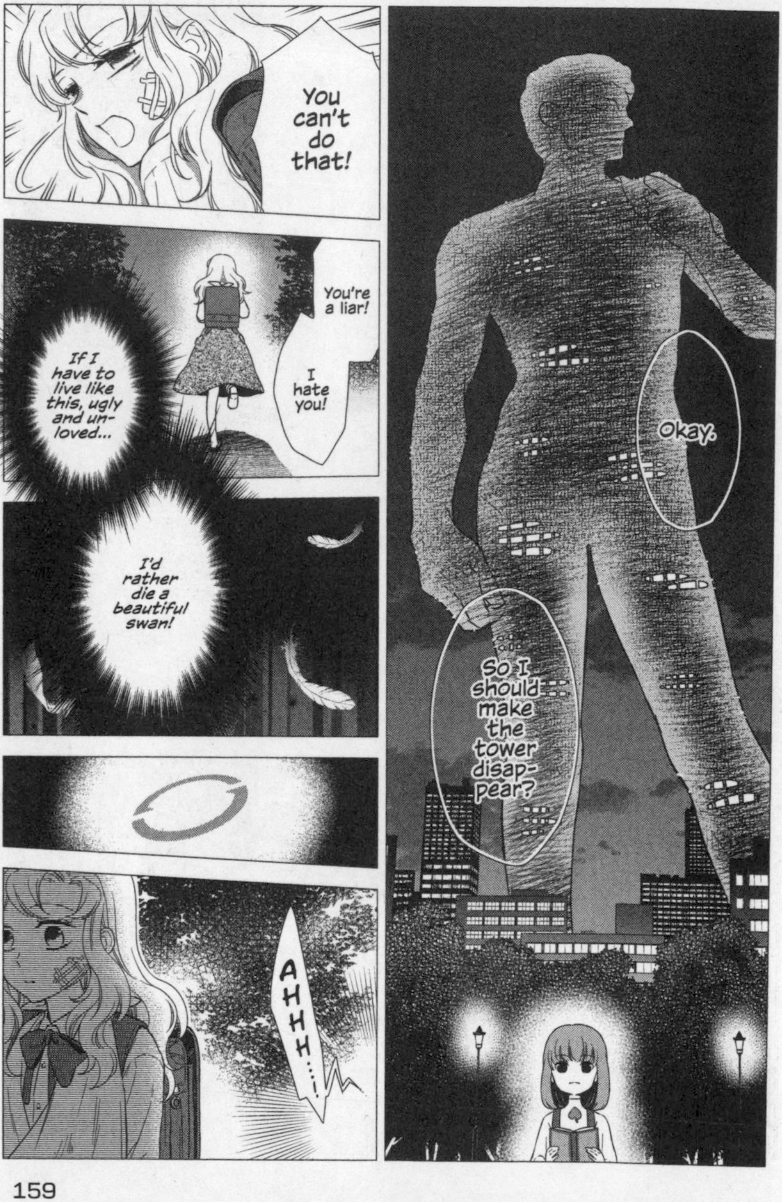
Okay.
So I should make the tower disappear?
You can't do that!
You're a liar!
I hate you!
If I have to live like this, ugly and unloved...
I'd rather die a beautiful swan!
AHHH...!

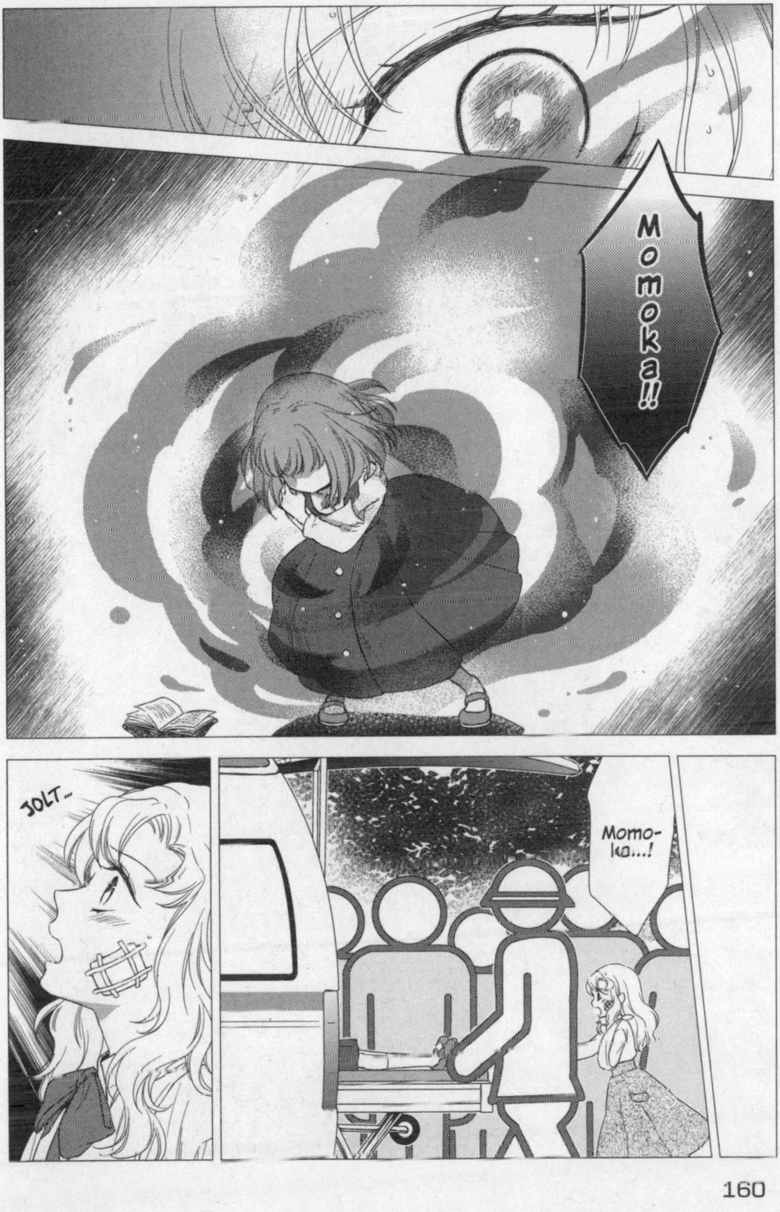
Momoka!!
Momo-ko...!
JOLT...

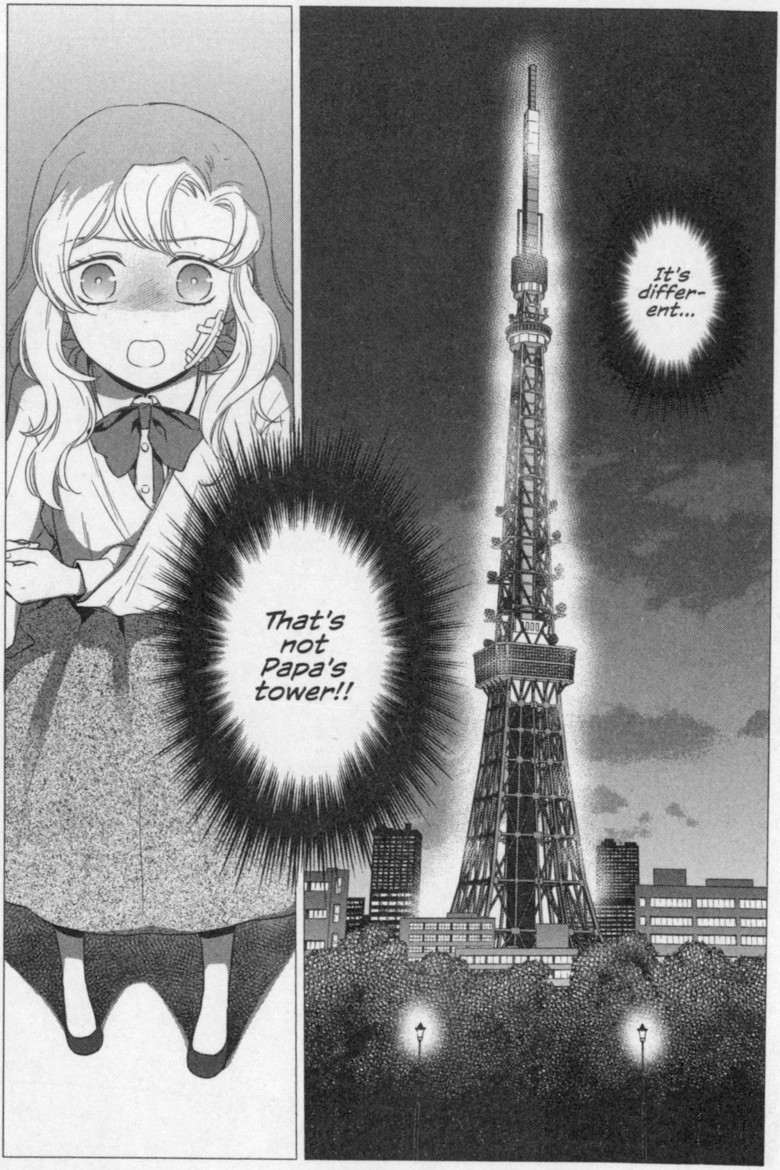
It's different...
That's not Papa's tower!!

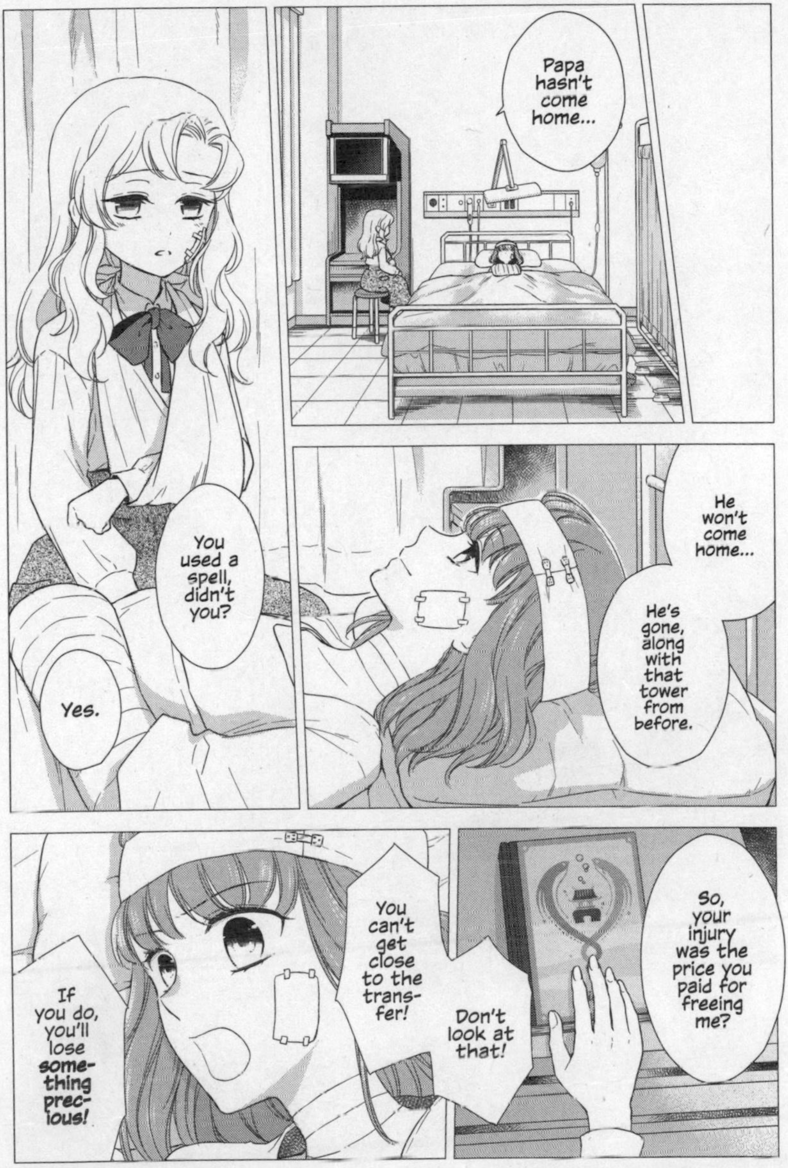

Papa hasn't come home...
He won't come home...
He's gone, along with that tower from before.
You used a spell, didn't you?
Yes.
So, your injury was the price you paid for freeing me?
Don't look at that!
You can't get close to the transfer!
If you do, you'll lose something precious!

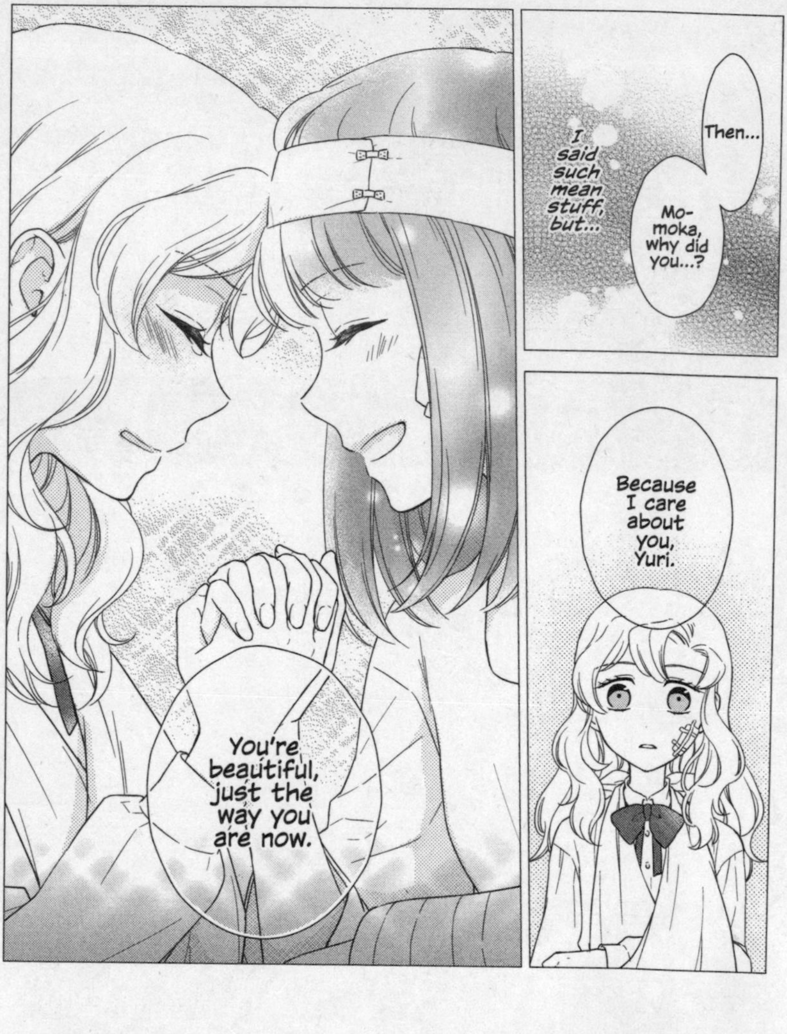
Then...
I said such mean stuff, but...
Mo-moka, why did you...?
Because I care about you, Yuri.
You're beautiful, just the way you are now.

NOT LONG AFTER THAT...

MOMOKA DISAPPEARED DURING THE INCIDENT.

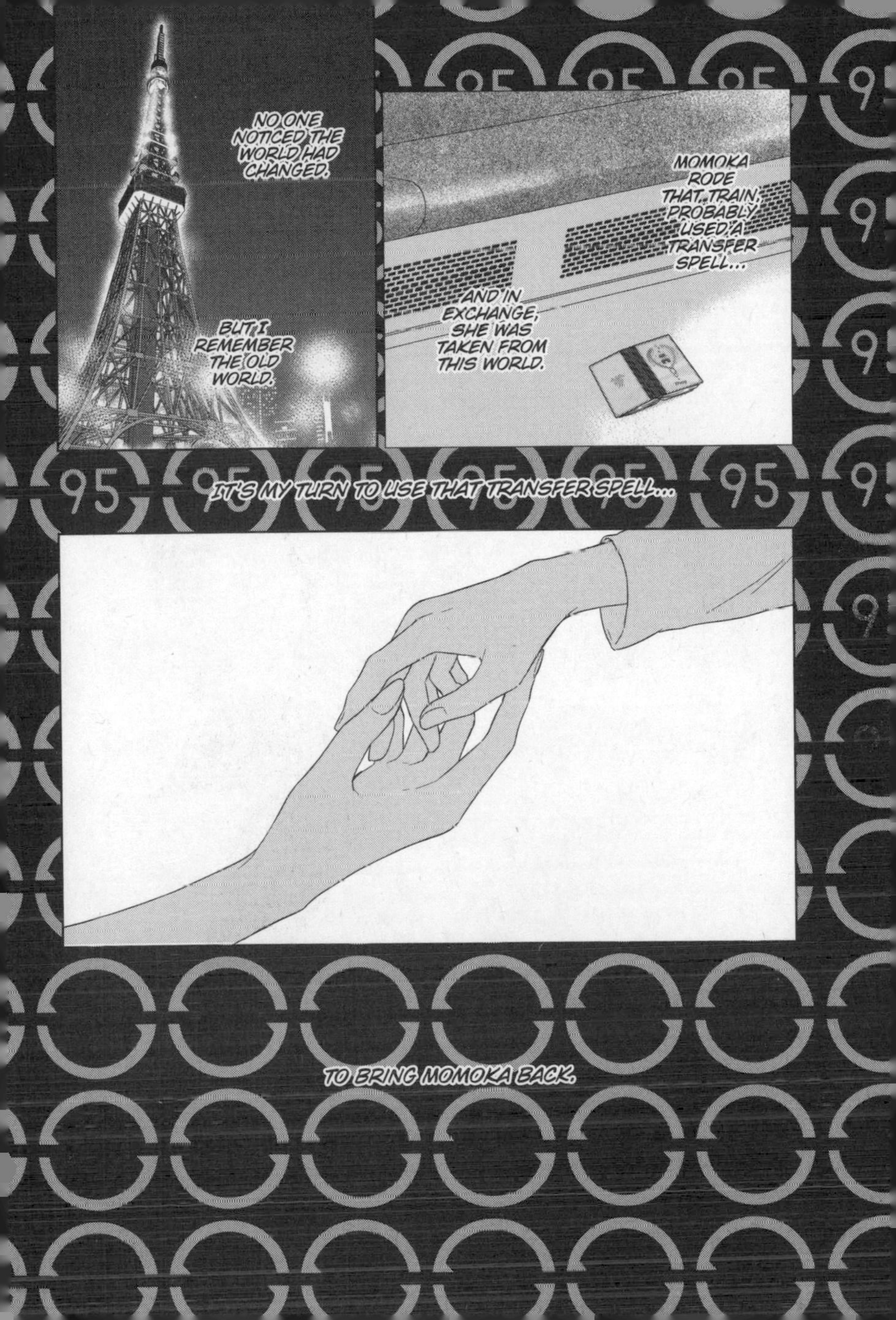
MOMOKA RODE THAT TRAIN, PROBABLY USED A TRANSFER SPELL...
AND IN EXCHANGE, SHE WAS TAKEN FROM THIS WORLD.
NO ONE NOTICED THE WORLD HAD CHANGED.
BUT I REMEMBER THE OLD WORLD.
IT'S MY TURN TO USE THAT TRANSFER SPELL...
TO BRING MOMOKA BACK.

20 20TH STATION

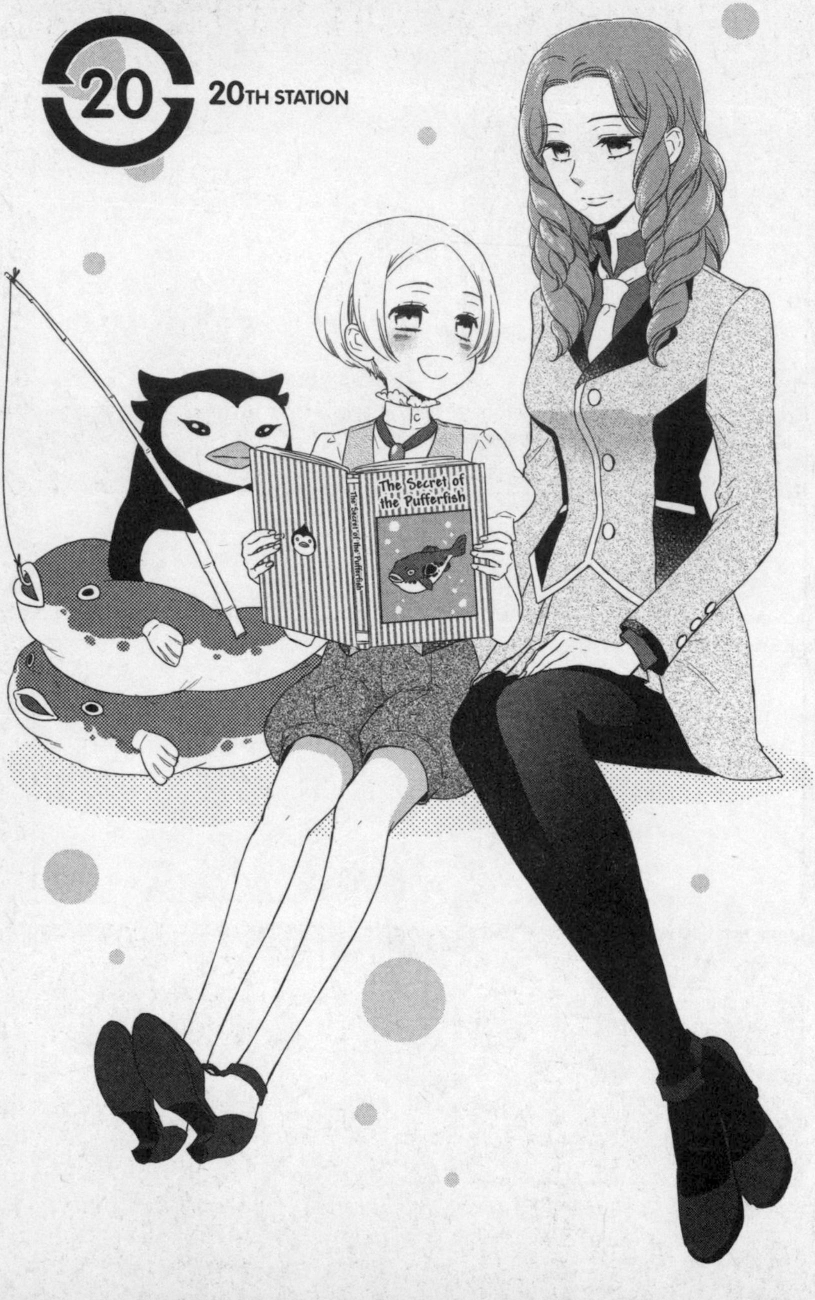
The Secret of the Pufferfish
The Secret of the Pufferfish

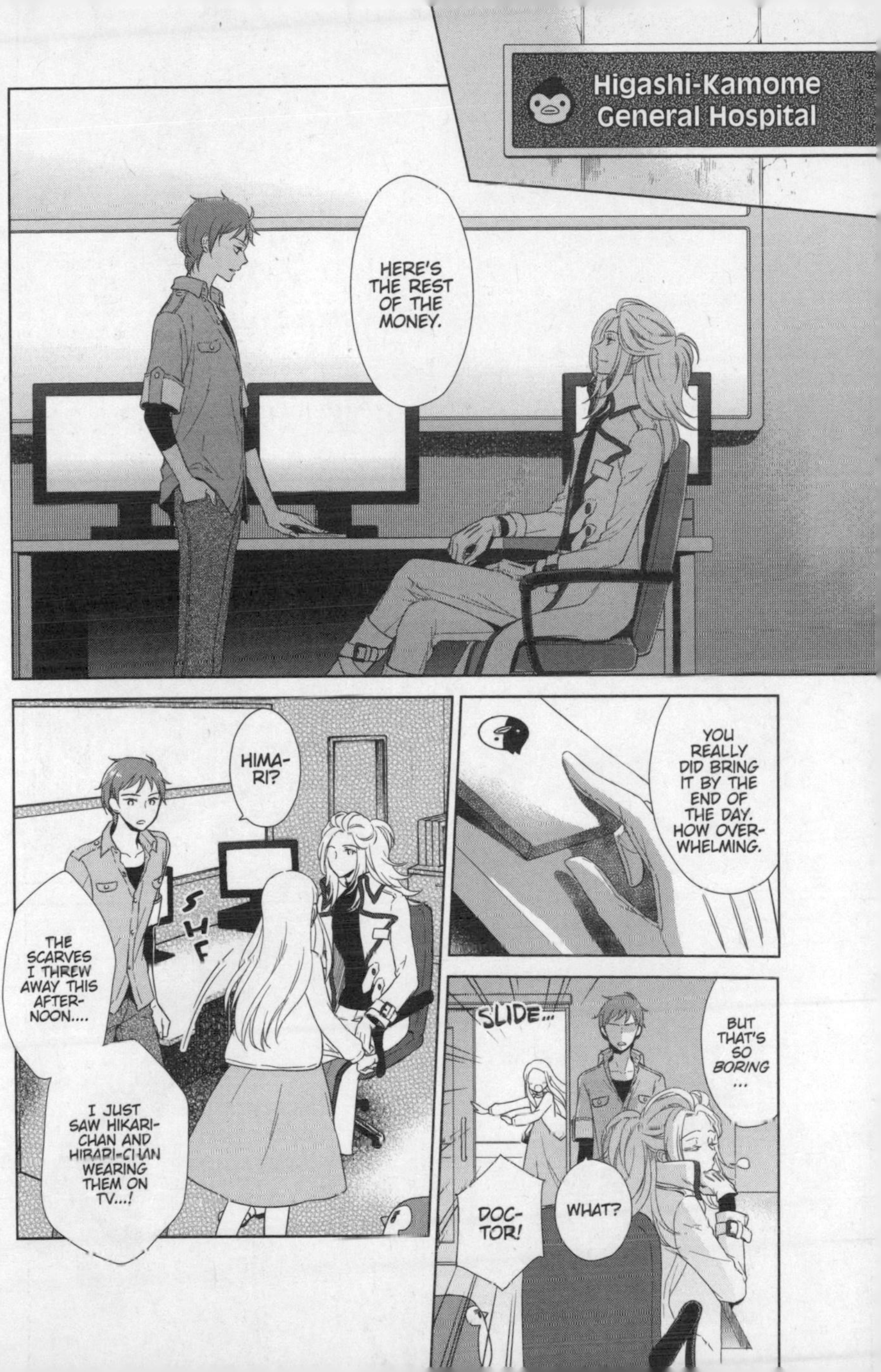
Higashi-Kamome General Hospital
HERE'S THE REST OF THE MONEY.
YOU REALLY DID BRING IT BY THE END OF THE DAY. HOW OVER-WHELMING.
BUT THAT'S SO *BORING*...
SLIDE...
WHAT?
DOC-TOR!
HIMA-RI?
SHF
THE SCARVES I THREW AWAY THIS AFTER-NOON....
I JUST SAW HIKARI-CHAN AND HIBARI-CHAN WEARING THEM ON TV...!

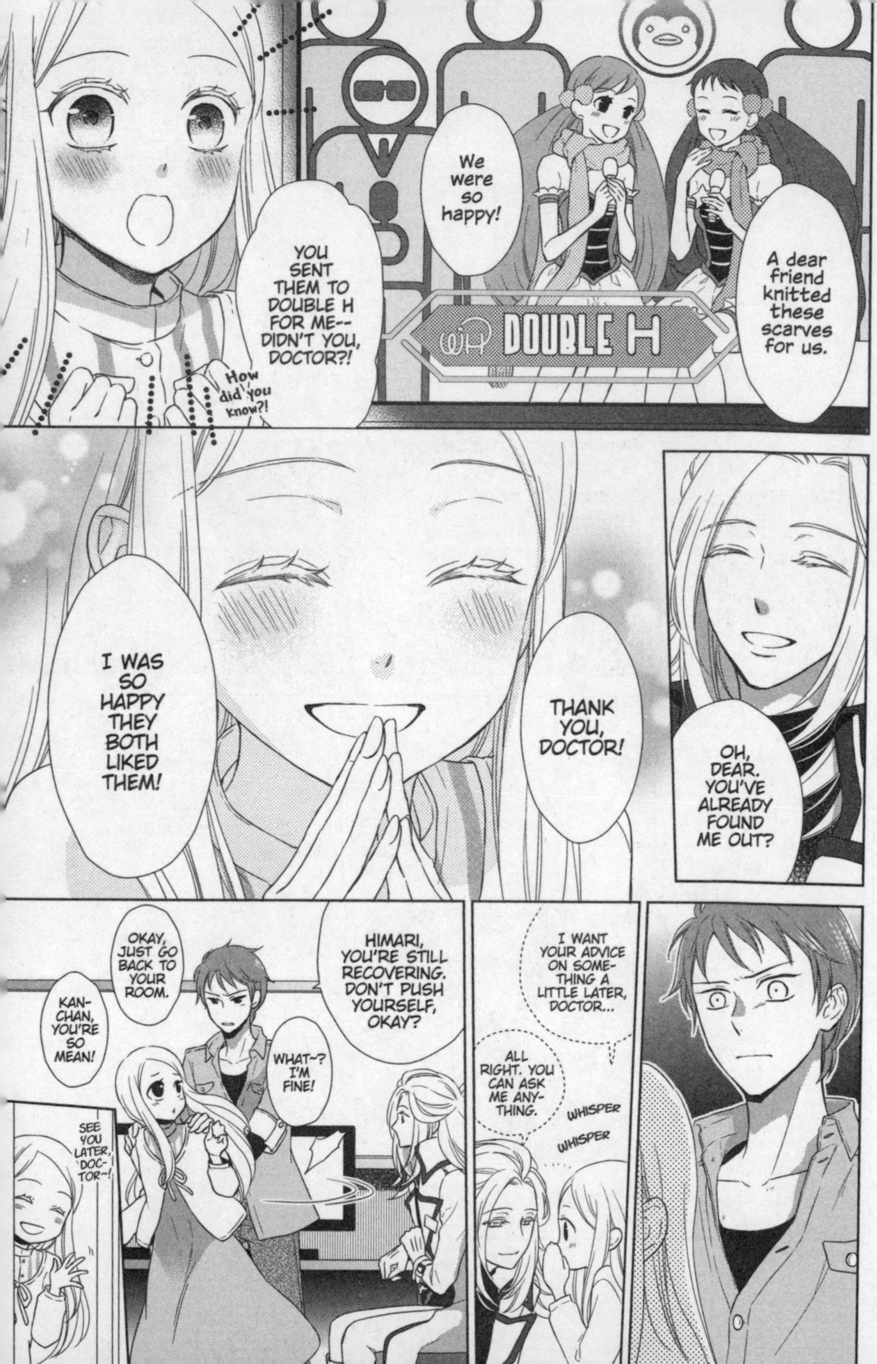
DOUBLE H
A dear friend knitted these scarves for us.
We were so happy!
YOU SENT THEM TO DOUBLE H FOR ME--DIDN'T YOU, DOCTOR?!
How did you know?!
OH, DEAR. YOU'VE ALREADY FOUND ME OUT?
THANK YOU, DOCTOR!
I WAS SO HAPPY THEY BOTH LIKED THEM!
I WANT YOUR ADVICE ON SOME-THING A LITTLE LATER, DOCTOR...
ALL RIGHT. YOU CAN ASK ME ANY-THING.
WHISPER
WHISPER
HIMARI, YOU'RE STILL RECOVERING. DON'T PUSH YOURSELF, OKAY?
WHAT~? I'M FINE!
OKAY, JUST GO BACK TO YOUR ROOM.
KAN-CHAN, YOU'RE SO MEAN!
SEE YOU LATER, DOC-TOR~!

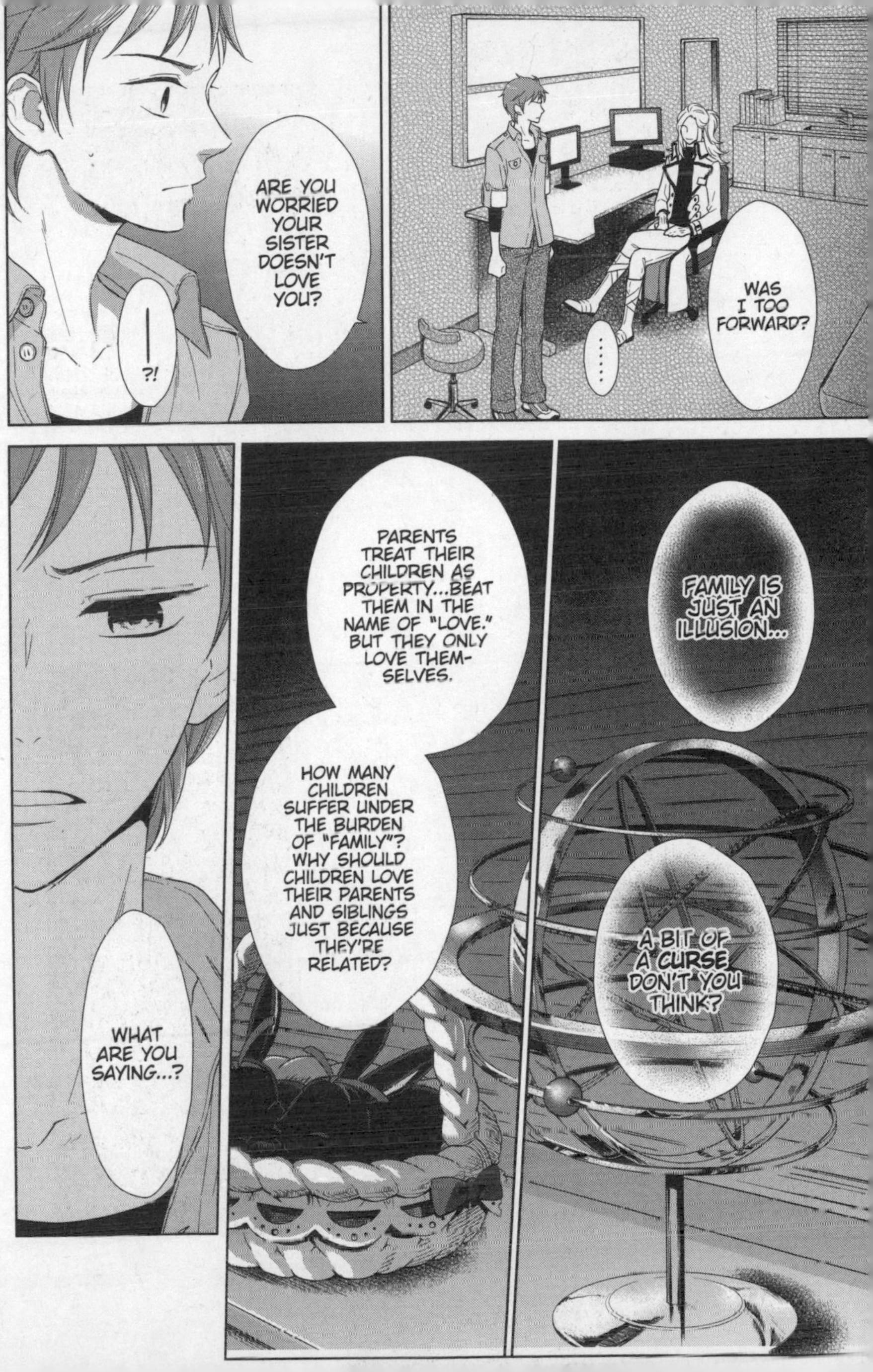
WAS I TOO FORWARD?
......
ARE YOU WORRIED YOUR SISTER DOESN'T LOVE YOU?
—?!
FAMILY IS JUST AN ILLUSION...
A BIT OF A CURSE DON'T YOU THINK?
PARENTS TREAT THEIR CHILDREN AS PROPERTY...BEAT THEM IN THE NAME OF "LOVE." BUT THEY ONLY LOVE THEM-SELVES.
HOW MANY CHILDREN SUFFER UNDER THE BURDEN OF "FAMILY"? WHY SHOULD CHILDREN LOVE THEIR PARENTS AND SIBLINGS JUST BECAUSE THEY'RE RELATED?
WHAT ARE YOU SAYING...?

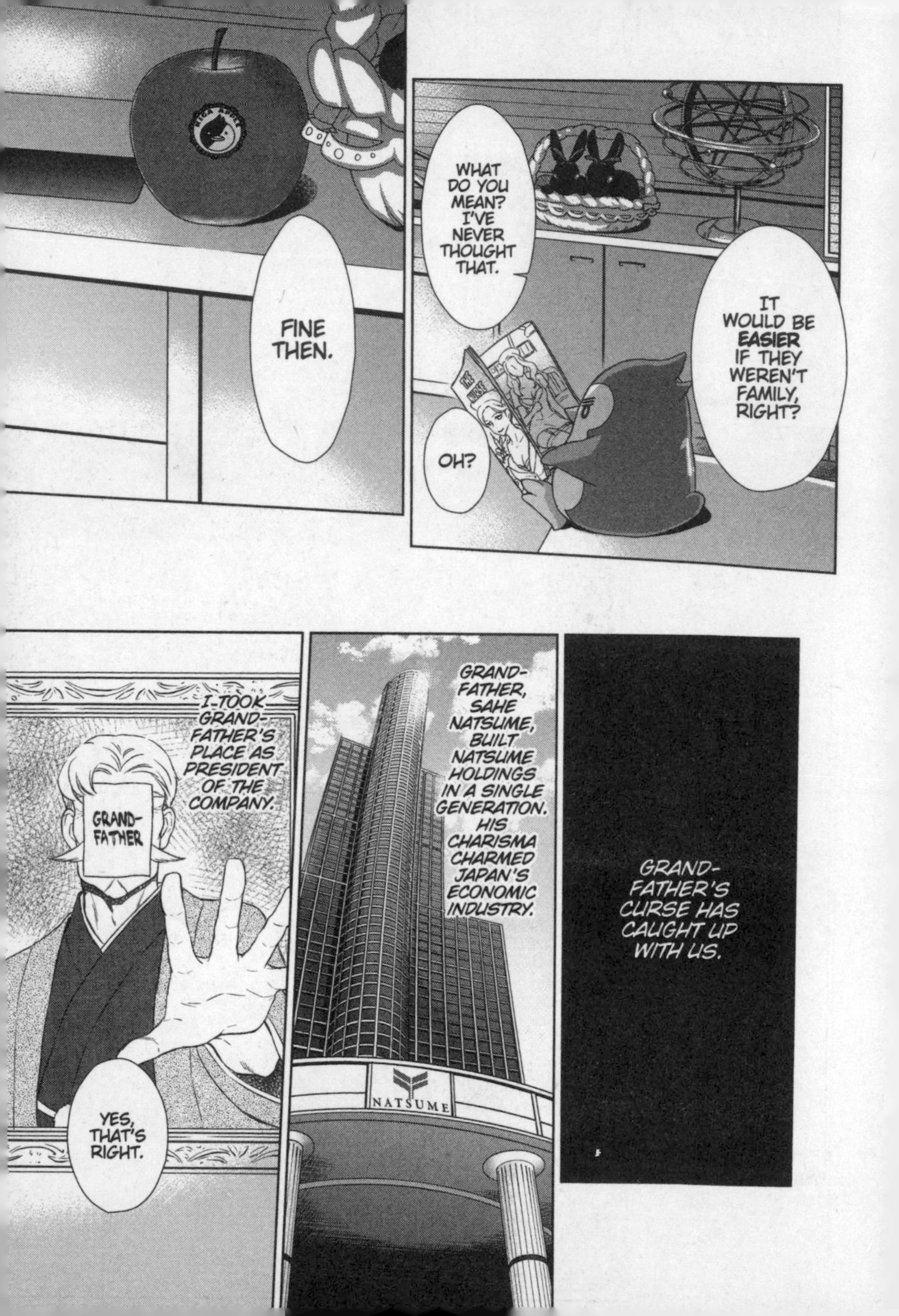
IT WOULD BE EASIER IF THEY WEREN'T FAMILY, RIGHT?
WHAT DO YOU MEAN? I'VE NEVER THOUGHT THAT.
OH?
FINE THEN.
GRAND-FATHER'S CURSE HAS CAUGHT UP WITH US.
GRAND-FATHER, SAHE NATSUME, BUILT NATSUME HOLDINGS IN A SINGLE GENERATION. HIS CHARISMA CHARMED JAPAN'S ECONOMIC INDUSTRY.
NATSUME
I TOOK GRAND-FATHER'S PLACE AS PRESIDENT OF THE COMPANY.
GRAND-FATHER
YES, THAT'S RIGHT.

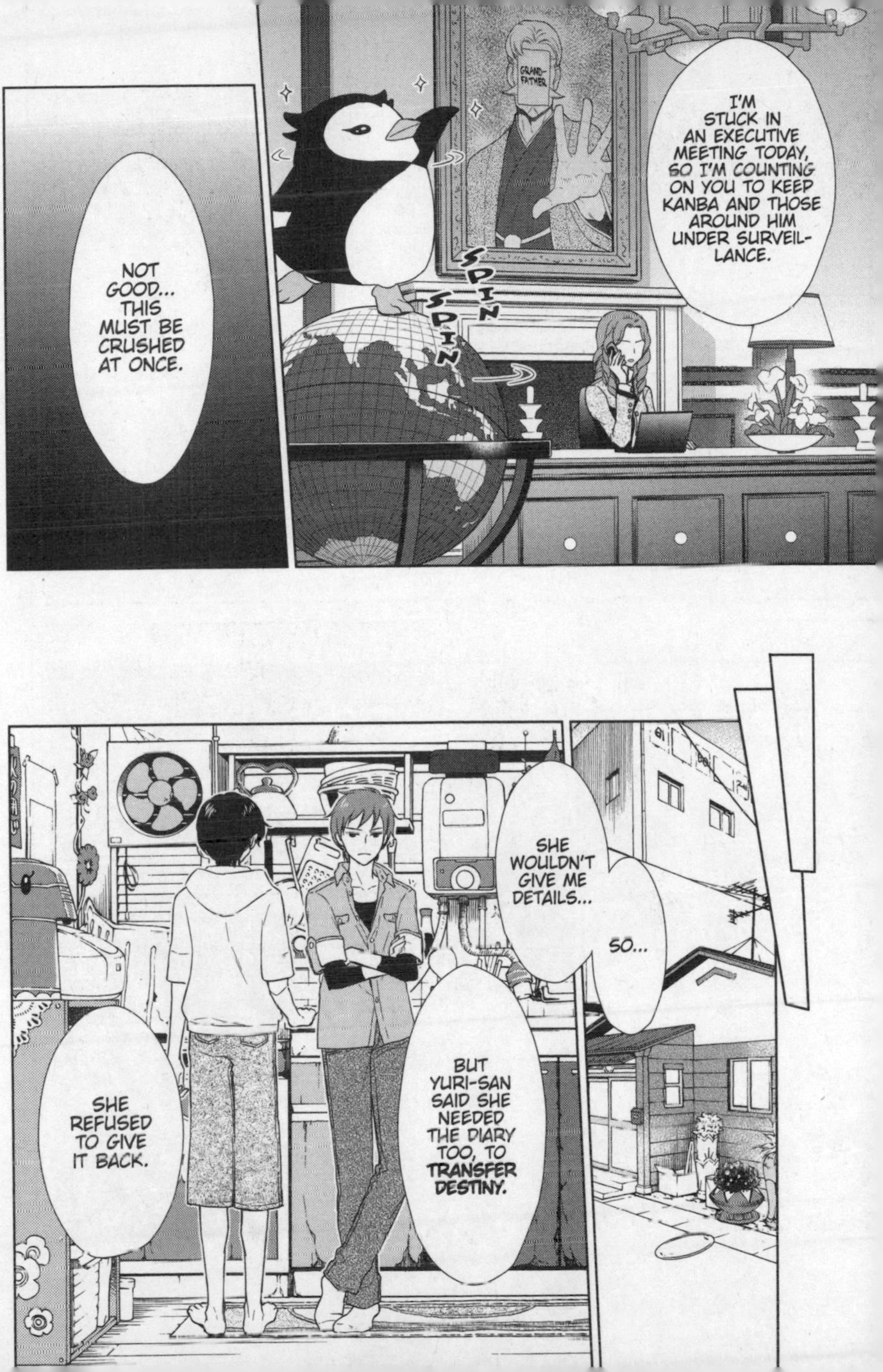
I'M STUCK IN AN EXECUTIVE MEETING TODAY, SO I'M COUNTING ON YOU TO KEEP KANBA AND THOSE AROUND HIM UNDER SURVEIL-LANCE.
GRAND-FATHER
SPIN
SPIN
NOT GOOD... THIS MUST BE CRUSHED AT ONCE.
SHE WOULDN'T GIVE ME DETAILS...
SO...
BUT YURI-SAN SAID SHE NEEDED THE DIARY TOO, TO TRANSFER DESTINY.
SHE REFUSED TO GIVE IT BACK.

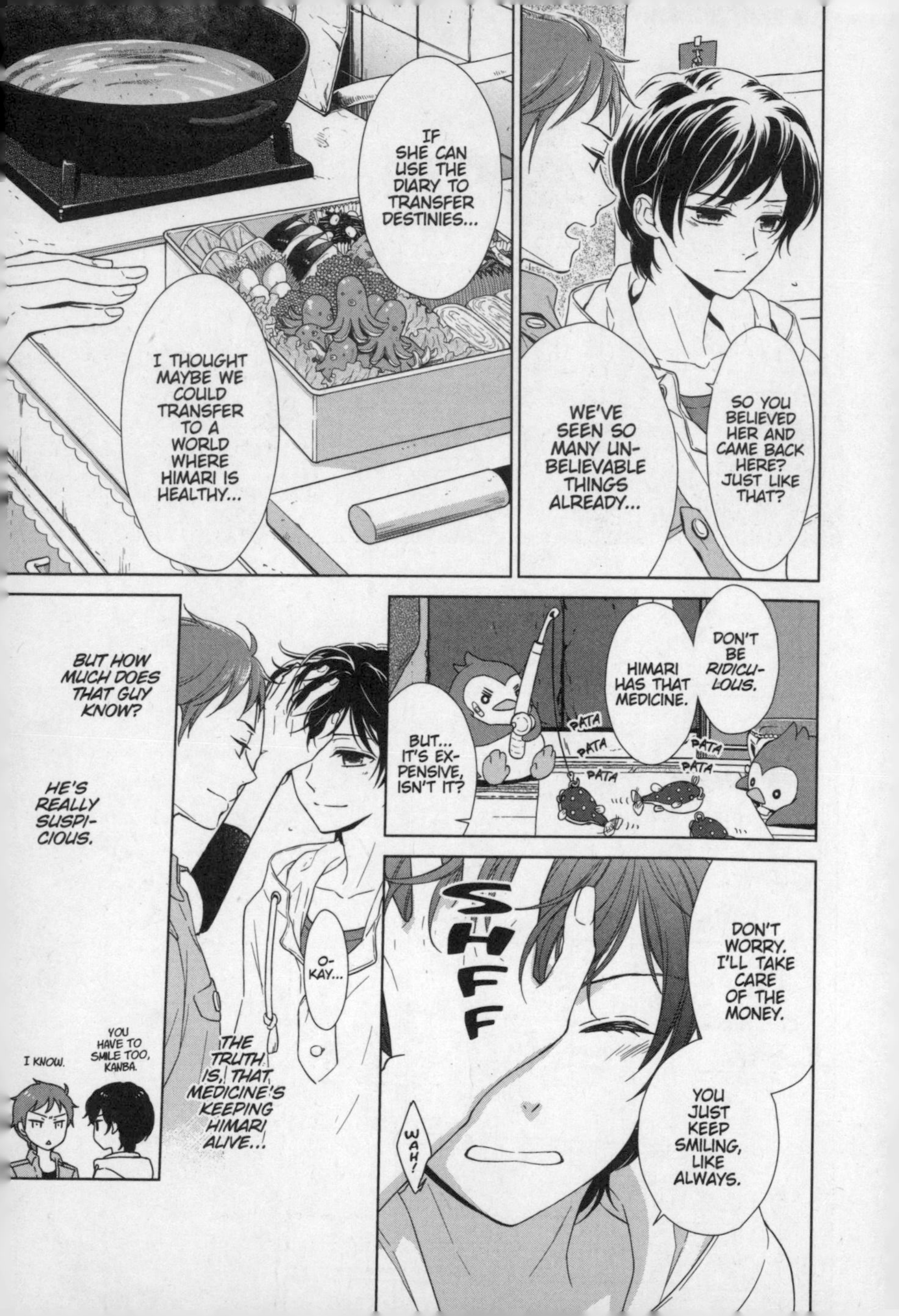
SO YOU BELIEVED HER AND CAME BACK HERE? JUST LIKE THAT?
WE'VE SEEN SO MANY UN-BELIEVABLE THINGS ALREADY...
IF SHE CAN USE THE DIARY TO TRANSFER DESTINIES...
I THOUGHT MAYBE WE COULD TRANSFER TO A WORLD WHERE HIMARI IS HEALTHY...
DON'T BE RIDICULOUS.
HIMARI HAS THAT MEDICINE.
PATA PATA PATA
PATA PATA
BUT... IT'S EXPENSIVE, ISN'T IT?
SHFF
DON'T WORRY. I'LL TAKE CARE OF THE MONEY.
YOU JUST KEEP SMILING, LIKE ALWAYS.
WAH!
BUT HOW MUCH DOES THAT GUY KNOW?
HE'S REALLY SUSPICIOUS.
O-KAY...
THE TRUTH IS, THAT MEDICINE'S KEEPING HIMARI ALIVE...
YOU HAVE TO SMILE TOO, KANBA.
I KNOW.

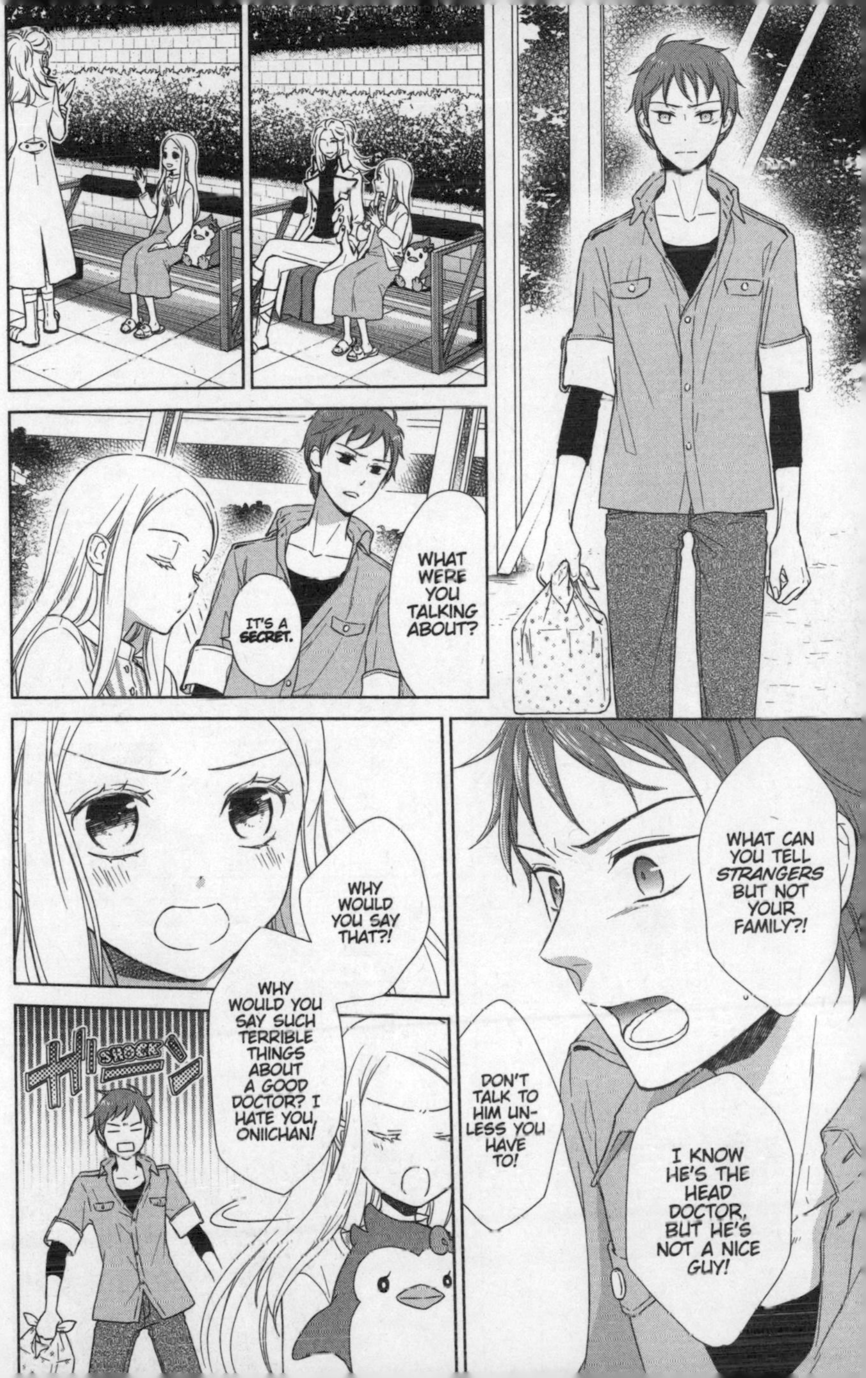
WHAT WERE YOU TALKING ABOUT?
IT'S A SECRET.
WHAT CAN YOU TELL STRANGERS BUT NOT YOUR FAMILY?!
I KNOW HE'S THE HEAD DOCTOR, BUT HE'S NOT A NICE GUY!
DON'T TALK TO HIM UNLESS YOU HAVE TO!
WHY WOULD YOU SAY THAT?!
WHY WOULD YOU SAY SUCH TERRIBLE THINGS ABOUT A GOOD DOCTOR? I HATE YOU, ONIICHAN!
SHOCK

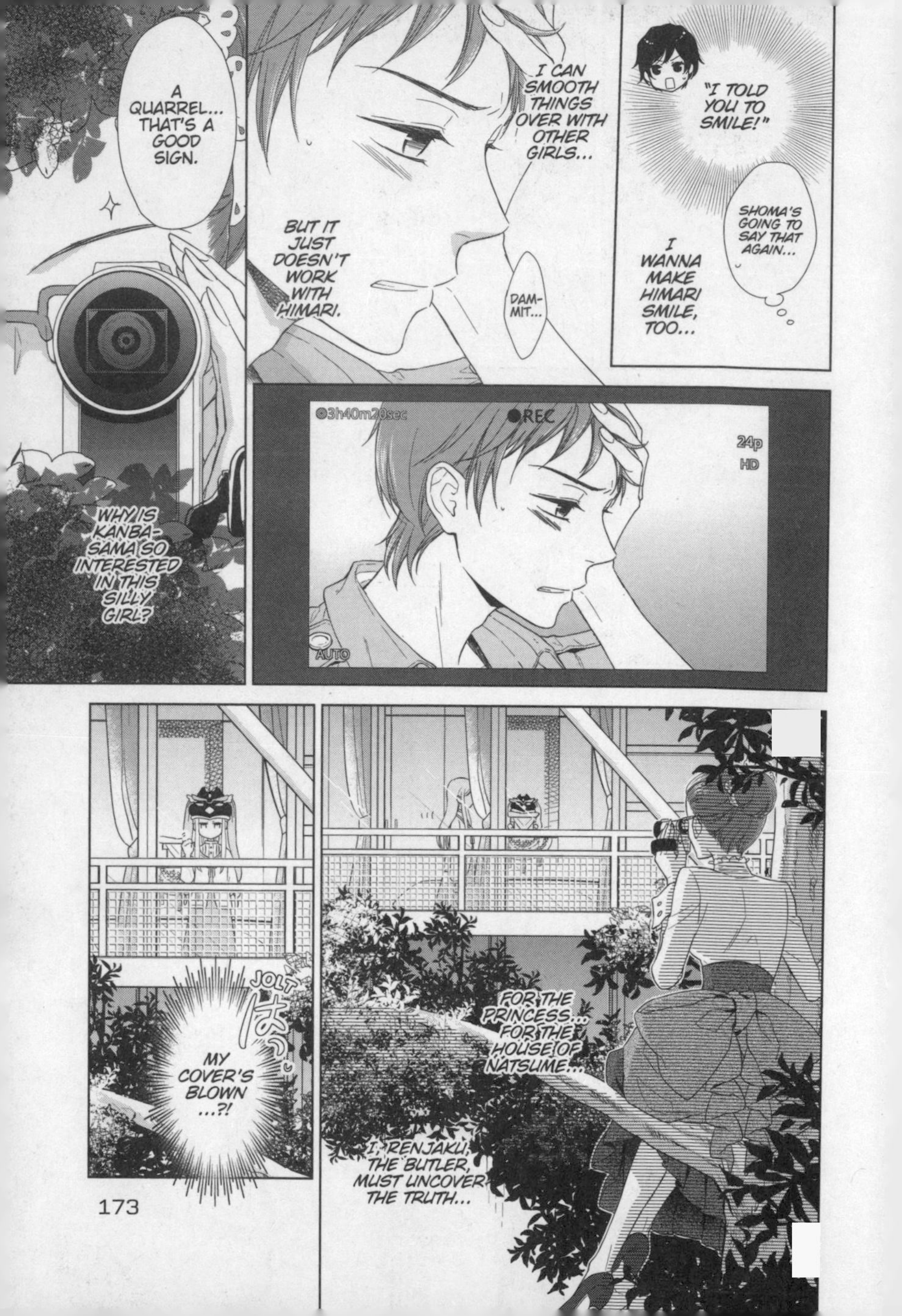
"I TOLD YOU TO SMILE!"
SHOMA'S GOING TO SAY THAT AGAIN...
I WANNA MAKE HIMARI SMILE, TOO...
I CAN SMOOTH THINGS OVER WITH OTHER GIRLS...
BUT IT JUST DOESN'T WORK WITH HIMARI.
DAM-MIT...
3h40m20sec
REC
24p
HD
AUTO
A QUARREL... THAT'S A GOOD SIGN.
WHY IS KANBA-SAMA SO INTERESTED IN THIS SILLY GIRL?
FOR THE PRINCESS... FOR THE HOUSE OF NATSUME...
I, RENJAKU, THE BUTLER, MUST UNCOVER THE TRUTH...
JOLT
はっ
MY COVER'S BLOWN...?!

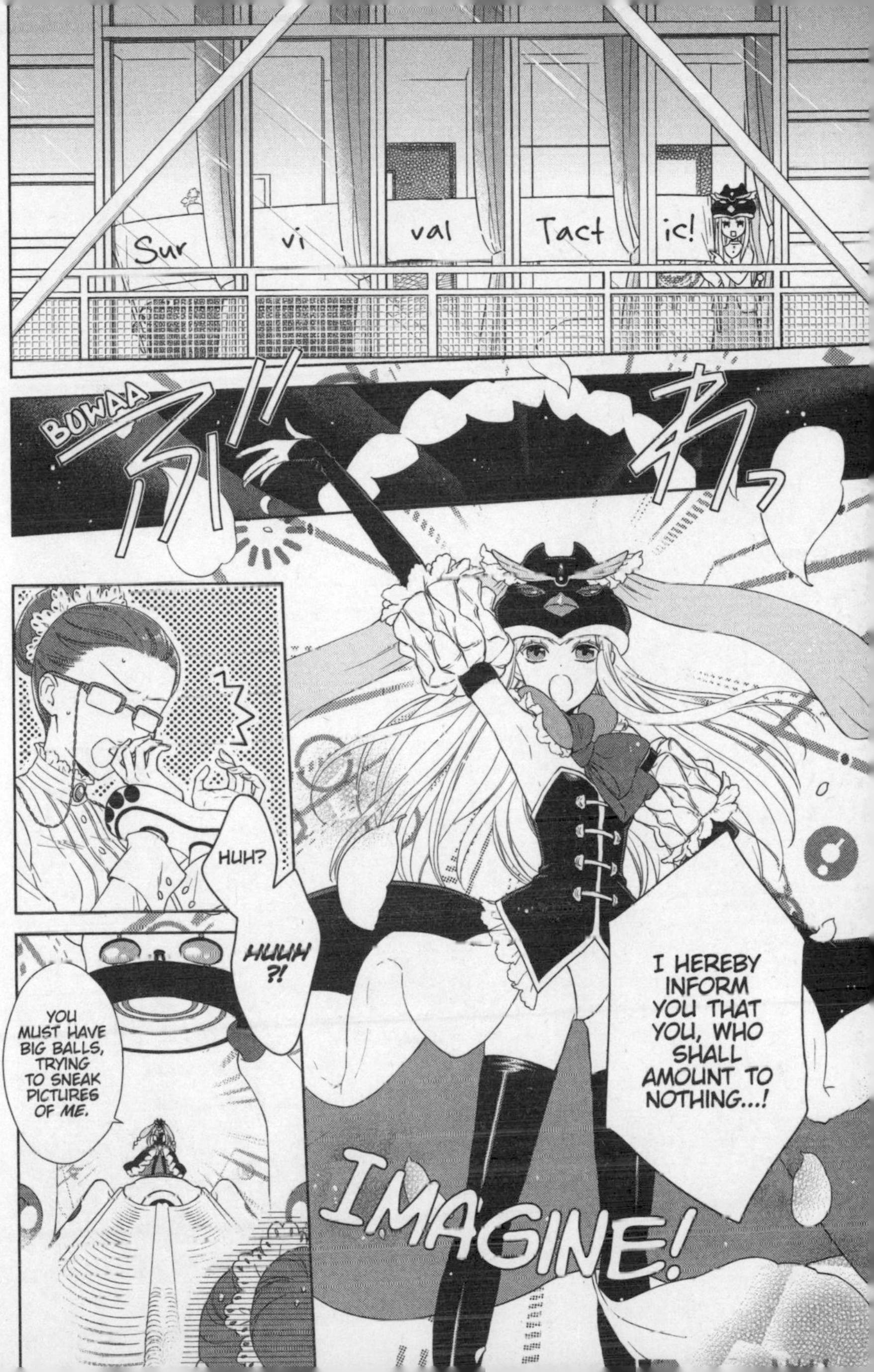
Sur vi val Tact ic!
BOWAA
I HEREBY INFORM YOU THAT YOU, WHO SHALL AMOUNT TO NOTHING...!
IMAGINE!
HUH?
HUUH ?!
YOU MUST HAVE BIG BALLS, TRYING TO SNEAK PICTURES OF ME.

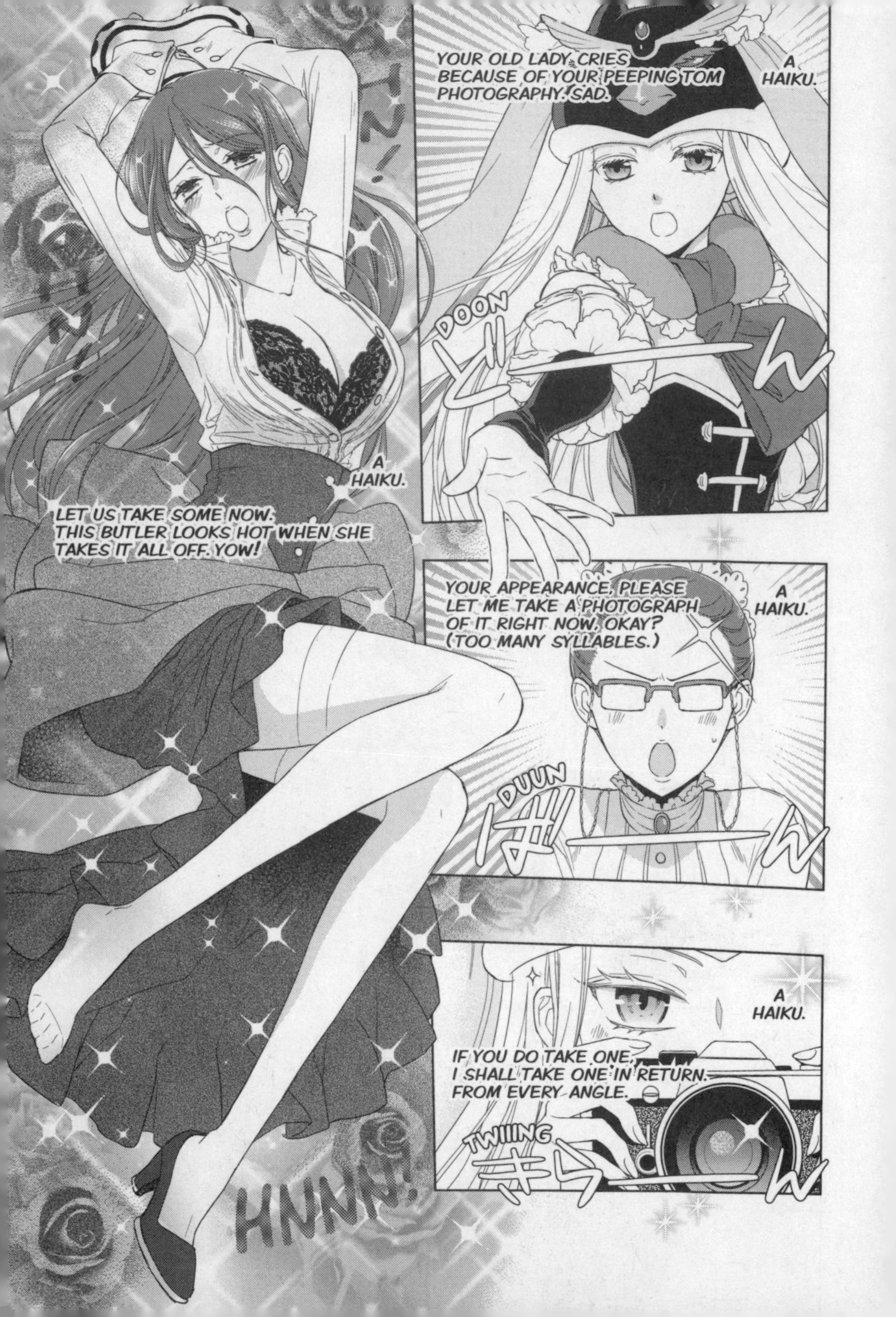
YOUR OLD LADY CRIES BECAUSE OF YOUR PEEPING TOM PHOTOGRAPHY. SAD.
A HAIKU.
DOON
YOUR APPEARANCE, PLEASE LET ME TAKE A PHOTOGRAPH OF IT RIGHT NOW, OKAY? (TOO MANY SYLLABLES.)
A HAIKU.
DUUN
A HAIKU.
IF YOU DO TAKE ONE, I SHALL TAKE ONE IN RETURN. FROM EVERY ANGLE.
TWIIING
A HAIKU.
LET US TAKE SOME NOW. THIS BUTLER LOOKS HOT WHEN SHE TAKES IT ALL OFF. YOW!
HNNN!

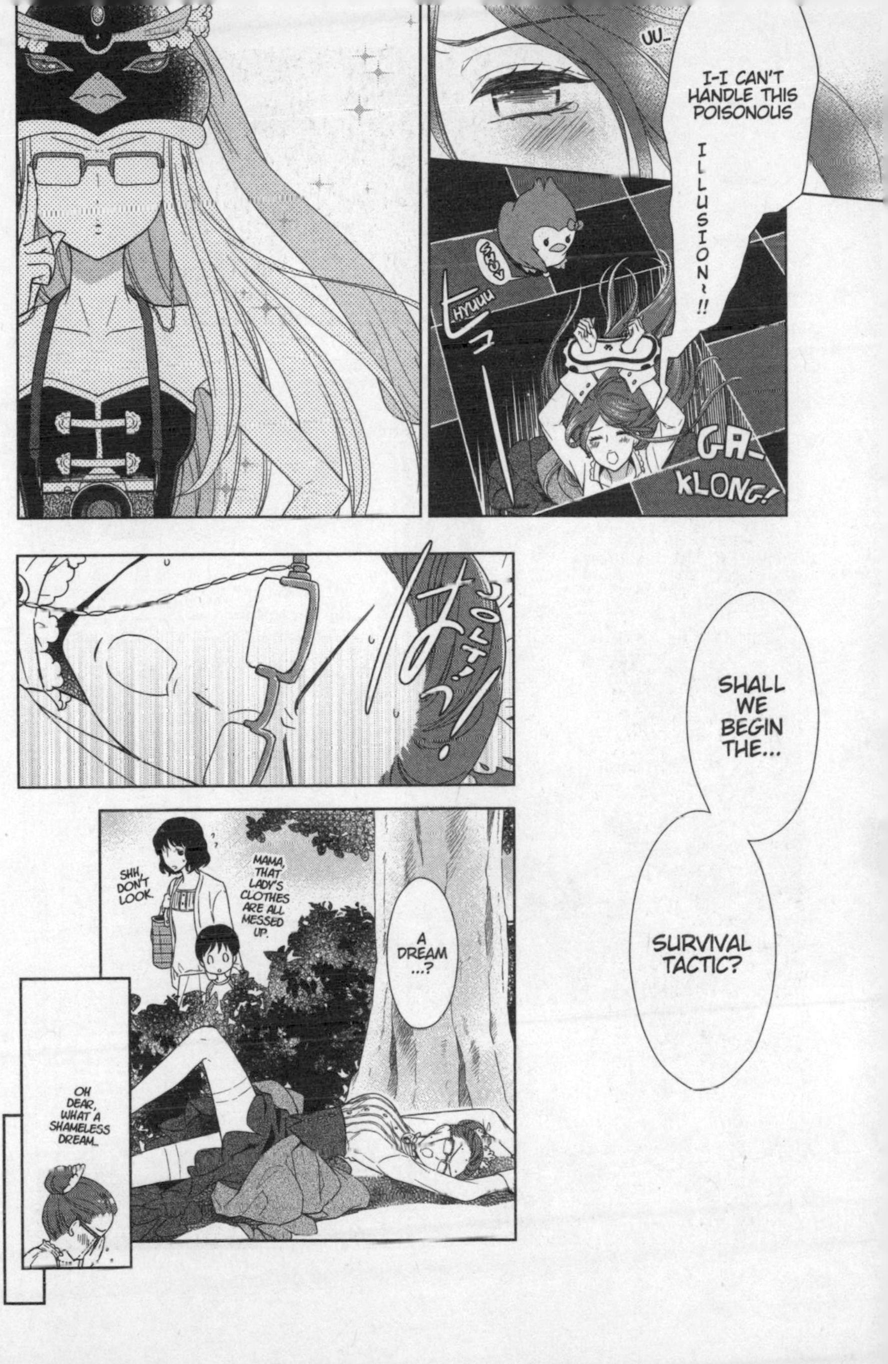
UU...
I-I CAN'T HANDLE THIS POISONOUS ILLUSION~!!
ヒュ HYUUU
GA-KLONG!
SHALL WE BEGIN THE...
SURVIVAL TACTIC?
はっ!
ビクッ!
A DREAM...?
MAMA, THAT LADY'S CLOTHES ARE ALL MESSED UP.
SHH, DON'T LOOK.
OH DEAR, WHAT A SHAMELESS DREAM...

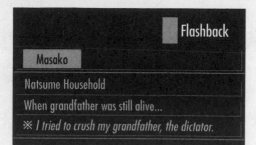

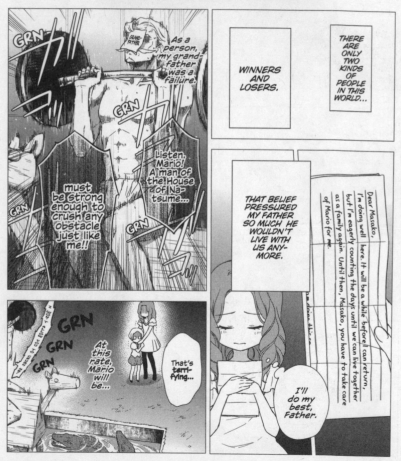

Flashback

Masako

Natsume Household

When grandfather was still alive...

※ *I tried to crush my grandfather, the dictator.*

THERE ARE ONLY TWO KINDS OF PEOPLE IN THIS WORLD...
WINNERS AND LOSERS.
THAT BELIEF PRESSURED MY FATHER SO MUCH HE WOULDN'T LIVE WITH US ANYMORE.
Dear Masako,
I'm doing well here. It will be a while before I can return, but I'm eagerly counting the days until we can live together as a family again. Until then, Masako, you have to take care of Mario for me.
I'll do my best, Father.
GRN
GRAND-FATHER
As a person, my grandfather was a failure.
GRN
Listen, Mario! A man of the House of Natsume...
must be strong enough to crush any obstacle just like me!!
GRN
GRN
GRN
GRN
GRN
That's terrifying...
At this rate, Mario will be...

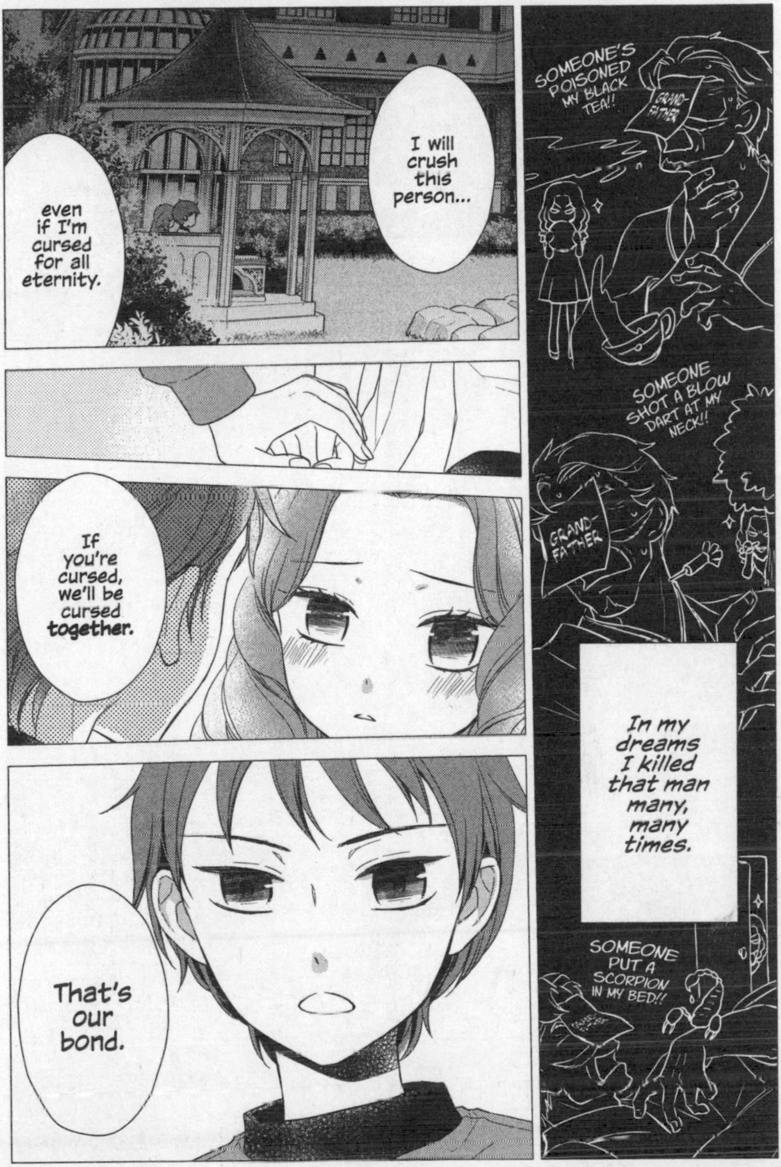

SOMEONE'S POISONED MY BLACK TEA!!
GRAND-FATHER
SOMEONE SHOT A BLOW DART AT MY NECK!!
GRAND-FATHER
In my dreams I killed that man many, many times.
SOMEONE PUT A SCORPION IN MY BED!!
I will crush this person...
even if I'm cursed for all eternity.
If you're cursed, we'll be cursed together.
That's our bond.

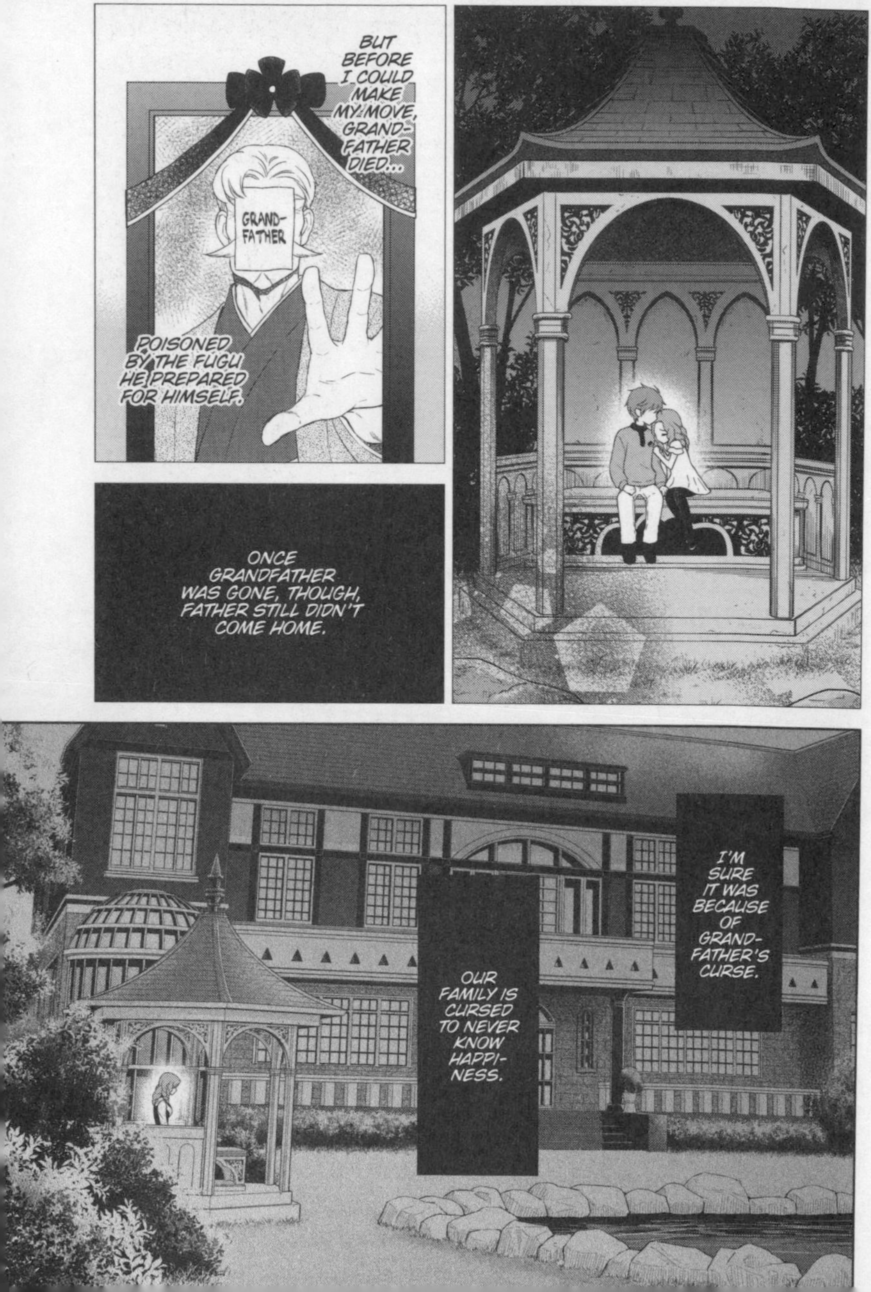
BUT BEFORE I COULD MAKE MY MOVE, GRAND-FATHER DIED...
GRAND-FATHER
POISONED BY THE FUGU HE PREPARED FOR HIMSELF.
ONCE GRANDFATHER WAS GONE, THOUGH, FATHER STILL DIDN'T COME HOME.
I'M SURE IT WAS BECAUSE OF GRAND-FATHER'S CURSE.
OUR FAMILY IS CURSED TO NEVER KNOW HAPPI-NESS.

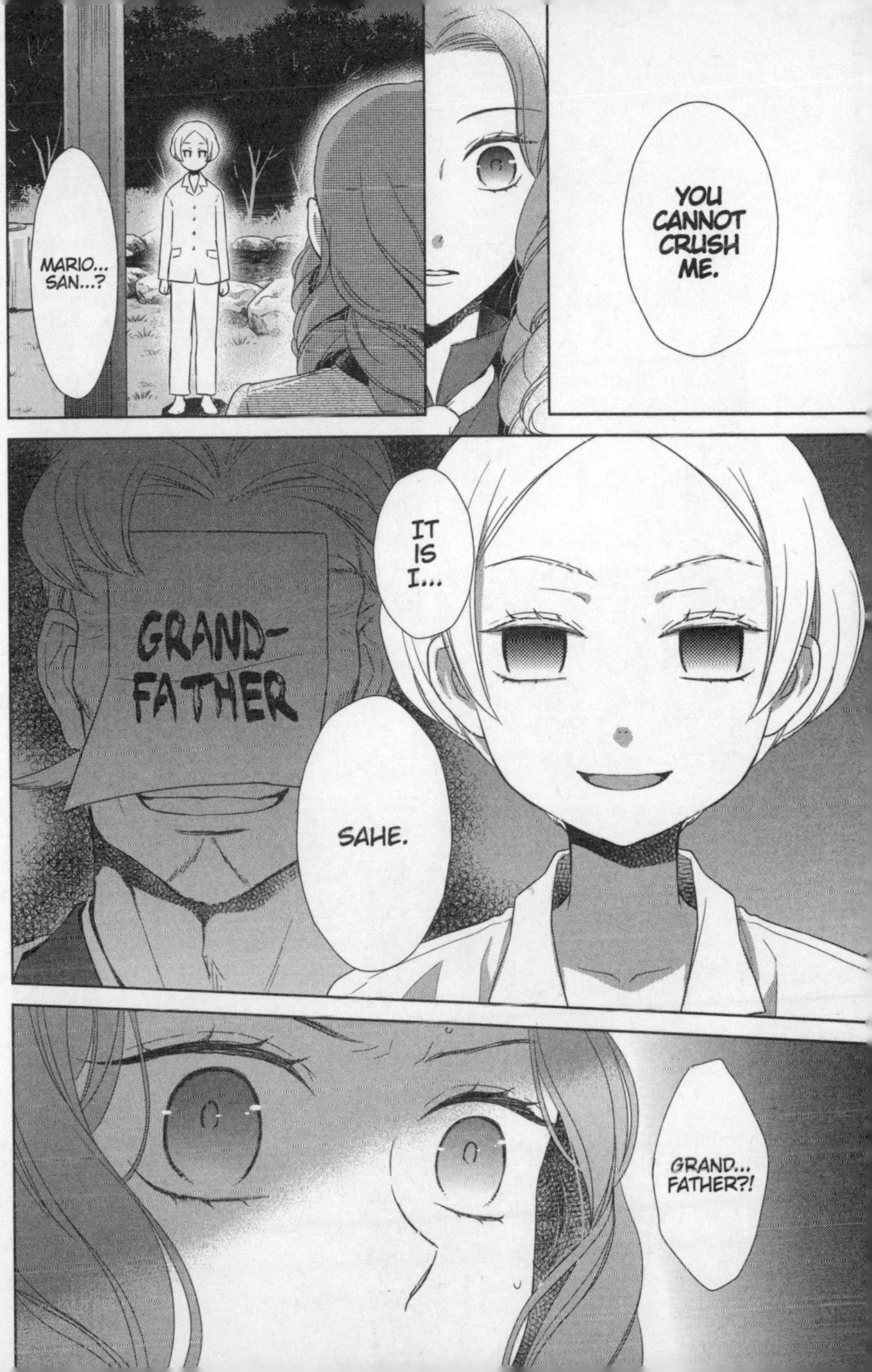
YOU CANNOT CRUSH ME.
MARIO... SAN...?
IT IS I...
GRAND-FATHER
SAHE.
GRAND... FATHER?!

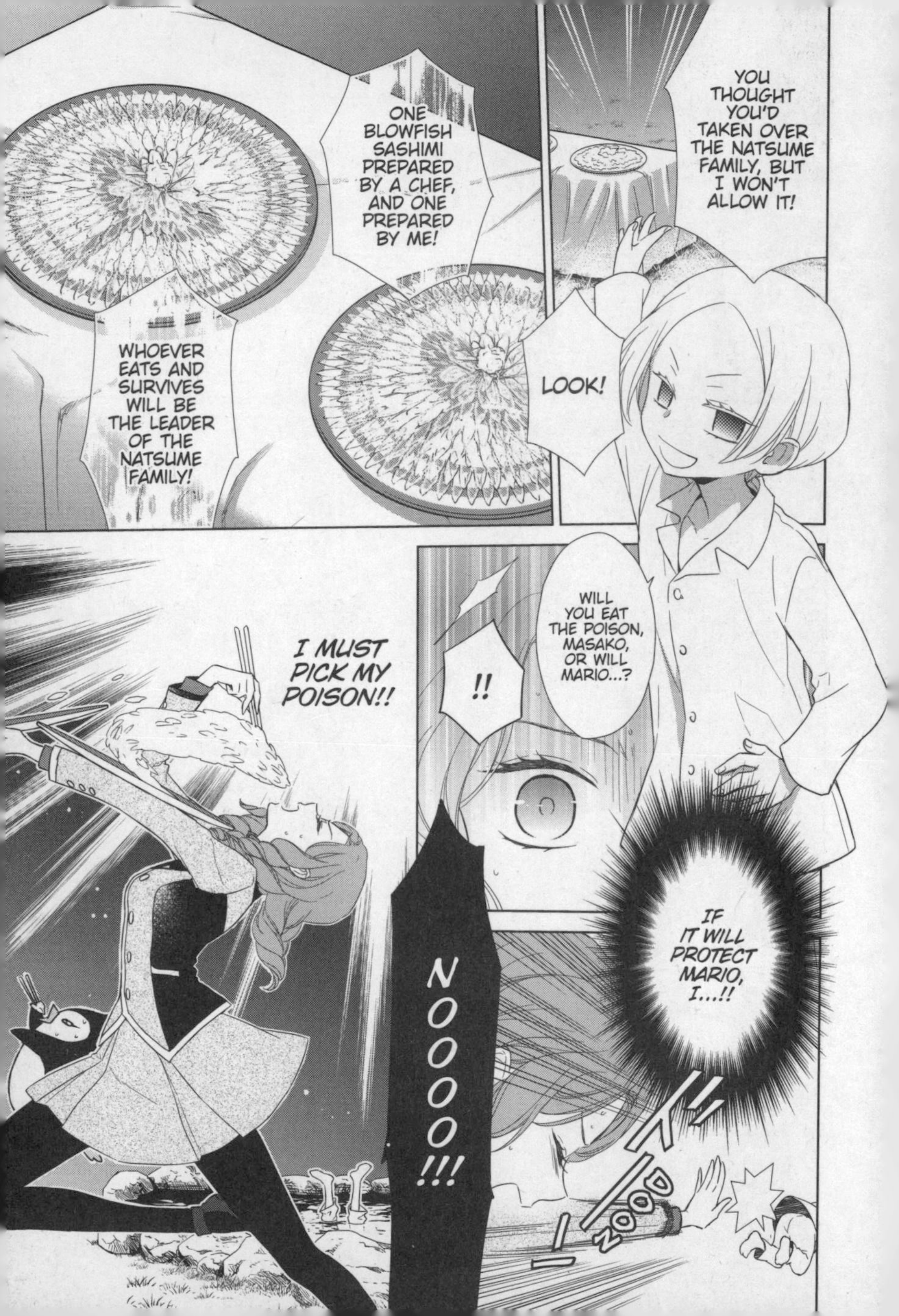
YOU THOUGHT YOU'D TAKEN OVER THE NATSUME FAMILY, BUT I WON'T ALLOW IT!
LOOK!
ONE BLOWFISH SASHIMI PREPARED BY A CHEF, AND ONE PREPARED BY ME!
WHOEVER EATS AND SURVIVES WILL BE THE LEADER OF THE NATSUME FAMILY!
WILL YOU EAT THE POISON, MASAKO, OR WILL MARIO...?
!!
IF IT WILL PROTECT MARIO, I...!!
I MUST PICK MY POISON!!
NOOOOO!!!

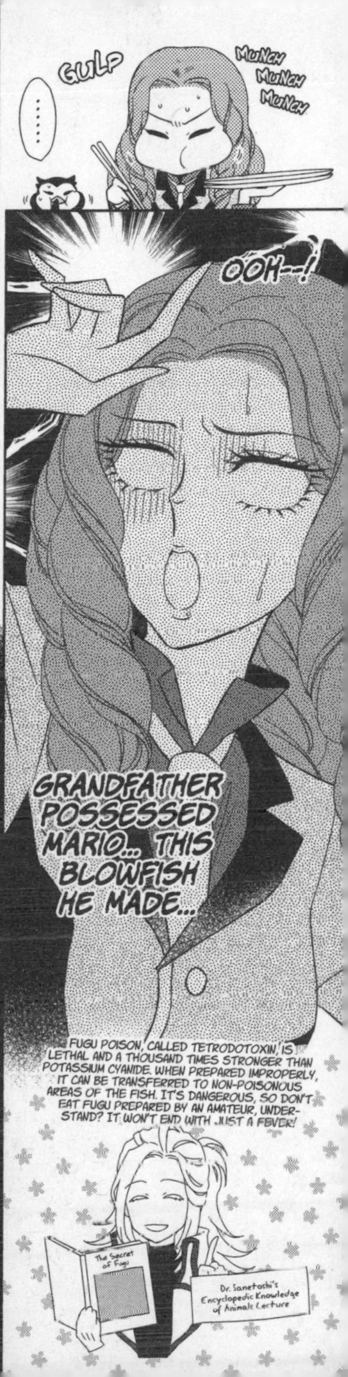
MUNCH
MUNCH
MUNCH
GULP
......
OOH--!
GRANDFATHER POSSESSED MARIO... THIS BLOWFISH HE MADE...
FUGU POISON, CALLED TETRODOTOXIN, IS LETHAL AND A THOUSAND TIMES STRONGER THAN POTASSIUM CYANIDE. WHEN PREPARED IMPROPERLY, IT CAN BE TRANSFERRED TO NON-POISONOUS AREAS OF THE FISH. IT'S DANGEROUS, SO DON'T EAT FUGU PREPARED BY AN AMATEUR, UNDERSTAND? IT WON'T END WITH JUST A FEVER!
The Secret of Fugu
Dr. Sanetoshi's Encyclopedic Knowledge of Animals Lecture
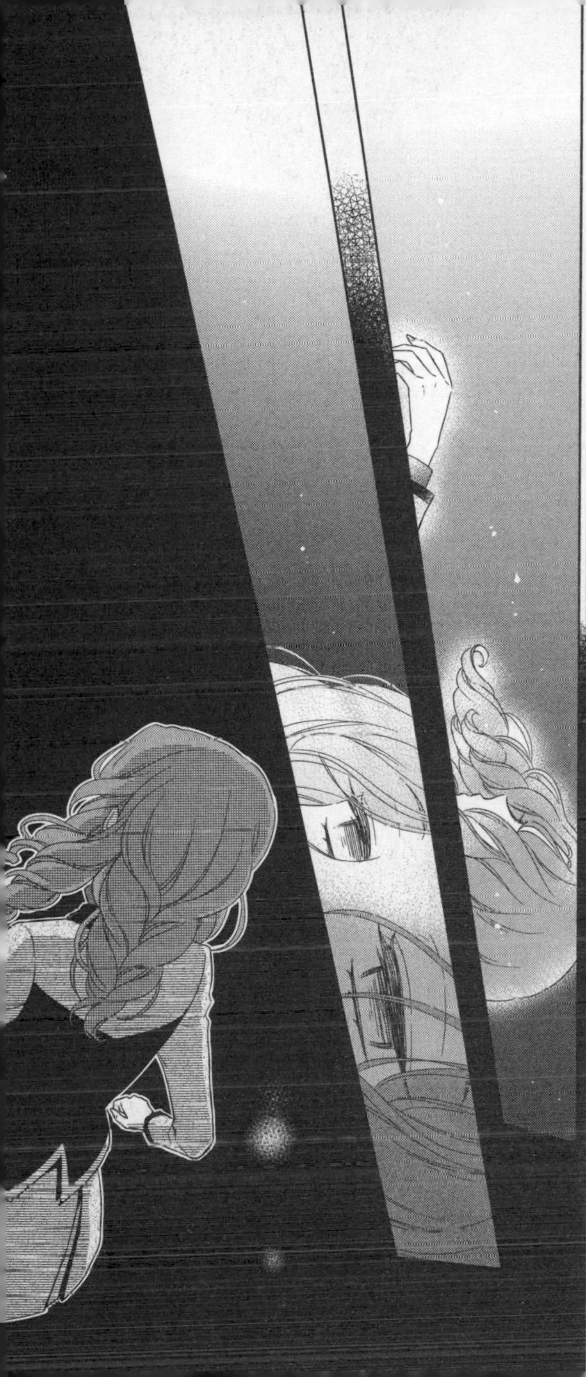

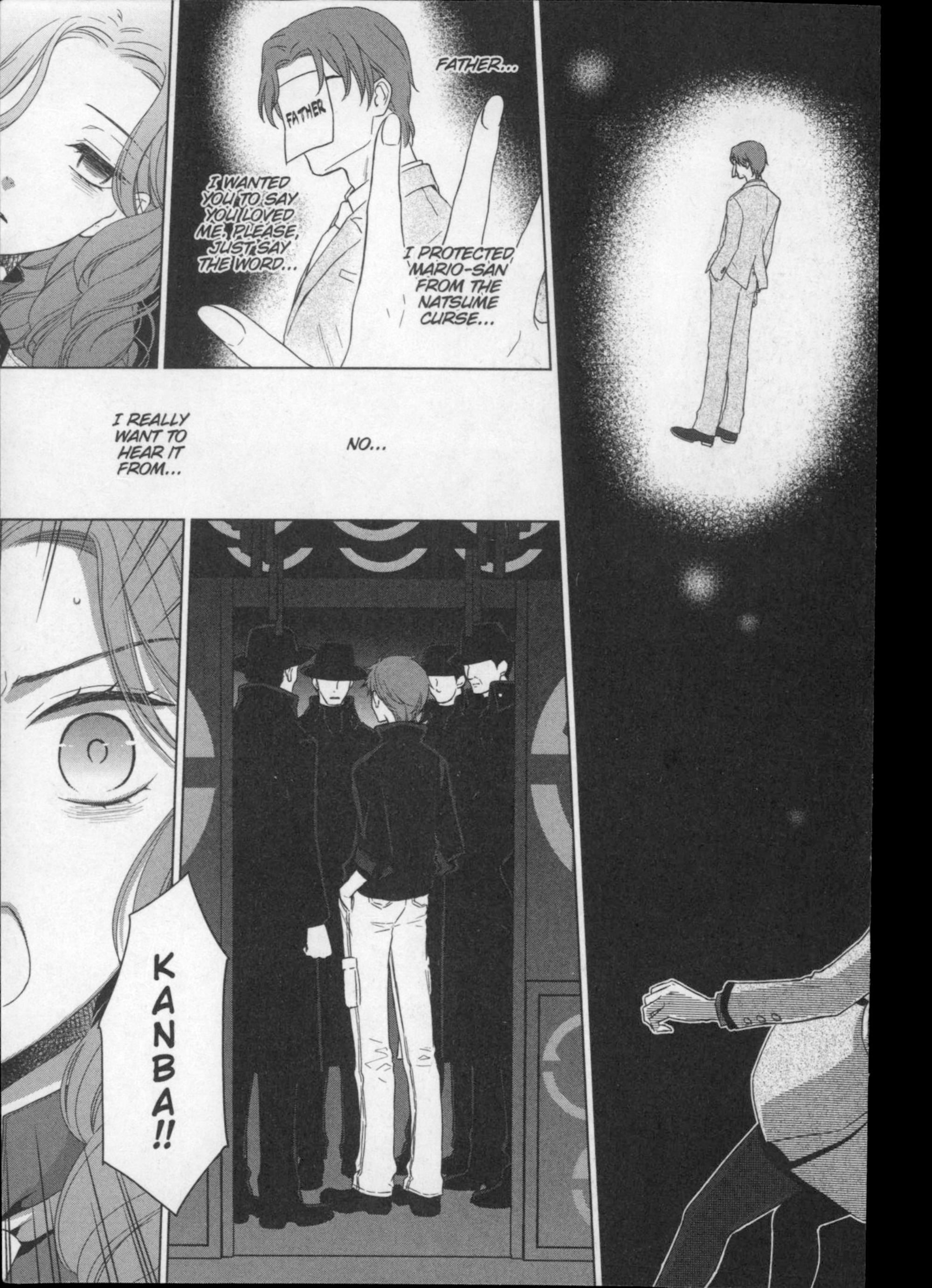
FATHER...
FATHER
I PROTECTED MARIO-SAN FROM THE NATSUME CURSE...
I WANTED YOU TO SAY YOU LOVED ME. PLEASE, JUST SAY THE WORD...
NO...
I REALLY WANT TO HEAR IT FROM...
KANBA!!

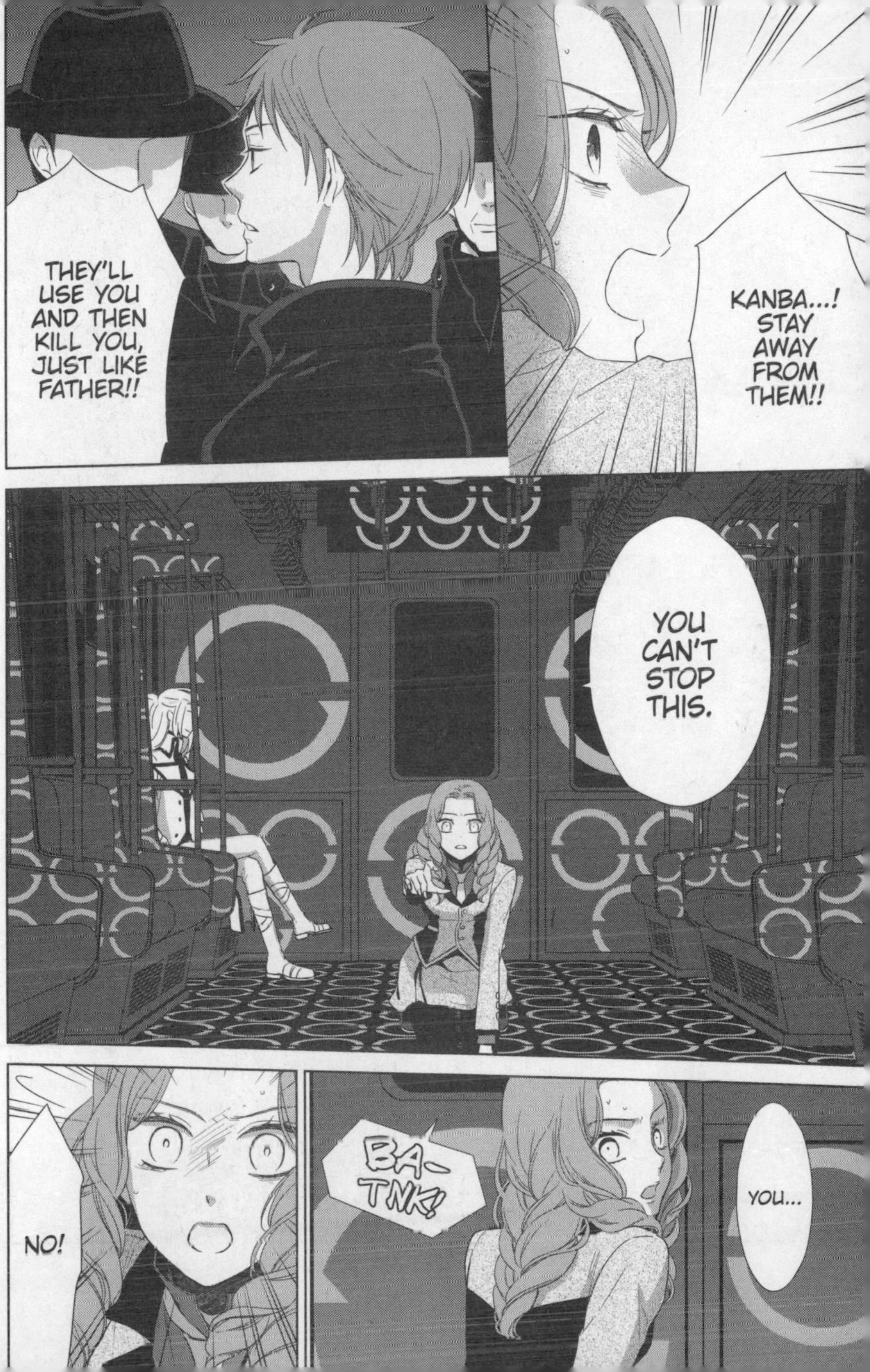
KANBA...! STAY AWAY FROM THEM!!
THEY'LL USE YOU AND THEN KILL YOU, JUST LIKE FATHER!!
YOU CAN'T STOP THIS.
YOU...
BA-TNK!
NO!

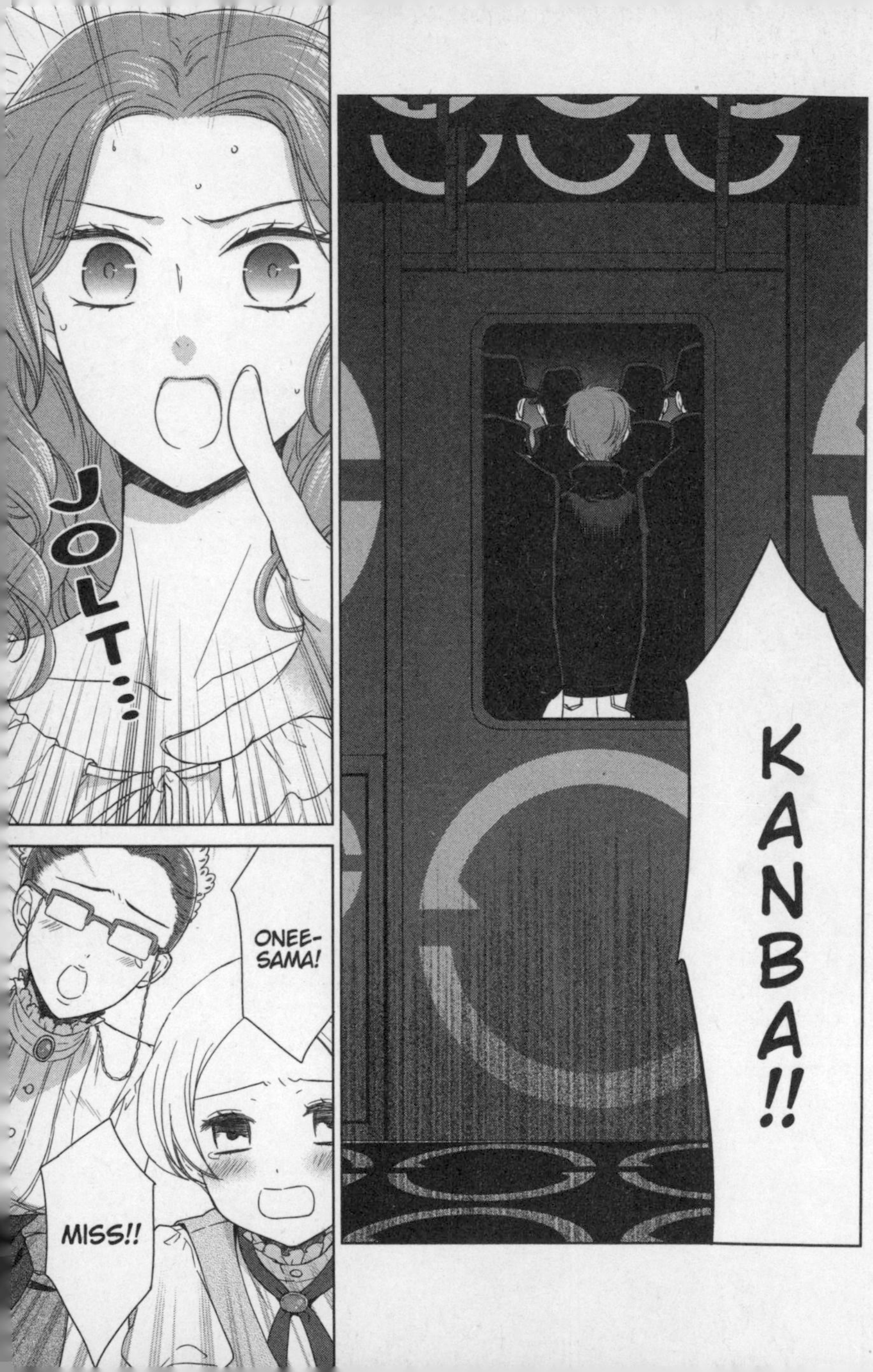
KANBA!!
JOLT...
ONEE-SAMA!
MISS!!

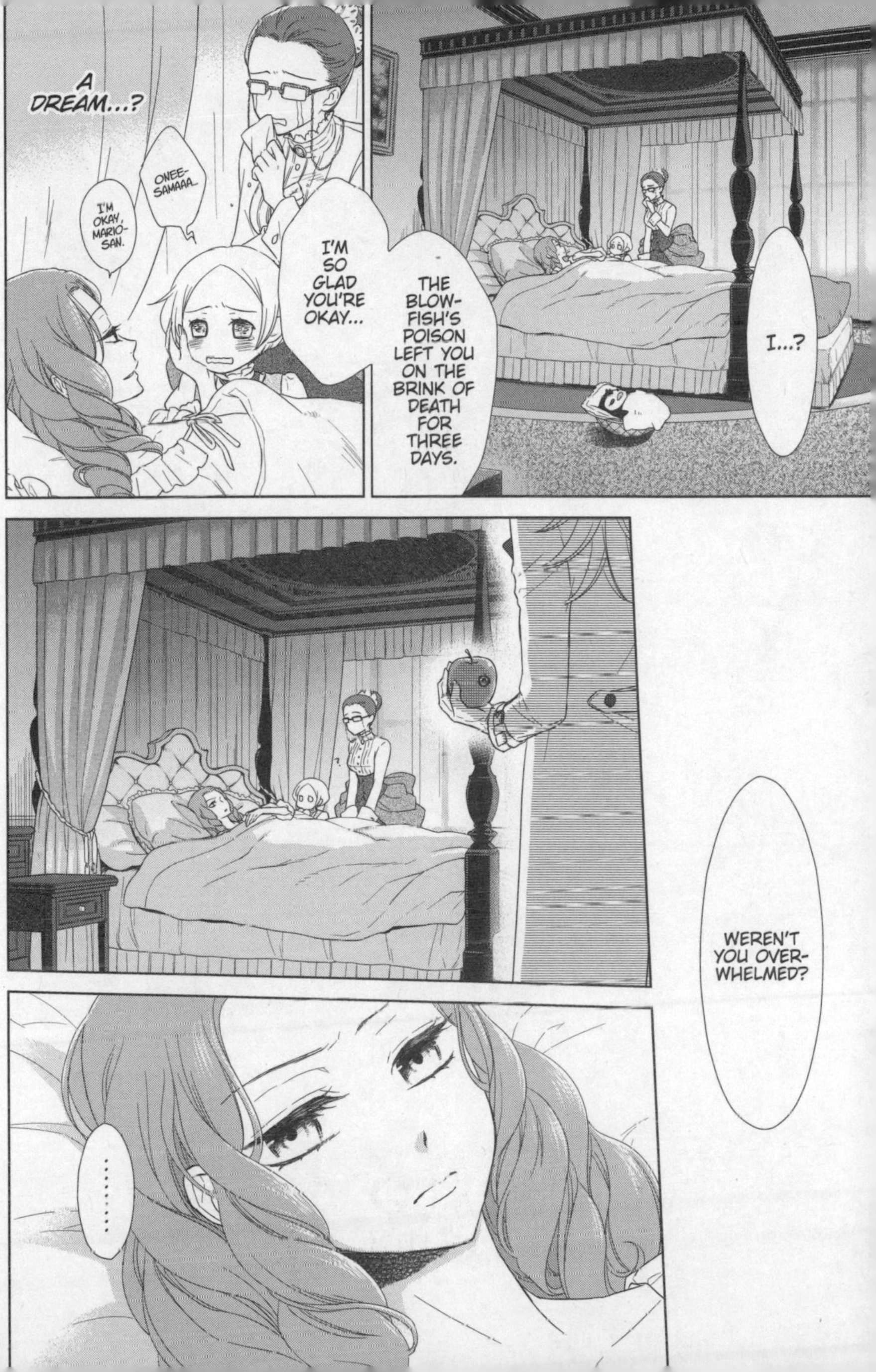
I...?
ONEE-SAMAAA...
I'M SO GLAD YOU'RE OKAY...
THE BLOW-FISH'S POISON LEFT YOU ON THE BRINK OF DEATH FOR THREE DAYS.
I'M OKAY, MARIO-SAN.
A DREAM...?
WEREN'T YOU OVER-WHELMED?
......

E N D

NEXT →
STATION
PENGUINDRUM

volume
#**4**

For Choosing This

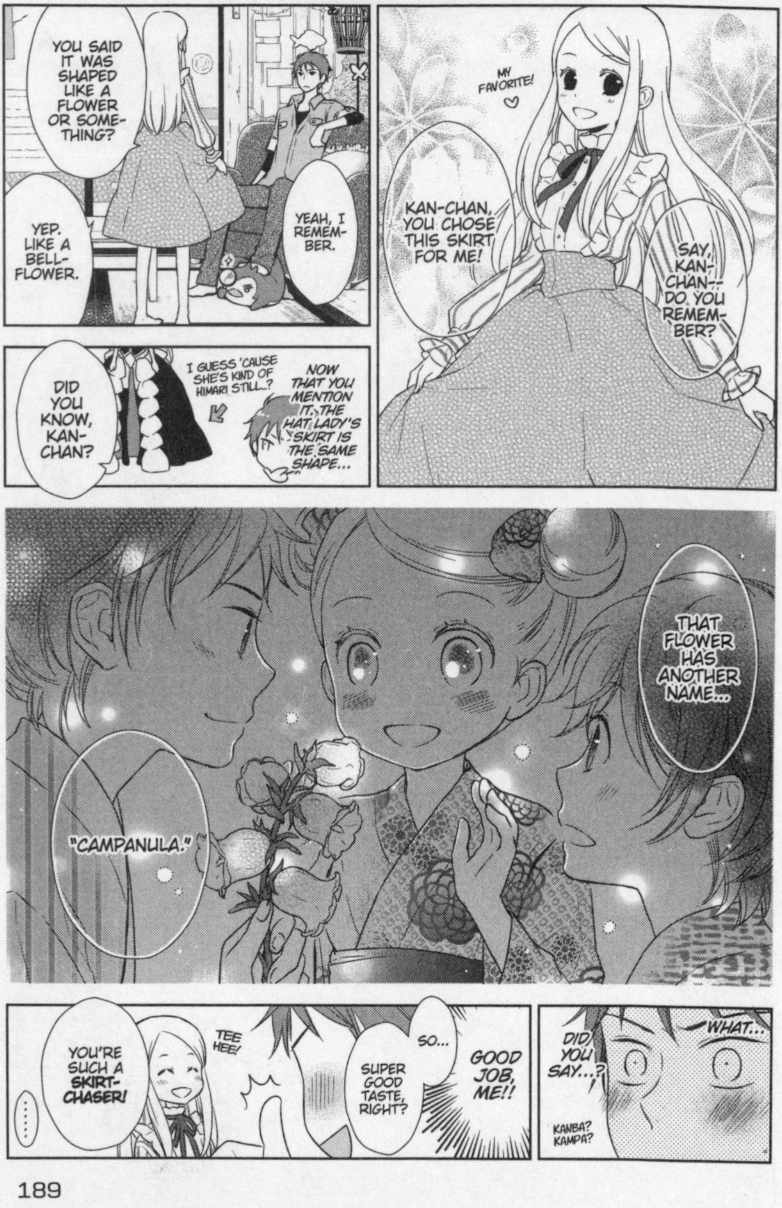
SAY, KAN-CHAN-- DO YOU REMEMBER?
MY FAVORITE! ♡
KAN-CHAN, YOU CHOSE THIS SKIRT FOR ME!
YOU SAID IT WAS SHAPED LIKE A FLOWER OR SOME-THING?
YEAH, I REMEMBER.
YEP. LIKE A BELL-FLOWER.
NOW THAT YOU MENTION IT, THE HAT LADY'S SKIRT IS THE SAME SHAPE...
I GUESS 'CAUSE SHE'S KIND OF HIMARI STILL...?
DID YOU KNOW, KAN-CHAN?
THAT FLOWER HAS ANOTHER NAME...
"CAMPANULA."
WHAT...
DID YOU SAY...?
KANBA? KAMPA?
SO...
SUPER GOOD TASTE, RIGHT?
GOOD JOB, ME!!
TEE HEE!
YOU'RE SUCH A SKIRT-CHASER!
......

Li'l Devil Mario

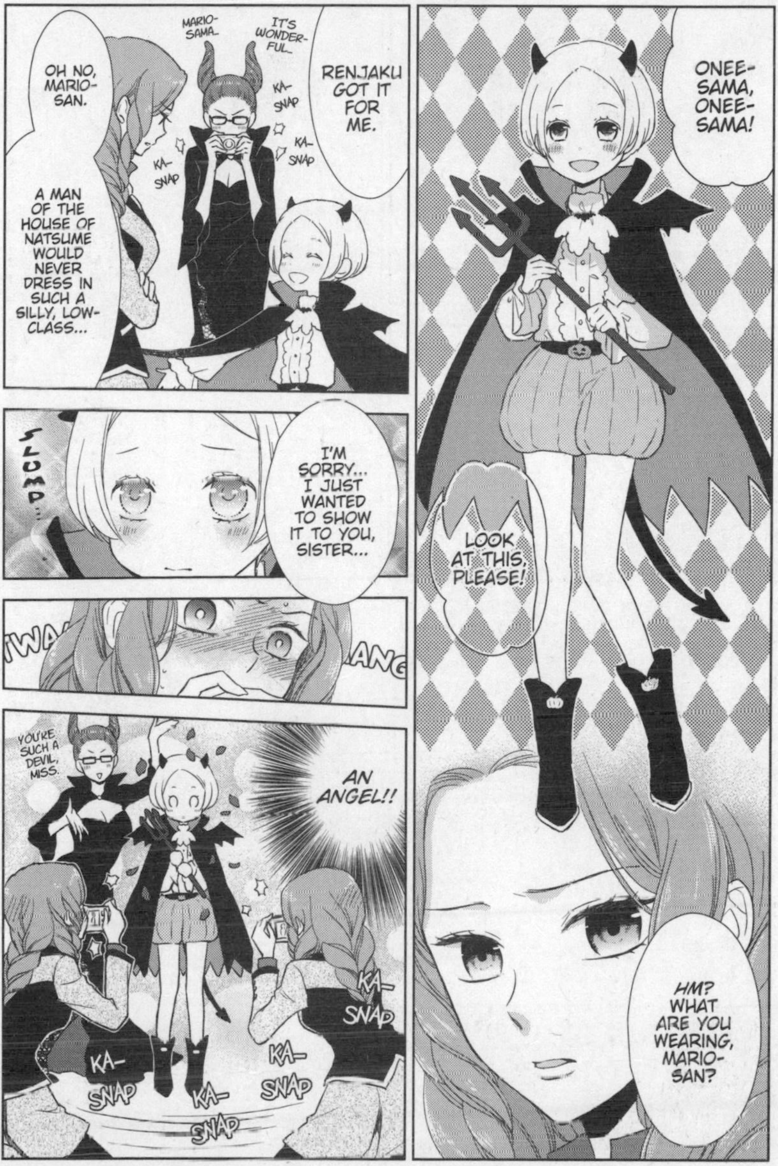
ONEE-SAMA, ONEE-SAMA!
LOOK AT THIS, PLEASE!
HM? WHAT ARE YOU WEARING, MARIO-SAN?
RENJAKU GOT IT FOR ME.
IT'S WONDERFUL...
KA-SNAP
KA-SNAP
MARIO-SAMA...
KA-SNAP
OH NO, MARIO-SAN.
A MAN OF THE HOUSE OF NATSUME WOULD NEVER DRESS IN SUCH A SILLY, LOW-CLASS...
I'M SORRY... I JUST WANTED TO SHOW IT TO YOU, SISTER...
SLUMP...
AN ANGEL!!
YOU'RE SUCH A DEVIL, MISS.
KA-SNAP
KA-SNAP
KA-SNAP
KA-SNAP

Half of the Ties That Bind

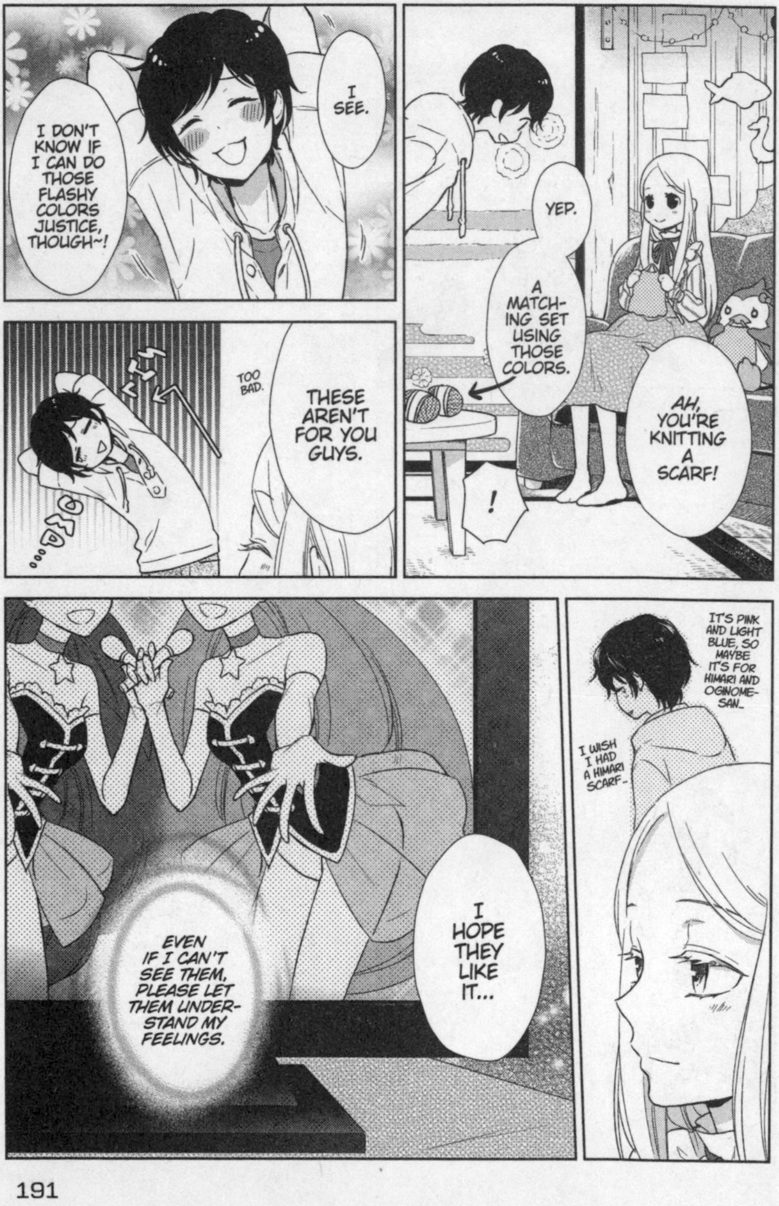
AH, YOU'RE KNITTING A SCARF!
!
YEP.
A MATCHING SET USING THOSE COLORS.
I SEE.
I DON'T KNOW IF I CAN DO THOSE FLASHY COLORS JUSTICE, THOUGH~!
THESE AREN'T FOR YOU GUYS.
TOO BAD.
IT'S PINK AND LIGHT BLUE, SO MAYBE IT'S FOR HIMARI AND OGINOME-SAN...
I WISH I HAD A HIMARI SCARF...
I HOPE THEY LIKE IT...
EVEN IF I CAN'T SEE THEM, PLEASE LET THEM UNDERSTAND MY FEELINGS.

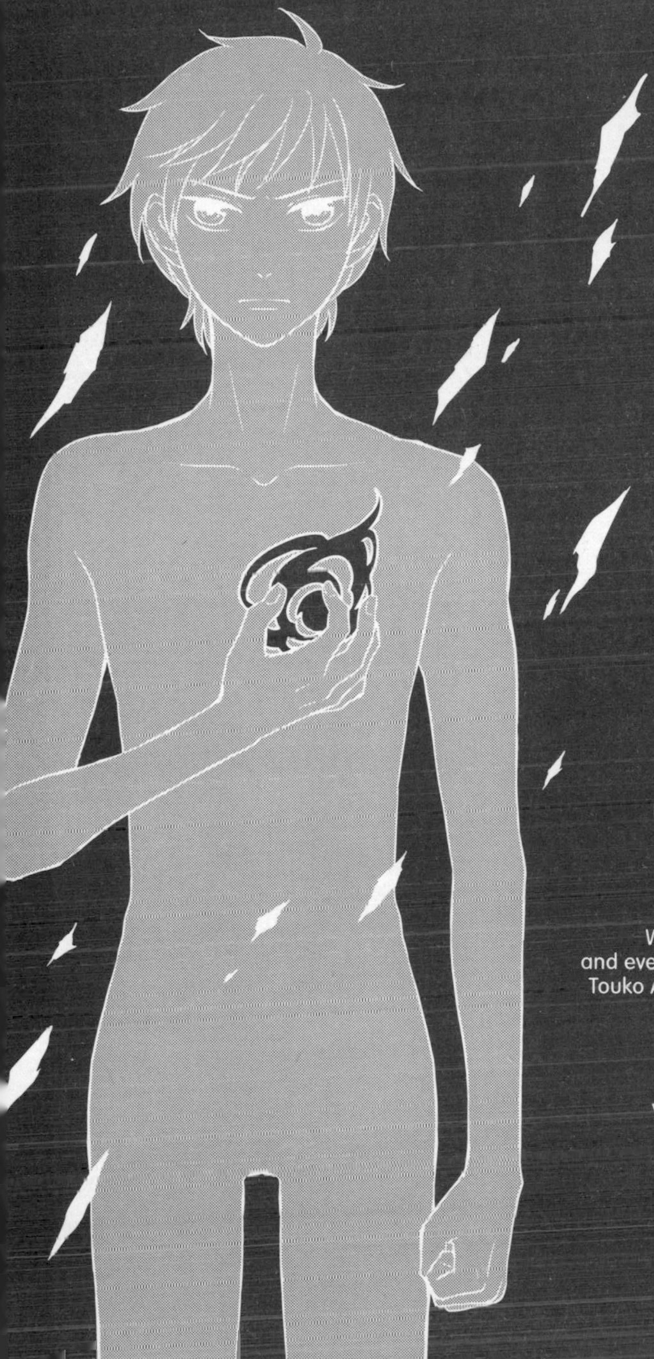

Spring, born...
Summer, found...
Fall, meeting...
Winter, fades away...

Kunihiko Ikuhara
the director,
Lily Hoshino
the mangaka...
my editor,
Fujimoto-san...
Kaneda-san
Mochitsuki-san...
Wataru Osakabe-san,
and everyone else involved...
Touko Akiba-san, my family,
my readers...

I'll be happy to see
you on the next train.
Thank you.

2015.10.

Isuzu Shibata

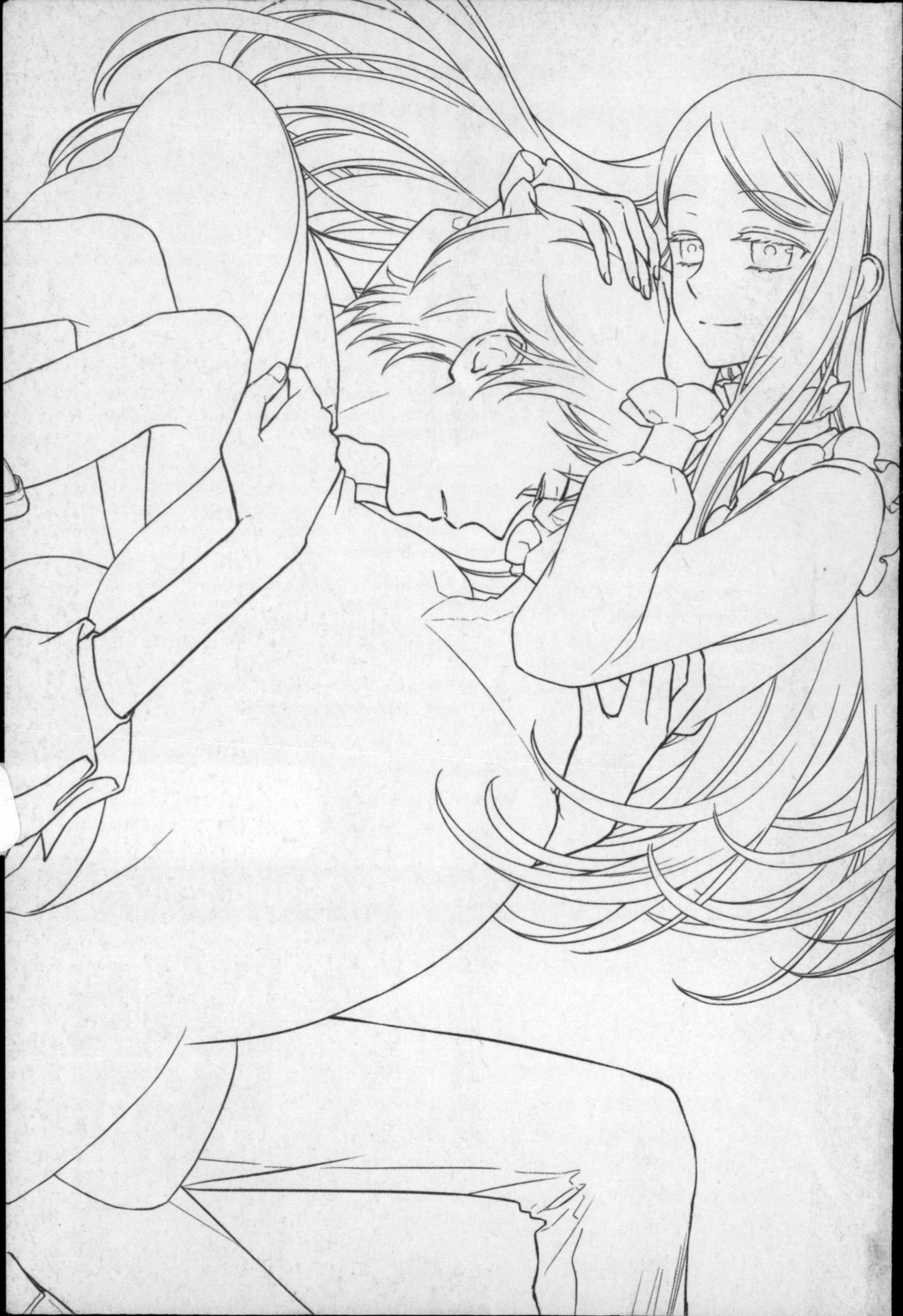

SEVEN SEAS ENTERTAINMENT PRESENTS

PENGUINDRUM

art by ISUZU SHIBATA story by ikunichawder character designs by LILY HOSHINO VOL. 3

TRANSLATION
Beni Axia Conrad

ADAPTATION
Lora Gray

LETTERING
Jennifer Skarupa

COVER DESIGN
Nicky Lim

PROOFREADER
Danielle King

EDITOR
Jenn Grunigen

PREPRESS TECHNICIAN
Rhiannon Rasmussen-Silverstein

PRODUCTION MANAGER
Lissa Pattillo

MANAGING EDITOR
Julie Davis

ASSOCIATE PUBLISHER
Adam Arnold

PUBLISHER
Jason DeAngelis

MAWARU—PENGUINDRUM Vol. 3 by ikunichawder, Isuzu Shibata, & Lily Hoshino

Original Japanese edition published in 2015 by GENTOSHA COMICS Inc.
English translation rights arranged worldwide with GENTOSHA COMICS Inc. through Digital Catapult Inc., Tokyo.

Seven Seas press and purchase enquiries can be sent to Marketing Manager Lianne Sentar at press@gomanga.com. Information regarding the distribution and purchase of digital editions is available from Digital Manager CK Russell at digital@gomanga.com.

ISBN: 978-1-64505-509-9

Printed in Canada

First Printing: November 2020

10 9 8 7 6 5 4 3 2 1

FOLLOW US ONLINE: *www.sevenseasentertainment.com*

READING DIRECTIONS

This book reads from ***right to left***, Japanese style. If this is your first time reading manga, you start reading from the top right panel on each page and take it from there. If you get lost, just follow the numbered diagram here. It may seem backwards at first, but you'll get the hang of it! Have fun!!

1
2
3
4
5
6
7
8
9

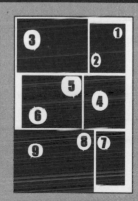